MW01027902

In this book, Michael Kuhn tacl ive
been and will continue to be a p ons
in both academic and societal circles, practiced both publicly and privately, almost everywhere and especially in the Middle East. Kuhn does this by probing the rich Arabic theological tradition in medieval Iraq and Syria and coming back to the present with invaluable insights and recommendations that also makes meaningful connections with important western scholarship. All that is topped with and engraved in a rich experience of academic ministry in the Middle East. This is a materially rich, intellectually nuanced, theologically responsible study in comparative theology, which will illumine and give depth to any current Christian–Muslim conversation on Christology and the trinity.

Hani Hanna, PhD
Associate Professor of Systematic Theology,
Evangelical Theological Seminary in Cairo, Egypt

Dr Michael Kuhn's study is not only a significant contribution to scholarship on medieval Arabic-speaking Christians theologizing under Islamic rule, but also a delightful guide full of practical insights and helpful information for today's peacemakers, who lovingly and willingly seek to share the power of the Triune God with their neighbours. I have already used Kuhn's valuable study in my Christian–Muslim Apologetics course.

Ayman S. Ibrahim, PhD
Bill and Connie Jenkins Associate Professor of Islamic Studies,
Director, Jenkins Center for the Christian Understanding of Islam,
The Southern Baptist Theological Seminary, Louisville, Kentucky, USA

The notions of "Abraham" and "Monotheism" are often used to qualify "the class" to which Judaism, Christianity, and Islam (in this order of their historical emergence) are said to belong. The essential character of Christianity as a monotheistic tradition has, however, been historically challenged by Judaism but more vociferously by Islam. The Trinity has been at the heart of this challenge. Rather than seeing it as a particularly intimate revelation of the one God to investigate as "insiders" should, it has often been seen as a weakness to attack and undermine. Michael Kuhn's work brilliantly juxtaposes two disparate medieval Christians whose input could potentially add a rich layer in the story of the "Christian–Muslim discourse" on God: one of these arguably embedding a cogent response to Muslims, another engaging in a candid dialogue with one of them. These cases highlight not just the humility of men who took initiatives to give an honest account of a revelatory faith but also the story of God who reveals his true nature so humanity can relate with him as sons and daughters and not as slaves and servants. I have no hesitation in recommending this excellent work to all honest people of faith, Muslim and Christian.

David Emmanuel Singh, PhD
PhD Stage Leader and Link Tutor,
Oxford Centre for Mission Studies, Oxford, UK

Mike Kuhn has established the importance of two theologians writing in Arabic in a Muslim context who both attempted to defend the oneness of God in the face of Muslim criticisms that the Trinity and Incarnation undercut God's oneness. This ground-breaking study of Iliyyā of Nisibis and ʿAbd Allāh Ibn al-Ṭayyib is the first sustained analysis of their work in English, and so will open up the significance of these theologians for the global dialogue with Muslims that is happening in our time.

Mark Beaumont, PhD
Research Associate,
London School of Theology, Northwood, London, UK

The society that had developed in the Middle East by the tenth century was both socially plural and intellectually diverse. Religious encounters demanded great mental resilience among Christians, as they sought to uphold fundamental teachings in a climate pervaded by belief in radical divine unity. The two eleventh-century theologians presented here, Iliyyā of Nisibis and Ibn al-Ṭayyib, were leading exponents of Christian apologetic in this setting, seriously engaging with new Muslim methods and confidently meeting the challenges they encountered. Michael Kuhn's analysis of their theologies shows how they explained and defended their beliefs in terms accessible to Muslims, and opens up a little-known but intensely rich and erudite intellectual world.

Rev David Thomas, FBA
Emeritus Professor of Christianity and Islam,
University of Birmingham, UK

Here is a compelling account of how two Christian theologians living under Islamic rule during the Abbasid era in the eleventh century engaged in serious theological dialogue with Muslim theologians about the divine unity and the nature of Christ. The thoroughness of this study makes one wonder whether Christian and Muslim scholars today are engaging in dialogue in the same depth. We can only hope that, inspired by studies of this kind, a new generation of Christians and Muslims will emerge – both in the Middle East and elsewhere – who can go beyond polemics and engage, both in

Arabic and in English, in rigorous theological dialogue that is relevant to our changing and politically sensitive contexts.

Colin Chapman
Former Lecturer in Islamic Studies,
Near East School of Theology, Beirut, Lebanon
Visiting Lecturer,
Arab Baptist Theological Seminary, Beirut, Lebanon

Mike Kuhn's erudite book, *God Is One,* may at first appear too academic and overwhelming for the general reader, but you will want to overcome that initial hesitation and pick it up anyway. Kuhn's motivation and purpose are eminently practical and the outcome particularly relevant for today. His analysis of the writings of two eleventh-century Arab Christian theologians on the doctrine of God is so carefully done that it does indeed make a significant contribution to the academic study of dialogue literature. But his constant concern for relevance and applicability, coupled with a very fluent writing style, also make his book vastly accessible and useful, not only for the Arab student of theology, but also for others everywhere who desire to engage in loving, profound, and inviting conversations about God with their Muslim neighbors. I celebrate Kuhn's unique contribution to taking the church's positive engagement with Islam one step further in the direction of loving understanding in a world where Christians and Muslim are living as neighbors in closer proximity than ever before.

Martin Accad, PhD
Chief Academic Officer and Associate Professor of Islamic Studies,
Arab Baptist Theological Seminary, Beirut, Lebanon

Michael Kuhn's *God Is One* is an outstanding contribution to scholarship on medieval Muslim–Christian relations with deep resonance for Muslim–Christian interaction in the present. Mike writes with unusual clarity and insight about two extraordinary Christian theologians, Ibn al-Tayyib and Iliyyā of Nisibis, and the impact of the Muslim milieu on their theology. The result is among the most thorough and nuanced explorations that I have read of the single most important topic in Muslim–Christian interaction, the doctrine of God.

Daniel Brown, PhD
Director,
Institute for the Study of Religion in the Middle East

Witnessing to the truth in love and with respect is a challenge for all Christians. *God Is One* by Michael Kuhn provides a masterful account of how two eleventh-century theologians from the church of the east defended their faith so eloquently and to the admiration of their Muslim audience. In this book, Kuhn offers a valuable example from a Middle Eastern context that ought to inform our engagement in Christian–Muslim dialogue today. This comes at a timely season when evangelicals in the Arab world are digging deeper roots in the region and developing contextual approaches for articulating their faith. This book is a great resource for anyone serious about witnessing from a minority setting.

Elias Ghazal
Executive Director,
Middle East and North Africa Association for Theological Education

Michael Kuhn's *God Is One: A Christian Defence of Divine Unity in the Muslim Golden Age* lays before us in prose that is both lucid and elegant a precise analysis of the defense of divine unity as undertaken by two medieval churchmen whose historical moment was rendered inconvenient by the dominance of the "religious other." Kuhn is at pains not to force from the legacy of his subjects a contrived relevance for those who witness to Christ in Islam-dominant contexts today. Nevertheless, one cannot help but imagine that the irenic discourse which his two theologians maintained when and as the opportunity was presented to them ought at the least to be carefully attended in these no less fitful days of Muslim–Christian exchange.

Kuhn is attentive both to the antecedents of Abū al-Faraj ʿAbd Allāh Ibn al-Ṭayyib (d. 1043/434) and Bishop Iliyyā of Nisibis (d. 1046/437) and to how each developed such legacy in a context where the Muslim notion of divine unity, captured by the word *tawḥīd*, set the unyielding agenda for any such conversation. He notes where his protagonists chose discretely not to name their respective Muslim counterparts, where their end game seems to have been less the persuasion of their Muslim interlocutors than the careful equipping of Christians with arguments that might allow them to survive in unfavorable and precarious circumstances, and where the quest to commend Christian faith as consonant with *tawḥīd* may have outrun both the biblical witness and conciliar/Trinitarian Christology.

Kuhn's assessments are in every case cautious, patient, generous, and unafraid. His final chapter is a *tour de force* of chastened hope as the author notes how the unbending lines of medieval conversation about divine unity, and indeed the manner in which Muslims and Christians are prepared to engage such themes, have lately softened in a manner that suggests that further and fruitful conversation and witness may lie just ahead.

David A. Baer, PhD
Director, Theological Education Initiative
Professor, Old Testament and Biblical Languages,
Seminario Bíblico de Colombia, Medellin, Colombia

Michael Kuhn's meticulous research and cogent reasoning bring to life two historical figures as models for those seeking to "embrace the life of the Trinity in a society where Islam is the majority faith." This book is a valuable resource for both Christian scholars in dialogue with Islam and Christians needing the life-giving knowledge that the incarnate God is with them in their day-to-day struggles.

Frank Newell
Professor,
Alexandria School of Theology, Egypt

Global Perspectives Series

God Is One

Langham
GLOBAL LIBRARY

God Is One

A Christian Defence of Divine Unity in the Muslim Golden Age

Michael F. Kuhn

Langham
GLOBAL LIBRARY

© 2019 Michael F. Kuhn

Published 2019 by Langham Global Library
An imprint of Langham Publishing
www.langhampublishing.org

Langham Publishing and its imprints are a ministry of Langham Partnership

Langham Partnership
PO Box 296, Carlisle, Cumbria, CA3 9WZ, UK
www.langham.org

ISBNs:
978-1-78368-576-9 Print
987-1-78368-577-6 ePub
978-1-78368-578-3 Mobi
978-1-78368-579-0 PDF

Michael F. Kuhn has asserted his right under the Copyright, Designs and Patents Act, 1988 to be identified as the Author of this work.

All rights reserved. No part of this publication may be reproduced, stored in a retrieval system or transmitted, in any form or by any means, electronic, mechanical, photocopying, recording or otherwise, without the prior written permission of the publisher or the Copyright Licensing Agency.

Scripture quotations are from The Holy Bible, English Standard Version® (ESV®), copyright © 2001 by Crossway, a publishing ministry of Good News Publishers. Used by permission. All rights reserved.

Unless otherwise noted, qur'ānic citations are from the *Sahih International Version* found at www.quran.com.

British Library Cataloguing-in-Publication Data
A catalogue record for this book is available from the British Library

ISBN: 978-1-78368-576-9

Cover & Book Design: projectluz.com

Langham Partnership actively supports theological dialogue and an author's right to publish but does not necessarily endorse the views and opinions set forth here or in works referenced within this publication, nor can we guarantee technical and grammatical correctness. Langham Partnership does not accept any responsibility or liability to persons or property as a consequence of the reading, use or interpretation of its published content.

This book is respectfully dedicated to friends and neighbors
from Syria and Iraq for whom the recent conflicts
have led to loss of family, friends and home.

Your struggle has deepened my concern for how God is understood among your people – the heirs of the subjects of this research. I am painfully aware that this does nothing to redress the injustices done to you or to restore peace and prosperity in your homelands. Yet it is a small token of my appreciation for your friendship and an expression of my hope that you will experience freedom and joy in the new lives you have found.

CONTENTS

Acknowledgments

"To the one who has taught me even one letter, I have become a slave." The Arabic proverb captures the sense of indebtedness to those who teach. I feel that debt of gratitude to a multitude of teachers stretching back to my childhood years. To record the names of all would be impossible. So I will be content to mention but a few names whose influence and encouragement have helped this book see the light of day.

As this work has been adapted from my doctoral thesis, I recognize the immense benefit afforded me by the scholarly environment of the Oxford Centre for Mission Studies. I am especially grateful to Dr David Singh for his patient input and assistance in locating excellent supervisors. Dr Damon So interacted with me on the subject of the Trinity. Brian Woolnough served as my "house tutor" and always took an active interest in my work. The discussions around the seminar tables helped me understand the nature of research and allowed me to connect with a scholarly community that spans the globe.

I would also like to express my thanks to the helpful staff of the Oriental Institute of Oxford University. The library became my home away from home where I was fortunate to meet and interact with other scholars who enriched my understanding of medieval Arab Christianity. Both Julian Faultless and Salam Rassi shared their work and resources, for which I am deeply grateful.

Le Centre de Documentation et de Recherches Arabes Chrétiennes located in Beirut played an important role through its library and staff. Aside from finding many resources there, I enjoyed the warm hospitality of Lena and Mona Dahaby as well as Father Ronney al-Gemayel, SJ. I also made the acquaintance of Father Samir Khalil Samir, SJ, whose influence appears in many citations.

The Arab Baptist Theological Seminary has been my institutional home through the course of this study. I should mention that every faculty member and student at ABTS has been the laboratory of my exploration of a Christian theological response in the Muslim context. Dr Martin Accad, Dr Hikmat Kashouh and Abd al-Karim Zein al-Dine have been my board of reference for understanding ancient Arabic vocabulary and sentence structure. I've benefited from conversations with Caleb Hutcherson in the area of historical theology. Elie Haddad, the President of ABTS, has been a source of encouragement in the research and in applying it in the contemporary Arab world. Other colleagues who have encouraged me along the way include Emad Boutros, Dr Walid Zailaa, Dr Wes Watkins, Dr Perry Shaw, Dr Karen Shaw, Dr Daniel Chetti and Dr Arthur Brown. My colleagues in "Teach-Learn" encouraged the thesis by making my work environment a delight. They include Elias Ghazal, Georgette

Tamer, Joyce Saddi and Marwan Chaaya. Through ABTS, I have had the privilege of co-laboring with Father Elia Khalife, a scholar-monk of the *Rūm* (Greek) Orthodox tradition. Fr Elia has provided a new depth of appreciation for the artistic, scholarly and spiritual heritage of the Eastern churches for which I am deeply grateful.

Dr Mark Beaumont, whom I first met ages ago in Morocco, served as a reader and advisor in this study. Beyond the joy of reconnecting, I appreciated Mark's scholarly understanding of Christology and his patient corrections and suggestions. His influence is seen in the number of citations of his work.

On an academic level, no one has been more involved in this work than Professor David Thomas. I have appreciated his ability to rein in my ideas when they ranged too far afield or when my claims exceeded the evidence presented. Simultaneous with my delving into his prodigious research in the field, he patiently assisted me to develop a clearer understanding of my role as a researcher, listening to texts penned by the ancients. Though David and Mark alerted me to a number of errors, I alone bear responsibility for those that remain.

The publication has benefited from the fine editorial work of the staff of Langham. Working with Vivan Doub, a long-time family friend, has been a joy. Special thanks are due to her for encouraging this publication and overseeing the editing process.

Aside from scholars and colleagues listed above, I would also like to express sincere thanks to friends and family members whose patience and encouragement have played a vital role in my research pursuits. Barbara Kuhn, my mother, has continued to encourage me despite my long absences from my homeland. I am grateful to my sister, Margaret Edwards, and her husband Randy, whose home has become a second home for my family and whose loving care, extended to us in myriad ways, has been a profound blessing. Though my father, M. F. Kuhn, is no longer alive, his memory often came to mind while poring over books or examining a manuscript. His determination to teach my brothers and me to plod through hard work and finish may be the best reason why this work has seen the light of day. My thanks also go to Ken and Jeff Kuhn, my brothers, and their spouses for their constant encouragement.

I would also like to thank Cedar Springs Presbyterian Church in Knoxville, Tennessee, for their support and encouragement in this work. In some ways, my current role in Beirut is a result of their vision for an articulate Christian theological response in the Muslim context. I am especially grateful to Piers Van de Merwe for urging me on. John Wood, Rod Huckaby, Doug Messer, Jim McKinney and Jon Woodroof also supported me through the gift of friendship.

The final thanks go to my immediate family. Though we are scattered as far as "East from West" their loving support is the stuff of life. Emily Joy Kuhn, my youngest daughter, also made her home in the Middle East while this book was being written. Her involvement in psycho-social development among displaced peoples provided another lens through which to view the complexity of Muslim–Christian engagement. Hannah Farkas and her husband Nick have offered hours of encouraging conversation to enrich and bless us. Bethany Giles and her husband Jake and their five sons have given us new life as we've experienced the renewal of generations before our very eyes. I would have found it impossible to complete a project of this scope without the rich relational support of my family.

My deepest gratitude goes to the person who has lived this research with me and hoped even more than I for its completion and blessing – Stephanie. Her love and perseverance are a source of joy, stability and hope. She read and corrected the drafts while they were still very rough. The endless hours of study have repaid her little, but some of my best memories of these years will be of long walks with her in the gardens of Oxford where she eagerly listened to my recent findings. This book represents but a small part of a long journey that I continue to share with her.

"The LORD is my shepherd." So wrote the psalmist, and I join millions who have acknowledged the loving rod and staff of a kind and gentle Shepherd guiding them along the way. In preparing this book, I sensed that the theologians of the Church of the East recognized the same Lord as their Shepherd, and it has been my privilege to sit at their feet as they expounded their understanding of him. So I give joyful thanks to the good Shepherd and confide the outcomes of this study into his generous hands.

Abstract

This study examines two prominent theologians of the Assyrian Church of the East who responded to Islam's perennial objections to the Christian Trinity and Christology. The theologians in question are Abū al-Faraj ʿAbd Allāh Ibn al-Ṭayyib (d. 1043/434) and Bishop Iliyyā of Nisibis (d. 1046/437). Both men were characterized by a remarkable literary production marking them out among the intellectual elite of their day as polymaths and among their ecclesial family as distinguished servants due to the wisdom they brought to their theological craft.

Ibn al-Ṭayyib, though recognized as an exegete, has not been noted for his contribution to Muslim–Christian discourse. This book identifies an implicit response to Islam in his theological treatises. Though he did not engage with a specific dialogue partner nor even mention Islam explicitly, the questions he considered correspond unmistakably to the themes of the Muslim–Christian interface which centered around the unity of divinity and the incarnation. This implicit defense of divine unity in Ibn al-Ṭayyib's theological formulations forms one wing of this study. The other is provided by Iliyyā of Nisibis who, unlike Ibn al-Ṭayyib, enjoyed a productive dialogue with the Shi'īte Vizier (Minister of State) of the Marwanid dynasty (located in eastern Syria and western Turkey today). The "agnostic inquisitiveness" of Abū al-Qāsim in tandem with the rhetorical skill and *tawḥīd* rhetoric of Iliyyā occasioned one of the most promising examples of Muslim–Christian discourse of the medieval period, known as the *Sessions*. The *Sessions* proved to be a rare exception to the acrimonious nature of the medieval Muslim–Christian exchange, portending hope through two men who transcended the confines of their time to listen to and engage with one another.

Both theologians dealt with critical questions posed by Muslim intellectuals concerning the Christian definition of divine unity in light of their Trinitarian and christological formulations. The Christians claimed divine unity (*tawḥīd*) as a correct moniker of their view as they sought to secure the inclusion of their community in the fold of monotheism. Key questions included the definition of the Trinitarian hypostases and their relation to the divine essence (How can God be one and three?). The nature of the union of divinity and humanity in Christ was equally critical given that Muslims viewed the incarnation as an egregious example of *shirk* (associating the Creator with the created – polytheism). The two theologians borrowed conceptually and lexically from their Christian predecessors to shape a cogent defense of Christian divine unity in the Muslim milieu. However, they were also well attuned to Islamic *kalām* (theological reasoning) and situated their formulations within the boundaries of that rhetorical style and lexicon.

Though the technical issues debated by medieval theologians continue to serve as points of interest and demarcation, the dimensions of the contemporary Muslim–Christian exchange must include them as part of a more broadly framed dialogue. In the final chapter we will consider the current existential angst which has engulfed the heirs of Iliyyā and Ibn al-Ṭayyib in their homelands of the Middle East with a view toward the ministerial benefits of a Trinitarian theology in a *tawḥīd* frame of reference. Can the Trinitarian God and the incarnate Christ offer hope in a context that has long endured the decline of the historic Christian faith?

1

Charting the Course

1. Introduction

The two faiths of Islam and Christianity hold much in common. Among their shared concerns is the belief in one God, also shared with their Jewish predecessors and elaborated in their respective revealed scriptures. The monotheistic ideal, though common to both faiths, is nevertheless an article of contention as the two Abrahamic faiths arrive at different conclusions concerning the conceptualization of the one God. The Christian concept is expressed classically in the historic creeds formulated by the Councils of Nicea-Constantinople and Chalcedon which advocated a Trinitarian God – Father, Son and Holy Spirit. Islam, on the other hand, has persistently retorted, "They have certainly disbelieved who say, 'Allāh is the Messiah, the son of Mary' . . . They have certainly disbelieved who say: 'Allāh is the third of three.' And there is no god except one God" (Q5:72–73).[1] The tenet of God's oneness, referred to in Arabic as *tawḥīd*, is codified in the first phrase of the Islamic creed (*al-shahāda*) stating: "There is no God but Allāh" and rigidly defined in the Islamic exegetical corpus (*tafsīr*).

Islam's insistence on the oneness of God is highlighted by the gravity of violating this article of faith. The sin of "association" (*al-shirk*) is that of associating any created being with the majesty of the eternal and unfathomable God. It is a form of unbelief (*kufr*) so great that it is unpardonable in Islamic thought. This is precisely the point of contention between the two faiths. The Trinitarian formulation of Christianity is often perceived by Muslims to be nothing more than "associating" the sublimity of Allāh with a created being, namely the second person of the Christian Trinity – Christ. Theology proper then is both the hope of rapprochement between the two religions and its greatest obstacle. This foundational doctrine of the nature of God, while it can be perceived as a source of kinship between the two faiths, must also be reckoned as

1. Unless otherwise noted, qur'ānic citations are from the Sahih International Version found at www.quran.com.

an element of differentiation. Indeed, contemporary theologians have recognized this dual potentiality in the two conceptions of deity.[2]

The object of this research is theology proper – a probing of one point along the jagged line of Muslim–Christian interaction spanning nearly fourteen centuries. In his discussion of the interface between the two faiths, Roman Catholic theologian Hans Küng has pleaded "neither for opposition to be swept under the carpet, nor for a syncretistic mixing of religions . . . [but] for an honest approach and an attempt at understanding, based on mutual self-awareness, on objectivity and fairness, and on the knowledge of what separates and what unites."[3] The current study is situated in the medieval Abbasid era and it is from this vantage point that I consider "what separates and what unites," assessing to what degree "self-awareness, objectivity and fairness" were in play.

But why this particular vantage point? Though others might be chosen, this one commends itself from multiple aspects. Most notably, I venture to examine theologians who spoke on behalf of a church under Islamic hegemony. The Assyrian Church of the East predated Islam and flourished in the lands that became Muslim centers of power – Damascus and Baghdad. Theologians nurtured by the Syriac theological heritage had long been employed in the service of their Muslim overlords, translating works of Greek philosophy, astrology, medicine and mathematics into Arabic, resulting in an intellectual revitalization unparalleled until the Enlightenment. There was also a discernible interest on the part of the early Abbasid Caliphs to hear the views of Christians and even to maintain an atmosphere of tolerance where the exchange of ideas was valued. Take, for example, the renowned dialogue of the Abbasid Caliph al-Mahdī with Church of the East Catholicos[4] Timothy I (781/165).[5] A subsequent Caliph – al-Ma'mūn (813/198 – 833/218) – founded the renowned *Bayt al-Ḥikma* (House of Wisdom) to promote translation efforts. In his interrogation of the Christian Abū Qurra (fl. 785/168 – 829/214), the former exhorts him to speak without fear of reprisal: "This is a court of justice and equity: none shall be wronged therein. So advance your arguments and answer without fear, for there is none here who will not speak well of you . . . Let everyone speak who has the wisdom to demonstrate the

2. Miroslav Volf suggests that the reality of the two faiths worshiping the same God proffers a hopeful coexistence but he also recognizes the difficulty as Islamic theologians such as Aref Nayad, director of Kalām Research and Media in Dubai, referring to the Athanasian Creed, declares that a Muslim "cannot accept, and must actually reject the entire creed" (Volf, "Common Word for a Common Future," 131).

3. Küng, *Islam*, xxv.

4. "Catholicos" is the title given to the Patriarch of the Assyrian Church of the East.

5. A dual dating system will be used in this research, beginning with the Gregorian Calendar (*Anno Domini* [AD] or Common Era [CE]) and followed by the Islamic Hejira date (AH). Thus 781 (CE) / 165 (AH).

truth of his religion."[6] Thus the era, at least initially, proffered a robust exchange of ideas between the Christian and Muslim communities.

Some observers have assumed that this degree of reciprocity characterized the long tenure of the Abbasids.[7] However, such an assumption proves to be ill-informed. The polemic quickly polarized around those doctrines which were so central to their distinctive communities and upon which Christians and Muslims could not agree: the unity of divinity especially in reference to the Trinity and the two natures of Christ – the human and the divine. The growing entrenchment in interfaith relations of subsequent centuries produced an atmosphere that was neither cooperative nor cordial.[8] Furthermore, Islam, with its staunch definition of divine unity, quickly gained the intellectual high ground. Not surprisingly, the churches of the East – Jacobite, Melkite and the Church of the East[9] – lost adherents to Islam.[10] While this development can be traced as a terraced line[11] rather than a steady progression, the end result is the same. The Syriac and Arabic-speaking churches became aware of a broad-scale defection and societal marginalization as Islam became the predominant faith in the region.[12]

Our research displays two intellectuals who, though competent in multiple fields of endeavor, turn their attention to the theological divide on the question of God's unity. Their erudition is enhanced by a native grasp of the language of their Muslim sovereigns – Arabic. Thus, the theologians observed interacted with Islam in its language, using its terminology, from within its societal systems of law, philosophy and rhetoric. In this sense, the study is one of contextualized theology where Christians under Islamic sovereignty, and from within a Muslim society, seek to explain their theology.

---

6. Goddard, *History of Christian–Muslim Relations*, 51–53.

7. Consider Abu-Nimer, *Interfaith Dialogue*. "Throughout most of the Abbasid era, Christians enjoyed security and freedom. . . . They wore the same clothes, played the same games and enjoyed many of the same comforts that the Muslims did" (73). Abu-Nimer seems to ignore much of the unpleasant reality that characterized interfaith relations later in the Abbasid era.

8. Thomas, "Early Muslim Responses to Christianity," 254.

9. The Assyrian Church of the East is often referred to as "Nestorian." In this research I will use the preferred self-designation of the church, "the Assyrian Church of the East." Sebastian Brock has noted that if "Nestorian" is taken to mean a Christology of "a divine and human person of Christ" the moniker is, in fact, a "misnomer" (Brock, "The 'Nestorian' Church"). Iliyyā of Nisibis was content to refer to his church as "Nestorian" although Ibn al-Ṭayyib pointed out that the moniker was not accurate.

10. Keating, *Defending the "People of Truth,"* 12.

11. This terraced line is referred to by Phillip Jenkins as "punctuated equilibrium" (Jenkins, *Lost History*, 114).

12. Chapter 2 will present evidence of changes in the religious demography of the Abbasid realm.

2. Research Questions

Essentially, the research question is: What contribution did the Church of the East theologians of the eleventh century make to the Muslim–Christian interface? The particular point of interest is divine unity. Were the theologians of the Church of the East able to elaborate their doctrine of divine unity so as to include themselves among the people of *tawḥīd*? In the case of one of these theologians – Abū al-Faraj ʿAbd Allāh Ibn al-Ṭayyib – I will endeavor to demonstrate that he was actively interacting with Islamic thought though seldom referring to his religious counterparts explicitly. This implicit interaction proffers some lessons as to how Christians, though on the defensive, were yet cognizant of the need to hold their distinctive views of divinity in the Muslim milieu. In the case of the second theologian under discussion – Iliyyā of Nisibis[13] – an explicit dialogue partner is present in the Marwanid Vizier[14] Abū al-Qāsim. Equally interesting observations unfold as a result of this explicit dialogue held under the aegis of a tolerant political regime which emerged only briefly through a window of history. The conciliatory Vizier allows Bishop Iliyyā to defend his Trinitarian monotheism in reference to his own Christian thought but also from a qur'ānic perspective. Thus both the implicit writings of Ibn al-Ṭayyib and the more explicit nature of Iliyyā's dialogue provide unique observation points for Muslim–Christian engagement of the period. The two theologians were selected in part due to their proximity chronologically and in part due to their prominence as Arabic-speaking and -writing theologians and intellectuals in the Muslim milieu. Additionally, their affiliation with the Assyrian Church of the East (i.e. "Nestorian") provides interesting points of contact in terms of their Christology.

Of course, the two theologians under discussion were part of a long chain of Christian intellectuals who had provided Christian responses to Islamic queries of their faith. These will be surveyed in a cursory fashion in chapter 2. Therefore, I will be interested to note how the themes of the ninth- and tenth-century debates resurface and develop in the eleventh century. To this end, I reflect on Muslim polemicists who were engaging Christians prior to the eleventh century in an attempt to discern the context of Muslim–Christian relations of the medieval period.

Under the rubric of this broad research question, I also pose secondary questions. First, did the position of the Church of the East geographically, theologically or linguistically proffer a more informed engagement with Islam, whether irenical or polemical in nature? I will note particular choices of Arabic terminology, rhetorical

---

13. His name is most commonly anglicized as "Elias of Nisibis." However, the transliteration of his name in Arabic yields "Iliyyā," which will be used consistently in the present work.

14. "Vizier" is the title of a high-ranking government official, similar to a Prime Minister or Minister of the Interior.

styles and Islamic theological concepts which the theologians under discussion employ to their advantage. Of particular interest is the Church of the East Christology which tended to emphasize the separate hypostases of Christ as a correlative to his distinct natures – his humanity and divinity – as stipulated by the credal formulations. The theologians felt this Christology secured for them an advantage in the Muslim milieu over their Christian counterparts – the Byzantines and miaphysite Jacobites.

Second, as the Church of the East existed in the Muslim Abbasid realm, I have a view to the social and legal status of Christians during the Abbasid period. The theologians will provide some clues as to what was at stake for the societal status of Christians in the interfaith exchange of the eleventh century. Given their status under Muslim hegemony, might one expect a more pliable theology capable of coexistence with Islamic *tawḥīd* (divine unity) or do Christians manifest a greater intransigence after centuries under Islamic dominance? I will note something of an eclipse of the public and explicit debates of the early Abbasid period as a greater reticence to engage in public polemics emerges. Is this attributable to the inherent risk of polemical debate?

Finally, the question of the Christians' success in their argument for divine unity must be posed. Can Trinitarian unity and an incarnate deity conform to Islamic *tawḥīd*? The scholarly literature has noted repeatedly that the Muslim–Christian interface offered little in terms of empathetic listening to the other. Practitioners on both sides of the divide appear intransigent in their defense of long-cherished religious formulations. The intransigence does not disappear in the eleventh century, but there is a noteworthy glimmer of success in the exchange which shall be observed in due course.

3. Significance: To What End?

The question must now be asked: What value does this study add to the scholarly field of Muslim–Christian relations? I consider the question under the categories of time and place. In terms of time, I am looking at the eleventh century – which follows what is generally considered a more illustrious period of Muslim–Christian interaction. As mentioned above, the early centuries of the Abbasid era portended hope of a more inclusive Islam, promising to dissolve the ethnic and tribal divisions which had characterized the previous Umayyad Caliphate.[15] With its new capital in Baghdad, the Abbasid revolution set the stage for the meeting of minds – Muslim, Christian and Jew. The Christians' participation with Muslims in philosophy and translation efforts made the early Abbasid era a watershed historical epoch in Muslim–Christian relations.[16] The various ecclesial families of the East had produced their own competent

15. Rissanen, *Theological Encounter*, 9.

16. Goddard, *History of Christian–Muslim Relations*, 54–55.

spokespersons: the Jacobite Ḥabīb Ibn Khidma Abū Rā'iṭa (fl. 810–830/194–215), Theodore Abū Qurra (c.785–829/168–214), the Melkite Bishop of Haran, ʿAmmār al-Baṣrī (early to mid-ninth century, also from the Church of the East) and Yaḥyā Ibn ʿAdī (893–974/280–363), a Jacobite philosopher and theologian who penned a renowned response to Abū ʿĪsā al-Warrāq's *Refutation of the Three Christian Sects*. The eleventh century follows this fecund period of Muslim–Christian exchange and may be considered less promising for study of the field. While a reluctance to engage in polemical debate has been noted, the period carries forward and develops the themes which were initiated by the preceding Christian spokesmen. Thus it is an important period in charting the course of Muslim–Christian engagement.

It is also noteworthy in terms of time that the period under discussion falls on the threshold of the infamous Crusades when Muslim–Christian relations degenerated into armed conflict. Although the Crusades will not figure large in this research, there is an interesting point of contact as Abū al-Qāsim had fled from the Faṭimid Caliph al-Ḥākim bi-Amr Allāh, whose antics played a role in unleashing the Crusades, before finding asylum in the Marwanid Emirate. The research will suggest that al-Ḥākim's staunch persecution of Abū al-Qāsim's family helped set the stage for his productive interaction with Bishop Iliyyā. Thus, it is of some interest to note the two distinct effects of al-Ḥākim's volatility.

Finally, in regard to time, the figures under study have received some scholarly attention through encyclopedic entries and critical editions. It appears a propitious time to embark on a critical analysis of their thought and contribution to the fields of theology and Muslim–Christian interaction. Iliyyā's *Sessions* has received limited scholarly attention with the result that little of the Bishop's thought is accessible to English readers, although accessible French versions have been provided by Delly and Samir. Ibn al-Ṭayyib is known primarily for his exegetical contribution with scant attention paid to his theological treatises and virtually no scholarly attempt to discern his contribution to Muslim–Christian relations. I will observe these aspects more fully in the literature review which follows.

In terms of place, it has been noted that the Church of the East existed under Islamic hegemony and the theologians wrote and thought in the Arabic language. There is more to say regarding the theological significance of the Church of the East. Although it has long been disregarded as "Nestorian" and therefore a heretical church, recent studies have challenged this position.[17] In light of these studies, the Church of the East must now be reintegrated into the study of historical theology. While their Byzantine counterparts (writing in Latin and Greek) have been the object of copious study, the Arabic theologians of the Church of the East are only now being

17. See Brock, "The 'Nestorian' Church."

appreciated. This research will shed some light on the theological contributions of the Church of the East while living under Islamic rule. The value of these contributions is brought into relief by their Islamic context. The theologians borrowed from the Islamic understanding of God's eternal attributes to convey their understanding of the Trinitarian persons. Their penchant, not unlike Islamic thought, was to shield deity from human imperfections through careful delineation of the divine and human hypostases in the person of Christ. These theological distinctions are of great interest in the contemporary climate of Muslim–Christian interaction that now spans several continents and numerous nations and people groups.

Indeed, as people of the modern era, and perhaps due to an overrating of the significance of our historical period, we anticipate that any research will bear on the contemporary situation. "Significance" by nature of the fact means significance to our day. After all, the period of interest, not unlike the contemporary era, was characterized by a rich and varied interface, ranging from the most reciprocal and respectful interfaith dialogue to the most violent vilification and militant rejection of opposing views. Though the threads of the tapestry of knowledge are interwoven, I will resist, for now, the penchant to make application to the modern period. The eleventh-century theologians of the Church of the East must first speak on their own terms, from their particular contexts. Only then, as I conclude this study, will some application for the contemporary period be derived.

4. Methodology: Integrated Textual Analysis

Our methodology is a comparative textual analysis of select writings attributed to the two theologians. It may be helpful to envision this methodology as a series of four concentric circles. The innermost circle is the textual study *per se*. The primary points of observation will be the structure and lexicon employed in these texts. I will seek to evaluate their internal coherence and persuasive value as well as discerning the intended audience and readership of the text in question. At some points, the attention is turned to questions of textual authenticity: to what degree can one trust that these texts are the product of the theologians in question? To what degree might they have undergone editing and amendment and how does that impact conclusions?

The next circle represents the extant Christian apologetic writings from the preceding period. As has been mentioned, considerable attention will be devoted to how these concepts and ideas have been carried forward by the two figures in question. As an example, in *Bayt al-Ḥikma* Ibn al-Ṭayyib demonstrates that he was influenced by his predecessor, Yaḥyā Ibn ʿAdī, both in his theological lexicon and in his rational argumentation. However, the texts also indicate that the former was selective in his references to Ibn ʿAdī's thought and made his own distinct contribution to the formulation.

The third circle pertains to the Islamic polemical texts from the period. The particular questions and points of attack that Muslims seek to exploit can be clearly discerned in both authors. Therefore, a number of Muslim polemicists who preceded the eleventh century will be surveyed, noting close lexical and rhetorical affinities between Muslim and Christian authors as well as similar argumentation.

The outermost circle represents the broader social and political context of the Buyid and Marwanid administrations. Though both men lived in the Abbasid era, the political vicissitudes of the period saw them under the sovereignty of two distinct regimes. This aspect of the study keeps an eye toward the social and legal status of Christians in the realm. Thus it will be necessary to dedicate some space to pertinent aspects of the *dhimmī* legal status and the Pact of ʿUmar as well as extant texts and secondary sources that give evidence of the status of religious minorities of the period. Again, a portion of chapter 2 will be devoted to this purpose. This concentric-circle approach focuses primarily on the textual evidence while integrating insights from Muslim–Christian relations of the period as well as historical and sociological works. For this reason, I refer to the methodology as "integrated textual analysis."

5. Limitations

Every research project has implicit limitations due to the subject matter or the competencies of the researcher. One limitation of the present work arises from its focus on Muslim–Christian relations. This emphasis makes a full theological analysis of the positions taken by the protagonists impractical. This would require a detailed survey of the ecumenical councils until Chalcedon against the backdrop of both the miaphysite and dyophysite[18] expressions of the faith. While reference is made to other expressions of the Christian faith as well as the Councils, I am conscious of the fact that the treatment could be significantly expanded.

A second and more obvious limitation is the selection of very specific texts as dictated by the research question. As mentioned, Ibn al-Ṭayyib is renowned for his work as a scriptural exegete and commentator. While this aspect of his work may have yielded some insight into the pertinent issues at the Muslim–Christian interface, the theological treatises are more productive sources for this study. This is largely due to Ibn al-Ṭayyib's stated purpose of preserving the Syriac exegetical heritage in

18. Here I opt for "miaphysite" rather than the commonly used moniker "monophysite" to describe the Christology of the Oriental Orthodox Church family. "Dyophysite" expresses the separation of the hypostases in Church of the East ("Nestorian") Christology. Later in this book I will opt for the more precise moniker "dyohypostatic."

the new *lingua franca* of the Caliphate – Arabic. Similarly, Iliyyā of Nisibis wrote an extensive historical chronology, a grammatical compendium and other documents of interest. However, the research must be limited to his *Sessions* and a few other diverse writings which treat the topic of interest. Sessions 1–3 and 5 were found to be germane to the research interests, although the treatment of Iliyyā's compelling monotheistic confession in Session 5 is drawn primarily from his correspondence with the Vizier due to the place of prominence it occupies in the correspondence.[19] In this selection of texts, the research was guided by the criteria of those topics which figured large at the Muslim–Christian interface of the era, namely the unity of God in the Trinitarian formulation and Christology – divinity and humanity in the one Christ.

At several points in this research, I was made aware of the lack of the relevant background in Greek philosophical thought. When reading the likes of Yaḥyā Ibn ʿAdī, it becomes clear that the erudite theologian was writing out of a Greek frame of reference. His choice of terms as well as the logical construction of his thought adhere closely to those of his Greek philosophical forebears. Ibn al-Ṭayyib and Iliyyā demonstrate a similar influence although to a lesser degree. No doubt the research could be enriched by a more thorough understanding of Aristotelian thought as well as of the lexical varieties of Arabic and Syriac translations of the Greek philosophers.

Finally, as the research is set within the medieval Islamic context, I sought a fair and objective understanding of Islamic texts based on their medieval commentators. Obtaining a thorough background in such a vast field requires a lifetime from the best of scholars. Therefore, I recognize that this research is necessarily limited in its treatment of the Islamic source material.

6. Interaction with Literature

The fields of Muslim–Christian relations and Arab Christian studies have undergone notable advancement in recent years. These are the primary fields of study this research incorporates while also touching on historical theology, apologetics and Islamic studies. Three prominent scholars of these fields – David Thomas, Samir Khalil Samir and Sidney Griffith – surface repeatedly throughout this book. To mention every work consulted would be tedious and render the bibliography superfluous. It may suffice to understand these three professors as standing at the head, though not exclusively, of genres of the academic corpus. In the following paragraphs, a cursory overview

19. Session 4 deals with the rational and miraculous proofs of the faith. Session 6 treats the topics of Arabic syntax, lexicography and calligraphy before exalting the merits of Christian theology (*'ilm al-kalām*). Session 7 deals with Christian views of astrology, Muslims and the soul (Caspar, Charfi and Samir, "Bibliographie du dialogue islamo-chrétien," 262–266).

of some major works is provided before discussing the approach of this research in interacting with the literary corpus.

6.1 Survey of the Literary Corpus

6.1.1 Critical Editions

Aside from the extant manuscript evidence of the authors which will be noted subsequently, Samir Khalil Samir has produced extremely reliable critical editions of some of the works studied herein. Most noteworthy in this genre is Samir's work on Session 1 – "Entretien d'Elie de Nisibe avec le vizir Ibn 'Alī al-Maghribī sur l'unité et la Trinité."[20] His excellent French translation and vigilant notation of variant readings and sectional and verse divisions of Iliyyā's first Session greatly facilitated further study. Louis Cheikho's pioneering work in providing Arabic editions of *Sessions* preceded Samir but suffered from insufficient manuscript evidence, especially in Session 2.[21] The intervening work of Emmanuel Karim-Delly provided a suitable French translation of the seven Sessions[22] accompanied by a substantial introduction to Iliyyā's life, work and thought. Although unpublished, David Bertaina provided a very helpful English translation of Session 3 which outlines Iliyyā's qur'ānic defense of Christian monotheism.[23] Another scholar whose French translations of Ibn al-Ṭayyib's Trinitarian treatises must be mentioned is Gérard Troupeau.[24] In addition to the editions, the research benefited from the excellent work of Samir and Faultless in assembling the known facts of the two figures' biographies.[25] These scholarly editions and biographical materials prepared the way for an integrated textual analysis of the works in question drawing on insights from the field of Muslim–Christian studies.

6.1.2 Comparative Theological Studies

David Thomas's extensive work on Muslim polemicists in the field of comparative Muslim and Christian theology provides a second genre which served as a conceptual lens for textual analysis. His works are numerous such that only a few seminal works are presented here. *Christian–Muslim Relations: A Bibliographical History* (*CMR*) is the foundational reference work in the field. His translation and analysis of Abū 'Īsā al-Warrāq and exploration of 'Alī ibn al-Rabbān al-Ṭabarī provide a lens through

20. Samir, "Entretien d'Elie de Nisibe."

21. Cheikho, "Majālis Iliyyā mutrān Naṣibīn."

22. Delly, *La théologie d'Elie bar-Senaya.*

23. See al-Niṣībīn and Bertaina, *Establishing the Proof.*

24. See Troupeau, "Le traité sur l'unité"; "Le traité sur la Trinité"; "Le traité sur l'union."

25. Caspar, Charfi and Samir, "Bibliographie du dialogue islamo-chrétien"; Faultless, "Ibn al-Ṭayyib."

which to approach the substantive Muslim objections to the Christian faith.[26] His work on "The Miracles of Jesus in Early Islamic Polemic," not to mention the entire Brill series The History of Muslim Christian Relations of which Thomas is the editor, supplied the critical background. Other works which elucidated the Muslim–Christian discourse of the period include Martin Accad's thesis "*The Gospels in the Muslim and Christian Exegetical Discourse from the Eighth to the Fourteenth Century*" and articles by Abdel Majid Charfī,[27] Mark Swanson[28] and Abd al-Munʿim Sirry.[29]

Mark Beaumont's seminal works, especially *Christology in Dialogue with Muslims: A Critical Analysis of Christian Presentations of Christ for Muslims from the Ninth and Twentieth Centuries*, are a substantive survey of the field prior to the era under study.[30] Many other authors contributed to the understanding of the salient theological issues at the Muslim–Christian interface, including Rachid Haddad's *La Trinité divine chez les théologiens Arabs: 750–1050*; Benedicte Landron's groundbreaking *Chrétiens et musulmans en Irak: attitudes nestoriennes vis à vis de l'Islam*; Samir's *Foi et culture en Irak au XIe siècle* offered excellent background and analysis of Iliyyā and the Sessions. Sebastian Brock is unparalleled in his understanding of the Church of the East. His works were also critical to this research.[31] Michel Allard added valuable insight to the Ashʿarī doctrine of the divine attributes[32] from which Joseph Cumming elaborated correlations to the Christian formulation.[33]

Many studies of various Muslim and Christian figures of the preceding era came into play in the research. Reynolds's work on Abd al-Jabbār was critical as the Muslim polemicist was a contemporary of the eleventh-century authors under study;[34] Beaumont, Mikhail and Hayek treated ʿAmmār al-Baṣrī;[35] Emilio Platti and Samir

26. al-Warrāq and Thomas, *Anti-Christian Polemic*; Thomas, *Early Muslim Polemic*; Thomas, "Ali Ibn Rabban al-Tabari."

27. Charfi, "La fonction historique."

28. Swanson, "Beyond Prooftexting"; "Folly to the *Hunafa*."

29. Sirry, "Early Muslim–Christian Dialogue."

30. See also Beaumont, "ʿAmmar al-Basri on the Incarnation"; *Christology in Dialogue with Muslims.*

31. See Brock, "The 'Nestorian' Church."

32. Allard, *Le probléme des attributs divins.*

33. Cumming, "Ṣifāt al-dhāt."

34. Reynolds, *Muslim Theologian*; Reynolds and Samir, *Abd al-Jabbar.*

35. Beaumont, "ʿAmmar al-Basri on the Incarnation"; Hayek, "ʿAmmār al Baṣrī"; Mikhail, "ʿAmmār al-Basrī's Kitāb al-burhān."

examined Ibn ʿAdī;[36] Griffith and others looked at Abū Qurra;[37] Mingana and Putman wrote on the dialogue of Timothy I with al-Mahdī;[38] and Keating analyzed Abū Rā'iṭa.[39]

6.1.3 History of Muslim–Christian Relations

Sidney Griffith's *The Church in the Shadow of the Mosque* falls under the third genre, that of the history of Muslim–Christian interaction, which also includes his "From Patriarch Timothy I to Ḥunayn Ibn Isḥāq." Goddard's masterful work and Phillip Jenkins's recent contribution also occupy places of prominence.[40] Other histories deal more specifically with the Church of the East, such as Brock's "Two Millennia of Christianity in Iraq," Baum and Winkler's *The Church of the East: A Concise History* and Allard's *Les Chrétiens à Baghdad.* Griffith's seminal article "The Monk in the Emir's Majlis" describes the contours of a subgenre to which Iliyyā's *Sessions* corresponds. I shall discuss this further below.

A final genre may be classified as political and social analysis, which has contributed to the social and demographic issues including various legal statutes and the reality of conversion of Church of the East adherents to Islam. These authors include Tritton, Dennett, Fattal, Yeor and Levy-Rubin.

6.2 Anticipated Contribution and Originality

Having surveyed in a cursory fashion the literature with which this study interacts, it remains to suggest the unique contribution and anticipated originality of this study. The authors under consideration are certainly known to researchers in the field. However, it is not unfair to suggest that the existing research is preliminary in nature. By this I mean that critical editions have been produced in some cases (e.g. Samir's work on Iliyyā's Session 1) and the authors have found their way into theological compendia such as Haddad's masterful work on the Trinity among the Arab fathers. Samir's "La place d'Ibn al-Tayyib dans la pensée Arabe," as well as his fine work introducing the first of Iliyyā's Sessions and other articles,[41] have made an excellent beginning in the analysis of the two authors. This research intends to build on this solid foundation by examining the work of the authors with a wider purview. Much

36. Platti, *Yaḥyā Ibn ʿAdī*; "Yaḥyā b. ʿAdī and His Refutation"; "Yahya Ibn ʿAdi and the Theory of *Iktisab*"; Samir, *Maqāla fī al-tawḥīd.*

37. Griffith, *Theodore Abu Qurrah*; "View of Islam from the Monasteries"; "Qur'an in Arab Christian Texts."

38. Mingana, "Apology of Timothy the Patriarch"; Putman, *L'église et l'islam sous Timothée I.*

39. Keating, *Defending the "People of Truth."*

40. Goddard, *History of Christian–Muslim Relations*; Jenkins, *Lost History.*

41. See Samir, "L'unicité absolue de Dieu."

remains to be done in assessing their value and contribution by situating their work within the context of the rich Muslim–Christian interface of the eighth to twelfth centuries. The research anticipates that the Arabic-speaking and writing theologians of the Church of the East, who are themselves immersed in the Muslim milieu, will have unique lexical and notional contributions which have yet to be recognized. The research proposes lines of connection to preceding theologians to suggest how the eleventh-century authors carried forward the dialogue but also made their own unique contributions. Additionally, the research will keep a view toward the Muslim polemical challenges which faced Christians in increasing measure, seeking to ascertain to what degree the authors remained engaged in and responsive to their Muslim milieu. An additional question concerns to what degree the pressure of the Muslim polemic against Christianity forced the theologians to go further than their predecessors. This will be particularly noted in Iliyyā's christological analogies.

There is a unique vantage point that this research will take toward Ibn al-Ṭayyib. This philosopher-physician-theologian has yet to be evaluated for his contribution to the Muslim–Christian interface. On the one hand, the prospect is challenging as Ibn al-Ṭayyib did not interact directly with a Muslim dialogue partner to my knowledge. Nevertheless, he lived an active public life during a tumultuous period in the Caliphate capital of Baghdad. His theological contribution was noteworthy especially in the field of exegesis and scriptural commentary, though some suggest he was preserving his Syriac heritage without adding to it significantly. His theological treatises have only been reproduced in their Arabic form, with French translations by Troupeau. The treatises hardly mention the religious other that must have been so prevalent in that time and place. Acknowledging this to be the case, this work probes whether or not Ibn al-Ṭayyib was cognizant of and responsive to his Muslim-dominated context. In this respect, the research proposes to assess the degree of public engagement in the polymath's theology. Was he engaged with the great debates of the period that surface repeatedly in the literature or was he reclusive, obsessed with the bygone glories of the once-great Assyrian Church of the East? To what degree does the intellectual probe, assess and contribute to his contemporary religious situation? If he is in fact engaging, why does he fail to mention this explicitly? What might explain this subtlety?

The *Sessions* of Bishop Iliyyā with the Marwanid-Shi'īte Vizier Abū al-Qāsim, unlike Ibn al-Ṭayyib's work, has received some attention in the scholarly world of Muslim–Christian studies. In fact, the dialogue figures large in a genre of the field which Griffith has entitled "The Monk in the Emir's *majlis*" where the monk was normally summoned to a *majlis* (session) with the Muslim authority. If the Christian acquitted himself well, the record of the *majlis* would be used by the church as much for its entertainment value as for its apologetical merit. Griffith lists five of these debates, of which Iliyyā's Sessions are the fourth, which have been preserved in the extant literature.[42] While Professor Griffith has identified the genre and pointed out the salient aspects of Iliyyā's *Sessions*, there is more to say. In addition to *Sessions* as text, there exists another written record of the historical meeting between the two men which is found in their personal correspondence (hereafter, *Epistle*) consisting of three exchanges: one letter from Abū al-Qāsim, an extensive reply from the Bishop and a final response from the Vizier.[43] Although much of the content of *Sessions* is also found in the *Epistle*, the latter adds significant aspects which will be examined further. Notably, the *Epistle* contains a ringing endorsement of Iliyyā's "Trinitarian monotheism." The positive declaration is uncharacteristic of the tenor and tone of the Muslim–Christian discourse of the era. The plot thickens as the *Epistle* also manifests an uncommon affection between the two protagonists. I will seek an explanation for this atypical affection and its relation to the Muslim's endorsement of Christian monotheism, whether suggesting Christian embellishment of *Epistle* and/or the Vizier's authentic acceptance and embrace of the Bishop's monotheistic argument.

It also bears mentioning that though Samir has done excellent work on the first of Iliyyā's Sessions, this research will also treat the second and third Sessions as these also bear on his monotheistic argument. In the second Session, Iliyyā expresses his Christology of a hypostatic duality in the one person of Christ through significant analogies. These analogies merit careful study as they express important aspects of the Christian's argument for monotheistic faith (*tawḥīd*) in the Muslim milieu. The third Session presents an argument for Christian divine unity, only from qur'ānic evidence. Needless to say, the Christian bishop's handling of the Qur'ān should excite scholarly attention in qur'ānic studies as well as Muslim–Christian discourse.

7. Defending Divine Unity in the Muslim Milieu: Structure of This Work

The following subheadings indicate the chapter titles. Each heading is followed by a brief synopsis of the chapter, indicating the sectional divisions.

42. The first is the dialogue of Timothy I (720–823) with the Caliph al-Mahdī (775–785). The second is the monk Abraham of Tiberias's encounter with several Muslim interlocutors in the *majlis* of Emir ʿAbd al-Raḥmān al-Hāshimī in Jerusalem in 820/205. The third is Theodore Abū Qurra's dispute with several Muslims before the Caliph al-Ma'mūn in Haran in 820/214. The fifth is the monk George's debate with several Muslim scholars in Aleppo in the early thirteenth century (Griffith, "Monk in the Emir's Majlis," 14).

43. al-Niṣībīn and al-Qasim, *Risāla ilā al-Wazīr.*

7.1 Charting the Course

This is the present chapter – the introduction.

7.2 Theologians in the Muslim Milieu

In this chapter, I discuss the sectarian, political and social context in which the theologians labored. I begin by introducing the two figures in addition to Iliyyā's Muslim dialogue partner through brief biographical sketches (section 2). This is followed by a discussion of the salient political and demographic factors which influenced each of the two writers' contexts in the early eleventh century (sections 3 and 4). In order to identify the predominant themes at the Muslim–Christian interface, several outstanding representatives are surveyed: Alī Ibn Rabbān al-Ṭabarī, al-Rassī, Abu ʿĪsā, al-Nāshi' al-Akbar, al-Ashʿārī, al-Bāqillānī and ʿAbd al-Jabbār (section 5). Finally, a few Christian respondents who interacted explicitly with Islamic objections are presented: Theodore Abū Qurra, ʿAmmār al-Basrī, Abū Rā'iṭa and Yaḥya Ibn ʿAdī (section 6). The purpose of these surveys is to identify themes and lexical elements which will resurface in the eleventh-century theologians.

7.3 Defining Trinitarian Unity: The Trinitarian Formulation of Abū al-Faraj ʿAbd Allāh Ibn al-Ṭayyib

In this chapter I examine three theological treatises penned by Ibn al-Ṭayyib on the subject of the Trinity. A tentative order and a plausible range of dates for the writing of the treatises are suggested. After defining key terms, a summary of the treatises is proposed, followed by interpretation and analysis (section 2).

Ibn al-Ṭayyib's Trinitarian formulation drew not only from Church of the East forebears such as ʿAmmār al-Baṣrī but also from representatives of other ecclesial families such as the Jacobite Yaḥyā Ibn ʿAdī (section 3). His topics of concern are consistent with the themes of the Muslim–Christian interface that became prominent in the ninth and tenth centuries. Evidence from three Muslim polemicists – al-Warrāq, Abū Bakr al-Bāqillānī and ʿAbd al-Jabbār – demonstrates thematic correlations with Ibn al-Ṭayyib's treatises (section 4).

7.4 Transcending Polemic: Iliyyā of Nisibis and Abū al-Qāsim on Trinitarian Monotheism

This chapter examines the Trinitarian formulation of Bishop Iliyyā of Nisibis. After addressing the criteria for selection of the texts and the issue of historicity (section

2), the Trinitarian works of Iliyyā are described and interpreted (section 3). In the analysis section, the reciprocal character of the exchange is a focus of interest and the reasons for this atypical tone are sought. The chapter proceeds to examine lexical-theological amendments made by the Bishop as a result of the Sessions and thereby demonstrates that the encounter of the two men had a reciprocal effect. Finally, the chapter considers Iliyyā's skillful interpretation of the Qur'ān (section 4).

7.5 Christological Reverberations: The Union of Human and Divine in Ibn al-Ṭayyib's Christology

This chapter begins with an extensive overview of the early christological dissensions and the credal resolutions that emerged before identifying the particular point of dissension of the "Nestorian" Church of the East. In this chapter, I suggest that the most appropriate moniker for the Church of the East christological position is "dyohypostatism" rather than the customary "dyophysitism." Furthermore, the careful avoidance of "theopaschitism" (suffering of deity) is identified as a key aspect of this dyohypostatic Christology (section 2). Five texts of Ibn al-Ṭayyib are selected as they portray his christological formulation. After introducing the source material, the description, interpretation and analysis follow. The source for much of the material of this chapter is the compendium of the Copt Abū Isḥāq Mu'taman al-Dawla Ibn al-ʿAssāl, entitled *Summa of the Principles of Religion*[44] (section 3). The conclusion presents Ibn al-Ṭayyib's christological formulation as "reverberating" with the Muslim milieu in which he lived and worked, demonstrated by careful attention to aspects of Ibn al-Ṭayyib's christological formulation.

7.6 Unblemished Deity Incarnate: The Christological Formulation of Iliyyā of Nisibis

This chapter assesses Bishop Iliyyā's christological formulation as expressed in the latter part of Session 1 and Session 2 in addition to a third document titled *The Book of Proof of the True Faith.*[45] Each document is attentively interpreted and analyzed (sections 2 to 4). The chapter concludes with an assessment of Iliyyā's christological formulation in the Muslim milieu with attention to his christological nomenclature, analogies and rhetorical strategy. The conclusion infers information relative to the social status of Christians and the role of the Sessions in ensuring that status.

---

44. The title is an English translation of the Arabic '*Majmūʿ uṣūl al-dīn wa-masmūʿ maḥṣūl al-yaqīn*' مجموع أصول الدين ومسموع محصول اليقين

45. The title translates the Arabic *Kitāb al-burhān ʿalā ṣaḥīḥ al-īmān* كتاب البرهان على صحيح الإيمان

7.7 Defending Divine Unity in the Muslim Milieu: Conclusion

The final chapter begins by summarizing the findings of the research. I discuss this narrowly, giving implications for subsequent study of Ibn al-Ṭayyib and Bishop Iliyyā, but also broadly, looking at the Muslim–Christian discourse of the medieval period. The chapter looks back at Ibn al-Ṭayyib's implicit engagement with Islamic thought as well as Bishop Iliyyā's unique engagement with Abū al-Qāsim. In conclusion, I venture to move beyond the conundrums of medieval Muslim–Christian relations to ask what benefit, if any, may be derived from this study for frank and open dialogue between Muslim and Christian communities today. The conclusion flags theological and missiological considerations from the perspective of Arab Christians living in the Muslim milieu of today's Middle East. The chapter explores the potential benefit of contemporary christological and Trinitarian expressions as applied to the Muslim milieu in the shadow of the existential angst that has gripped the region through the "Arab Spring" and the prolonged conflict in Iraq and Syria.

2

Theologians in the Muslim Milieu

Ibn al-Ṭayyib and Iliyyā of Nisibis

1. Introduction

Theologians are both influenced by and engaged with their religious, social, political and economic context. If their theology is credible, they do not work in a vacuum but respond to the burning questions of their day. The eleventh-century theologians of the Church of the East lived within and responded to their contexts. They interacted with many of the great themes that had dominated the eminent examples of Muslim–Christian interaction of the ninth and tenth centuries. Ibn al-Ṭayyib (d. 1043/434) and Iliyyā of Nisibis (d. 1046/437) were carrying the dialogue forward, providing, at times, responses for their Muslim interlocutors but always a theological perspective for their ecclesial family which continued to live in lands where Islam was dominant politically and, increasingly, socially.

In the present chapter the sectarian, political and social contexts in which the theologians labored are studied. First, the two figures are introduced in addition to Iliyyā's Muslim dialogue partner through brief biographical sketches (section 2). This is followed by a discussion of the salient political and demographic factors which prevailed in each of the two writers' contexts in the early eleventh century (sections 3 and 4). In order to identify the predominant themes at the Muslim–Christian interface, several outstanding voices of that interface are surveyed. First, Muslim spokesmen are observed, seeking to identify the issues which loomed large in Islamic polemic directed toward Christianity (section 5). Finally, attention is given to a few prominent

Christian spokesmen who attempted to respond to Islamic polemic (section 6). In each section, the work is necessarily cursory with an eye to the tone of Muslim–Christian relations before the eleventh century, focusing on issues which Ibn al-Ṭayyib and Iliyyā will address. Subsequent chapters will develop these themes further and refer to both Muslim and Christian voices that influenced the eleventh-century Muslim–Christian interface.

2. The Theologians

2.1 Abū al-Faraj ʿAbd Allāh Ibn al-Ṭayyib (d. 1043/434)

Abū al-Faraj ʿAbd Allāh Ibn al-Ṭayyib attained renown in his era and beyond as a polymath – physician, philosopher, professor and priest, a man who attained eminent learning while retaining a steadfast religious commitment. His written works in philosophy, medicine and religion number forty-two, most of which are no longer extant.[1] He lived in Baghdad as a scriptural commentator and scholar-monk-priest of the Church of the East.[2]

2.1.1 Exegetical, Theological and Ecclesial Contribution

He was prolific, though not perceived as innovative, as a scriptural commentator seeking to preserve the Antiochene exegetical tradition in the new medium of Arabic as he observed his native Syriac receding in importance. His translation of his predecessors' work into Arabic extended their influence among the Coptic churches of Egypt and Ethiopia. His commentary on the Bible titled *The Paradise of Christianity*[3] draws from Moshe bar Kepha (ca. 813–903) and Isho'dad of Merv (a ninth-century Syrian church father). The works of John Chrysostom (347–407) and Theodore of Mopsuestia (ca. 350–428) also find their way into his commentaries.[4] He penned over a dozen treatises of varying length on aspects of the Christian faith, many of which are no longer extant. Judging from his references to his own work, Ibn al-Ṭayyib

1. Samir states that many of his works were dictated and penned by his understudies. This may explain Avicenna's complaint about the weakness of Ibn al-Ṭayyib's style. It was actually the writing of his students (see Samir, "La place d'Ibn al-Ṭayyib dans la pensée arabe," 181–182).

2. The Assyrian Church of the East is popularly known as "Nestorian." In this work I avoid this moniker in favor of the preferred self-description of this ecclesial family – "Church of the East" or the "Assyrian Church of the East." I explain the reasons for this disassociation from Nestorius in chapter 5.

3. *Firdaws al-Naṣrāniyyā* فردوس النصرانية

4. His commentary on the Gospels is published in Arabic (see al-Ṭayyib, *Tafsīr al-Mashriqī*).

considered his *Treatise on Religious Principles*[5] as his *Summa Theologica.* Although it is no longer extant, extensive portions have been preserved in a Coptic recension.[6]

He was a committed churchman of the Church of the East serving as secretary of the Catholicos (Patriarch) Yuḥannā Ibn Nazūk (1012–1022) but also convening and leading the synod that elected the subsequent Catholicos Elias I (1028–1046) after six intervening years without a Patriarch due to the destruction of the patriarchal residence and unrest in the Christian quarter of Baghdad known as Dār al-Rūm.[7] After the synod, Elias I (also known as Elie of Tirḥan) renewed Ibn al-Ṭayyib's commission as secretary to oversee all religious publications for theological probity. In this capacity, Ibn al-Ṭayyib read Iliyyā of Nisibis's *Sessions* and approved its publication.[8] In addition, he made a notable contribution to the understanding of Canon law in the Church of the East through *The Law of Christendom*[9] in which he systematized early sources beginning with Nicea until the Church of the East patriarchs of his own era.[10]

2.1.2 Medical and Philosophical Contributions

As a physician, Ibn al-Ṭayyib attracted students from distant Persia and was esteemed as the leading physician in the 'Adūdiyya Hospital of Baghdad (established by 'Adūd al-Dawla). He was privy to a superior training in philosophy as a student of al-Ḥasan ibn al-Khammār, who studied under the renowned Yaḥyā Ibn 'Adī.[11] Ibn al-Ṭayyib has been referred to as the final link in a chain of Christian Arab Aristotelians in Baghdad where he was esteemed as the leader of the school of philosophy known as "The House of Wisdom" (*Bayt al-Ḥikma*). We find him explaining a *Book of Questions* – a presumed philosophical work of Ḥunayn ibn Isḥāq (d. 873) – as early as 1014/405 and offering a course shortly thereafter on Galen. His commentary on Porphyry's *Isagoge* was presumed to have been written by al-Fārābī until the detachment of one page from another revealed the true author.[12] In fact, he translated the works of several Greek philosophers and commented on others including Aristotle, Hippocrates and Galen.[13] One of his students – Ibn Buṭlān – recounts that he was engrossed for twenty years seeking to explain Aristotle's *Metaphysics.* The same student suggests that his unfettered assiduity contributed to the illness from which he ultimately died.

5. *Maqāla fī al-usūl aldīniyya* مقالة في الأصول الدينية
6. The recension is that of Abū Isḥāq Ibn al-'Assāl (Ibn al-'Assāl, *Majmū' Usūl al-Dīn*).
7. Samir, "La place d'Ibn al-Ṭayyib dans la pensée arabe," 186.
8. Landron, "Apologétique, polémique et attitudes Nestoriennes," 108.
9. *Fiqh al-Naṣrāniyyā* فقه النصرانية (see al-Ṭayyib, *Ibn aṭ-Ṭayyib Fiqh*).
10. Baum and Winkler, *Church of the East*, 72–73.
11. Landron, "Apologétique, polémique et attitudes Nestoriennes," 185.
12. Landron, 185, 187.
13. Faultless, "Ibn al-Ṭayyib," 667–669.

Ironically, Ibn al-Ṭayyib's contemporary Avicenna (Ibn Sīna) held his work in derision, even suggesting that he was mentally inept.[14] Perhaps the animosity stemmed from jealousy within the circle of philosophers or from Ibn al-Ṭayyib's prominence in a rival philosophical school.[15]

2.1.3 Ibn al-Ṭayyib and Islam

Recent studies have highlighted the lack of explicit reference to Islam in the work of Ibn al-Ṭayyib.[16] Circumstantially, one might infer that Ibn al-Ṭayyib was well versed in the polemic of his predecessors. He was fully conversant with Greek philosophy, highly stationed in Abbasid society as secretary to the Catholicos (the Patriarch of the Church of the East) and the most renowned physician of his day.[17] How, then, does one explain the near absence of explicit reference to the dominant religion?

In response, we note Ibn al-Ṭayyib's keen awareness of and intellectual engagement with the topics which dominated the Muslim–Christian interface of his day. His *Treatise on Religious Principles* treats the following topics:

> Proofs of the non-eternity of the world, the unity of God, the Trinity and the Union; that the Law of Jesus abrogates all other Laws and cannot itself be abrogated; proofs of the truth of the coming of Christ and of the Gospels; proofs that the pleasures of the righteous after resurrection are not eating and drinking but union with God, and that the punishment for the ignorant (*al-juhhāl*) is estrangement from God.[18]

Other themes that received a great deal of attention from Ibn al-Ṭayyib include the superiority and finality of the "law of Christ" and the veracity of the Gospels.[19] The presence of these themes suggests that Ibn al-Ṭayyib took interest in the critical issues of the Muslim–Christian interface of his era.

---

14. Landron, "Apologétique, polémique et attitudes Nestoriennes," 187, 192.

15. Samir quotes Bayhaqi, p. 42: من حق تصنيفه أن يُردّ على بائعه، ويُترك عليه ثمنه "His works deserve to be returned to the seller and one should relinquish to him what he has paid for them" (Samir, "La place d'Ibn al-Ṭayyib dans la pensée arabe," 183).

16. Julian Faultless writes, "The present writer has not come upon any explicit mention of Islam or Muslims in Ibn al-Ṭayyib's works (although he does mention Judaism by name). This in itself is remarkable for an intellectual living in Baghdad who must have thought daily about the position of Christians within the Islamic world" (Faultless, "Ibn al-Ṭayyib," 670).

17. Landron, *Chrétiens et musulmans en Irak*, 108.

18. Faultless, "Ibn al-Ṭayyib," 683.

19. Faultless, 679. Samir Khalil Samir suggests that Ibn al-Ṭayyib's discussion of the law in Psalm 19 invokes a classic theme of medieval Christian apologetics. "Ibn al-Ṭayyib addresses the theme of the Law of the Lord being perfect. He contrasts three types of law (*nāmūs*): natural (*ṭabīʿī*), biblical (*kitābī*) and surpassing (*ifḍālī*)" (S. K. Samir, "ʿAbdallâh b. aṭ-Ṭa yyib, Abû l-Farağ'," *Islamochristiana* 2 (1976): 203–204).

In this work, evidence is presented to demonstrate that Ibn al-Ṭayyib's lack of explicit mention of Islam does not indicate his ignorance thereof or his flight from the battleground of ideas. The precise reasons for this lack in his writings are difficult to discern, but we offer two considerations which may assist in arriving at a more balanced appreciation of his contribution to the Muslim–Christian interface. First, the battle of polemics had affected interfaith interaction such that any hope of reciprocity was extinguished. As a keen theological mind, Ibn al-Ṭayyib was aware of the barren and interminable conundrums to which Muslims had pushed their Christian counterparts. He avoids impasses deriving from the binary nature of polemic in previous centuries, nourishing his own flock which lived in a milieu now dominated by Islam. Second, Baghdad in the era of Ibn al-Ṭayyib was fraught with sectarian strife (discussed below) effectively narrowing the horizon of interfaith dialogue. Incentive to enter into direct polemical engagement was at a low ebb, especially as Christians risked social and financial loss if they did not prevail in public debate. Ibn al-Ṭayyib set forth the intellectual foundations of his Christian doctrine in response to the pervasive assault thereupon in sectarian Baghdad. His theology is his implicit apologetic. This research will examine select theological texts of Ibn al-Ṭayyib in light of the prevailing religious environment in order to provide a more accurate assessment of Ibn al-Ṭayyib.

2.1.4 Concluding Anecdote

A surviving anecdote related by Ibn Abī Uṣaybiʿa provides insight into Ibn al-Ṭayyib's approach to faith and science. Two Persian students arrived in Baghdad seeking the savant whose renown had reached their homeland. They repaired to a church where they were astonished to find Ibn al-Ṭayyib leading prayers in clerical robes with head uncovered, holding a censor. After the conclusion of the prayers, he observed their surprise but refrained from responding. He proceeded to teach them the arts of medicine. However, when the season of the Muslim pilgrimage arrived, he asked if they had completed their religious duty. Ascertaining they had not, Ibn al-Ṭayyib sent his Persian understudies on pilgrimage to Mecca. Upon their return, he asked if they dressed in humble garb, hurled stones at the devil and ran the course as required by the rite of pilgrimage. Upon their affirmative response, the master delivered a lesson to his Persian disciples instructing that in matters related to divine law, ritual (correct observance derived from divine law) takes precedence over rationality. Indeed, we shall encounter again Ibn al-Ṭayyib's penchant to subject rationality to revelation.[20]

20. Landron, "Apologétique, polémique et attitudes Nestoriennes," 186; Samir, "La place d'Ibn al-Ṭayyib dans la pensée arabe," 179.

2.2 Iliyyā of Nisibis (975/364–1046/437)

Iliyyā of Nisibis was a beloved bishop of the Church of the East. Presumably, his childhood home was in Sinn – the town of his father in the latter part of the tenth century. Sinn was located on the left bank of the Tigris River at its confluence with the Smaller Zab River. For this reason he is often referred to as Iliyyā bar Sennaya (*ibn al-Sinnī*). His intellectual capacities were quickly manifest such that he was ordained a priest by the tender age of nineteen. Early in life, Iliyyā took monastic vows at the nearby Monastery of Abba Simeon which was renowned for the healing properties of water drawn from its well. He also resided at the Monastery of Saint Michel near Mosul (996–1001/386–391) where he became the disciple of a venerable old monk, John the Lame (*al-a'raj*). This monastery was a favorite of Muslim visitors who often told of its picturesque promenades and lavish wine production.

Iliyyā drew the attention of his superiors through his piety, intelligence and wisdom. He was appointed the Bishop of Bayt Nūhadhra (near Dahuq) at the age of twenty-seven, only eight years after his ordination as priest (15 February 1002/392). He administered the affairs of the diocese for six years. By the relatively young age of thirty-two, occasioned by the death of the former Metropolitan Yahbalaha, Iliyyā was consecrated Metropolitan (Bishop) of Nisibis on 26 December 1009/399. The city of forty thousand gardens was famed for its theological school. While in Nisibis, he enjoyed the beneficence of the Marwanid Princes of Diyarbakir.[21] He resided in Nisibis until his death ostensibly in 1046 and was buried in Mayyāfāriqīn beside his brother – Abū Saʿīd Manṣūr Ibn ʿĪsā.[22]

Abū Saʿīd was also the physician of Abū al-Qāsim ibn ʿAlī al-Maghribī who mentioned the physician's name in the presence of his brother Iliyyā requesting that the Bishop reprimand his brother who had recently withdrawn from offering medical care to Abū al-Qāsim. When Iliyyā spoke to the doctor about this matter, Abū Saʿīd related to his brother a cryptic dream in which he was warned that Abū al-Qāsim would soon die and that he need no longer offer his services to him.[23]

21. Delly, *La théologie d'Elie bar-Senaya*, 9–12; Landron, *Chrétiens et musulmans en Irak*, 112–113. Many have dated Iliyyā's death to 1049. The more likely date is 1046 (Samir, *Foi et culture en Irak*).

22. This brother also achieved renown in the field of medicine and was the personal physician of Naṣr al-Dawla Ibn Marwan – Amīr of the Marwanid dynasty. Abū 'Saʿīd Manṣūr Ibn ʿĪsā is credited with the construction of a hospital in Mayyāfāriqīn. The story is that Naṣr al-Dawla's daughter had fallen ill and in his desperation to find a cure, the Marwanid sovereign said the reward for her cure would be the daughter's weight in *dirhams*. When Abū Saʿīd was credited for the cure, he directed Naṣr al-Dawla to use the sum for the construction of a hospital that all might benefit. Abū Saʿīd apparently shared the religious devotion of Iliyyā as he was known as Zāhid al-ʿŪlemā' ("the most ascetic scholar"). Samir, *Foi et culture en Irak*, 170.

23. Samir, 175–177. Abū Saʿīd also penned a treatise on the interpretation of dreams and visions (Samir, 170, 180).

2.2.1 Iliyyā's Literary Production

Iliyyā was one of the most illustrious and prolific intellectuals of the eleventh century whose written corpus extends beyond theology to the fields of history and linguistics.[24] His writings include the renowned *Chronography*[25] which was esteemed by both Muslims and Christians, a thorough grammar of his native Syriac as well as a Syriac–Arabic glossary, works in canonical law, as well as a work of pastoral interest entitled *Dispelling Anxiety*.[26] He also wrote *The Demonstration of the Correctness of the Faith*[27] which defended his Church of the East theology in the sectarian milieu.[28]

This research will focus on a text produced by Iliyyā in a gracious dialogue with a Muslim vizier[29] who, by all appearances, enjoyed a reciprocal friendship with the Bishop. One writer deems Iliyyā's *Sessions* to be "the most beautiful Muslim–Christian apologetic in our possession from the golden age of Arabic Christian literature in the Oriental Church of the East."[30] From the outset, there is a warm reciprocity in the dialogue which merits our attention as an outstanding example of eleventh-century interfaith interaction. As mentioned above, the dialogue was reviewed by Ibn al-Ṭayyib as he had become the official editor of materials penned by Church of the East clergy. Iliyyā includes a subscript stating:

> After completing this letter, O dear brother and excellent *Shaykh*, I deem it proper to send it before you and the others have become aware of it, to the excellent *Shaykh*, priest, doctor and philosopher, Abī al-Faraj Ibn al-Ṭayyib, the secretary of the Patriarch so that he will contemplate it and inform me of his opinion. Ecclesial laws enjoin the author of a book on dogma to show it first to the reigning patriarch as well as to the savants. But as there is no patriarch presently and given that the *Shaykh* is the only man of his time, the organ of all who live there and all clerics, I send to him this letter. After reading it and examining its contents, he wrote in his hand on the bottom of the letter what follows: "I have read it and prayed for the life of its composer and for the continuation of his prayers for the world. The letter is extremely beautiful, orthodox

24. For an overview of Iliyyā's literary output with bibliography see Monferrer Sala, "Elias of Nisibis," 727–741.

25. *Kitāb al-azmina* كتاب الأزمنة 1019.

26. Samir, "Deux cultures qui s'affrontent," 619. *Kitāb daf' al-hamm* كتاب دفع الهم

27. *Kitāb al-burhān 'alā ṣaḥīḥ al-īmān* كتاب البرهان على صحيح الإيمان

28. Baum and Winkler, *Church of the East*, 70–71.

29. The Vizier was a high-ranking government official whose duties corresponded to those of a Minister of the Interior or Prime Minister.

30. Delly, *La théologie d'Elie bar-Senaya*, 15.

and in harmony with the ecclesial books. It is impossible for him who loves the truth to reject a single word thereof."[31]

2.2.2 Abū al-Qāsim al-Ḥusayn ibn ʿAlī al-Maghribī (995–1027/334–418)

Abū al-Qāsim – Iliyyā's Muslim interlocutor – was a historical figure whose accomplishments were detailed by the Islamic scholar and historian Shams al-Dīn Abū Al-ʿAbbās Aḥmad Ibn Muḥammad Ibn Khallikān (1211/608 – 1282/681). He hailed from a highly stationed family of the Fāṭimid dynasty where he received a noteworthy intellectual and theological formation having memorized the Qur'ān and a few works of grammar and ancient Arabic poetry.[32] Thus, he was not unaware of the issues which figured large at the Muslim–Christian interface of his era and his dialogues with Iliyyā bear this out. The Vizier and his family entered into conflict with one of the most renowned figures of the Fāṭimid dynasty – al-Ḥākim bi-Amr Allāh (d. 1021/412) – whose antics are legendary in Islamic history. His mindless destruction of Jerusalem earned him the epitaph "the mad Caliph" and was one factor among others that provoked the disastrous Crusades. It was this al-Ḥākim who executed Abū al-Qāsim's father,[33] uncle and two brothers (1010/400), resulting in Abū al-Qāsim's flight from Fāṭimid Cairo at the age of twenty-nine.[34] Later, he would attempt a coup to replace the Fāṭimid Caliph with the Alīd Amīr of Mecca. As the attempt failed, Abū al-Qāsim sought refuge in Iraq where he served the Uqaylids of Mosul as well as the Dailemites of Baghdad. Due to ongoing intrigue and the persistent loss of favor from the Fāṭimid Caliph, he was forced to seek refuge with the Amīr of Diyārbakīr – Naṣr al-Dawla Aḥmad ibn Marwān.[35]

Abū al-Qāsim was a man of considerable education and literary output. His writings include a work of verse and prose, an abridgment of the *Reformation of Morals*,[36] *Familiar Discourses*[37] and *Refinement of the People of Distinction*.[38] His father left a record of his education in a copy of his abridgment of the *Reformation of Morals*. Therein he noted his son's accomplishments in memorizing the Qur'ān

31. Delly, 16.

32. Landron, *Chrétiens et musulmans en Irak*, 114.

33. One source states that Abū al-Qāsim was arrested in Cairo but escaped, joining his father in Iraq (Amedroz, *Marwanid Dynasty*, 138).

34. R. Caspar, A. Charfi and S. K. Samir, "Bibliographie du dialogue islamo-chrétien (XIe–XIIe siècles)," *Islamochristiana* 3 (1977): 256–284.

35. Khallikan, *Ibn Khallikan's Biographical Dictionary*, 453; Landron, *Chrétiens et musulmans en Irak*, 114; Samir, *Foi et culture en Irak*, 181–183.

36. *Islāḥ al-mantiq* إصلاح المنطق

37. *Kitāb al-ināš* كتاب الإناس

38. *Adab al-khawāṣṣ* أداب الخواص

and a number of grammatical and philological books as well as mastering fifteen thousand verses from ancient Arabic poetry and excelling in orthography, algebra and composition.[39]

While occupying his post in Diyārbakīr, he came into contact with Iliyyā of Nisibis and engaged in a dialogue with the Bishop over three successive visits from July 1026/417 to June 1027/418.[40] Iliyyā recorded the substance of the Sessions in response to a request from Abū al-Qāsim. Abū al-Qāsim died on the eleventh day of Ramadan (15 October) 418/1027, only four months after his third visit to Iliyyā. By his request, his body was interred in Kufā, near the Chapel of ʿAlī Ibn Abī Tālib, confirming his Shiite inclinations.[41] He requested the following inscription on his tomb: "I have long traveled on the way of error and ignorance. It was time for me to arrive at the end of my journey. I have repented of my sins and this latter part of my journey will perhaps erase the first part. After forty-five years, I would have hoped for a longer respite had I not known that my Creditor is generous."[42]

Although Abū al-Qāsim read the personal correspondence of Iliyyā before knowledgeable Muslims who praised Iliyyā's knowledge of their faith, he would not have seen Iliyyā's account of the Sessions as they were finalized three months after his death.[43] In their correspondence, Abū al-Qāsim requested that Iliyyā send to him a written account of their dialogue as well as *Dispelling Anxiety*,[44] a work penned by the Bishop in response to Abū al-Qāsim's existential struggle.[45]

3. Buyid Ascendancy in the Abbasid Realm

In this section, the political and social context in which Ibn al-Ṭayyib labored is examined. Section 4 will deal with the political context of Bishop Iliyyā.

3.1 Abbasid Loss of Political Hegemony (850–945)

Ibn al-Ṭayyib labored in early eleventh-century Baghdad at a time when the powerful and centralized Abbasid administration had begun to wane. Abbasid authority was challenged both externally and internally through the late ninth and early tenth

39. Khallikan, *Ibn Khallikan's Biographical Dictionary*, 451.

40. Samir, "Deux cultures qui s'affrontent," 620. We will discuss the possibility of fabrication of *The Sessions* in chapter 4.

41. Khallikan, *Ibn Khallikan's Biographical Dictionary*, 454.

42. Khallikan, 454; Landron, *Chrétiens et musulmans en Irak*, 114.

43. Landron, 116–117.

44. *Daf' al-hamm* دفع الهم

45. Samir, "Le Daf' al-hamm d'Elie de Nisibe," 116.

centuries.[46] By the period of our interest, Abbasid hegemony had eroded such that the Shiʿīte Buyids were now holding the reins of political power. Though political sovereignty slipped from the hands of the Abbasids, they maintained prominence in matters of religion and jurisprudence and at intervals commanded the allegiance and awe of their subjects.[47] Indeed, at the particular moment of our interest, the Abbasid Caliph was reasserting his authority, with implications for the interfaith environment in Ibn al-Ṭayyib's Baghdad.[48]

3.2 Buyid Sovereignty (923–1062)

The Buyids – a Persian people of Kurdish ethnicity – held the reins of power in the Abbasid realm from 945/344 till 1062/454 (Ibn al-Ṭayyib's death was in 1043/434). Because the Buyids held only Iraq and western Persia, their dominance did not rival that of the Abbasids at their pinnacle of power.[49] Though the Caliph retained his title, the Buyids essentially took over the administration of the empire, maintaining or deposing Abbasid Caliphs as figureheads.

Religiously, the Buyids were Shīʿites of some variety.[50] They were marked primarily by their attentiveness to political and economic exigencies. They never attempted to install a Shīʿite (*'Alīd*) Caliph but were content to give fealty to the Abbasid Caliphs who reciprocated by providing a religious cloak of legitimacy to their rule.[51]

---

46. Montgomery Watt suggests three reasons for the decline of the Abbasids. First was the complexity of maintaining relations of trust amidst administrators and governors across such an extensive region. "The rewards of office were enormous, but the chances of enjoying them in a leisurely old age were slight." Watt's second factor is the Abbasid reliance on a mercenary military force. The Abbasids attempted to leverage loyalty through financial remuneration of soldiers. Keeping the mercenary forces supplied required increasing taxation – Watt's third factor (Watt, *The Majesty That Was Islam*, 160).

47. "ʿAḍūd al-Dawlah approached the Caliph Ṭā'iʿ with reverence, kissing the ground before him, whereupon he received his commission" (Arnold, *Caliphate*, 66–67).

48. Lewis, "Abbasids," 19–20.

49. Points eastward were under the Sāmāmids before the Ghaznavids. The Fāṭimids ruled Egypt and North Africa from 969 and also controlled a considerable portion of Syria (Watt, *The Majesty That Was Islam*, 193).

50. Some have discerned Zaydī tendencies while others have suggested Twelver Shīʿite characteristics. They may have adopted Imāmism (the forerunner of Twelver Shīʿism) as a political move to gain the support of the wealthy echelons of Baghdad or to counter the rigidity of the Sunnī *'ulamā* (religious scholars) (Watt, 202, 212). Also, the occultation of the Imām (*al-ghaiba al-kubrā*) would have been convenient, facilitating their puppet control of the Abbasid Caliphs (Kraemer, *Humanism*, 41).

51. Lewis, "Abbasids," 20. Indeed, some view their administration more as an effort to reinvigorate Sassanian leadership than a strictly Shīʿite coup. Beginning with ʿAdūd al-Dawla (978–983/367–372), who represents the pinnacle of Buyid power, their supreme leader was styled in Sassanian fashion *shāhanshāh* ("King of kings") rather than by the previous epithet *amīr* ("ruler") (Kraemer, *Humanism*, 45).

3.2.1 The Decline of the Buyids

Around the turn of the millennium, the Buyid grip on administrative reins began to loosen. A maritime trading crisis weakened their administration and contributed to the economic superiority of the Fāṭimids of Cairo.[52] Additionally, the Buyids inherited the challenge that had contributed to the downfall of the Abbasids – maintaining an army. This costly proposition proved unwieldy for a Buyid powerbase that was, by this time, split into three sections plagued by the family infighting of three brothers.[53]

Social indicators paint a picture of a city that was struggling to maintain its former prestige. Though intellectual currents flourished, the Buyid rulers sought to check the degradation of security due to "the high cost of living, lack of government funds, famine, epidemic, pestilence, inefficient administration, and a general breakdown of authority and of law and order."[54] The Buyid ascendancy was rather short-lived. The Seljūqs – a Turkish people new to the fold of Islam – were rapidly advancing.[55]

3.2.2 Status of Christians in Buyid Iraq

By all appearances, Christians were well treated during the initial Buyid tenure.[56] However, such good fortune for Christians under Buyid administration was not a constant. The weakening Buyid powerbase gave the Sunnī Abbasid Caliph al-Qādir bi-llāh (991–1031/381–422) sufficient leverage to mobilize a Ḥanbalī[57] Sunnī resurgence

52. Watt suggests this might have been the implementation of a Fāṭimid policy or possibly the influence of the Carmathians (Watt, *The Majesty That Was Islam*, 201). Trade was re-routed from the Persian Gulf to the sea route.

53. Cahen, "Buwayhids or Buyids," 1350–1356. Sulṭān al-Dawla ("Authority of the State") assumed leadership in 1012 and proceeded to fight with his brother Musharrif al-Dawla ("Bestower of Honor of the State") around 1019. Jalāl al-Dawla (a third Buyid brother – "Majesty of the State") came to power in 1025. By this time, the Buyid powerbase had weakened to the point that he was incapable of relocating his governorship from Baṣra to Baghdad. With no more brothers to fight, he battled his nephew (Abū Kālījār) for sovereignty. By the time the former died and the latter took over, it was all too clear that the Seljuqs were the portending power in the region (Watt, *The Majesty That Was Islam*, 198–199). Abū Kālījār must have recognized the obvious for he made a treaty with Tughril-Beg, the Seljūq leader, and sealed the deal with a double marriage alliance. Upon Abū Kālījār's death (1048/439), political chaos ensued in Baghdad.

54. Kraemer, *Humanism*, 51.

55. Their leader Ṭurghil-Beg proclaimed himself Sultan and proceeded to overpower Jurjān, Ṭabaristan (1041), Hamadhan, Rayy (1042), Mosul and beyond (1043), Ispahan (1050) and Aserbaijan (1054) (Watt, *The Majesty That Was Islam*, 200).

56. The renowned Buyid Amīr ʿAdūd al-Dawla (978–983/367–372) installed the Christian Naṣr Ibn-Harūn as his administrator (Vizier) and authorized him to refurbish and rebuild churches and monasteries that had fallen into disrepair in Mesopotamia and Persia.

57. This school of jurisprudence held that divine law can never be subject to human reason. For the Ḥanbalī, the will of Allāh is inscrutable and can be known only insofar as Allāh reveals himself. Moreover, Ḥanbalī conceptualization of the balance of human action and divine sovereignty was weighted heavily toward the latter. Human actions result from divine predestination. This tendency was also apparent in Ḥanbalī interpretation of the Qur'ān. Allegoric interpretation was rejected, as was rational theological speculation (Lapidus, *History of Islamic Societies*, 166). For the Ḥanbalīs, the role of rationality, though

in Baghdad. He gained political power, witnessed by his wresting a Shīʿite mosque from the Buyid leadership and returning it to the Sunnī fold. In 1019/410, he publicly condemned the view that the Qur'ān was created as well as any exegesis of the Qur'ān that resorted to allegory, consigning offenders to infidel status and permitting the shedding of their blood with impunity.[58] He was allowed a free hand politically and shrewdly used his authority to foster a strident Hanbalī resurgence.[59] Around 1012, al-Qādir compelled Christians to wear distinctive clothing invoking clauses from the Pact of ʿUmar, which will be discussed below. Reports of stoning and mobs breaking up Christian funerals appear at this time and many rank-and-file Christians embraced Islam[60] while others migrated to more congenial areas.[61] Such moments of chaos resulted in a shifting religious demographic:[62]

> And in the year three hundred and ninety two of the Arabs [1001 AD] the Arabs rose in a tumult against the Christians in Baghdad and they looted their houses. And they also put forth their hands against the churches to destroy them. And having set on fire that church of the Jacobites which is by the side of the place where flour was ground, it fell down on a very large number of Arabs, men, and women, and children, and it suffocated them and burned to death those who set it on fire; and the onlookers became terror stricken.[63]

3.2.3 *Dhimmī* Laws and the Pact of ʿUmar

Discerning the broader social status of Christians in eleventh-century Baghdad is no small challenge. On the one hand, some Christians in Abbasid Baghdad maintained a very high social standing.[64] Christians still held positions of influence as intellectuals (doctors, translators, and the like). We have observed Ibn al-Ṭayyib's prominence

---

not entirely unimportant, was a subordinate one of defending the faith and persuading others to embrace it (Rissanen, *Theological Encounter*, 73).

58. Kraemer, *Humanism*, 62.

59. Sourdel, "Al-Kadir bi'llah," 378–379.

60. Moffett, *History of Christianity*, 380.

61. Wilmshurst, *Martyred Church*, 190.

62. Al-Qādir also labored to suppress remnants of Muʿtazilī thought, demanding penance of Ḥanafī jurisprudents with Muʿtazilī affinities. He sponsored the public reading of *al-risāla al-qādiriyya* (1018/409) – apparently named after himself – a profession of faith which condemned Shīʿism, Muʿtazilism and even Ashʿarism. In his latter years he sponsored other documents which further reinforced Ḥanbalī tenets chiefly by denouncing divergent views such as the creation of the Qur'ān (Sourdel, "Al-Kadir bi'llah," 378–379).

63. Budge and Hebraeus, *Chronography of Gregory Abul Faraj*, 183.

64. Within recent history, Christian statesmen such as the renowned Yaḥyā Ibn ʿAdī (d. 974/363) wrote and interacted with great freedom amongst Baghdad's elite.

and it is not difficult to adduce evidence for some Christians' high social standing. However, the status of the Christian elite of Baghdad may not accurately reflect the social conditions of less-privileged Christians.

A legal code known as the Pact of ʿUmar was invoked at intervals throughout the Abbasid era. The Pact is a summary statement of the principles applied by Muslim leaders to the non-Muslim communities (*dhimmī*) under their care, regulating their social and economic status. The historical development of the Pact is disputed although it likely originated with the Muslim victory over the Christians of Damascus or the Arabian Peninsula in the late seventh century and underwent editorial amendments subsequently. The Pact replaced earlier surrender agreements and implemented more stringent stipulations on the conquered peoples. At least by the mid-ninth century, when the Caliph al-Mutawakkil published a renowned edict regarding the non-Muslim communities under his sovereignty, the Pact represented a consensus as to how non-Muslims should be treated.[65]

The Pact's stringent terms should not be read as a detailed portrayal of Christian treatment during the period. Levels of implementation varied depending upon the region of implementation, the policy and practice of Muslim governors and the economic conditions prevailing at the time in question.[66] Implementation of the Pact was an intermittent rather than perennial feature of the period.[67] The severity of the Pact[68] – surprising by modern standards but usual for medieval times – is difficult to reconcile with the fact that Christians benefited from the good graces of their rulers, holding high positions, studying under Muslim masters and amassing wealth.[69] Nevertheless, for the purpose of this research, it is noteworthy that the Caliph al-

65. Levy-Rubin, "Pact of 'Umar."

66. Dennett, *Conversion and the Poll Tax*, 12.

67. Even during times of known implementation of the Pact, surprising incongruences appear in the literature. For instance, the Caliph al-Mutawakkil who implemented the most severe laws against *dhimmīs*, including the destruction of all new churches, was thoroughly conciliatory and civil toward his Christian doctors. The laws were reinvoked by Harūn al-Rashīd in 807/191 and al-Mutawakkil in 849–50/234–35. The fact that the laws of the Pact were reinstated suggests that their enforcement could grow lax (Thomas, *Early Muslim Polemic*, 9).

68. For example, Abū al-Faḍl, Vizier in Rayy (972/361), prohibited all worship in churches. Reports of Christians leaving or being deported from Islamic lands, attacks on churches, mob violence against Christians, etc., are documented. The multiplication of monasteries and convents during the period may indicate a mentality of refuge-seeking among Christians. During Ibn al-Ṭayyib's active life, the Buyids detained Metropolitan John VI in Baghdad (1001/391) and demanded a ransom (Reynolds, *Muslim Theologian*, 71).

69. Tritton, *Caliphs and Their Non-Muslim Subjects*, 50, 231–232.

Qādir (991/381 – 1031/422) reintroduced the Pact in Baghdad concurrently with the productive period of Ibn al-Ṭayyib.[70]

It is difficult to aver specific implications on Muslim–Christian relations of the period owing to the Caliph's Ḥanbalī proclivities. Nevertheless, for the first thirty years of the eleventh century, the period during which Ibn al-Ṭayyib flourished, the Abbasid Caliph aggressively pressed his Ḥanbalī views, including the implementation of legal clauses from the Pact of 'Umar, while regaining political influence in Baghdad.

4. The Marwanids

While Ibn al-Ṭayyib labored under the Buyid administration, Iliyyā of Nisibis enjoyed a more congenial leadership under the Marwanids – a Kurdish dynasty which flourished in eastern Turkey from 990/380 to 1085/478. The first ruler was Abū ʿAlī al-Ḥasan Ibn Marwān, who seized the city of Mayyāfāriqīn[71] after the demise of the Buyid Amīr Adūd al-Dawla (983/373). However, it was a later brother of Ibn Marwān – Naṣr al-Dawla Aḥmad – whose fifty-year reign (1011–1061/401–453) brought the dynasty to an unprecedented level of prosperity and cultural refinement. Upon his accession, he was congratulated by the three surrounding regional powers – the Byzantines of Constantinople, the Fāṭimid Caliph of Cairo (al-Ḥākim) and the Buyids of Baghdad now ruled by Sultān al-Dawla. Naṣr al-Dawla was a skilled politician who accommodated the large surrounding powers while simultaneously carving out a sphere of influence for the Marwanid dynasty. His court was frequented by scholars, historians and poets and his reign was the apogee of the Marwanid dynasty in terms of social, cultural and commercial prosperity. To his credit, Naṣr al-Dawla chose two able viziers, one of whom figures large in our story – Abū al-Qāsim al-Ḥusayn Ibn ʿAlī al-Maghribī (referred to above). It is possible that the majority of the Marwanid populace was Christian of some variety. This may explain the Amīr's establishment of two houses for Christian pilgrims in Jerusalem in 1053/445 as revealed by a marble slab inscription. Though he was pious in personal practice, religion was not Naṣr al-Dawla Aḥmad's primary concern. He was known for his immense wealth, his 360 concubines and his gastronomical pleasures. Under Nasr al-Dawla's beneficent leadership, Mayyāfārikīn became a cultural *point de rencontre* for philosophers, poets and religious scholars. He was able to annex the city of Edessa in 1026/417, although he was later forced to cede Edessa and Nisibīn to the Bedouin Arab dynasties of

70. Thomas, "Muslim Regard for Christians," 15. Interestingly, the Fāṭimid Caliph al-Ḥākim (996–1021/386–412) reinvoked the Pact of ʿUmar as well from Cairo impacting Christian communities on the flanks of the Buyid/Abbasid realm.

71. Mayyāfāriqīn was a city in the Diyarbakir province of eastern Turkey. Contemporary Silvan has been identified as one possible site; another is Arzan.

Northern Syria.[72] The prevailing religious attitudes of the Marwanids likely contributed to the air of reciprocity that dominated Iliyyā's Sessions with Abū al-Qāsim.

5. Islamic Voices of the Abbasid Era

By the early ninth century the polemic of Muslim scholars toward Christians was concerned primarily with two doctrines: the Trinity and the incarnation.[73] If any movement is noticeable in the tenth century, it is a continual sharpening of these two focal points of polemic interest.[74] The confident refutation of these doctrines reveals a supreme confidence of Muslims in their system of belief and the philosophical coherence of Islam. The title *A Refutation of the Christians* appeared repeatedly in the early *kalām* literature demonstrating that the refutation of the Trinity and the incarnation had become a common exercise in which Muslim polemicists engaged with vigor. The high bar of intellectual rigor was set by the Islamic doctrine of *tawḥīd* (divine unity). In this sectarian environment, any intimation that an Islamic *mutakallim* (theologian) was sympathetic to Christian ideas was tantamount to the charge of heresy.[75] In the following pages, a few of the leading Islamic voices are surveyed, highlighting aspects of the polemic with which Ibn al-Ṭayyib and Iliyyā engaged.

5.1 The Trinity

5.1.1 Abū ʿĪsā Ibn Hārūn Ibn Muḥammad al-Warrāq (d. soon after 864/250)

Abū ʿĪsā[76] was active in Baghdad in the early to mid-ninth/third century. Although his precise Muslim affinities are not clear, he had fully imbibed the Muslim doctrine of God's complete separation from creation – a view explicated at length by the

72. Hillenbrand, "Marwanids," 626.

73. A third major issue under attack by Muslim polemicists was the veracity of the Christian Scriptures, inspired, at least in part, by the apparent absence of prophecy pointing to Muḥammad. This issue is present in the ninth century but was most fully elaborated in the eleventh century by the Muʿtazilī ʿAbd al-Jabbār who developed an elaborate narrative of Christian origins to explain how the apostle Paul had effectively derailed the Christian community, diverting it from the true gospel of Christ (see Reynolds, *Muslim Theologian*).

74. Thomas, "Early Muslim Responses to Christianity," 250.

75. Swanson, "Early Christian–Muslim Theological Conversation," 5.

76. Of Abū ʿĪsā's works, his *Refutation of the Three Christian Sects* (الرد على الثلاث فراق من النصارى *al-Radd 'alā al-thalāth firaq min al-Naṣārā*) has survived through Ibn ʿAdī's *Manifest of the Errors of Muhammad Ibn Harūn*. It provides the most detailed and extensive attack on Christian doctrine prior to the fourteenth century and it served as a reference point for Muslim polemicists for a century after its composition (Thomas, "Abū ʿĪsā l-Warrāq," 700). The fact that no Christian response become apparent until Yaḥya Ibn ʿAdī's nearly a century later may indicate the intense challenge that his work posed to Christian intellectuals.

Muʿtazilī.[77] He is known for his relentless interrogation of religious tenets. Although he manipulates Christian thought, language and sectarian divisions with ease, his mentality is antithetic to concepts such as "Trinity" and "incarnation" which are an affront to his rational view of God as transcendent and other. His detailed knowledge of the faith afforded him an opportunity to demonstrate fissures in Christian thought using its doctrinal constructs, addressing his polemic to the various Christian sects and their specific distinctions. The sheer volume of objections that Abū ʿĪsā raised and the scope of doctrinal issues he contested rendered a thorough Christian response virtually impossible.[78]

He insists on the internal inconsistency of Christian doctrines such as the Trinity, pressing Christians into a logical conundrum concerning the differentiation of the persons of the Trinity which Christians had located in the hypostases. Abū ʿĪsā reasons that these hypostases must be either "substance" of the divinity or non-substance. If the hypostases are substance then God is "internally differentiated," defying divine unity. If the differentiation of the hypostases does not derive from the substance, then the cause thereof lies outside God. This is equally problematic suggesting some cause which is coeternal with God and acting upon the divinity. In either case, the unity of God is violated.[79]

5.1.2 Abū Bakr Muḥammad al-Bāqillānī (d. 1013/403)

Al-Bāqillānī (d. 1013/403)[80] was a judge residing in tenth-century Baghdad who adhered to the Mālikī school of jurisprudence. Thus he was an older contemporary of Ibn al-Ṭayyib residing in the same city. An outstanding student of al-Ashʿārī's disciples,[81] he was renowned for his prodigious literary output (writing thirty to forty pages after evening prayers) as well as his trenchant polemic directed at other religious faiths including Christianity. His prolific nature (writing some fifty-five works, most of which are no longer extant) is accompanied by a penchant for contention. His incisive responses earned him the title "sword of the Sunna and spokesman of the

77. Thomas, "Christian Theologians," 272. Muʿtazilism was an intellectual movement within Islam that flourished from the eighth to tenth century in Baṣra and Baghdad. It was devoted to the rational defense of Islam against any other intellectual or religious claim. The Muʿtazilī are known for their denial of the eternality of the Qur'ān as well as their emphasis on divine unity and justice.

78. Thomas, *Early Muslim Polemic*, 75.

79. Thomas, *Christian Doctrines*, 270.

80. The *Kitāb tamhīd al-awā'il wa-talkhīṣ al-dalā'il* (composed around 980/369) of al-Bāqillānī is the earliest extant systematic exposition of the Ashʿarī system of belief and contains his response to Christianity entitled *bāb al-kalām 'alā al-naṣārā.*

81. Al-Bāqillānī was educated by immediate disciples of al-Ashʿarī having been born (941–942/330) only six years after the latter's death (935/324) (Thomas, *Christian Doctrines*, 119).

nation."[82] The narrative of his voyage to the Byzantine capital provides an anecdotal perspective on al-Bāqillānī's agitated rejection of Christian views. He was brought into the presence of the Christian emperor through a low door, forcing him to stoop, ostensibly in homage to the Byzantine sovereign. Al-Bāqillānī's colorful response was to enter posterior first.[83] Accordingly, one is not surprised to find an acrimonious tone in al-Bāqīllanī's views on Christianity. His discussion is limited to the doctrines of the Trinity and incarnation as the theological specimens that contradict Islamic *tawḥīd* (unity of God).[84]

He rejects the Christian discussion of the *jawhar* (substance) of God, a reference to the Aristotelian thought of Christians such as Yaḥyā Ibn ʿAdī who categorized God as "substance" since he could not be conceived of as "accident." Thomas points out that the term bore different meanings in Christian and Islamic thought. Christians defined it essentially as "a self-subsistent agent." In the Muslim context the term denotes "a basic element of the material world upon which the constituent parts of physical reality are constructed."[85] Al-Bāqillānī, presupposing the Islamic concept, sees the attribution of substance to God as an anthropomorphism – a prohibited category in his Ashʿārī frame of reference.[86] Both Ibn al-Ṭayyib and Iliyyā will clarify the meaning of *jawhar* (substance) at the Muslim–Christian interface.

He also rejects the limitation of the hypostases to three, satirically suggesting that Christians should not limit the plurality to three but could increase it to four or fourteen.[87] Some had identified the three attributes as existence, knowledge and life. By suggesting that the number be increased, proposing "power" as an additional attribute, Al-Bāqillānī posited what, for him, was a natural Christian reaction that power is included in the attribute of life. That being the case, the attribute of "knowledge" might also be included in the attribute of "life," ostensibly demonstrating an arbitrary designation of the eternal attributes.[88]

Christians had attempted to relate the concept of the Trinity to the Islamic discussion of the attributes (*al-ṣifāt*) citing the assertion of the Ashʿārīs that God's attributes are "neither identical with him nor different from him."[89] In like manner,

82. *Sayf al-sunna wa-lisān al-umma* سيف السنّة ولسان الأمّة

83. W. Haddad, *Christian–Muslim Encounters*, 85.

84. Thomas, *Christian Doctrines*, 124.

85. Thomas, 128.

86. In this, he is likely following al-Kindī's *Refutation of the Trinity* (W. Haddad, *Christian–Muslim Encounters*, 88) and the *Radd* of Abū ʿĪsā (Thomas, *Early Muslim Polemic*, 78–79).

87. The seven attributes held by the Ashʿārī are life, knowledge, power, will, speech, vision and hearing. Al-Bāqillānī posited an eighth: *baqā* – eternality (W. Haddad, *Christian–Muslim Encounters*, 86).

88. W. Haddad, 89.

89. The precise formula used by the Ashʿārī is that the attributes are "neither God nor other than him" (*lā hiya huwa wa-lā hiya ghayruh* لا هي هو ولا هي غيره) (Thomas, *Christian Doctrines*, 165).

the three hypostases of the Trinity are neither identical with him nor different from him. Al-Bāqillānī, however, will not allow the equivocation because Muslims do not assert that God is "other than" his attributes in the sense that he could not replace them or be their substitute.[90] One of the key contributions of Ibn al-Ṭayyib is the definition of the hypostases as the attributes belonging to the essence of deity, which are of necessity limited to three for reasons which we shall observe later.

5.2 The Incarnation

5.2.1 ʿAlī Ibn Rabban al-Ṭabarī (d. ca. 855/241)

Muslim–Christian interaction received new impetus during the Abbasid era with the rise of Muslim polemicists who had converted from East Syrian Christianity. Al-Ṭabarī converted to Islam late in life (around the age of seventy).[91] He was an atypical Muslim apologist of the period specifically because he brought such a developed knowledge of Christianity to his polemical task.[92] His arguments fuelled future generations of Muslim apologists such as ʿAbd al-Jabbār in his account of the temptation of Jesus[93] as well as the tenth-century convert from Christianity al-Ḥasan Ibn Ayyūb whose work survived in *The Correct Answer*[94] of Ibn Taymiyya (d. 1328/728).[95]

Christians confidently referred to Christ's numerous miracles as proof of his divine nature. Al-Ṭabarī's counter-perspective on the miracles of Christ placed him on a par with other prophets who worked miracles equal to those of Christ. Was Christ born of a virgin? Adam was brought into existence with neither father nor mother. Elijah raised the dead as did Christ. Moses fed a multitude. Yet in no case do these miracles substantiate a claim to divinity on the part of the prophet.[96] Iliyyā gave his response to this specific claim in the Sessions.

Al-Ṭabarī adduced scriptural proofs to substantiate the claim that Jesus was a mere man. One example of such is John's report of Jesus's retort to the Jewish leaders

---

90. Thomas, 164–165.

91. His *Radd 'alā al-Nasārā* was written as an explicit retraction of his Christian faith while the *Kitāb al-dīn wa al-dawla* (*The Book of Religion and Empire*) is an apologetic of Muḥammad's prophethood based on his virtues and fulfillment of biblical prophecies (Thomas, "ʿAlī l-Ṭabarī," 669–670, 672).

92. Thomas, *Early Muslim Polemic*, 17.

93. Reynolds, *Muslim Theologian*, 139. Reynolds also points out that Goldziher's *Über Muhammed: Polemik gegen ahl al-Kitab* preserves evidence that Muslim writers (cited on pages 374–379) are using biblical texts which al-Ṭabarī collected and translated centuries earlier (Reynolds, *Muslim Theologian*, 200; cited from A. Mingana, "Remarks on Tabari's Semi-Official Defence of Islam," *Bulletin of the John Rylands Library* 9 [1925]: 236).

94. *al-Jawāb al-ṣaḥīḥ* الجواب الصحيح

95. Thomas, "ʿAlī l-Ṭabarī," 671.

96. Thomas, "Miracles of Jesus," 222.

in John 8:37: "You want to kill me, but I am a man who told you the truth that I heard from God."[97] His claim is that although a handful of references in the Gospel could lead to the false conclusion of Christ's divinity, the greater weight of evidence (over 20,000 references) favors his humanity.[98]

He refers to Old Testament messianic prophecies to insist that the Messiah was to be human, not divine. Furthermore, he insists that the use of Father/Son language is figurative, connoting respect but not divine origin.[99] He refers to the transfiguration as a further proof of Christ's humanity as God declares his pleasure in Christ. The verse as quoted by al-Ṭabarī is consistent with Islamic claims concerning the Messiah, referring to Christ as a "servant": "This is my servant, whom I have declared pure, and my beloved, in whom I take rest."[100] If a servant, then he could not be God. "This is my servant whom I have chosen, and my beloved with whom I myself am satisfied. Behold I place my spirit upon him and he will call the nations to the truth."[101] Al-Ṭabarī gave a great deal of attention to John 20:17 which, for him, is a clear statement of Christ's non-divinity and his submission to God.[102] The verse reflects qur'ānic declarations made by Christ, such as Qur'ān 3:51, 5:117 and 19:36.

5.2.2 Abū ʿĪsā Ibn Hārūn Ibn Muḥammad al-Warrāq

Abu ʿIsā explores questions related to why the Son (as opposed to the Father or the Spirit) was united with human nature and whether or not this unity was an act of the three hypostases or only the Son, as Christians claim.[103] The second section deals with particular challenges to the concept of the unity occasioned by the birth and death of Christ. Attention is given to the period of Jesus's gestation in the womb as well as his childhood years. The ideas of God being carried in the womb of a woman

97. Reynolds, *Muslim Theologian*, 152.

98. Thomas, *Christian Doctrines*, 59, fn 45. Al-Ṭabarī, at times, seems to overplay his hand, insinuating Christ's inferior spiritual stature: "One who said 'O Lord, if it is possible to make this tribulation pass from me then do so' is one who doubts the capability of God. It cannot be that the one who says this knows that God is capable of everything" (Reynolds, *Muslim Theologian*, 153, cited from 'Ali al-Tabari, *Radd*, 145).

99. Beaumont, *Christology in Dialogue with Muslims*, 107; "Muslim Readings."

100. Reynolds, *Muslim Theologian*, 162, cited from 'Ali al-Tabari, *Radd*, 144. The verse as quoted by al-Ṭabarī bears only slight resemblance to Matthew's account: "He was still speaking when, behold, a bright cloud overshadowed them, and a voice from the cloud said, 'This is my beloved Son, with whom I am well pleased; listen to him'" (Matt 17:5).

101. Thomas, "Ali Ibn Rabban al-Tabari," 143.

102. Martin Accad notes that John 20:17 is the most-often-quoted passage of Scripture by Muslims in anti-Christian polemic (see Accad, "Ultimate Proof-Text," 200): "But go to my brothers and say to them, 'I am ascending to my Father and your Father, to my God and your God'" (John 20:17). This verse also received attention from Jāḥiẓ, b. Ayyūb, Nāshī al-Akbar, Kaʿbī and Rāzī (see Reynolds, *Muslim Theologian*, 156).

103. See fn 76 for information on Abū ʿĪsā's written work.

or nurtured and fed by her are inadmissible as rational belief concerning deity. He borrows Christian terminology related to their descriptions of the incarnate Word – rest, movement, expression of emotions, and so on – ridiculing the idea that the divine and the human intermingled in a "unique way." Later the crucifixion and burial are considered, each receiving a detailed treatment of the problems deriving from the claim of Christ's divinity at these phases of his life. The thrust of the argument is to demonstrate the rational incoherence of implicating the divine nature in the human experiences of Jesus at every phase of his life.[104]

Abū ʿĪsā offers a trenchant critique of how the two natures united, citing significant difficulties concerning the metaphors employed by Christians. Christians maintained that the Word was non-physical and yet used terms of physicality to describe the unity with humanity. Abū ʿĪsā sought to demonstrate the ridiculous nature of divine and human intermingling across the broad spectrum of human emotions and actions. This argument demonstrated, at least to any thinking Muslim, that the divine and human simply could not "mingle" in some unique fashion.[105] Abū ʿĪsā's concern here is with the rationality of the doctrinal formulations promoted by the various Christian sects to express the unity of the two natures. The third part of his refutation seems to be a slight departure in that Abū ʿĪsā's critique tends toward the hypothetical as he deals with issues Christians have not actually addressed, namely the Messiah's participation in his own creation and theoretical implications of Christ's bearing a son. Throughout his work, Abū ʿĪsā demonstrates a detailed and comprehensive understanding of the various Christian sects.[106]

Abū ʿĪsā sought to demonstrate internal inconsistency in Christian thought. He suggested that the incarnation rendered Christ distinct from the Father and Spirit because he possessed something that was not possessed by the Father. On this basis, the equality of the three hypostases in all respects – a doctrine held by Christians – could no longer be sustained. On the surface, the attack appears sophisticated and indefensible. However, it could hardly have been a death-blow to Christians as the latter might well retort that equality concerns the divine worth, moral purity, and so on, and need not imply precise correspondence. He relentlessly pursued a detailed knowledge of the Christian sects and exposed incongruence in each. He highlighted a perceived inconsistency in the dyohypostatic view of the union as they held the divine and human to have united before birth. This implies that deity endured a human birth – a manifest contradiction to their separation of the hypostases. The same is true for the death of Christ. Must not the union be obliterated at his death or else deity

104. Thomas, *Early Muslim Polemic*, 64.

105. Thomas, 68–69.

106. Thomas, 65.

is united with the deceased?[107] Abū ʿĪsā's argument is to prove the irrationality of Christian doctrines, not through comparison with Islam, but through its own internal inconsistency. In doing so he provides a wealth of polemical responses for those wishing to engage Christians in disputation.[108]

5.2.3 Abū Bakr Muḥammad al-Bāqillānī

Al-Bāqillānī shows the conflict between the various Christian schools of thought on the incarnation. As one would expect, he rejects any merging of the divine with the temporal as this would make God subject to change and decay.[109] Furthermore, he insists the act (*fi'l*) of unity of the two natures must, of necessity, have been accomplished by an agent (*fā'il*). Who is the agent to whom the act of unity is to be attributed? He systematically eliminates possible responses concluding that the unity of Christ's divine and human natures is not viable intellectually. His other point of attack on the duality of Christ's nature focuses on the crucifixion. According to al-Bāqillānī, if the two natures remained united in death, this would necessitate the death of both the Father and the Spirit, who share the Son's essence. If, on the other hand, the two were separated, then the doctrine of the unity would be negated.[110]

Al-Bāqillānī then turns to various scriptural references to sustain his conclusions relative to Christ's humanity. He invokes Christ's prayer before raising Lazarus as well as the Gethsemane prayer of Jesus that this cup (of his passion) might pass from him. Al-Bāqillānī may be following al-Maturidī in suggesting that this prayer is representative of a prophet, not of divinity – an argument that had become widely known due to its incorporation in the commentary of Abū Jaʿfar al-Ṭabarī.[111] He uses Christian Scripture to suggest that Christ's references to himself as God (e.g. John 14:9) do not imply that Christ is divine. A similar mention is made of Moses acting as "God" to Aaron and to Pharaoh. The application of the name "God" to a human being does not justify attributing divinity to human beings in the view of al-Bāqillānī.[112]

5.2.4 ʿAbd al-Jabbār al-Hamadhānī (d. 1025/415)

ʿAbd al-Jabbār, a contemporary of Ibn al-Ṭayyib and Iliyyā, was a renowned Muʿtazilī judge who lived in Buyid Rayy, but also moved in and out of Baghdad. He was appointed chief judge of Rayy (south of contemporary Tehran) in 977. While in

107. Thomas, 108–109, 118–119.
108. Thomas, 66.
109. Goddard, *History of Christian–Muslim Relations*, 61–62.
110. W. Haddad, *Christian–Muslim Encounters*, 90–91.
111. W. Haddad, 91; Reynolds, *Muslim Theologian*, 154.
112. Reynolds, 156.

Rayy, al-Jabbār drew disciples from many distant lands and ensured his notoriety as a Muʿtazilī theologian and jurisprudent of the Shāfiʿī school.[113]

In his *Establishing the Proofs of Prophethood*[114] he argues that Muḥammad, though he had no contact with Christians, was enabled by God to correctly diagnose their error. He quotes the Nicene Creed in full arguing that Christians cannot claim that God is both begetter and begotten and yet hold that he is one. He specifically attacks Nestorian Christology and their attempts to segregate the divinity of Christ from humanity. In ʿAbd al-Jabbār's view, Christ did not cease to be divine, whether in a state of sleeping, eating, urination, defecation, sickness or death.[115] At several points ʿAbd al-Jabbār accuses the Christians of pure *shirk* (associating divinity with created things).[116] He also rebuts the Christian claim that their view of Christ is the same as that of Islam: "a word of God and a spirit from him" (Q3:45; 4:171), pointing to their "speculative interpretations" which depart from the clarity Muḥammad revealed.[117] Throughout, ʿAbd al-Jabbār demonstrates a wholesale dismissal of Christian tenets, even preserving the accusation, despite persistent Christian disavowals, that God the Father had intercourse with Mary, desiring her as a man lusts (*shawa*) for a woman.[118]

ʿAbd al-Jabbār's *Summa*[119] also dealt extensively with the Trinity and incarnation. One issue that arrests our attention is his discussion of the manner of the union of the divine and human in Christ. As both doctrines contradict ʿAbd al-Jabbār's Muʿtazilī frame of reference, he finds the union of the divine and human a logical impossibility. He attacks the various means by which Christians assert that the divine and human were united in volition – a particular emphasis of Church of the East dyohypostatic Christology.[120] His concluding summary is to dismiss the christological formulations of both the Melkites and the Church of the East due to their insistence on the preservation of the two natures.[121]

113. Reynolds, 50–51; Thomas, "ʿAbd al-Jabbār," 595.

114. *Tathbīt dalāʾil al-nubuwwa* تثبيت دلائل النبوة

115. Reynolds and Samir, *Abd al-Jabbar*, 3, 12. As we will see in subsequent chapters, the dyohypostatic theologians set forth a hard and fast division between the human actions of Christ (e.g. being born, eating, sleeping, tiring, dying) and the divine actions (e.g. performing miracles, resurrecting, ascending).

116. Reynolds and Samir, 8, 31.

117. Reynolds and Samir, 39.

118. Reynolds and Samir, 85.

119. His *Summa* is *al-Mughnī fī abwāb al-tawḥīd wa-al-ʿadl* (*Summa on Monotheism and Divine Justice*) intended to be a comprehensive theological textbook of the Muʿtazilī. The work is only partially extant (see Reynolds and Samir, xxxvii–xxxviii).

120. Thomas, *Christian Doctrines*, 303–317.

121. Thomas, 356–357. While in Rayy, he also dictated his famous work titled *Summa on the Matters of Divine Unity and Divine Justice* (*al-Mughnī fī al-tawḥīd wa-al-ʿadl*) over a period of twenty years, 970–990/359–380. It is the fifth section of the *Summa* which treats Christian theology in detail,

5.3 Conclusion: The Battle for Divine Unity

The authors in the preceding paragraphs were chosen as they are deemed to be representatives of the kinds of polemic Muslims used in their dialogue with Christians. They represent both parties of the burgeoning intellectual life of Muslims in the Abbasid era – the Ashʿārīs and the Muʿtazilīs. The fact that one of the authors was a convert from Christianity demonstrates the dynamic nature of the Muslim–Christian interface. All held places of influence in public life rendering their writings influential in their own day; and these writings remain extant today as pre-eminent examples of Islamic polemics in the medieval period.

The Islamic polemic surveyed in cursory form can be fairly subsumed under the title "a defense of divine unicity" (*tawḥīd*).[122] In brief, the doctrine upholds the utter uniqueness of God – that nothing can be conceived which approximates him or shares in his being in any sense. The contravention of divine unicity is the sin of *shirk* – associating anything created with the divine. It is the often-asserted verity of the Qur'ān that "[there is] no divinity other than He."[123] The concept had grown to such prominence among the medieval Islamic theologians that the Muʿtazilīs were labeled "the people of divine unity." The Ashʿārīs were no less preoccupied by it. It is no exaggeration to state that divine unicity had become the intellectual standard for theological reasoning. With this background, it is not difficult to understand why the particular Christian tenets – incarnation and Trinity – were under severe scrutiny. They are the concepts which contradict the pre-eminence of divine unicity as understood and practiced by the medieval Muslim theologians and jurisprudents. For this reason, these doctrines become the intellectual battleground of choice for Muslim polemicists.

---

notably the Trinity and incarnation, following the format of Abū ʿĪsa al-Warrāq. Predictably, al-Jabbār argues that Trinity is polytheism. Perhaps ʿAbd al-Jabbār's most trenchant polemic was his reconstruction of Christian origins in which he laid the blame for Christianity's aberrant doctrines (e.g. the Trinity and Christ's divinity) at the feet of the great innovator the apostle Paul. According to ʿAbd al-Jabbār, the original gospel was corrupted by the apostle Paul and others in collusion with a corrupt Roman administration. The true version of the gospel made its way to Arabia and served to prepare Muḥammad's first followers to believe his prophetic message (see Kuhn, "Ibn al-Ṭayyib's Trinitarian Formulation," 150–173; Reynolds, *Muslim Theologian*).

122. "Unicity" is often used in the literature as a better representative of the concept than "unity." It stresses the utter impossibility of any approximation to the being of Allāh. He is "that like which there is no other" (see Gimaret, "tawḥīd," 389).

123. *Lā ilāh ilā huwa* لا إله إلا هو . The statement is asserted twenty-nine times in the Qur'ān (Gimaret, 389).

6. Christian Voices of the Abbasid Era

It is helpful to form an idea of how Christians had responded to Muslim polemical accusations prior to the time of Iliyyā and Ibn al-Ṭayyib. A few outstanding Christian voices that engaged with the Muslim–Christian interface are surveyed below.

6.1 Timothy I's Dialogue with Caliph al-Mahdī (781/165)

Timothy I was the highly revered Catholicos (Patriarch) of the Church of the East (780–823/163–208). His dialogue with the Caliph al-Mahdī (775–785/158–169) took place in 781/165 in the form of a series of questions posed by the Caliph to Timothy.[124] The questions covered a broad range of issues including the Trinity, the incarnation and the Christian Scriptures.[125] We can identify, at this very early stage of the Abbasid era, the incipient Muslim repudiation of Christian doctrines. For instance, there are hints that the Johannine references to the *paraclete* (Comforter) were already being understood as a prophetic announcement of Muḥammad.[126] The title "Son of God" was thought by Muslims to connote a biological relationship between God and the Virgin, despite persistent Christian disavowals. The idea of two natures residing in one person was inherently illogical to al-Mahdī. Indeed, for al-Mahdī, the purported death of Christ intensified the conundrum as the nature of God could never die. Timothy I referenced Christ's death in the Qur'ān (19:33) but al-Mahdī held that Christ's ascension to heaven (mentioned in 19:33) preceded his death which would be a future event. Such an ignominious death, alleged al-Mahdī, would impugn Christ's status as a prophet. Timothy's apologetic stated that Christ's death concerned his humanity but not his divinity – a common response that is echoed by later apologists. It is noteworthy that, even at this early stage of Muslim–Christian interaction, al-Mahdī shows a willingness to dismiss the Christian Scriptures when they contravene his Muslim belief system.[127]

6.2 Theodore Abū Qurra (ca. 755–829/138–214)

Theodore Abū Qurra (c. 785–829/168–214) was the Greek-speaking Bishop of Haran (Melkite) who was one of the first Christian spokesmen to write in Arabic. Theodore

124. The fact that the dialogue is recorded in Syriac and Arabic shows that Arabic – the language of Islam and the Arabs – was gaining prominence in the area and was used increasingly by the Church of the East.

125. Beaumont, *Christology in Dialogue with Muslims*, 23; Brock, "Two Millennia."

126. Accad, "Gospels in the Muslim Discourse," 75.

127. Beaumont, *Christology in Dialogue with Muslims*, 24–26.

debated the Abbasid Caliph al-Ma'mūn (813–833) in the year 829/214. The tone of the dialogue displays a high degree of reciprocity as the Caliph charged Theodore to speak his mind freely without fear of recrimination.[128] Theodore was innovative, seeking a fresh language to communicate Trinitarian concepts in the new medium of Arabic. He reasons that God's greatest excellences derive from his "capacity for relationship with others like himself." These virtues are "begetting" (*wilāda*), "procession" (*inbithāq*) and headship (*riyāsa*).[129] From here, Theodore proceeds to establish the Trinitarian nature of God the Son (the begotten one), the Spirit (proceeding) and the Father (headship).[130]

Furthermore, he makes use of Islamic anthropomorphic language to convey the concept of incarnation.[131] Theodore asks rhetorically, "If God is able to hear, does this imply that he has physical ears?" In the same way his begetting does not necessarily imply a physical act.[132] He exploits the Islamic idea of Mary's purity to show that Jesus was given a body that was free of corruption and, therefore, suitable for God's indwelling.[133] Rather than God's "taking a son" (denied in Q23:91), the eternal Son "takes a body." God's session on a throne, also expressed in the Qur'ān, does not limit him to time and space. So, argues Theodore, his indwelling of a body must not be seen as limiting his divine prerogatives. Abū Qurra demonstrates a desire to make his Christian faith accessible to Muslims. He also plunges into the Islamic debate on the use of anthropomorphisms when speaking of God.[134]

6.3 Ḥabīb Ibn Khidma Abū Rā'iṭa (fl. 810–830/194–215)

Abū Rā'iṭa is a Jacobite (miaphysite) representative of the ninth-century apologists. He likely occupied the office of Bishop in his native Tikrit and was a contemporary of ʿAmmār al-Baṣrī (Church of the East), Timothy I (Church of the East Catholicos) and Theodore Abū Qurra (Melkite).

128. Goddard, *History of Christian–Muslim Relations*, 51–53.

129. See Abū Qurra's credal definition of the Trinitarian hypostases in Dick, "Deux écrits inédits."

130. Swanson, "Early Christian–Muslim Theological Conversation," 9.

131. The Qur'ān's insistence on God's absolute unity and utter transcendence while describing him in anthropomorphic terms pushed the *mutakallimūn* (theologians) to delineate an understanding of human attributes ascribed to God (e.g. hearing, sitting) such that his unique nature was not impugned.

132. Beaumont, *Christology in Dialogue with Muslims*, 30.

133. *Ḥulūl* is the qur'ānic term for indwelling. This is yet another example of Theodore's use of Islamic terminology to the extent possible to capture his interlocutor's attention and approval.

134. Among Abū Qurra's works was one titled *Against Those Who Claim That the Word of God Was Created* – evidently written as a response to Muʿtazilī *kalām* (Allard, "Les Chrétiens à Baghdad").

Although we know little of Muslim response to Theodore, we do know that his views received a response from 'Isa Ibn Sabih al-Murdar (d. 840) entitled *Against Abū Qurra the Christian* (Beaumont, *Christology in Dialogue with Muslims*, 30).

Abū Rā'iṭa offered a systematic apologetic toward Muslims in defense of the Trinity as well as the incarnation, taking an "encyclopedic approach" to Islamic objections in Arabic.[135] He was direct enough to challenge the Islamic view of God's unicity. Abū Rā'iṭa innovatively used the question of al-Kindī (an Islamic philosopher, d. ca. 870/256) on the nature of God's oneness to his advantage, asking how Islam viewed God's oneness in terms of Aristotelian categories.[136] If God is one in number, his oneness is indistinct from that of a human being, thus belittling God. Abū Rā'iṭa remonstrated that the Trinity respected both the oneness of God and his distinction from all that is created.[137]

His *Letter on the Incarnation* is composed of forty-four questions in response to a host of Islamic objections to the incarnation. Abū Rā'iṭa repeatedly links his responses to the concepts and phraseology of the Qur'ān. He selected terms that Muslims could understand and would associate with qur'ānic teaching, which may indicate the author's personal engagement with Muslims.[138] In some instances, he uses qur'ānic concepts to cross-examine his reader. For example, question 29 raises a similar issue to that of Abū Qurra: if God's session on a heavenly throne does not limit him, neither should his indwelling of a human body.[139]

In his essay titled "Demonstration of Christianity and the Holy Trinity" Abū Rā'iṭa is content to refer to Christ's divinity and humanity as two attributes (*ṣifatān*) rather than "natures." Christ, the eternal Word, is joined with a human body so as to become one substance. In his body he suffers and feels pain, but his divinity does not.[140] As a miaphysite, Abū Rā'iṭa wields this defense more awkwardly than his dyophysite counterparts. The suffering of Christ, that doctrine so prized by Christians, posed an insuperable obstacle to Muslims for whom a suffering divinity was unconscionable. Thus, one finds attempts to isolate the Divine from any semblance of human suffering. Such attempts would flourish under the dyohypostatic Christology of the Church of the East.

---

135. Abū Rā'iṭa wrote in Arabic although his community of a generation earlier would have been Syriac-speaking, illustrating the rapidly spreading influence of the Arabic language.

136. Al-Kindī (the father of Arabic philosophy, d. ca. 870/256) employed Aristotelian categories to ask if Christians viewed God's oneness as a oneness of "number (as an individual object is one), species (as all human beings are one) or genus (as animals are all one)." Al-Kindī's point was that the first category disallowed the Trinity while the last two were an admission of plurality in God.

137. Swanson, "Early Christian–Muslim Theological Conversation," 11–12. One analysis of Abū Rā'iṭa suggests that his methodology was to firmly ground Christian thought in the unity of God – a move away from the Cappadocians, whose emphasis was on the "triune economy in the one God" – arguably evidence of the pervasive influence of Islam on Christian doctrinal formulation (Keating, *Defending the "People of Truth,"* 11).

138. Beaumont, *Christology in Dialogue with Muslims*, 57.

139. Beaumont, 57.

140. Beaumont, "'Ammar al-Basri on the Incarnation," 59.

At times, the reader senses that Abū Rā'iṭa's thought is robust, such as his insistence that the pronunciation (*nutq*) of God's word is an eternal emanation as is the procession (*inbithāq*) of the Spirit.[141] However, his retreat to analogy muddies the waters he has labored to clarify. His reference to Eve's proceeding from Adam's side and Abel's birth as analogous to the Trinity seems to falter under the theological weight of the concept.[142]

One feature of Abū Rā'iṭa's writing is that he is clearly seeking to arm Christians against a rising tide of Islamic polemic. Abū Rā'iṭa's apologetic may in fact grow out of societal developments that are forcing Christians to ever deeper levels of definition of faith:

> In the period between Harun ar-Rashid and al-Mutawakkil (232–247/847–861), exactly the time during which Abū Rā'iṭa is writing, relations between Muslim and Christians had become decidedly strained and Christian chroniclers such as Dionysius of Tell Mahre began to identify their situation as one of religious persecution. Now the policy of the Abbasid caliphs to promote conversion to Islam through the promise of full participation in political and cultural life, coupled with the added incentive of relief from the *gizyah* [taxation of religious minorities], and religious and social restrictions, made it increasingly attractive for non-Muslims to abandon their ancestral religions.[143]

6.4 *'Ammār al-Baṣrī (Early- to Mid-Ninth Century)*

'Ammār al-Baṣrī labored in the early ninth century and, like Timothy I, hailed from the same Church of the East as Ibn al- Ṭayyib and Iliyyā with its dyohypostatic Christology.[144] He dedicated his *Book of Questions and Answers* to the Caliph al-

141. His treatment of the incarnation in *On the Proof of the Christian Religion* is a strong Christocentric statement that the divine mandate through Christ was a re-creation of humankind who had fallen into death and depravity. Though our human minds may not fathom the rationale behind the incarnation, argues Abū Rā'iṭa, it behooves human beings to accept it as it has been revealed (Keating, *Defending the "People of Truth,"* 121, 125). The reference to the two natures of Christ as *ṣifatān* (two attributes) represents an accommodation to Islamic thought and terminology which will reappear in subsequent theological expressions.

142. Keating, 112–114.

143. Keating, 19.

144. We have eschewed the common use of "dyophysite" in reference to the Church of the East. While it is true that the church held to two *physeis* (natures) of Christ, the moniker does not serve well to distinguish their Christology from that of other ecclesial families which were also dyophysite (e.g. adherents of Chalcedon). The Church of the East held specifically to two *qnume* – a Syriac word commonly translated as "hypostases." Thus we elect to describe Church of the East Christology as dyohypostatic. We will elaborate the Church of the East's Christology in chapter 5.

Ma'mūn who ruled from 813/197 to 833/218. This work treats the prominent issues of contention between Muslims and Christians in four sections: God and the creation, the four Gospels, the Trinity and the incarnation. The *Book of Questions and Answers* taken with his *Book of Proof*[145] provides the most thorough defense of the Christian faith in the ninth century. The two works mentioned above earn for ʿAmmār al-Baṣrī a place of prominence alongside Abū Rā'iṭa as one of the first Arabic-writing systematic theologians.[146]

6.4.1 Incarnation

Al-Baṣrī resorted to analogy to defend the concept of the embodiment of deity. As the sun shone its light on the earth, so the deity took a human temple to indwell. As the light is not entirely contained by the earth, so God's glory overflows the embodiment of Christ – the temple. In his dyohypostatic frame of reference, al-Baṣrī does not speak of "the embodiment of God" but of God the Word becoming human.[147]

His discussion of the incarnation is substantial – nearly three times the length of Abū Rā'iṭa's *Letter on the Incarnation* – answering fifty-one questions on the topic in the *Book of Questions and Answers.*[148] He frames the incarnation within the generosity of God in an attempt to appeal to Muslims, identifying four motivations which demonstrate the giving nature of God. First, the human form of God in the incarnation allowed humanity to receive and appreciate this revelation. Second, God became visible in response to the human longing to see with physical eyes. Third, God revealed himself prior to the day of judgment as an act of mercy toward those who would be judged. Fourth, since God has given dominion to man, his appearance as a man demonstrates how man should rule.[149] One discerns an attempt to render the incarnation more accessible to Islamic understanding. A similar tendency is

---

145. The complete title is كتاب البرهان على سياقة التدبير الإلهي *Kitāb al-burhān 'alā siyāqa al-tadbīr al-ilāhī* (date after 838/223) (see Beaumont, "ʿAmmar al-Basri," 606). The work is divided into twelve subject areas, most of which represent live issues at stake at the Muslim–Christian interface, and is likely intended to equip Christians to answer Muslim objections (Beaumont, *Christology in Dialogue with Muslims*, 68).

146. Beaumont, "ʿAmmar al-Basri on the Incarnation," 56. ʿAmmār also tackled the accusation of *taḥrīf* – corruption of the Christian Scriptures – demonstrating that *taḥrīf* loomed large in the interfaith equation in the early ninth century. It is noteworthy that fourteen of his 102 questions in the *Book of Questions and Answers* deal with the authenticity of the Gospels. It is the most far-reaching defense of the Gospels from the ninth century and therefore indicates that the accusation of intentional *taḥrīf al-lafẓ* (corruption of the text) of the Gospels had overtaken the former accusation of misinterpretation (*taḥrīf al-ma'nā*) (Beaumont, "ʿAmmar al-Basri," 605).

147. Beaumont, "ʿAmmar al-Basri on the Incarnation," quoting from ʿAmmar al-Basri, "Kitab al masa'il wa al-ajwiba," 194. *Allāh al-kalima ta'annasa* الله الكلمة تأنّس

148. ʿAmmār is deftly exploiting a Church of the East pedagogical method of question and answer to instruct in theology, i.e. catechism. He weaves catechesis into apologetic, addressing both Muslim and Christian (Beaumont, "ʿAmmar al-Basri on the Incarnation," 56–57).

149. Beaumont, "ʿAmmār al-Baṣrī," 608.

observable in his discussion of the Christian debate on the issue of hypostatic union. He refers to the disagreement among Christian traditions, but passes over the details, presumably for the sake of facilitating understanding for Muslims. "They agree that the Creator appeared in a body like theirs . . . but they disagree over how to describe the body; some say it is one hypostasis and others that it is two hypostases."[150] His care to present the truth of the incarnation in fresh terms so as to render the doctrine accessible to Muslims commands respect and serves as a benchmark for subsequent interfaith interaction.

6.4.2 Christ's Death

Al-Baṣrī's response as to why Christ would suffer and die is unique in this time period in that Christ, by his self-sacrifice, is enabled to give eternal life to others. He is like a doctor who swallows poison to reassure his patient that he will not die or a champion fighter whose strength is expended to defeat his opponent.[151] The death of Christ demonstrates that those who follow him will overcome death through a victorious resurrection.[152]

He felt his dyohypostatic Christology gave him an advantage over and against his miaphysite and Byzantine peers[153] and even implicitly appealed to Muslims for corroboration.[154] The perceived separation between the human and divine hypostases in Christ provided al-Baṣrī with a validation for denying the death of divinity in Christ's person. It also gave him leverage to argue that the deity was not exposed to suffering as this was endured by the human nature of Christ – an argument wielded less convincingly by Jacobites and Byzantines. Might this have been a plausible argument to Muslims, or were they listening only to the degree necessary to sharpen their rejoinders? Whatever the case, ʿAmmār provides an intriguing twist in the interfaith equation by elevating the benefits of his dyohypostatic Christology to appeal to Islamic rationality. Indeed, Iliyyā of Nisibis and Ibn al-Ṭayyib continue to press these advantages in a Muslim context. One ironic footnote to the history of Muslim–Christian relations is that Nestorius (anathematized at Ephesus in 431) and the Church of the East which revered him offered a degree of promise, however slight, for communicating the mysteries of the Christian faith in a Muslim context. The discussion of Christ's death takes a familiar trajectory – a defense against the Muslim

150. Beaumont, *Christology in Dialogue with Muslims*, 71, quoting from al-Basri, *Kitab al-Burhan*, 62.

151. Beaumont, "ʿAmmār al-Baṣrī," 605.

152. Beaumont, "ʿAmmār al-Basri on the Incarnation," 61.

153. Both Abū Qurra, the Melkite, and Abū Rā'iṭa, the Jacobite, had attempted to exclude the divine nature from suffering.

154. Beaumont, "ʿAmmar al-Basri on the Incarnation," 58.

accusation that such a reprehensible death could not be worthy of a prophet of Allāh. Beaumont makes the interesting observation that neither ʿAmmār al-Baṣrī nor any ninth-century apologist tackles the forthright denial of Christ's death in Q4:157 – an explicit denial of the crucifixion.[155] Contrary to expectations of a thorough apologetic compendium, al-Baṣrī does not even mention this verse in his discussion of the death of Christ. Beaumont suggests that Islamic rule, of necessity, placed a limitation on the type of arguments Christians could put forward. Al-Baṣrī resorted to "more congenial territory," meaning the Muslim accusation that Christ's passion belittled his prophetic status as opposed to the overt denial of his death.[156]

6.4.3 Trinity

ʿAmmār insisted that Muslims had no right to question Christians who were upholding the teachings of their revealed Scriptures which had been confirmed to them through many wondrous signs. He defends the veracity of the Christian Scriptures before proceeding to a defense of the Trinity. Questioning the legitimacy of the Trinitarian formulation once the Christian Scriptures have been demonstrated to be true is illegitimate. ʿAmmār based his argument for the choice of terms used to express the Trinitarian persons on Scripture – a practice which Ibn al-Ṭayyib also adopted.[157]

ʿAmmar also labored to supply a defense for the common Islamic objection that there could be more than two attributes of essence. For ʿAmmār, these two attributes were life and word. He responded to the assertion that God's seeing and hearing as well as other attributes should be considered attributes of the essence. Sight and hearing are used anthropomorphically as the eyes and ears are physical members of composite bodies. Thus their intent is to attribute knowledge to God. Other attributes such as justice, compassion, generosity, favor, kindness and mercy are actions which flow from the essential attribute of word. Any of the above-mentioned actions can change although the divine essence is unchanging. Indeed, the one substance can have both sight and non-sight, hearing and non-hearing, goodness and its opposite,

155. "We killed Christ Jesus the son of Mary, the Messenger of Allāh, but they killed him not, nor crucified him, but so it was made to appear to them, and those who differ therein are full of doubts, with no (certain) knowledge, but only conjecture to follow, for of a surety they killed him not" (Q4:157 Youssef ʿAlī translation).

156. Beaumont, *Christology in Dialogue with Muslims*, 73. Subsequently, Beaumont suggests a correlation between 4:157 and al-Baṣrī's reference to Matt 27:42 (in reference to question 37 of *The Book of Questions and Answers*). In this passage, the Jewish onlookers are taunting Jesus, suggesting that he come down from the cross if he is, in fact, the Christ. Beaumont's suggestion is that al-Baṣrī may be intentionally confronting Muslims with the fact that even Christ's enemies acknowledged his death by crucifixion, rendering the veracity of his death unquestionable (Beaumont, *Christology in Dialogue with Muslims*, 86). An additional implication is that the enemies of Christ failed to grasp the necessity of the crucifixion as the preliminary to his glorification and victory and, therefore, sought to divert Christ from it.

157. Hayek, "ʿAmmār al Baṣrī," 102, 114; Mikhail, "ʿAmmār al-Basrī's Kitāb al-Burhān," 169–170.

and so on. So these concepts are to be considered actions, not essential attributes. The essential attributes are differentiating attributes. Without these attributes the essence would be other than it is. Word and life differentiate between essences. The attribute of life differentiates an animate body from the earth of which it is composed. In like manner, the attribute of word (or knowledge) differentiates animate life from human life. ʿAmmār's defining of the attributes of essence as word and life laid formative groundwork for Ibn al-Ṭayyib's Trinitarian concept.[158]

Ibn al-Ṭayyib identified not two, but three essential attributes. Furthermore, ʿAmmār's difficulty in selecting terminology for the hypostases and clearly defining the concept may have been an incentive to Ibn al-Ṭayyib to look beyond his Church of the East forebear.[159] ʿAmmār's formulation was critical in the distinction between the attributes of action and those of essence and his influence on Ibn al-Ṭayyib is noted. However, the influence of another defender of Trinitarianism was even more prominent than that of ʿAmmār.[160]

6.5 Yaḥya Ibn ʿAdī (893–974/280–363)

Yaḥyā Ibn ʿAdī was a Jacobite philosopher and theologian who was born in Tikrit but lived in Baghdad. He was the forebear of Ibn al-Ṭayyib as the head of the Baghdad school of philosophy known as The House of Wisdom. He studied at the feet of Abū Bishr Mattā (d. 940) and his more renowned student Abū Naṣr al-Fārābī (d. 950). Ibn ʿAdī's *Treatise on the Unity (of God) according to the Doctrine of Christians*[161] gives a defense of plurality in divinity based on the definition that is attributed to God as the "First Cause." Essentially, by the way the First Cause is defined, oneness may be attributed to God as well as plurality. The substance of God remains hidden but his attributes (*ṣifāt*) are evident through his actions and their effects (*āthār*). The three attributes of bounty (*jūd*: named the Father), wisdom (*ḥikma*: named the Son) and power (*qudra*: named the Spirit) are essential (*yuḍṭarru ilayhā*) to God as well as sufficient (*yustaghnā bihā*).[162]

Ibn ʿAdī's response to Abū ʿIsā al-Warrāq's refutation of the three Christian sects preserves almost the entirety of al-Warraq's argument. There is a noticeable

158. Mikhail, 162–165.

159. Mikhail, 172–173.

160. It is noteworthy that a scribal editorial comment at the end of ʿAmmār's *Kitāb al-masā'il wa-al-ajwiba* suggests that the interested reader who desires to study these issues further should consult the work of Yaḥyā Ibn ʿAdī and his response to Abū ʿĪsā al-Warrāq (Mikhail, 176).

161. *Maqāla fī al-tawḥīd 'ala madhhab al-Naṣāra* مقالة في التوحيد على مذهب النصارى

162. al-Khoury, *Ibn Rushd*, 93–94; Platti, "Yaḥyā Ibn ʿAdī," 403. This conceptualization of the Trinity also appears in his refutation of al-Kindī's treatise against the Trinity (961/350) (Platti, 411–412).

maturation in his view of the essential attributes of God. Although he conceptualizes the three attributes as bounty, wisdom and power, his more robust expression of the three essential attributes as intellect, intelligent and the intelligible[163] is critical for our purposes. Ibn ʿAdī affiliates with a line of Christian intellectuals who gravitated toward this conceptualization, including Ibn al-Ṭayyib.[164] The argument that sustains this conceptualization can be expressed as follows: God is the essence of knowledge that knows all things. As he is among the "all things" known, it follows that God knows himself. Thus, he is characterized as "knowing one" and "one known." Therefore, we have the three attributes of God conceptualized as (1) "the essence of knowledge" (*jawhar al-'aql*); (2) "the knowing one" (*al-'āqil*); and (3) "the one known" (*al-ma'qūl*). In a separate treatise, Ibn ʿAdī explains why it is reasonable to say that "the Creator is one substance with three properties, called hypostases by the Christians." In this treatise, as well as some others, he refers to the Trinity as paternity, filiation and procession[165] – terminology which Ibn al-Ṭayyib will employ.

Though it is difficult to reconstruct the chronological order of his writings, there is a development in the thought of Ibn ʿAdī in reference to the Trinity. The three descriptors of Zayd (doctor, accountant, writer) leave the Christian tenet exposed and vulnerable as Ibn Taymiyya (d. 1328/728) demonstrated subsequently. The triad of the essence of knowledge, the knowing one and the one known has a stronger intellectual currency. The reference to the Trinity as paternity, filiation and procession holds promise in terms of a robust reflection on the Trinitarian conception and fidelity to the scriptural revelation despite its obvious drawbacks for communication with Muslims.

6.6 Conclusion

The Christian theologians surveyed entered into the interfaith fray of the medieval Abbasid period. We have surveyed some leading voices in cursory form not limiting our discussion to Church of the East theologians as influences from both Jacobite and Melkite theologians will become apparent in Ibn al-Ṭayyib and Bishop Iliyyā of Nisibis. The examples suffice to indicate both the methodologies that Christians employed (Aristotelian logic, scriptural proofs, analogy, etc.) and common themes

---

163. *'aql* عقل – intellect; *'āqil* عاقل – intelligent [one]; *ma'qūl* معقول – intelligible;
"يشيرون باسم الآب إلى الجوهر الذي سمّوه الباري إذا عُقل عاقلا لذاته. ويشيرون بإسم الإبن إلى الباري إذا عُقل عاقلا لذاته. ويشيرون باسم الروح القدس إلى الباري إذا عُقل معقولاً لذاته."
(al-Khoury, *Ibn Rushd*, 79–80).

164. Boulos al-Khoury states that we find this tenet first in Ibn ʿAdī, later in his student Ibn Zaraʿ (d. 1008/398) then al-Isfihānī (13th c.) and with Ibn al-Ṭayyib (also attributed mistakenly to the 13th c.) (al-Khoury, *Ibn Rushd*, 79). This view of the Trinity is further developed in Ibn ʿAdī's *Epistle of the Validity of the Belief of the Christians That the Creator is One Substance Endowed with Three Attributes* (Platti, "Yaḥyā Ibn ʿAdī," 419–420).

165. Paternity: *ubūwa* أبوة، ; filiation: *bunūwa* بنوة، ; procession: *inbi'āth* إنبعاث،

which dominated the Muslim–Christian interface. The unique angle derived from ʿAmmār al-Baṣrī's dyohypostatic Christology in his discussion of Christ's death was briefly observed. This aspect of the Church of the East's Christology will reappear in chapters 5 and 6 when the respective christological contributions of Iliyyā and Ibn al-Ṭayyib are discussed. ʿAmmār's definition of the attributes of essence may be considered a precursor to Ibn al-Ṭayyib's views although Yaḥyā has a more profound influence. In summary, the eleventh-century theologians assimilated the themes and issues which Christians had discussed with their Muslim counterparts. They employed similar responses but also added their unique contribution to further develop the Christian theological response in the Muslim milieu.

7. Conclusion

From the contexts in which Ibn al-Ṭayyib and Iliyyā lived and labored, some preliminary conclusions may be drawn which inform our subsequent study. The two theologians were men of eminent culture and education. They were models of the Johannine ideal of being "in the world but not of it" (John 17:14–19). They were cultured men, well attuned to the ideological currents wafting through their era. Though I will engage in a critique of their work, they were astute theologians and men of learning, having earned their place of influence among their people.

Although the two men were contemporaries, their contexts were different. Iliyyā's context was characterized by a general *détente* in religious matters and the presence of an explicit dialogue partner while Ibn al-Ṭayyib lived in a milieu of strident Ḥanbalī resurgence. Thus, we will not be surprised to find that the two men, though discussing similar issues, take different contextual approaches.

The critical theological issues at the Muslim–Christian interface of the period were the Trinity (as opposed to divine unicity of Islam) and the incarnation. Together, the two issues were the polemical target of Islamic practitioners of *kalām* – virtually the "exhibit A" of aberrant religious doctrine. The reason for the prolific debate concerning these issues is not difficult to discern given that *tawḥīd* (divine unity) had become the hallmark of Islamic *kalām* and the intellectual standard bearer of Islamic philosophy. It was the criterion by which all thought was measured and it was the Trinity and the incarnation which provided its most focused and public challenge. The third issue which came to a boiling point in the eleventh century[166] was the question of scriptural authority, notably, the accusation of *taḥrīf* (corruption) of the Jewish

166. We consider the eleventh century to be a defining moment in the development of the accusation of *taḥrīf* largely due to two Muslim polemicists – ʿAbd al-Jabbār and his "critique of Christian origins" and Ibn Ḥazm of Andalusia who also subjected the Christian Scriptures to the explicit charge of *taḥrīf* (see Accad, "Gospels in the Muslim Discourse," 73; Reynolds, *Muslim Theologian*).

and Christian Scriptures. Although this research focuses on the previous two issues, scriptural corruption will appear from time to time in our analysis. Indeed by the eleventh century, Muslim polemicists were increasingly assuming the corruption of the Christian and Jewish scriptures as they were resistant to reconciliation with the Qur'ān and prevailing perceptions that Muḥammad was prophesied in previous revelations.

In this chapter I have surveyed the context in which the eleventh-century theologians lived as well as the legacy of attack and defense they inherited from leading Muslim and Christian thinkers in earlier centuries. It remains to demonstrate their active engagement with Islam through a detailed study of their writings. In the following chapters, I highlight the features of this engagement in the explicit interaction of Iliyyā with Abū al-Qāsim in the *Sessions* as well as the implicit engagement of Ibn al-Ṭayyib through his theological treatises.

3

Defining Trinitarian Unity

The Trinitarian Formulation of Abū al-Faraj ʿAbd Allāh Ibn al-Ṭayyib

1. Introduction

In this chapter I examine three theological treatises penned by Ibn al-Ṭayyib on the subject of the Trinity. I suggest a tentative order and a plausible range of dates for the writing of the treatises. Although Ibn al-Ṭayyib did not respond to a specific Muslim dialogue partner, he clarified the Christian doctrine in an Islamic hermeneutical context and plunged into the long-running debate between Muʿtazilīs and Ashʿārīs concerning the relation of the attributes (*al-ṣifāt*) to the essence (*al-dhāt*). His Trinitarian formulation drew not only from Church of the East forebears such as ʿAmmār al-Baṣrī but also from representatives of other ecclesial families such as the Jacobite Ibn ʿAdī. Ibn al-Ṭayyib's contribution was to refine the Trinitarian formulation, rendering it more concise and accessible. His definition responded to explicit Islamic polemic although he did not write in a polemical vein. His topics of concern are consistent with the themes at the Muslim–Christian interface that became prominent in the ninth and tenth centuries. Evidence from three Muslim polemicists – Abū ʿĪsā al-Warrāq, Abū Bakr al-Bāqillānī and ʿAbd al-Jabbār – demonstrates thematic correlations with Ibn al-Ṭayyib's treatises. These include the definition of the attributes of essence as well as their number and names, the distinction of attributes of essence from those of act, defining the hypostases relative to the attributes of essence, the question of attributing action to the essence or the hypostases, and preserving the authority of revelation as the arbiter in Christian belief. Ibn al-Ṭayyib emerges as a responsive theologian laboring in the Islamic milieu to mitigate the force of Islamic polemic against Christianity and provide a succinct formulation for his coreligionists in Buyid Baghdad.

2. The Documents

Ibn al-Ṭayyib's extant work on the Trinity is preserved in three treatises. His treatise titled "Treatise on the Unity and the Trinity"[1] is preserved in MS Huntington 240 in the Bodleian Library, Oxford. Gérard Troupeau has provided an excellent edition of the treatise with an accompanying French translation. The copyist of Huntington 240 referred to this treatise as "the second treatise."[2] In order to avoid confusion due to the similarities in Troupeau's titles, I will use the shorthand "M2" when referring to this *maqāla* (treatise). A separate treatise is entitled "Treatise on the Trinity and Unity."[3] Again, a critical text has been provided by Gérard Troupeau accompanied by a French translation. The work is based on two manuscripts of Ibn al-Ṭayyib's text. The first is preserved in the Bodleian Library, Oxford.[4] The second is in the Vatican Library (Arabic 145, fol. 50v–67r). The title of the treatise, as recorded by the copyist of Huntington 240, is ironic given that neither the word "Trinity" nor "unity" is used in the treatise (although they are used in the former treatise). Once again, to avoid confusion among the treatises, I will maintain Huntington 240's designation as "the third treatise'[5] using the shorthand "M3." I provide an English translation with section and verse divisions in appendix 2. A briefer treatise is entitled "Treatise on the Hypostases and Substance and That the Act Belongs to the Substance."[6] Troupeau's edition with introduction and French translation is based on a Vatican Library manuscript (Arabic 145, fol. 72r–75v). I shall refer to this treatise using the shorthand "MM" (*maqāla mukhtaṣara*). Thus, the three Trinitarian treatises of Ibn al-Ṭayyib are "M2," "M3" and "MM." A final source for Ibn al-Ṭayyib's Trinity is preserved by the Copt Abū Isḥāq Mu'taman al-Dawla Ibn al-ʿAssāl and presented in a critical edition by Samir.[7] This work is referred to by Ibn al-ʿAssāl simply as "A Treatise of Fourteen Chapters." Though it is not thoroughly examined herein, its parallels with the works mentioned above will be noted.

---

1. *Maqāla fī al-tawḥīd wa al-tathlīth* مقالة في التوحيد والتثليث

2. *al-Maqāla al-thāniyya* المقالة الثانية

3. *Maqālat al-tathlīth wa al-tawḥīd* مقالة التثليث والتوحيد

4. Ibn al-Ṭayyib, *Epistle on the Oneness of the Creator and Threeness of His Hypostases*, in Huntington 240, Bodleian Library, 1549.

5. *al-Maqāla al-thālitha* المقالة الثالثة

6. *Maqāla mukhtaṣara fī al-aqānīm wa al-jawhar wa anna al-fiʿl lil-jawhar* مقالة مختصرة في الأقانيم والجوهر وأنّ الفعل للجوهر

7. Samir, "Ṣafaḥāt min maqāla."

Troupeau's editions facilitate a more in-depth analysis comparing Ibn al-Ṭayyib's Trinitarian thought to that of his Christian predecessors as well as his Islamic counterparts in the sectarian milieu of Baghdad and Abbasid Iraq. This is the objective of the present work. In the following sections of this chapter, I provide a brief exposition and analysis of the three treatises, followed by a discussion of the author's Christian influences and an examination of Ibn al-Ṭayyib's Trinitarian thought in the context of the Muslim–Christian discourse of the period.

2.1 Chronology and Logical Order

There are few reference points by which to date Ibn al-Ṭayyib's theological treatises. Faultless suggests that M3 develops themes found in M2 and, therefore, postdates that work.[8] M3 mentions the author's commentary on John (section 8). This may aid in dating the work later than 1018/409; however, this is inconclusive due to the fact that the author uses the future tense in reference to his commentary.

By comparing the two treatises, one can easily discern the development of the author's thought, with M3 showing evidence of being the later work of the author. Part 3 in M2 corresponds to section 1 in M3, albeit the latter is significantly more detailed. Part 4 in M2 corresponds roughly to section 3 in M3. In M3 the author gives a more detailed treatment of the various objections. He also divides his demonstration that the attributes of essence are only three into two types: a legal demonstration and a rational demonstration. While there are hints at both of these in M2, it is M3 that provides a clear demarcation. This may indicate that Ibn al-Ṭayyib has become more aware of objections to M2 in the Muslim milieu and seeks to provide further elaboration in M3. (This is not to suggest that Muslims were interacting directly with M2.) Furthermore, M3 contains a section on the objection that the hypostases are three only. The author is also aware that his explication of the attributes may lead to an objection that these attributes assume a separate essence. His division of reality into two categories of potentiality and actuality enables him to show that God's attributes were existent within him as potentialities prior to creation.

In summary, M2 does in fact precede M3 chronologically based on four considerations:

- M3 adds definitions and concepts as well as responding to objections which are not raised in M2. M3 represents a more developed expression of Trinitarian thought.
- The copyists of Huntington 240 entitled M2 "the Second Treatise" and M3 "The Third Treatise." Although it is impossible to know if these

8. Faultless, "Ibn al-Ṭayyib," 692.

titles were carried over from an earlier copy, Huntington 240 remains a primitive witness to the anteriority of M2.

- M3 begins with an introductory section which presents in summary form the argument laid out in M2; thus it is reasonable to assume that M3 is a further elucidation of Ibn al-Ṭayyib's thought on the doctrine of the Trinity.
- There are significant variations in vocabulary between the two treatises. Notably M3 avoids the specific words "Trinity" and "unity," despite the fact that these are major topics of discussion. This is accomplished by the use of expressions such as "three hypostases," "three attributes," "the essence of the Creator is perceived in three ways," or "one essence." The presumed earlier treatise, M2, uses both words liberally, as does MM. The avoidance raises the question whether Ibn al-Ṭayyib may have intentionally circumvented use of these words. Might the reason be problems encountered in the use of the terms in M2 in an Islamic hermeneutical context? We also note the avoidance of the specific term "attributes of act" (*ṣifāt al-fiʿl*), again referred to through circumlocutions such as "an attribute that extends beyond the essence to created things."

MM may be a further clarification of section 5 of M3. If this is true, we are left with an enigma as to why Ibn al-Ṭayyib avoids the use of "Trinity" and "unity" in M3 but reverts to these terms in MM. Perhaps the intended audience is different or the avoidance of "Trinity" and "unity" in M3 was inadvertent. The latter seems unlikely. If MM is an elucidation of M3 section 5, I infer the following tentative sequential order of the three treatises: M2, M3, MM. The reference to the commentary on John in M3 indicates the treatise's posteriority to the commentary, and that it was written after 1018/409. Thus M3 and MM may be dated in the twenty-five-year period between 1018/409 and 1043/434 (the date of Ibn al-Ṭayyib's death) whereas M2 could possibly have preceded 1018/409.

For clarity's sake, I refer to the sections of the treatises with Roman numerals and to the paragraphs with Arabic numerals; thus M3 IV.2 is the treatise M3 section 4, paragraph 2.

2.2 Definition of Terms

An exposition of the treatises will be facilitated by an understanding of certain terms which Ibn al-Ṭayyib uses repeatedly. In this section, the Arabic term is supplied accompanied by a transliteration and English translation. This will facilitate the use of

English translations in subsequent sections.[9] For other key terms used by the author, see appendix 1.

2.2.1 Trinity (التثليث *al-tathlīth*) and Unity (التوحيد *al-tawḥīd*)

"Trinity" is used consistently with the historic creeds of the church indicating that the one God exists in three hypostases. The form used by Ibn al-Ṭayyib and other Arab theologians of the period highlights the contrast between the Christian and Muslim concepts. *Tathlīth* is literally "making three" while *tawḥīd* is "making one."[10] The definition of *tawḥīd* is the crux of the treatises as Ibn al-Ṭayyib argues for a unity that includes the plurality of the hypostases. From the outset, the vocabulary chosen by the Christian was problematic in the Muslim milieu. However, this deficiency shows a lack of standardization in Christian Arabic terminology which also resulted from the imposition of Islamic meanings in the Arabic medium.[11] Ibn al-Ṭayyib uses neither of these words in M3 but does so liberally in M2 as well as in MM.[12] "Oneness" (وحدانية *waḥdāniyya*) is also used, albeit rarely.[13]

2.2.2 Substance (الجوهر *al-jawhar*) and Essence (الذات *al-dhāt*)

"The substance" or "essence" is the true nature of a being: in M3, M2 and MM the author refers to the synonymous relation of the two words.[14] For clarity's sake, I have translated *jawhar* as "substance" and *dhāt* as "essence" but it should be remembered that the author does not make a clear delineation. "Essence" is used more often by the author. Indeed "substance" is rarely used other than to clarify that the church uses it synonymously with "essence."[15] Two exceptional uses of the word deserve mention. In M3 IV.3, the author speaks of the communicable attributes as extending beyond the "substance of the essence" (*jawhar al-dhāt*). In the same paragraph, the author refers to the "substance" three times, each time referring to the substance of a created being.[16] Thus, the author prefers the use of "substance" referring to created things and

9. See also appendix 1, which is a glossary of common theological terms used by both Ibn al-Ṭayyib and Iliyyā of Nisibis.

10. Contemporary Arab theologians prefer the word *thālūth* (ثالوث) as it connotes both the oneness of God and the Trinitarian persons. The word is never used by Ibn al-Ṭayyib.

11. R. Haddad, *La Trinité divine*, 181.

12. M2 I.2, II.3, III.1, III.4, IV.1, IV.3; MM 1.

13. M2 IV.1.

14. See M3 I.1 and M2 V.1. Occasionally, when referring to the church's belief, the author will use the word *jawhar*, suggesting it is the preferred nomenclature of the church (*al-bay'a*).

15. M2 V.1.

16. See M3 IV.3.

"essence" referring to the divine essence which is manifestly one.[17] Furthermore, he indicates that "substance" is the common terminology used by the church.

2.2.3 Attribute/s (صفة ج صفات *ṣifa*, pl. *ṣifāt*)

Ṣifa is the term commonly used by Ibn al-Ṭayyib for "attribute." It differs from the use of the word by the Muslim *mutakallimūn* (theologians) only in that the attributes' number is limited to three. The *ṣifāt* are entities present in the essence and not essences in and of themselves.[18] He refers to the synonym *khāṣṣa*, plural *khawāṣṣ*, only rarely, associating it with the church's nomenclature.[19] *Ṣifa* is the most commonly used word in M3 leading to the conclusion that a major objective of the treatise is to define the Christian understanding of the attributes. The attributes divide into two categories: those that do not extend beyond the essence[20] (referred to herein as incommunicable) and those that extend beyond the essence to the creatures[21] (referred to herein as communicable).[22] The former are limited to three attributes[23] (paternity, filiation and procession)[24] which are revealed, not inferred. Thus God is one in essence though this essence is perceived through the three perceptions of the eternal attributes.[25] The communicable attributes are not limited to a specific number[26] and can be perceived from the created order. Examples of these include bounty, power, wisdom and eternality.[27] Furthermore an attribute is an eternal entity (*ma'nā*) within the essence, not merely in the mind of the one speaking about God. It is the attribute taken with the essence that yields the hypostasis.[28] This coexistence of the attribute with the essence is referred to as a joining (*jumla*)[29] or ensemble (*mujtam'*).

17. M3 III.2; M2 III.2.

18. *al-ṣifāt yushār bihā 'ilā ma'ānin mawjūda li-hādhihi al-dhāt* الصفات يُشار بها إلى معان موجودة لهذه الذات . M3 I.1.

19. M2 V.1.

20. *fa-minhā ṣifāt takhuṣṣuhu lā tata'addāhu* فمنها صفات تخصه لا تتعدّاه

21. *ṣifāt tata'addā dhātahu ilā makhlūqātihi* صفات تتعدّى ذاته إلى مخلوقاته

22. M3 II.2.

23. M3 II.1.

24. M3 I.1. See also *A Treatise of Fourteen Chapters* where the author refers to the attributes of essence as *awṣāf* (descriptors) but also limits their number to three (Samir, "Ṣafaḥāt min maqāla," 250).

25. *fa-dhāt al-bāri' yunẓar fīhā thalātha anẓār* فذات البارئ يُنظَر فيها ثلاثة أنظار. M3 I.3.

26. M2 VIII.1.

27. M3 II.2, VII.2.

28. This concept is introduced in M2 where the attributes of power, goodness and wisdom are "taken with" (اخذت مع) the essence (الذات). See M2 III.3.

29. M2 IV.2.

2.2.4 Paternity, Filiation and Procession (أبوة، بنوة، إنبعاث *ubuwwa*, *bunuwwa* and *inbiʿāth*)

"Paternity," "filiation" and "procession" are the three attributes of the essence. Their names are given by the Lawgiver and thus express his intent and the precise meaning he desires. Furthermore, they are not to be understood with the meanings attributed to them in common parlance.[30] Thus, Ibn al-Ṭayyib assigns a technical meaning to each of these attributes of essence. The author belabors his understanding that the eternal entity of filiation, when taken with the essence, is rightly called "Son." So the eternal entities of fatherhood and procession, when taken with the essence, are rightly called "Father" and "Holy Spirit."[31] Furthermore there is no precedence among the three, whether essential or temporal. The overflow (*ifāḍa*) of the essence within itself is the Son and the overflow of the essence upon others is the Spirit.[32]

2.2.5 Hypostasis (أقنوم ج اقانيم *uqnūm*, pl. *aqānīm*)

Uqnūm is the only word used for "hypostasis" or one of the "persons" of the Trinity – Father, Son and Holy Spirit. Though a Syriac word, it is likely a derivative of the Greek *oikonomos* (οικονομος).[33] The hypostasis is a joining or an ensemble of the essence with each of the attributes of essence.[34] Thus, there are three hypostases and no more[35] relative to the three attributes of the essence: paternity, filiation and procession. It is the attributes which distinguish one hypostasis from another.[36]

2.2.6 Other Terms

*2.2.6.1 Cause and Caused (*علة ومعلول ʿilla *and* maʿlūl*)*

The "cause" is the ultimate reason for a proposition, which humankind will only arrive at in the hereafter.[37] In a related meaning, the word also refers to the source or origin. Ibn al-Ṭayyib refers to the Father as the essence who is the "cause" of the Son and Spirit who are "caused." The author is careful to stipulate that this does not mean that the Father was at one time unknowing and then began to know, for these titles are

30. Note that this is precisely al-Ashʿarī's argument against the Muʿtazila when he insists that the "hand of Allāh" must be understood in a way that is neither metaphorical (e.g. the blessing of God) nor literal (as though Allāh possesses material hands) but analogical. That is to say, the mention of the "hand of Allāh" refers to a reality in God which is related to his essence in the way that a man's hand is related to the man (Allard, *Le problème des attributs divins*, 282).

31. M3 I.2.

32. MM 4.

33. R. Haddad, *La Trinité divine*, 171.

34. M3 I.2, IV.1; M2 V.1; MM 1.

35. M3 II.1, IV.4.

36. MM 1.

37. M3 II.4.

given their technical, theological meaning in Scripture and must not be understood as in common parlance.[38] Nor does this mean the Father is the source of the Son and Spirit's existence because all share the eternal essence.[39]

*2.2.6.2 Knowledge, Knowing One and Known One (*العلم والعالم والمعلوم al-ʿilm wa-al-ʿālim wa-al-maʿlūm*)*

In Ibn al-Ṭayyib's rational argument for God's Trinitarian nature, he uses the argument for God's self-knowledge following Ibn ʿAdī; however, the word used is *'ilm* (knowledge) rather than *'aql* (intelligence) – Ibn ʿAdī's choice. Thus the ability to know pertains to the attribute of fatherhood (the hypostasis of the Father). The knowledge of self is spoken of as the "knowing one" and pertains to the attribute of filiation (the hypostasis of the Son). The attribute of being known pertains to the procession (the hypostasis of the Spirit).[40]

*2.2.6.3 Revealed (*وقف عليه توقيفا waqqaf ʿalayhi tawqīfan*)*

This term refers to the assurance of truth and especially truth supplied by divine revelation.[41] The same terminology was used among *mutakallimūn* to assert that "we must not presume to know about God anything more than exactly what God has said about Himself in the Qur'ān and Sunna."[42] The human mind does not require a revealer of the attributes that extend beyond the essence to the creation because these communicable attributes (e.g. goodness, power and wisdom) are inferred by the human mind from the creation.[43] Revelation is the only basis for the knowledge of the attributes of essence numbering three, no more or less. This is due to the fact that the human mind cannot apprehend the attributes of essence apart from revelation.[44] One must believe the revelation as God demonstrates its authenticity through miracles.[45] One may also be assured of a truth through creation and inference although this is

38. M3 III.4, VIII.1; MM 3.

39. M3 VIII.1.

40. M3 III.3.

41. M2 V.2: *wa-innamā summiyat bi-hādhihi al-asmā tawqīfan lā min al-'āda li'anna kitāb al-sharī'a sammāhā bi-hādhihi al-asma'*

وإنما سمّيت بهذه الأسماء توقيفاً لا من العادة لانّ كتاب الشريعة سمّاها بهذه الأسماء

42. Cumming, "Ṣifāt al-dhāt," 123.

43. M3 II.2.

44. M3 IV.4: *li'ana ṣāḥib al-sharī'a innamā waqqafanā 'alā al-ṣifāt allatī lā tafī al-'uqūl al-bashariyya bi-alwuqūf 'alayhā wa-lā istiqṣā'ihā wa-hādhihi hiyya allatī takhuṣṣ al-dhāt.*

لان صاحب الشريعة إنما وقّفنا على الصفات التي لا تفي العقول البشرية بالوقوف عليها ولا إستقصائها وهذه هي التي تخصّ الذات

45. M3 II.6.

limited to what our senses can explore and our mind infer and, therefore, does not include God's self-knowledge.[46]

*2.2.6.4 Potentiality and Actuality (*القوة والفعل al-quwwa wa al-fiʿl*)*

The author divides all things into two categories: those that have potentiality (*al-quwwa*) and those that have both potentiality and actuality (*al-fiʿl*).[47] He introduces these terms in M3 section 5 to respond to the objection that an attribute, of necessity, requires the existence of an object. Thus, if God's attributes are eternal, there must be other essences that existed with him in eternity past. Action is not ascribed to the attributes, but to the essence to which the attributes belong. If action were ascribed to the attributes, each hypostasis would have an action distinct from the other hypostases; therefore, action is ascribed to the essence.[48]

*2.2.6.5 Innate Entity (*المعنى ج. المعان al-maʿnā, *pl.* al-maʿāni*)*

This word is sometimes used with its common definition "meaning"[49] but it also takes on a more technical definition and can be translated as "innate entity," synonymous with the hypostases as "innate entities" within the essence.[50]

2.3 Second Treatise (M2)

2.3.1 Contents

The second treatise is entitled by the copyist of Huntington 240 "The Second Treatise concerning the Trinity of Abū al-Faraj ʿAbd Allāh bin al-Ṭayyib."[51] Troupeau divides M2 into nine sections (including the introduction). The division follows the logical contours of the treatise as all sections commence with some form of the verb *qāl* (to say). I have chosen to depart from Troupeau in labeling the introduction as section 1 (thus nine sections in total) and have made other minor amendments as noted. I suggest the following titles and accompanying summaries for the nine sections:

1. Introduction – the precious pearl of religious truth: The author asserts the superiority of the Christian Trinity over rival religious concepts. As

46. M3 VI.3.

47. M3 V.2.

48. MM I, 2.

49. M3 VII.2, VIII.4.

50. M3 V.5. Ibn Zurʿa and Iliyyā of Nisibis used the term in similar ways (see R. Haddad, *La Trinité divine*, 168–169).

51. *al-Maqāla al-thāniyya fī al-tathlīth li-Abī al-Faraj ʿAbd Allāh bin al-Ṭayyib* المقالة الثانية في التثليث لأبي الفرج عبد الله بن الطيب Troupeau's titles are confusing as the only distinction between M2 and M3 is the juxtaposition of the two words *tathlīth* and *tawḥīd*.

in searching for a precious pearl, the researcher must not be upset by the proliferation of the false, but trust that the authentic will displace the impostor by its superior qualities.

2. The manner by which Christ's message was accepted: The elite Greeks accepted the message of Christ, being convinced of its principles, while the masses accepted it due to the miracles of the evangelists. By contrast, other religions were accepted by people of inferior intellectual capacities.
3. The Creator is one and many: This is not objectionable as the Creator is one in essence and three in attributes and these are two different aspects of the Creator. The two descriptors are not illogical as they are applied to different aspects of God – his essence and attributes.
4. The triad of knowledge: "Knowledge, knowing one and known one" are attributes of the essence which, when taken with the essence, each yields a distinct entity (*ma'nā*). This reference to the triad of knowledge is an attempt to render the doctrine in acceptable philosophical jargon as Ibn 'Adī had done previously. This is Ibn al-Ṭayyib's embryonic articulation of the attributes which is more fully developed in M3.
5. Terminology: Christians speak of the essence as "substance," the attributes as "properties" and the combination of the attributes with the essence as "the hypostases." Furthermore, the terms "Father," "Son" and "Spirit" arise from the Christian law (*sharī'a*) and debating their legitimacy is pointless.
6. Analogy from the visible realm: Socrates is white, warm and a savant. The essence of Socrates is one while his attributes are many. The author marshals evidence from the visible realm (e.g. Socrates and Zayd) to show that it is not uncommon to view three as one.
7. Objection to limiting God's attributes to three:[52] The author categorizes God's attributes into attributes of essence and attributes of act. The attributes of essence are three and no more as they do not extend beyond the essence to any other being. The attribute of paternity is the cause of filiation and procession. Thus, the attribute is a real entity inherent in the essence. The attributes of act are of an unspecified number. Ibn al-Ṭayyib

52. I opt to begin this section a paragraph earlier than Troupeau. This is due to the fact that the paragraph included in section 7 lays out the objection to which section 7 responds. Troupeau includes the objection in the preceding section (VI).

uses a creative expression to suggest their number is still being discovered: "the quantity of them runs along as we make our way."[53]

8. Objections concerning the attributes:[54] Christians share some aspects of their faith with other religions while other aspects are not held in common. Some say the attributes are many but do not posit a separation between the attributes of act and essence. Those who say the attributes are not other than the essence but a mere description of the essence are in error. This is proven by the fact that the attributes which describe the essence are not one and the same. If it is assumed that the attributes are describing something other than the essence, then the attributes are appropriate to something other than the essence.
9. Conclusion: God is one in essence, many in attributes. When the essence is taken with different attributes, it yields a different result.

2.3.2 Interpretation and Analysis

From the outset, the treatise bears the marks of production in an Islamic milieu. The religious concepts the author refers to are consistent with Islam, the influence of which is now ubiquitous in his native Baghdad. The author is urging his readership not to be unsettled by the proliferation of a false religion: "The inestimable ideal among religious concepts is indeed like a precious pearl among worldly objects" (section 1). Section 2 of the treatise refers to the acceptance of the Christian religion by superior minds as well as by the masses. The superior intellects in question are the Greeks among whom the gospel story proliferated. As for the masses, their persuasion was not based on rationality or argumentation but on the miracles which accompanied the preaching of the gospel. While Ibn al-Ṭayyib's argument may garner little resistance among his Christian co-religionists, it is strictly an in-house response to the proliferation of Islam. He is grasping at the straws of an argument that has long lost traction in the intellectual circles of Baghdad. *Tawḥīd* has become the intellectual standard among the *mutakallimūn* and the Arabs, presumably those "inferior intellects" to whom he refers, have occupied the seats of power and spread their language and religion east and west.

Fortunately, Ibn al-Ṭayyib abbreviates his critique of opposing religions and their adherents and returns to an argument for the rationality of the Trinity (section 3).

---

53. *wa hādhā al-miqdār yajrī fīmā naḥnu bi-sabīlihi* وهذا المقدار يجري فيما نحن بسبيله

54. As in the preceding section, I opt to begin section 8 one paragraph earlier than Troupeau. In this paragraph, the author states that various groups have defined the attributes in various ways. He then proceeds to lay out the errors of these views. The errors are treated in the following paragraphs. For that reason, I include this introductory paragraph with section 8.

Those who attribute both unity and trinity to God must not be accused of irrationality but should demonstrate the separate aspects of his unity and trinity. Ibn al-Ṭayyib undertakes to do this by showing that divergent attributes exist within the one God, yet the divergence of descriptions does not imply a multiplicity of essence. The attributes Ibn al-Ṭayyib has chosen at this stage are wisdom, power and goodness – commonly used attributes of God among Muslims and Christians. He pursues his argument by stating that if the essence is taken with each of the descriptions, three divergent results are yielded: the wise One, the powerful One, the good One. Yet no rational person would thereby assert a plurality of essence: "Yet no one claims that its (the essence of the Creator) being powerful is the same as its being wise . . . As the descriptions differ, though the essence is one, the descriptions are not the essence but other than it. So the essence is one and its descriptors are many" (section 3).[55] Thus, the assertion of God's unity and trinity conforms to the formal rules of logic as the unity and trinity apply to separate aspects of God – essence and attributes.

Ibn al-Ṭayyib elaborates by employing the triad of knowledge: The Almighty must be knowing for he is the Creator of knowing minds: "The essence whose attribute is knowledge must know. Therefore, the divine essence knows, knows itself [*ta'lam dhātahā*] and is known" (section 4). The three attributes, when taken with the essence, yield one with knowledge, a knowing one and a known one. The essence is one with three attributes. Ibn al-Ṭayyib is adapting the well-known triad of intellect used by his predecessor Ibn ʿAdī (see section 3.2 below). Additionally, the concept of God as intellect was common currency in Muslim discourse, having been popularized by Ibn Sīnā.[56]

From here, Ibn al-Ṭayyib transfers these attributes to the Trinitarian names. Knowledge is named "fatherhood" by Christians while the knowing one is named "filiation" and the known one "procession." The joining of the essence with these attributes is called the hypostases, named Father, Son and Spirit – names supplied by revelation and, therefore, not open to debate: "The names are instruments used to indicate the named entities. Since existence testifies to the correctness of the named entities, debate over them is nothing more than sophistry and those who enter that debate are in error, neither belonging to the people of truth nor adhering to true religion" (section 5). Further on, the author reverts to another Ibn ʿAdī argument referring to Zayd and Socrates to show that multiple attributes can be attributed to one essence. It is an unfortunate regression in the logic of Ibn al-Ṭayyib's argument. He has made progress in delineating the Christian concept but fails to acknowledge that human analogies are inadequate to bear the weight of the concept. The insufficiency

55. See also *A Treatise of Fourteen Chapters*, section 5 (Samir, "Ṣafaḥāt min maqāla," 250).

56. Afnan, *Avicenna*, 170–171.

of the analogy is somewhat pardonable given that both Muslims and Christians were using human analogy (e.g. Zayd) in the discussion of the divine attributes.[57]

Section 7 reveals the differentiation of the attributes of essence from the attributes of act – a similar division to that made by al-Ashʿarī.[58] Here, Ibn al-Ṭayyib is approaching a safer haven. However, he takes a risk in the preceding argument by employing Ibn ʿAdī's triad of intellect. The author establishes a communicable attribute (knowledge) as the defining characteristic of God's attributes of essence. He then proceeds to state that the attributes of essence are those which are not communicated beyond the essence to other essences.[59] Yet knowledge is such a communicable attribute. The author is open to the criticism that he has arbitrarily selected the attributes of knowledge though knowledge itself does not accord with his own definition of the attributes of essence. Two considerations may assist us in assessing this apparent lapse of logic. First, Ibn al-Ṭayyib's definition of the attributes of essence is cited in the same paragraph as his reference to knowledge (M3 VII.1). Apparently, he sees no inconsistency. His concern is with the self-knowledge of the deity. Although knowledge is a human trait, it can be fairly claimed that human knowledge of the divine is liable to error as it is neither innate nor complete. Indeed, the author clarifies this point in M3 VI below. Second, the discussion may be due to a common theme in Muslim–Christian discourse where the attributes of essence were defined as those attributes without which God would not be God. "Knowledge" was one such attribute as an unknowing god would be an absurdity.[60] In M3, Ibn al-Ṭayyib will further elucidate his view of the attributes and their relation to the hypostases. He will hold to the scriptural revelation and its terminology as the unique revealer of the attributes of essence, thereby strengthening his argument.

Section 8 refers to varying views on the attributes which are held by other religions. Although the author does not specify the religious group in question, he is almost certainly referring to the disagreement between the Ashʿarīs and the Muʿtazilīs relative to the attributes. The first group cited does not agree on the limitation of the attributes of essence to three:

> A group among the possessors of the ancient laws believe as we, saying that the essence of the Creator is one and his attributes are many and can be described as power, bounty, wisdom and the like. However, they do

57. Gimaret, "Sifa," 552.

58. This bears resemblance to early Islamic division of the attributes into attributes of essence and attributes of act (see Cumming, "Ṣifāt al-dhāt," 7–8).

59. فمنها صفات يوصف (البارئ) بها ولا تتعدّى ذاته بأن تتعلّق بغيرها "Among them are attributes by which he [the Creator] is described which do not surpass his essence to adhere to others."

60. ʿAmmār al-Baṣrī, for example, adopted this understanding of the attributes of essence (Mikhail, "ʿAmmār al-Basrī's Kitāb al-Burhān," 162–165).

> not limit the attributes to three but go beyond that number. So that is the nature of our disagreement with them. However, we have divided [the attributes] into attributes of essence and act. The attributes of essence are limited to three and as for the attributes of act, we agree with them that they are not limited to that number (section 8).

The reference appears to be to the Ashʿārīs. Al-Ashʿārī himself spoke of seven attributes of essence but did not consider the number fixed. The second group asserts that the attributes are all descriptions of the essence and the divergence of description reflects only the mind of the describer, not the essence.[61] This appears to be a description of the Muʿtazilī view of the attributes to which Ibn al-Ṭayyib expresses strong dissent.[62] Although the author makes no explicit reference to Islam, remarks like these show that he is intentionally interacting with Islamic thought relative to the attributes and providing a Christian perspective on the weighty theological issues of his day.

2.4 Third Treatise (M3)

2.4.1 Contents

The copyist of Huntington 240 entitles this document "The Third Treatise of Sheikh ʿAbū Faraj ʿAbd Allāh bin al-Ṭayyib concerning Trinity and Unity."[63] Troupeau's division of M3 into ten sections will be followed in the main with slight amendments noted. Appendix 2 is an Arabic–English version of M3 with section and verse divisions.

1. Statement of the doctrine: The author supplies a succinct summary of the doctrine as stated in his previous treatise. God is one in essence, three in attributes. The attributes are entities in the essence while the hypostases are the essence when taken with each of the three attributes of essence.
2. The legal demonstration that the attributes of essence are three only: The three essential attributes are those which do not extend beyond the essence to be communicated with other created beings. Thus, they cannot be known by inference from creation but must be revealed by the Lawgiver (they are inferred from Scripture, thus a "legal demonstration"). Specifically, these three attributes are paternity, filiation and procession.[64] God has revealed

61. Cumming says of the Muʿtazilī view of the *ṣifāt*, "Thus God's knowledge and power, of which the Qur'ān speaks, do not have any real existence. To say 'God has knowledge' is simply a circumlocution for 'God is knowing.' God's knowledge and power then are nothing more than verbal terms used as a way of speaking. They have no underlying reality" (Cumming, "Ṣifāt al-dhāt," 121).

62. Gimaret, "Sifa," 551–552.

63. *al-Maqāla al-thālitha li-al-Shaykh Abī Faraj 'Abd Allāh bin al-Ṭayyib fī al-tathlīth wa-al-tawḥīd* المقالة الثالثة للشيخ ابي فرج عبد الله بن الطيّب في التثليث والتوحيد

64. *ubuwwa, bunuwwa, inbi'āth* أبوة، بنوة وإنبعاث

these attributes in the measure that he deemed appropriate to each epoch, confirming the revelation through miracles. A fuller understanding of them awaits the hereafter when human minds will be elevated to a more complete state and, therefore, able to assimilate these truths.

3. The rational demonstration that the attributes of essence are three only: The triad of knowledge is demonstrated by the undeniable assertion that God is knowing.[65] He knows himself and is known. These three attributes (knowledge, knowing one and known one), which can neither be reduced to two nor increased to four, correlate with God's paternity, filiation and procession. When they are each taken with the essence, they yield three hypostases. The names "Father," "Son" and "Spirit" were given by God in "the Law" to correspond with the precise intention of the Lawgiver. Moreover, the church understands the designation "Father" to refer to the essence as cause of the Son and Spirit who are effects (or "caused," *ma'lūlān*). The terms used derive their meanings from the Law and must not be equated with their usage in common parlance.
4. Objection that the hypostases are three only: If the hypostases are derived from the joining of the essence with the attributes, they must be more than three. Attributes such as bounty, power, wisdom and eternality must also yield a hypostasis when joined with the essence. The author responds by categorizing the attributes into two types: (1) those attributes which extend beyond the essence to draw in other substances; and (2) the attributes of essence which are only known through revelation. The hypostases are only three because they are derived from the joining of the attributes of essence, which are only three, with the essence.
5. Objection that attributes which extend beyond the essence require a separate substance:[66] If the attributes that extend beyond the essence draw in other substances, then they require the existence of other substances.[67] How can this be if God alone is eternal? The author responds by dividing all things into two categories: (1) those having potentiality; and (2) those having both potentiality and actuality. These attributes exist in God in potentiality. Thus their objects also exist in potentiality. No separate substance is

65. See also *A Treatise of Fourteen Chapters* (Samir, "Ṣafaḥāt min maqāla," 253).

66. Note that in this section, Ibn al-Ṭayyib does not use the term "attribute of act" (*ṣifat al-fi'l*) as in M2. In his "Treatise of Fourteen Chapters," he uses the terms *ṣifāt al-dhāt* and *ṣifāt al-ta'addī* suggesting that these attributes extend into the realm of the created world (Samir, 254).

67. Note that Ibn al-Ṭayyib's use of "essence" (الذات) in this section refers to the essence of God. When he speaks of entities other than God, he uses the term "substance" (الجوهر).

required. God brought forth when he did according to his beneficence. Thus the attributes that existed in God in potentiality came into actuality at the appropriate time according to God's beneficent purposes.

6. Objection that one may infer God's attributes of essence from the creation: Some of God's attributes are obvious to our senses. Others are derived from rational inference. God's being a "knowing one" falls into this latter category. Although it may be inferred from the creation, that inference is liable to error as God's self-knowledge is not available to us through observation of the created order. It must be known through revelation.
7. Two views regarding the attributes: Christians view the attributes as eternal entities in God. Philosophers[68] view them as attributes which are present only in the mind of the describer, with no corresponding reality within God. In this view, God is pure essence and the attributes are nothing more than the means by which inferior minds speak of him. The Christians are correct whereas the philosophers are incorrect. The author establishes his view by asking if the meaning of bounteous and wise is the same. They are not the same; therefore, the difference lies either in the thing described or in the mind of the describer. If the latter is true, the description does not correspond to reality and is, therefore, nullified. As the essence is one, the different descriptions cannot apply to the essence *per se*, but to entities eternally present within the essence.
8. The names of the hypostases: The church calls these three properties paternity, filiation and procession. The Father begets. The Son is begotten. The Spirit proceeds. All of these refer to the one God who is the cause of all creation. The names denote their particular meanings in the Law, not the meanings associated with them in common usage. The Father's being "cause" while the Son and Spirit are "effect" does not mean that the Father is the cause of their existence as the essence is one.
9. The objection of compositeness in God: The author's response is that compositeness divides into two types: pseudo-composition and authentic composition. Authentic composition is seen in the human body as it is composed of the essential elements being mixed together. This is not true of God. As for pseudo-composition, it may be referred to as concurrence. For example, the essence and the attribute exist concurrently from eternity

68. Although the author uses the word "philosophers," his description is more in line with Muʿtazilī thinking.

past without compositeness and without an assembler. This is the view held by the church.

10. The objection that accidents are attributed to the Creator: The author responds that of what is found in a thing, some may be called "accident" and some "property." These are called properties, following the essence.

2.4.2 Interpretation and Analysis

In considering how Ibn al-Ṭayyib interacted with his Islamic hermeneutical context, it is helpful to note points of variation between M2 and M3. It is noteworthy that M3 avoids the denigration of other faiths which was evident in M2. The author moves directly into his subject matter, summarizing succinctly the contents of M2. He avoids any reference to the triad of knowledge in the introduction referring to the three attributes of essence as "entities within the essence, not essences." These attributes are paternity, filiation and procession. The author's intention is to demonstrate that the attributes can only be three – no more and no less. He quickly states his view that the hypostases are simply the attributes of essence when taken with the essence. Section I.4 gives a brief analogy to Zayd but the analogy is not as protracted as it was in M2. Ibn al-Ṭayyib is content to demonstrate that Zayd's attributes when considered separately lead to a different description of his person. Zayd is a mathematician, Zayd is white, and so on (V.9–11). The treatise quickly moves past the human analogy (compare with M2 VI.1).

In sections 4, 5 and 6, the treatise entertains important objections to the doctrine of the attributes of essence. The first question concerns why the attributes of essence are limited to three only – a topic of concern to both Ashʿārīs and Muʿtazilīs during the period. The second concerns a philosophical objection regarding the relation of the attributes and the essence. Here, the author divides all things into two categories – those with potentiality and those with actuality. It is noteworthy that Ibn Sīnā uses the same categorization.[69] The final objection in section 6 is that the attributes of essence may be inferred from the created order without reference to revelation.

In speaking of the attributes, I will use the titles "communicable" and "incommunicable." Ibn al-Ṭayyib's definitions differ from the contemporary meanings of those titles. Communicable attributes are those which extend beyond the essence to other created beings and are, therefore, accessible to unaided human reason: "The essence of the Creator and those communicable attributes do not require one who reveals a revelation to human minds. Indeed, the earth and its assembly lead to the declaration of a Creator, having the attributes of bounty, power and wisdom as well

69. Bertolacci, *Reception of Aristotle's Metaphysics*, 121.

as other communicable attributes" (M3 II.18).[70] Incommunicable attributes are those which are inaccessible to human reason and must be revealed. Specifically, this latter category consists of paternity, filiation and procession: "As for the essential attributes that are particular [to the essence] and do not go beyond it, they are hidden to human minds. There is no means to arrive at or perceive them. These three attributes are paternity, filiation and procession. The exalted Lawgiver bestows their knowledge upon us bringing us to rest upon them" (M3 II.19–21). This definition of the attributes not only portends the author's original contribution to Trinitarian thought but also a significant flaw in his argument which is discussed below. Two demonstrations of the doctrine are provided. The first is titled a "legal" demonstration because it is drawn from and revealed only in the Law or revelation (section 2). In the author's view, it was the Old Testament that revealed God's essence and the New which revealed the aforementioned attributes of essence. He holds that the reason for the timing of the revelation of the three attributes is locked within God's divine purposes: "The Old Testament led human beings to declare the divine essence alone without the attributes of essence. The New Testament granted human beings knowledge of the attributes of essence from the essence so that human beings would arrive at knowledge of the 'most blessed of all beings' in essence and attributes according to humanity's capacity" (M3 II.23–24). Furthermore, human beings will not be able to understand why there are only three attributes of essence and no more until God's purposes are more fully apprehended in eternity.

The second demonstration is a "rational demonstration" (section 3). Ibn al-Ṭayyib moves into the triad of knowledge as a separate, "rational proof" of God's Trinitarian nature. He builds on the supposition that God is one and that he is a knowing being. Therefore, God is both known and self-knowing. Although Ibn al-Ṭayyib has separated the legal from the rational proof, he quickly melds them into one argument stating that the "power to know" is paternity. God's "self-knowledge" is correlated with filiation which, when taken with the essence, yields the hypostasis of the Son. "Being known" is correlated with procession which, when taken with the essence, yields the hypostasis of the Spirit.

This rational demonstration may weaken the force of Ibn al-Ṭayyib's argument. He began by binding the attributes of essence to the necessity of revelation stating that these attributes are hidden from human minds as they do not extend beyond the essence to created things. However, his link between the triad of knowledge and the attributes of essence leaves him vulnerable to criticism which he himself recognizes in M3 section 6. This objection is that one may infer God is a knowing being through

70. In his "Treatise of Fourteen Chapters," Ibn al-Ṭayyib suggests the number of communicable attributes is on the scale of created beings but they may be grouped under three headings: bounty, power and wisdom (Samir, "Ṣafaḥāt min maqāla," 254).

observing the created order. Indeed, this is precisely the point that philosophers have established and upon which Ibn ʿAdī has built his triad of intelligence. If God's knowledge may be inferred, God must also possess self-knowledge. The author has recognized this implication in III.2. To his credit, the author recognizes the impasse and proceeds to respond in section 6, where he concedes that God's knowledge may be inferred without the grace of revelation, but states that human rationality is liable to error and, therefore, needs the corrective of revelation to properly understand God's self-knowledge: "We have conceded that the creation leads us to [perceive] God as knowing the creation based upon its inherent effects made known by Him. (As for His self-knowledge), there is no means for us to ascertain it from the effects of creation as it does not extend beyond his essence. What does not extend beyond His essence is concealed from human minds and senses such that revelation [of it] is necessary" (M3 VI.89–91). In essence, God's knowledge of creation may be inferred; God's self-knowledge may not. The point appears to run counter to the preceding argument of God's self-knowledge in III.2. Either God's self-knowledge requires revelation or it does not. Perhaps the contradiction might have been avoided had he referred to the triad of knowledge as an illustration rather than making a direct correlation with the scriptural attributes of essence. Indeed, the correlation is somewhat contrived. He was on safer ground in his contention that the scriptural terms (paternity, filiation and procession) could not have been derived from the created order. It was precisely the paternity, filiation and procession of God that required the benefit of divine revelation. Moreover, these attributes were at stake in the Muslim–Christian interchange concerning *tawḥīd* and Trinity. The correlation of those attributes with the triad of knowledge in both treatises brought Ibn al-Ṭayyib into a logical impasse which he himself recognized. I surmise that he felt it necessary to make this connection given the philosophical context in which he labored and the intellectual currency of the triad of knowledge. Not only did Ibn ʿAdī the Jacobite refer to the triad, but Ibn Sīnā the Muslim philosopher and contemporary of Ibn al-Ṭayyib made it foundational to his understanding of God.[71] In a theological vein, his reference to his own commentary on John 1 – the *logos* doctrine – suggested an obvious connection between the hypostases and the triad of knowledge.

Despite this apparent incongruity, a careful tracing of Ibn al-Ṭayyib's thought demonstrates an underlying coherence. In M3 section 4, the author argues that the attributes that extend beyond the essence entail another substance. The attribute of power, for example, entails the thing acted upon in power.[72] The attribute is known

71. Afnan, *Avicenna*, 170–171.

72. *ka-ṣifat qādir fa-innahā ṣifat lilāh ta'alā tajurr ma'hā jawhar al-maqdūr*
كصفات قادر فإنّها صفات لله تعلّى تجرّ معها جوهر المقدور

by observation of its effect in the visible realm. This aspect of the author's view of the attributes provides perspective on his use of the triad of knowledge. Although paternity and filiation are attributes shared with humanity, the paternity and filiation of God could not be derived apart from revelation. This is due to the fact that the object of God's filiation – the Son – could not be known apart from revelation. Nor would the object of paternity – the Father – be known apart from revelation. The same is true of the attribute of procession, the hypostasis of which is the Spirit. Whereas other objects of God's communicable attributes are observable in creation, the objects of the attributes of essence can only be observed in revelation. Thus, revelation is a necessity for humanity to come to a true understanding of these particular attributes of God. Ibn al-Ṭayyib's understanding of the attributes and their objects sheds light on his reference to the triad of knowledge. Though the author initially indicates that the attribute of God's self-knowledge is readily inferred, he later amends his argument to say that God's knowledge of the creation is inferred while his self-knowledge must be revealed. This is explicitly stated in M3 section 6. In parallel fashion, while paternity and filiation are human attributes, they could not be attributed to God apart from revelation because their objects remain hidden unless revealed by revelation. The objects are the hypostases – the Father, Son and Holy Spirit. Ibn al-Ṭayyib is forging a link between the well-known triad of intellect and the scriptural terminology of paternity, filiation and procession. While other attributes are discernible by the human mind interacting with the created order, these attributes of essence may only be known through revelation precisely because their outworking – the hypostases – are only revealed in revelation.

Despite the noted incongruity, the author's contribution to Trinitarian thought is quite remarkable. In seeking to demonstrate that the attributes of essence can be only three, no more and no less, he ties his argument to a division of the attributes into two types: attributes of essence and attributes that extend beyond the essence (i.e. communicable). The human mind can only attain to the attributes of essence through revelation which reveals them to be no more or less than three. The author's exclusive reliance on revelation as the only means to know the attributes of essence carried intellectual currency in his day as Ashʿārīs often deferred to revelation and its mysteries as the final arbiter of their *kalām* (theological deductive reasoning). Indeed, Ibn al-Ṭayyib's identification of the Trinitarian attributes as the attributes of essence is striking. Furthermore, his definition of the hypostases as the ensemble of the essence and the corresponding attributes of essence is clear and accessible, preserving both the eternality of the hypostases and their consubstantiality with the divine essence. As a theologian laboring in an Islamic milieu, Ibn al-Ṭayyib has provided a concise and accessible understanding of the Trinitarian hypostases – Father, Son and Holy Spirit.

2.5 *Short Treatise (MM)*

2.5.1 Content

The final Trinitarian work of Ibn al-Ṭayyib under consideration is his "Treatise on the Hypostases and the Essence," referred to herein as "MM."[73] The treatise consists of approximately 350 words. The focus of this treatise is to clarify whether the acts of God belong to the substance/essence or to the hypostases. The question of the attribution of the act may well arise from the author's former treatises and, therefore, I presume this treatise to be subsequent to the former two. It is noteworthy, however, that the question is also a favorite topic of Muslim polemical works, as will be seen in section 4.2 below.

The following is an outline summary of the contents of the treatise:

1. The confession of the church: The church confesses that God is one in substance and three in attributes. The hypostases are the joining of the essence with the attributes. Act is not attributed to the attributes, but to the essence, acting through the hypostases.

2. Act is attributed to the essence: If different acts are attributed to the attributes, each hypostasis would have a particular act, thus dividing the essence. Therefore, act is attributed to the essence.

3. The relationship of the hypostases to act: The appropriate acts of each hypostasis are ascribed to it though it is the essence acting through the hypostasis. Thus cause is ascribed to the Father. Effect is ascribed to the Son, as well as mediation in creation and union with humanity. Procession is ascribed to the Spirit.

4. All[74] are one principle, distinguished by the attributes: There is no temporal order within the essence. Therefore, one must not assume temporal priority of one over the other as they are from one substance. The distinction derives from the attributes.

5. Resemblance of the Christian doctrine to the view of philosophers: Self-existence is understood by the philosophers to be the first perfection[75]

73. The article is titled *maqāla mukhtaṣara* (مقالة مختصرة "Short Treatise") by the copyist of Huntington 240. Both Arabic terms *dhāt* (essence) and *jawhar* (substance) are used in this article. As *dhāt* is used more often, we have opted to use the word "essence" (*dhāt*) in the title of the treatise as opposed to "substance" (*jawhar*).

74. The word "all" translates a feminine pronoun without a clear antecedent (وهي كلها بالجوهر أصل وبالصفات متميزة *wa-hiyya kulluhā bi-al-jawhar aṣl wa-bi-al-ṣifāt mutamayyiza*). It appears to refer to the hypostases from the preceding paragraph.

75. *al-kamāl al-'awwal* الكمال الأول

resembling paternity. The second perfection is the reception of the emanation of the first perfection within the essence. This is referred to as filiation. The overflowing to others is the procession, which is called the Spirit. The church has amended the terms to facilitate their use but the meanings are the same.

2.5.2 Interpretation and Analysis

This last treatise follows the same purpose as the former and that is to defend and clarify the Christian doctrine stating that God is one in essence, three in hypostases. This particular treatise deals with only one question relative to the doctrine. Are acts attributed to the attributes or to the essence? Ibn al-Ṭayyib contends that the acts flow from the essence and thus have one source. Thus the essence remains undivided: "The attributes alone [*bi-mufradihā*] do not act. So the act is from the essence [*al-dhāt*] to which the attributes belong. If the act belonged to the attributes which are varied, then each hypostasis would have its own act distinct from the act of the other which would nullify the unity of the essence" (section 1).[76] The act, however, is distinct when viewed from the perspective of the hypostases. Act takes on its own particularity according to the hypostasis through which it is wrought.

The language used bears resemblance to that of Ibn Sīnā who spoke of God as a necessary being who emanates the good to his creation with no multiplicity in his being.[77] Furthermore, the whole question of whether action pertains to the essence or to the hypostases had been discussed by Muslim polemicists. ʿAbd al-Jabbār and Abū ʿĪsā al-Warrāq argue that if the substance alone is acting then the hypostases are ineffective, whereas attributing action to the hypostases implies the risk of multiple agents acting in potentially contradictory ways. It is reasonable to understand MM as Ibn al-Ṭayyib's response to this challenge, though not as a direct polemical confrontation.

The author is laboring in an Islamic context to solidify the foundation of God's unity of essence and trinity of attributes of essence. The actions of God must be attributed ultimately to the essence though they are wrought through the hypostases as emanations from the essence. Ibn al-Ṭayyib safeguards the unity of God's acts and thereby preserves the unity of the essence.

76. ولو كانت الأفعال للصفات وهي متغايرة لكان لكل أقنوم فعل يخصه غير فعل الأقنوم الآخر فكان توحيد الذات يبطل

77. Afnan, *Avicenna*, 172–173.

3. Ibn al-Ṭayyib and Christian Trinitarian Discourse

3.1 ʿAmmār al-Baṣrī (Early- to Mid-Ninth Century)

It will not be surprising to find Ibn al-Ṭayyib standing on the shoulders of his Christian predecessors who have amassed a long history of articulating the complexities of the Trinity, including John of Damascus, Abū Rā'iṭa, Abū Qurra and ʿAmmār al-Baṣrī.[78] Of these, ʿAmmār is noteworthy for having identified filiation and paternity as two attributes of the divine essence. Ibn al-Ṭayyib was certainly not the first to find a door of opportunity to explicate the Trinity in the Islamic controversy concerning the attributes.[79] In chapter 2, I stated that ʿAmmār's defense of the Trinity bears certain affinities with that of Ibn al-Ṭayyib. We summarize them in the following three points:

1. Both pointed to the illegitimacy of questioning the Trinitarian formulation and the names of the Trinitarian persons as these derive from Scripture.[80]
2. Both identified the Trinitarian persons with the attributes of essence.
3. Both provided a rationale for limiting the number of the attributes of essence.[81]

Although ʿAmmār's influence is noteworthy, Ibn al-Ṭayyib was by no means simply repeating his predecessor's ideas but rather amended and elaborated the Trinitarian formulation in the Islamic context.

For ʿAmmār, the attributes of essence were two: life and word. They were distinguished from the attributes of action because they are differentiating attributes. Neither "non-life" nor "non-word" could be attributed to God without making him other than he is.[82] Attributes such as justice, compassion, generosity, favor, kindness and mercy are actions which flow from the essential attribute of word and are liable to change. Because the divine essence is unchanging, these are considered actions, not essential attributes.

Ibn al-Ṭayyib does not seek to define the essential attributes but describes them as "eternal entities within the divine essence." Moreover, for Ibn al-Ṭayyib, the essential

---

78. ʿAmmār al-Basrī eschewed the use of *shakhs* (person) as a suitable moniker for the hypostases and used the Syriac *qnoma.* His definition of the hypostases is as follows: "*Al-qunūm* is a Syriac word as we have reported, and its meaning is 'individual' (*al-'ayin*), 'particularity' (*al-khāṣṣ*), 'perfect entity' (*al-kāmil*), independent in itself, rejecting from itself any need for something else in the subsistence (*qiwām*) of its essence (*al-dhāt*)" (Griffith, "Concept of al-Uqnūm," 190).

79. It seems that ʿAmmār is exploiting a Muʿtazilī view of the attributes whereas the Ashʿārīs have become dominant by the time of Ibn al-Ṭayyib (Mikhail, "ʿAmmār al-Basrī's Kitāb al-Burhān," 176).

80. Hayek, "ʿAmmār al Baṣrī," 102, 114; Mikhail, "ʿAmmār al-Basrī's Kitāb al-Burhān," 169–170.

81. See chapter 2, section 6.4.3.

82. Mikhail, "ʿAmmār al-Basrī's Kitāb al-Burhān," 162–165.

attributes are not two but three. They are entities which are eternally present in the essence. Their names – paternity, filiation and procession – are given by Scripture and are, therefore, not open to debate. He produces a rational argument for the attributes of essence, but his primary proof is the "legal" or scriptural proof. Furthermore, the definition of the hypostases is clarified by Ibn al-Ṭayyib. They are any of the three attributes of essence when taken with the essence. Thus paternity taken with the essence yields the Father; filiation taken with the essence yields the Son; and procession taken with the essence yields the Holy Spirit.

For these reasons, we find that ʿAmmār's thinking did not figure as large in Ibn al-Ṭayyib as did that of his nearer Jacobite predecessor Ibn ʿAdī.

3.2 Yaḥyā Ibn ʿAdī (893–974/280–363)

In his later years Ibn ʿAdī moved away from the triad of bounty, wisdom and power toward a formulation of rationality – Intelligence, Intelligent One and Intelligible.[83] The triad of rationality was likely viewed as a means of facilitating understanding in a Muslim hermeneutical context heavily influenced by Greek thought which deemed the intellect to be the eternal essence. The triad of intellect acting upon itself, the subject of the intellect and the object of the intellect as a reflection of Trinitarian reality became Ibn ʿAdī's most enduring legacy to Christian Trinitarian discourse. In his response to al-Warrāq, Ibn ʿAdī states that Christians "give the name 'Father' to the substance they call the Creator, intelligent as a pure intellect;[84] they give the name 'Son' to the Creator, intelligent as acting the intellection of his essence;[85] and they give the name 'Holy Spirit' to the Creator, intelligent as object of the intellection of his essence."[86] This conception of God was important for expressing the possibility of human intellectual union with the divine.[87] It is quite clear that, in the main, Ibn

83. Samir, *Maqāla fī al-tawḥīd*, 129. *'aql*, *'āqil* and *ma'qūl*: This manner of speaking is attributed to al-Farābī, Ibn ʿAdī's teacher, and its roots can likely be traced to Aristotle. Ibn ʿAdī translated his *Metaphysics* (R. Haddad, *La Trinité divine*, 229–230). Ibn Sīnā also spoke of God as pure intellect (Afnan, *Avicenna*, 170–171). Samir asserts that this move in Ibn ʿAdī's thought is observable twenty years after his authorship of his *Maqala fī al-tawḥīd* (Samir, *Maqāla fī al-tawḥīd*, 100).

84. Arabic: *idhā 'aqala 'āqlan mujarradan* إذا عقل عقلًا مجرّدًا

85. Arabic: *idhā 'aqala 'āqilan li-dhātihi* إذا عقل عاقلًا لذاته

86. Arabic: *idhā 'aqala ma'qūlan li-dhātihi* إذا عقل معقولًا لذاته . Platti, "Yaḥyā b. ʿAdī."

87. Ibn Zurʿa, Ibn ʿAdī's disciple, wrote a treatise on the intellect, stressing that the intellect is composite having the aspect of power which allows it to conceive of knowable beings. Curiously, Ibn Zurʿa relates a vision of his teacher Ibn ʿAdī who questions him on the nature of the intellect. He proceeds to instruct the disciple to write a treatise and attribute it to himself (see R. Haddad, *La Trinité divine*, 223).

al-Ṭayyib followed the formulation of Ibn ʿAdī although the former preferred the triad of "knowledge" whereas Ibn ʿAdī typically spoke of the triad of "rationality."[88]

The use of "intellect" for both the divine essence and the hypostasis of the Father by Ibn ʿAdī fails to differentiate between the hypostasis of the Father and the divine essence. In so doing, he tends to emphasize the unity of the essence at the expense of the distinctiveness of the hypostases. Ibn Zurʿa, a student of Ibn ʿAdī, labored to clarify the relation of the Father to the divine essence.[89] For Ibn al-Ṭayyib, the hypostasis of the Father, though the source[90] of Son and Spirit, is conceived in a parallel fashion to the other hypostases: "The attribute of the ability to know, referred to as fatherhood, when taken with the essence, is spoken of as a knowing essence[91] and called Father. The attribute of self-knowledge,[92] referred to as filiation, if taken with the essence, yields the knowing one spoken of as the hypostasis of the Son. The attribute of being known, taken with the essence, yields an ensemble spoken of as the Spirit" (M3 section 3). Thus, he clarified the triad of knowledge by linking each aspect to an attribute of essence and clearly demarcating it from the essence, which is consistent with his understanding of the hypostases.

Ibn ʿAdī's formulation was the intellectual framework which Ibn al-Ṭayyib adopted for his "rational proof" of the Trinitarian hypostases. Ibn ʿAdī also preceded Ibn al-Ṭayyib in speaking of the Father as the essence of deity taken with paternity. In the same way, the Son is this being when one superimposes self-knowledge. The Holy Spirit is the same entity as the object of the intellect – the intelligible. Ibn ʿAdī also suggested that the attributes may be joined to the substance forming an ensemble[93] distinct from the ensemble formed by the joining of the substance with a different property.[94]

Ibn al-Ṭayyib's formulation clearly draws on his Jacobite predecessor. Although Ibn ʿAdī refers to paternity, filiation and procession as attributes of God, it is precisely at this point that Ibn al-Ṭayyib takes the formulation a step forward.[95] It is these three attributes and no others which constitute the attributes of the divine essence. These

88. The triad of knowledge is *'ilm, 'ālim, ma'lūm* (علم، عالم، معلوم) while the triad of rationality preferred by Ibn ʻAdī is *'aql, 'āqil, ma'qūl* (عقل، عاقل، معقول). See M3 III.2 for Ibn al-Ṭayyib's formulation. Ibn al-Muqaffa (d. ca. 756) referred to the triad of *'ilm, 'ālim, ma'lūm* as a defective view of the Nestorians. Therefore Ibn al-Ṭayyib may be returning to a Church of the East tradition which used this formula although Ibn ʿAdī (the Jacobite) also used similar language (R. Haddad, 228–229).

89. R. Haddad, 222–225.

90. Arabic: *'illa* علّة

91. Arabic: *dhāt min sha'nihā an ta'lam* ذات من شأنها أن تعلم

92. Arabic: *'ilmihā li dhātihā* علمها لذاتها

93. Arabic: *mujtama'* مجتمع

94. Ibn Adī, "Maqāla al-Shaykh Yaḥyā Ibn ʿAdī," 74; Perier, *Petits traités apologétiques*, 22.

95. Platti, "Yaḥyā b. ʻAdī," 183.

three alone are eternally existent entities within the essence. Furthermore, it is these attributes alone which require revelation in order to be ascertained. They are not observable from the created order as they are not attributes of act. In summary, Ibn al-Ṭayyib refined Ibn ʿAdī's properties, thereby defining them as attributes of essence.

There is another aspect of Ibn al-Ṭayyib's contribution which should be highlighted. By comparison, it becomes apparent that Ibn al-Ṭayyib is a master of succinct formulation. In few words, he manages to express robust Trinitarian thought drawing on the Greek intellectual heritage articulated by Ibn ʿAdī permeated with a theological awareness that subjects the mind to revelation. Ibn ʿAdī was primarily a philosopher expressing Trinitarian thought in Greek philosophical terms, at times so esoteric as to render the formulation impenetrable.[96] Ibn al-Ṭayyib was a churchman who synthesized Greek thought and brought it to the service of his ecclesial community in lucid language.

3.3 Conclusion: Ibn al-Ṭayyib and Christian Trinitarian Discourse

Ibn al-Ṭayyib drew from the intellectual heritage of the Church of the East as seen in his forebear ʿAmmār al-Baṣrī. Like ʿAmmār, he links his discussion of the Trinitarian persons to the attributes of God. However, he diverges from him in his understanding of their number and names. Like ʿAmmār, his understanding of God's Trinitarian nature derives from theology proper – the nature of God as magnanimous, generous, self-giving and self-disclosing.

The theologian who most profoundly influenced Ibn al-Ṭayyib was his predecessor at the helm of the House of Wisdom, the school of Aristotelian thinkers that so influenced intellectual life in Baghdad: Ibn ʿAdī. Though embracing much of his philosophical understanding of the Trinity, Ibn al-Ṭayyib made his own contribution in terms of clearly defining the attributes of essence and their corresponding hypostases. He held forth the authority of revelation over that of philosophical deduction and produced a robust and succinct formulation of the Trinity.

Our understanding of Ibn al-Ṭayyib is crystallizing to demonstrate a responsive theologian laboring in the Islamic context. He drew from but also elaborated the Eastern theological heritage and its Trinitarian discussions. Furthermore, he was able to refine, synthesize and condense the views of his predecessors in order to

96. In Samir's excellent treatment and critical text of Yaḥyā's *Risāla al-Tawḥīd* (Samir, *Maqāla fī al-tawḥīd*, 196–207), he acknowledges that Yaḥyā's treatise is the most difficult Arabic text he has ever grappled with and that understanding Yaḥyā requires a thorough knowledge of Aristotle and medieval philosophy (Samir, 21). R. Haddad also points out that Ibn ʿAdī's formulation tends to emphasize the unity of the essence at the expense of the distinctiveness of the hypostases (R. Haddad, *La Trinité divine*).

provide accessible statements of Trinitarian thought in the service of his church now surrounded by a burgeoning presence of the Islamic other.

The long history of infertile polemic between the two faiths enabled Ibn al-Ṭayyib to realize the limitation of rational arguments. He invoked scriptural authority when rationality could no longer provide adequate justification. This invoking of revelation as the final arbiter was not uncommon among Ashʿārīs. His definition of the hypostases also has clear affinities with the Ashʿārī view of the attributes as eternal realities in the divine essence. I shall now turn our attention to several Muslim polemicists who pressed Christians on this particular issue. My goal is to gain an appreciation of Ibn al-Ṭayyib as a responsive Christian theologian laboring with a keen awareness of the Islamic milieu which surrounded him.

4. Ibn al-Ṭayyib's Trinity at the Muslim–Christian Interface

Although Ibn al-Ṭayyib is not reputed for having contributed to the Muslim–Christian discourse of the period, his treatises fit well within its parameters. I shall follow two lines of evidence to establish this fact. The first line consists of Ibn al-Ṭayyib's explicit expressions in his writings. The second line is the correlation of his subject matter to the prominent themes of Muslim–Christian discourse of the period. I will demonstrate this correlation through an examination of various Muslim polemicists drawing comparison and contrasts where necessary.

4.1 Explicit References in Ibn al-Ṭayyib

Ibn al-Ṭayyib's avoidance of explicit mention of Islam is mysterious; however, the introduction to M2 includes an explicit reference to "people of religions that contradict us":

> And before commencing our research (which is the necessity of holding to the Trinity in the exalted Creator whilst holding to His Unity), it is necessary to expose the difference between us and the people of religions that contradict us in other areas of research. [The difference is that] we establish their intention appropriately before remonstrating against it, which they do not do. (author's translation, M2 I.2)[97]

The author proceeds to speak of the apostles having preached to both the elite and the masses. The elite (e.g. Greeks) were convinced by the content of the gospel as they possessed the intellectual competency to scrutinize the book for its truth. The masses

97. Troupeau, "Le traité sur l'unité," 75.

were convinced of the truth of the gospel through the miracles of its proclaimers. According to Ibn al-Ṭayyib, such was not the case for other religions. The receptors of those religions were not equipped with sufficient wisdom to faithfully discharge the duties of their religion. Therefore, one must not receive their proclaimer's message nor the book which is revered as it has "frozen their hearts[98] by its action."[99] He quickly brings the topic to a close, resisting a deeper plunge into polemics. Nevertheless, it is sufficient to reveal that Ibn al-Ṭayyib is working within a sectarian context and is concerned to establish the church's views faced with the onslaught of contrary doctrines. He likens religious truth to a precious pearl amidst profane items and says the truth of such an idea must not be shaken amidst doubts that come against it.[100] Although one might counter that Ibn al-Ṭayyib could be referring to Jews – the other religious faction in Baghdad – such would hardly be the case as Jews and Christians shared a common book. It is doubtful that the author would have referred to it as a book that congeals the heart.

A second explicit reference to Islamic thought can be found in M2 VII.1 where Ibn al-Ṭayyib refers to "ancient possessors of the Law." He notes that they describe the Creator as having multiple attributes but they do not limit the attributes of essence to three. While Jews and Muslims might well fit this description, the second paragraph (M2 VII.2) reveals a narrower field of interest. He again refers to another group of law possessors who claim that the attributes are not other than the essence – a phrase that had been employed by Ashʿārīs to describe the relationship of God's attributes to his essence. The difference in the attributes is situated in the mind of the describer represented by different words. So the difference is in the describer's description but not in the divine essence, as it is one. Ibn al-Ṭayyib points out the irrationality of attributes with different meanings describing the same essence. Therefore, the description must refer to entities other than the essence which differ and for whom the descriptions are apt. Clearly the "entities" referred to are the attributes of essence which the author will later delineate as "paternity, filiation and procession." My point is simply that Ibn al-Ṭayyib is grappling with an Islamic expression of the attributes. He argues against the attributes existing only in the mind of the one who describes. They must be discrete entities for their description to carry meaning.

One other explicit reference in Ibn al-Ṭayyib demands attention. In M2 V.2, he posits a theoretical objection. The objector concedes that the attributes are many while the essence is one but proceeds to attack the Christian view that the attributes of essence are only three (knowledge, knowing one and known one). Because God's

98. Arabic: *ṣudūr* صدور

99. Troupeau, "Le traité sur l'unité," 75.

100. Troupeau, 75. Christians of Baghdad had converted to Islam in significant numbers by this time.

attributes are many, the Christians must not insist on only three attributes. The objector states, "we describe the exalted Lord [*al-bāri'*] as Creator [*khāliq*], Provider [*rāziq*], Wise One [*ḥakīm*],[101] Bounteous [*jā'id*] and others while you have stopped at a Trinity."[102] The objection itself is consistent with the Muslim–Christian discourse of the day. Beyond this, however, the similitude to the ninety-nine names of God is striking relative to the number of attributes. Three of the titles ascribed are among the ninety-nine names (*bāri', khāliq, ḥakīm*); a fourth one is derived from the same root (the Islamic title is *razāq* while the name listed is *rāziq*). The argument could be made that Ibn al-Ṭayyib is using generic attributes widely known in Arabic. Nevertheless, given the nature of the objection and the resemblance to the ninety-nine names, it is a reasonable assertion that the author is aware of the Islamic milieu in which he writes and chooses his material accordingly.

Though Ibn al-Ṭayyib does not engage in explicit polemical arguments against Islam, the preceding evidence is sufficient to demonstrate that the author is aware of his Islamic milieu. He is writing with an eye to the issues in his context. The lack of explicitness in his treatises may lie in the lack of a defined dialogue partner, sectarian tensions in Baghdad or other reasons of which we are unaware. Nevertheless, his theological treatises show clear evidence of the author's response to issues contested at the Muslim–Christian interface of his predecessors and contemporaries. I will proceed to demonstrate correlations between Ibn al-Ṭayyib's thought and the arguments of Muslim polemicists before evaluating his contribution to the Muslim–Christian interface.

4.2 Correlations with Muslim Polemicists

4.2.1 Abū ʿĪsā Muḥammad Ibn Hārūn al-Warrāq (d. ca. 864/250)

No other Muslim polemicist questioned Christians more intensively on the relation of the divine substance to the hypostases than Abū ʿĪsā al-Warrāq. His polemical concern is to oblige Christians to admit incongruence between their profession of three hypostases and a single divine essence.

In his *Refutation of the Three Sects*,[103] he glossed over subtleties of the Christian formulation which led him to the mistaken assumption that the hypostases are the

101. Huntington 240, in our view, reads حليم *ḥalīm* rather than *ḥakīm*. Both are from the ninety-nine names, *ḥalīm* meaning "the forbearing One."

102. Troupeau, "Le traité sur l'unité," 85.

103. *al-Radd 'alā al-thalāth firaq min al-Naṣārā* الرد على الثلاث فراق من النصارى . The work has survived through Ibn ʿAdī's *Manifest of the Errors of Muḥammad Ibn Harūn* (see ch. 2, fn 76).

substance.[104] He then carried his assumption to the logical conclusion that any differentiation in the hypostases is tantamount to differentiation in the substance:

> The Nestorians and the Jacobites should be asked: Tell us about the one substance [*al-jawhar al-wāḥid*] which you claim is eternal. Is it differentiated? They will say: No, for they do not apply differentiation or number to it when referring to one substance. Say to them: Tell us about the hypostases, are they differentiated? They will say: Yes, for according to them differentiation [*al-ikhtilāf*] and number [*al-'adad*] apply when referring to the hypostases (by number they mean the Trinity). Say to them: Then if you claim that the substance is the hypostases you are claiming that what is differentiated is what is not, which is contradictory.
>
> Say to them, Tell us about the hypostases. Are they differentiated because they are substance or because of another cause? If they say: Because they are substance, they impose differentiation upon the substance. And if they say: Because of another cause, they affirm a cause other than the substance and hypostases, which is opposed to their views.[105]

The author places the hypothetical Christian on the horns of a dilemma in that he claims differentiation in the hypostases and singularity in the substance while asserting that the hypostases are the substance. Abū ʿĪsā will continue to press his argument against the Christian in an inescapable predicament. Of course, the defect in the argument is in the assumption that Christians assert that the hypostases are the substance when, in fact, the Christian approach to the relationship between the hypostases and the substance is more sophisticated and nuanced than the author is prepared to recognize.

David Thomas underlines that in some cases Abū ʿĪsā's proclivity toward Islamic concepts prevents him from dealing with Christian ideas on their own terms. For instance, the attribute, in Islamic thought, qualifies a single subject. Thus it is illogical that the divine substance shares the attribute "Father" as well as the attribute "Son." Within this construct, Abū ʿĪsā presses his argument stating that fatherhood must be an attribute either of essence or of act. If it is an attribute of essence, only the hypostasis qualified thereby can be divine. The other hypostases cannot be (according to Abū ʿĪsā's presupposition that the attribute qualifies a single subject). If it is an attribute of act, then God is not eternally Father. The argument is sound in so far as one accepts

104. al-Warrāq and Thomas, *Anti-Christian Polemic*, 63.

105. al-Warrāq and Thomas, 77, 79.

the premise that one attribute qualifies one subject. However, his premise is foreign to the Christian conception which "locates the characteristic in the relationship between the progenitive and generated Persons."[106]

This intense interrogation concerning the relation of the substance and the hypostases serves to demonstrate that the topic was of keen interest at the Muslim–Christian interface of the period. Of course, Abū ʿĪsā preceded Ibn al-Ṭayyib by nearly two centuries, but the fact that Ibn ʿAdī provided an extensive response just prior to Ibn al-Ṭayyib's productive years enlivened the debate in the intellectual circles of Baghdad. Also, given Ibn ʿAdī's influence on Ibn al-Ṭayyib it is reasonable to assume that the latter would have studied Abū ʿĪsā's polemic. Additionally, Abū ʿĪsā influenced subsequent Muslim polemicists to a great degree.[107] As we shall soon see, the debate over the relationship of the hypostases to the essence did not wane in the ensuing decades.

Ibn al-Ṭayyib provides a useful clarification, though not a polemical rebuttal, to this particular issue in that he defines the relationship of the hypostases to the essence. The two are not identical but the hypostases are the ensemble of one of the three attributes of essence together with the essence. Thus it is the three attributes of essence – paternity, filiation and procession – that are eternal entities within the essence which constitute the differentiation. Their instantiation takes place when each of these attributes is taken with the essence yielding the three hypostases – Father, Son and Spirit.

Ibn al-Ṭayyib clarifies the relationship of the essence to the hypostases – the precise question about which Abū ʿĪsā is concerned. In the face of the accusation that differentiation within the essence leads to separate essences, Ibn al-Ṭayyib lays hold of the Ashʿarī understanding of the attributes: these are eternal entities existent within the essence. Although this would not have been Abū ʿĪsā's view, it would have been the common currency of theological discussions among the Ashʿarīs of Ibn al-Ṭayyib's day. The attributes do not divide the essence but are eternally present within it.[108] He consistently refers to the essence as *al-dhāt*, the commonly understood Muslim term. He works under the scriptural revelation to establish that the attributes of the essence are three, no more and no less, and that these terms are used in their meanings supplied by the Lawgiver and must not be confused with their connotation in common speech. This knowledge of the essence is only available by means of divine *tawqīf* –

106. al-Warrāq and Thomas, 62.

107. Thomas demonstrates Abū ʿĪsā's influence on two fourth-/tenth-century theologians: al-Bāqillanī and ʿAbd al-Jabbār: "It appears that by the latter part of the fourth/tenth century, Abū ʿĪsā's *Radd* had become an important source of information about Christian beliefs, and to some extent, of arguments against them" (Thomas, *Early Muslim Polemic*, 77–81).

108. Arabic: *qā'ima bi dhātihi* قائمة بذاته

the assured knowledge of scriptural revelation. There is no logical contradiction as the differentiation and unity are considered under different aspects of the Divine. Ibn al-Ṭayyib provides a succinct and useful definition to the interrelatedness of the essence, attributes and hypostases while protecting the Christian from the accusation of a differentiated essence – *shirk*, in effect.

Ibn al-Ṭayyib has declined to enter the fray of explicit Muslim–Christian polemics. However, he recognizes that the Ashʿārī view of the attributes, unlike that of the Muʿtazilī, supplies categories to Christians which enable them to sustain Christian concepts in the Islamic milieu. He confirms the nature and number of the attributes of essence based on scriptural *tawqīf* (assurance of belief by means of revelation). He then proceeds to show that the attributes of paternity, filiation and procession are indeed attributes of the essence and can qualify a single, undivided divine substance, differentiated in the hypostases by the three essential attributes. Ibn al-Ṭayyib was, therefore, not disengaged from the Muslim–Christian interface of his era but his theological treatises engaged with Islamic thought in an implicit rather than an explicit manner.

4.2.2 Abū Bakr al-Bāqillānī[109] (d. 1013/403)

Abū Bakr al-Bāqillānī's *Introduction*[110] contains a lengthy section refuting the various claims of Christianity. This section follows the progression of thought as al-Bāqillānī has just completed his presentation of God as a single, all-powerful being; thus his refutation of the Christians concerns their substandard view on the nature and unity of God.[111]

Al-Bāqillānī commences his argument by charging that the Christians are in error by referring to God as "substance." Thomas has pointed out that al-Bāqillānī is using his own definition for substance ("a basic component of material objects that can be characterized by accidents") whereas the Christians intend a meaning derived from Greek philosophy ("a self-subsistent entity").[112] Ibn al-Ṭayyib is at pains to clarify this fact. His first assertion in M3 I.2 is that the substance and the essence are one and the same.[113] Perhaps this confusion of terms lies at the root of Ibn al-Ṭayyib's preference for the term "essence" over "substance" when referring to the divine being.[114]

109. See chapter 2, section 5.1.2 for biographical information on al-Bāqillānī.

110. *Kitāb al-tamhīd* كتاب التمهيد

111. Thomas, *Christian Doctrines*, 124.

112. Thomas, 145.

113. *yushār bihi ilā dhāt al-bāri'ta'ālā* يُشار به إلى ذات البارئ تعالى. Is it coincidence that Ibn al-Ṭayyib addresses this issue first while it is also al-Bāqillānī's first criticism? Although the former does not follow the precise sequence of the latter, some parallels in the topics treated are observable.

114. Arabic: essence, *al-dhāt* الذات ; and substance, *al-jawhar* الجوهر

Al-Bāqillānī attacks the Christians' insistence on limiting the divine hypostases to three, suggesting they could be four, ten or more. He cites a Christian exposition of the Trinitarian persons as the existent one, knowledge and life and proceeds to point out that the attributes need not be three, for they are a random selection with no basis in rationality. Al-Bāqillānī congratulates himself that Christians have no answer to his polemic and must, therefore, abandon the Trinity.[115] Ibn al-Ṭayyib provides a twofold proof – revelation and rationality – of the attributes numbering three, no more and no less. The rational argument is built upon the triad of knowledge (M3 II & III) and may be vulnerable to al-Bāqillānī's criticisms. However, Ibn al-Ṭayyib anchors his argument in revelation and the names given to the attributes of essence in the Christian Scriptures. While it was by no means a rebuttal of the Ashʿārīs, it was certainly a deflection of the blow as Ashʿārīs themselves would defer to revelation "without asking why"[116] in the matter of the attributes.

Another concern of al-Bāqillānī, by now familiar to Christians, is that if the substance is "not other than the hypostases"[117] (held by Jacobites and Nestorians), there can be no differentiation between them. In *kalām* fashion, directing his reader to pose questions and anticipating the responses of his opponents, he states that the substance is "undifferentiated because it is substance, and because it is uncountable, and because it is not particularities which are diverse in significance." Christians are obliged to confirm this assertion. He then points out that the hypostases are differentiated particularities, diverse in significance and countable. The Christian is also obliged to confirm this. Thus the contradiction is established. The claim that the substance is not other than the hypostases cannot be sustained.[118] If, on the other hand, the substance is not identical to the hypostases (the view of Melkites), the differentiation of the substance implies multiple divinities.

It is noteworthy that Ibn al-Ṭayyib avoids the language, which, in fact, gained currency among the Kullābiyya,[119] that the attributes are "not other than God." In fact, he states explicitly in M2 II.2, "the essence is one and the descriptors [*al-awṣāf*] are not the essence but other than it. So the essence is one and the descriptors are many."[120] We do not understand from this that Ibn al-Ṭayyib viewed the attributes as having a separate, eternal existence (as al-Bāqillānī would later accuse the Melkites). Rather, perceived from the aspect of the essence, the Creator is one while viewed from the

115. Thomas, *Christian Doctrines*, 152–159.

116. *bi-lā kayf* بلا كيف

117. *laysa al-jawhar bi ghayr al-aqānīm* ليس الجوهر بغير الأقانيم

118. Thomas, *Christian Doctrines*, 158–159.

119. The Kullābiyya, named after ʿAbd Allāh ibn Kullāb (d. 240/854), held, contra the Muʿtazilīs, that the divine attributes had real existence within God's essence. The Ashʿārīs held the same view.

120. Troupeau, "Le traité sur l'unité," 79.

aspect of the attributes, three. Ibn al-Ṭayyib dismisses the accusation that the doctrine is abhorrent showing that the unity and plurality are understood from different aspects. It is a simple statement of non-contradiction. God is one in the sense of his essence; he is plural in the sense of his attributes. The author states that no rational person should refuse such a demonstration.

Al-Bāqillānī passes on to his argument concerning the nature of the term "hypostases." His first point of attack is the claim that the hypostases are attributes of the substance. This was a Christian claim which portrayed the relationship of the substance to the hypostases as parallel to the relationship of essence and attributes in Greek thought.[121] He puts the Christian before one of two alternatives. As the hypostases are not particularities to themselves, they must be particularities to something else. This necessitates a substance with three particularities, in effect, an affirmation of four eternal realities. The second alternative is to see the hypostases as particularities to themselves. In this scheme, the Son must be Son of himself, the Father, Father of himself, and so on. In fact, this divides the substance. Both alternatives collapse.

Ibn al-Ṭayyib does not claim that the hypostases are the attributes of essence/substance. Rather, throughout M3, he inserts an additional logical step. The attributes themselves are of the essence, eternally present. The hypostases are defined as the joining[122] of a particular attribute with the essence. He has already demonstrated that he sees no contradiction between the unity of the essence and the plurality of the attributes as these are taken in different senses.

The following paragraphs in the *Rebuttal* of al-Bāqillānī deal with the question of the Son and Spirit being particularities of the Father – how could they be equal in substance and yet hierarchically ordered? Al-Bāqillānī understands the Father is the cause of the existence of the Son and Spirit. Ibn al-Ṭayyib clarifies that the essence, being knowledge, known and knowing, is the cause of itself, not the cause of the existence of another (M3 VIII.2). But what is it, al-Bāqillānī asks, that makes the Father, Father (what distinguishes him from the other hypostases)? Is it nothing more than a random designation? Ibn al-Ṭayyib does in fact say that Christian theologians "make the attribute of the Father that he begot and that of the Son, that he was begotten and the Spirit . . . that he was emanated" (M3 VIII).[123] What might seem a random designation is not random, for these names, given by revelation, express the precise meanings the Lawgiver intends. Once again, the Christian defers to revelation: "All these names are from revelation and divine law and are not at all to be understood to

121. Thomas, *Christian Doctrines*, 132.

122. Arabic: *mujtama'* مجتمع

123. The Father begot (*awlada* أولَدَ); the Son was begotten (*wulida* وُلِدَ); and the Spirit was emanated (*'unbu'itha* أنبُعِثَ).

any effect or reason as intended in common parlance. It is necessary that these refer to a singular essence that is the reason for all existence and all that has been formed. This essence has three attributes spoken of using these terms" (M3 VIII).

Ibn al-Ṭayyib hesitates to enter the fray of confrontational polemic. Nevertheless his concern is to provide his Christian constituency with concepts which serve as intellectual armament in the Muslim milieu. It is precisely al-Bāqillānī's Ashʿarism from which he draws to elaborate these concepts.

4.2.3 ʿAbd al-Jabbār Ibn Aḥmad al-Hamadhānī[124] (d. 1025/415)

ʿAbd al-Jabbār attacks the Christian Trinitarian concept vehemently and attempts to force Christians to reckon with its inherent contradictions. Indeed, his argument is not unlike that of his Muʿtazilī predecessor Abū ʿĪsā, who is one source of his information though not explicitly acknowledged.[125] He asserts that if the hypostases are co-eternal with the substance, then "it cannot be right for the Father to be particularized by what is impossible for the Son and Spirit, and it is not right for them to be particularized[126] by what is impossible for him."[127] Thus, for ʿAbd al-Jabbār, the distinction of the hypostases cannot be maintained given the singularity of the divine substance. Whatever particularizes the Father must also be true of the Son given that the substance of Father and Son is one. So, if the Father is begetting, this must be equally true of the Son. Therefore, the Son who is begotten is also the Father who is begetting. This leads to an infinite regression where the particularity of the hypostases is lost. The reader recognizes Abū ʿĪsā's influence and indeed ʿAbd al-Jabbār refers to "our masters" who compelled the Christians to concede contradictions within their Trinitarian thought.[128]

Given that ʿAbd al-Jabbār's arguments are similar in nature to those of Abū ʿĪsā examined previously, I will not repeat those particular points but refer to other aspects of ʿAbd al-Jabbār's thought to which Ibn al-Ṭayyib provided a plausible response. For instance, the former relates that his predecessors have forced the Christians to confess that God was an agent in eternity as he became a Father by the bringing forth of a Son.[129] Ibn al-Ṭayyib answers, as have others, that the generation is not the cause of existence. The Father was the cause of the Son and Spirit, not in the sense of time,

124. See chapter 2, section 5.2.4 for biographical information on ʿAbd al-Jabbār.

125. Thomas, *Christian Doctrines*, 208.

126. *ikhtiṣāṣuhumā* إختصاصهما

127. Thomas, *Christian Doctrines*, 241.

128. Thomas, 243. According to David Thomas the verbal parallels between ʿAbd al-Jabbār and Abū ʿĪsā in particular sections (e.g. sections 3, 21–31) are so close that the latter must have formed the basis (Thomas, 220).

129. Thomas, 259.

but in the essence. "By this, I mean that the essence, in that it is knower and known, is one essence causing itself, but not its existence" (M3 VIII).

ʿAbd al-Jabbār also obliges his hypothetical Christian counterpart to acknowledge that the hypostases must act as agents[130] which necessitates each being alive and powerful and, if eternal, divine. In his estimation, this is tantamount to three divinities. The alternative is that the action is one action which negates the differentiation of agents, as it is impossible for one to perform action while the other does not. Therefore, this negates the hypostases.[131] Ibn al-Ṭayyib concedes the point of ʿAbd al-Jabbār that the unity of God is negated if the divine action is carried out by different agents, stressing that it is not carried out by the hypostases but by the essence (MM section 2) (both *al-jawhar* and *al-dhāt* are used). However, the action is associated with[132] the hypostases according to suitability:[133]

> So "the source" and "the Creator" are associated with the Father, not as Father, but as essence. And his being an effect, the mediation of creation and the union with it is associated with the Son because through this aspect, [filiation] it is suitable for the essence to unite with humanity and act. In its perfection, it is perfected. And procession is associated with the Spirit because the last of the Creator's acts is the effulgence on the other[134] because he was first existent, then related to himself by his self-knowledge and to his creation by effulgence (MM section 3).

I am not suggesting that Muslim readers would have found Ibn al-Ṭayyib's response persuasive. Likely, ʿAbd al-Jabbār would have found it maddening and irrational, due not to the irrationality of the construct but to the opposing presuppositions concerning the singularity of the act belonging to the essence. Our point is simply that Ibn al-Ṭayyib's subject matter fits nearly perfectly into the Muslim–Christian interface of his era. He is responding to quite specific objections raised by Muslim polemicists to the Christian Trinitarian formulation and, in fact, pens a brief treatise (MM) precisely as a response to this objection. Given that he responds so specifically, it is remarkable that he shows no inclination toward explicit polemics. Though one might speculate as to the reasons for this, plainly Ibn al-Ṭayyib chooses not to enter the arena of polemic neither for lack of intellectual acumen nor for lack of suitability of his subject matter.

---

130. *fā'ilūn* فاعلون

131. Thomas, *Christian Doctrines*, 257.

132. *yunsabu 'ilā* يُنسَبُ إلى

133. *'alā sabīl al-munāsaba* على سبيل المناسبة

134. Arabic: *al-ifāḍa 'alā ghayrihi* الإفاضة على غيره

An interesting aspect of ʿAbd al-Jabbār's *Summa*[135] is that he likens the Christians' Trinitarian views to that of the Kullābiyya who held, contra the Muʿtazilīs, that the divine attributes had real existence within God's essence (sections 10, 11, 12, 19). Although he refers to them as the Kullābiyya (named after ʿAbd Allāh Ibn Kullāb d. 240/854), his Ashʿārī contemporaries held the same view. Given that Christians were now referring to the hypostases in similar language to the Muslim attributes, such a comparison is not surprising. Ironically, Ibn al-Nadīm, a Christian writer, suggests that it was Fathiūn – also a Christian – who taught Ibn Kullāb that the Word of God is God, ostensibly tying the *kullābī* view of the attributes to Christian origins.[136] By the same token, it is not surprising that Ibn al-Ṭayyib borrowed from the Ashʿārī construct of the *ṣifāt* in expressing a thoroughly Christian understanding of the hypostases.

ʿAbd al-Jabbār was quite familiar with the debaters of Baghdad and even mentions in *Establishing the Proofs of Prophethood*[137] several of Ibn al-Ṭayyib's predecessors, after which comes this curious comment: "after him was Yaḥyā b. ʿAdī from whom came the heretics who are in your area, the sect[138] that does not engage in debate."[139] Who were this sect that resisted debate? Ibn al-Ṭayyib followed Ibn ʿAdī as the leading philosopher of Baghdad, so is he a candidate? Precise dates are difficult to pin down, but by 406/1016, Ibn al-Ṭayyib was well ensconced in his medical-professorial role in the Adud Hospital of Baghdad.[140] As ʿAbd al-Jabbār was writing his *Tathbīt* in 385/995,[141] Ibn al-Ṭayyib may have been too young to be considered a candidate. If we assume he lived to eighty years of age (d. 434/1043), he would have been thirty-two years old as ʿAbd al-Jabbār was writing, so it is not outside the realm of possibility. It is certain, however, that he was at least influenced by those "debate resistors" as he is considered the "final important link in the chain of Aristotelian philosophers working

135. His Summa *al-Mughnī fī abwāb al-tawḥīd wa-al-ʿadl* (*Summa on Monotheism and Divine Justice*) is intended to be a comprehensive theological textbook of the Muʿtazilī. The work is only partially extant (see Reynolds and Samir, *Abd al-Jabbar*, xxxvii–xxxviii).

136. Thomas, *Christian Doctrines*, 245, fn 37.

137. *Tathbīt dalāʾil al-nubuwwa* تثبيت دلائل النبوة

138. *Madhhab* مذهب

139. Reynolds, *Muslim Theologian*, 211 (from "Tathbit," p. 92, 11.8–10). In the *Critique of Christian Origins*, Reynolds and Samir opt for a translation of this statement which does not preserve the meaning referred to above. After referring to "Qusṭa b. Lūqā, Ḥunayn b. Isḥāq, his son Isḥāq, Quwayrā and Matta Grammatikos, also known as Abū Bishr b. Yūnus who commented on the books of the atheists," the author continues stating: وبعده يحيى بنُ عدي، وعنه أَخَذَ هؤلاء المُلحِدة الذين في زمانِك، ومذهبُهُم لا يقومُ بِالجَدَلِ. Thus a straightforward translation would be "and after him Yaḥyā b. ʿAdī and from him draw those atheists who are in your time and their sect does not engage in debate." (Reynolds and Samir translate: "Yet teachings are not established by debate.") N.B. al-Jabbār has already demeaned the Christians by referring to them as "atheists" so he is referring to Christians, not literal atheists (Reynolds and Samir, *Abd al-Jabbar*, 153).

140. Samir, "La place d'Ibn at-Ṭayyib dans la pensée arabe," 179.

141. Thomas, *Christian Doctrines*, 207.

in Baghdad" which includes the names to which ʿAbd al-Jabbār refers – Ḥunayn ibn Isḥāq, Isḥāq Ibn Ḥunayn, Mattā Ibn Yūnus and Yaḥyā Ibn ʿAdī.[142]

In summary, Ibn al-Ṭayyib was not attempting an explicit refutation of contemporary polemicists like ʿAbd al-Jabbār. He was providing perspective and clarity for his Christian parishioners and readers situated in the Islamic milieu of eleventh-century Buyid Baghdad and its environs. His topics of interest and the objections he deals with clearly arise from the conundrums of Muslim–Christian discourse of the period. He is crafting his treatises to enhance Christian intellectual plausibility in a Muslim hermeneutical context. Ibn al-Ṭayyib was a Christian theologian and statesman, responsive to his Islamic milieu, laboring to enhance the plausibility of the Christian faith for the church he served.

5. Conclusion: Ibn al-Ṭayyib's Value to the Muslim–Christian Interface

Ibn al-Ṭayyib is by no means the first Arab theologian to speak of God's attributes as *ṣifāt*, as the term is used by both Ashʿārīs and Muʿtazilīs. Although Ibn ʿAdī used the term, he generally preferred *khawāṣṣ* (properties). Other terms used include *ma'ānī* (entities), employed by ʿAmmār al Baṣrī for God's being both living and speaking. Abū Rā'iṭa made extensive use of *ṣifa* as opposed to other terms, perhaps in an intentional effort to foster communication with Muslims. While Ibn al-Ṭayyib is not the first to do so (Ibn al-Muqaffa also preceded him), the fact that he uses extensively a term with significant currency in Islam signals his recognition that its meaning falls within the parameters of his Christian understanding. Furthermore, he uses it consistently throughout both Trinitarian treatises. Gimaret has pointed out that the Ashʿārī concept of the *ṣifāt* diverges from that of the Muʿtazilīs: "When a Sunni [i.e. Ashʿārī] theologian speaks of God's attributes . . . substantives (power, knowledge life) . . . are not for him mere words but represent real entities, meanings joined to the divine essence, existent as it is and eternal as it is. For Ashʿārī the attributes are nothing other than positive realities, existents."[143] Gimaret's observation assists the English-speaker to understand that the word *ṣifa*, as used by the Ashʿārī *mutakallimūn* and indeed by Arab theologians of the Church of the East, carried more weight than the English word "attribute." His view that the attributes of essence taken with the

142. Faultless, "Ibn al-Ṭayyib," 668.

143. Gimaret, *La doctrine d'al-Ash'ārī*, 236, 243. French: "Quand un théologien sunnite [i.e. Ashʿārī] parle des *ṣifāt allāh* . . . les substantifs (*qudra, 'ilm, ḥayāt*) . . . ne sont pas pour lui de simple mots, ils représentent des entités réelles, des *ma'ānī* conjointes à l'essence divine, existantes comme elle, éternelles comme elle . . . Pour Ashʿārī ne sont véritablement *ṣifāt allāh* que des réalités positives, des existants."

essence yield the hypostases bears noticeable resemblance to the Ashʿārī formulation of the *ṣifāt*. The quote from Ibn Farūk below, as one summary statement of al-Ashʿārī's thought, reveals how the essential attributes were conceptualized:

> He [al-Ashʿārī] said, "The *ṣifāt* of God (exalted is He) fall into two categories: 1) those which cannot be said to be other than He (these are subsistent in His essence [*qā'ima bi dhātihi*], and 2) those which must be other than He because of their subsisting in something other than Him [*li-qiyāmihi bi-ghayrihi*]. . . ." He used to say, "The word of God (exalted is He) is a preeternal *ṣifa* belonging to Him, eternally subsisting in his essence."[144]

My point is merely that Ibn al-Ṭayyib's use of *ṣifāt* is situated squarely in the discussion of the divine attributes which had occupied the minds of Ashʿārīs (as well as Muʿtazilīs). His division of the *ṣifāt* into attributes of essence and those that go beyond the essence would have struck a familiar chord with Muslims and Christians conversant with their theology. We understand Ibn al-Ṭayyib as a Christian theologian, keen to systematize and communicate the church's dogma of the Trinity derived from Scripture in an Islamic milieu where Islamic forms of expression are increasingly predominant.

Ibn al-Ṭayyib benefited from precedent Christian explications of the Trinitarian hypostases. He provided succinctness and clarity to Ibn ʿAdī's formulation as well as a more clearly defined adherence to scriptural revelation. He recognized the Ashʿārī understanding of the attributes as consistent with the Christian understanding and willingly drew from it to elaborate both the definition of the hypostases and the necessity of their being three and no more.

In light of these considerations, we are in a better position to understand the purpose of Ibn al-Ṭayyib's theological treatises. Though he eschews direct and explicit polemical engagement, he nevertheless remains quite attuned to the issues that predominate the Muslim–Christian discourse of the period. Much as the strings of a musical instrument reverberate with the tones of another instrument in its vicinity, so Ibn al-Ṭayyib's Trinitarian formulation reverberates in the Muslim–Christian interface of his day. Given his own intellectual and ecclesial prominence in the most important Islamic city of the day, Baghdad, one would expect him to demonstrate his awareness of these issues through his writing and teaching. It is not at all difficult to see that Ibn al-Ṭayyib is in fact responding to the pressing issues through which Muslims have repeatedly confronted their Christian counterparts. These issues include the

---

144. *inna kalām Allāh ta'ālā ṣifa lahu qadīma lam yazal qā'im bi-dhātihi.* إنّ كلام الله تعالى صفة له قديمة لم يزل قائم بذاته (translation from Cumming, "Ṣifāt al-dhāt," 134; original: Ibn Furak, *Mujarrad Maqālāt*, 40, 59).

relationship of the hypostases to the divine substance or essence, the number and nature of the divine attributes and their categorization into attributes of act and essence, the number of hypostases issuing from the attributes of essence and the question of action – is it attributed to the essence or to the hypostases? To all of these questions, Ibn al-Ṭayyib provided substantive responses.

Was the explication of Ibn al-Ṭayyib persuasive to a Muslim audience? In all probability, the answer is no. We have no idea if it was ever read by a Muslim audience. But it does not detract from the fact that Ibn al-Ṭayyib was providing a cogent and theologically informed response to the pressing intellectual issues dividing Christians and Muslims. His response was intended for Christians who daily observed the ascendancy of Islamic thought in Buyid Baghdad and felt themselves at the mercy of the intellectual rigor of the *mutakallimūn*.

Thus, Ibn al-Ṭayyib can be understood as a Christian intellectual laboring in the Islamic milieu by fortifying his Christian constituency with intellectual armaments to both understand and mitigate the intensity of the Islamic polemic directed against their faith. The succinct nature of the treatises yields the impression that they are for the purpose of training, used among Church of the East clerics as educational tractates.

4

Transcending Polemic

Iliyyā of Nisibis and Abū al-Qāsim on Trinitarian Monotheism

1. Introduction

The medieval period presents few surprises in the realm of Muslim–Christian interaction. The rhetoric revolves around the primary issues of Christology and Trinity and secondarily the proofs of revelation.[1] The two sides present their assumptions with little empathy or will to understand the other even if the Church of the East was deemed more irenic in its interactions with Islam than were the Melkites or Jacobites.[2] One need not progress far into the Abbasid period to find Muslim polemicists exploiting the key Christian doctrines as exhibits of defective thought in regard to the absolute unity of Allāh in the Islamic conception.[3] Christians attempt to explain their theology and Christology but Muslims remain convinced that their formulations are substandard rationally. Moreover, the discussions are not merely academic but impact the social status of Christians through the medieval period.[4]

1. Allard, "Les Chrétiens à Baghdad," 386–387; Thomas, *Early Muslim Polemic*, 16.

2. Landron, *Chrétiens et musulmans en Irak*, 11.

3. One objective of *kalām* was to deconstruct and thereby destroy theological opponents. 'Abd al-Jabbār is an example from this time period. His intention was to deconstruct Christianity point by point. Christianity's being in error is assumed by the *mutakallimūn* who wrote to disprove it (see Reynolds, *Muslim Theologian*, 244).

4. Abdel Majīd Charfī points to multiple factors that influenced the polemical literature at the Muslim–Christian interface. One of the seven factors he indicates is "social antagonism" provoked by economic downturns. He mentions the work of al-Jāhiẓ, writing in the time of al-Mutawakkil, censoring

Iliyyā[5] ibn Shīnā al-Naṣībī's encounters with the Vizier Abū al-Qāsim al-Ḥusayn ibn ʿAlī al-Maghribī reflect the intransigent nature of the Muslim–Christian interface but manage to transcend it, taking on a distinctly different tone.

This chapter analyses the Trinitarian formulation of Bishop Iliyyā of Nisibis from the perspective of Muslim–Christian relations. Analysis of Iliyyā's extant Trinitarian works reveals the Bishop's contribution from three vantage points. First he had a unique dialogue partner in Abū al-Qāsim. The interchange between the two statesmen goes beyond the well-worn polemics of their era. The mutual appreciation and reciprocity displayed by the two men is uncharacteristic of the medieval period and portends the positive results of their dialogue as portrayed in the literature. In fact, the cordial relationship between the two men represented in *The Sessions* and their correspondence may be seen as an oasis of reciprocity in this medieval desert of polarization in Muslim–Christian relations.[6] Second, Iliyyā made effective though restricted use of the Qur'ān and its exegetes for a defined purpose: establishing that his Christian community was monotheist. His argument was persuasive enough to command the respect of the Muslim scholars of Abū al-Qāsim's court. Third, the Bishop adroitly used a combination of rational arguments and rhetorical skills which secured a unique reception for his Trinitarian formulation. Rationally, he sought to link his own Christian conviction with well-known Islamic formulations to demonstrate that his views were not aberrant. Rhetorically, Iliyyā skillfully wielded Islamic monotheistic phraseology to claim parity with his Muslim counterparts in monotheistic faith. The chapter further demonstrates how the Church of the East's intellectual leaders skillfully defended their Christian faith in Arabic as responsive theologians in an Islamic milieu dominated by Islamic *tawḥīd* (divine unity). The presence of an empathetic dialogue partner in Abū al-Qāsim afforded the Bishop a unique opportunity to explicate his Trinitarian views in the attempt to render them palatable to Muslim sensitivities.

---

the Christians for their way of life. Interestingly, the *Epistle* of Iliyyā mentions his rebuttal of al-Jāhiẓ (Charfi, "La fonction historique," 54).

5. I have chosen to use the transliteration of his name, thus "Iliyyā" rather than "Elias." This choice is based on the ancient orthography إليّا (Iliyyā) rather than إيليّا (Īlīyā). 'ibn Shīnā refers to his place of birth (al-Sinn or Shennā in Syriac). Also I opt for al-Naṣībī following Samir, though I commonly use the anglicized equivalent of the place name, "Nisibis" (Caspar, Charfi and Samir, "Bibliographie du dialogue islamo-chrétien," 258).

6. Thomas states, "there is no evidence at all that any Muslims reacted positively to Christian attempts to explain their doctrines, or thought them anything but flawed and misguided" (Thomas, "Early Muslim Responses to Christianity," 253).

2. The Documents

2.1 Selection Criteria for Works

We have seven or perhaps eight works of Iliyyā on the Trinity, each one shedding further light on Iliyyā's explication of the Trinity in *Kitāb al-majālis* (*Book of the Sessions*). From these works, I have selected those which demonstrate Iliyyā's unique contribution to the Muslim–Christian interface. *The Sessions* – renowned as an example of Muslim–Christian exchange – is complemented by the *Epistle* which provides a more personal account of the two men's interaction. Therefore, these two works will constitute our primary interest. Two of the Sessions (1 and 3) are pertinent to our argument and will be discussed below. In all, three works of Iliyyā (*Epistle*, Session 1 and Session 3) constitute our primary sources for this chapter. Other works which complement Iliyyā's Trinitarian formulation are the *Epistle on the Oneness of the Creator and Threeness of His Hypostases*[7] and his treatise on substance (*Kiyān*).

2.2 Question of Historicity

Whereas the *Epistle* as well as *The Sessions* portrays Abū al-Qāsim's enthusiastic and uncharacteristic acceptance of Christian *tawḥīd*, it is necessary to entertain the question of embellishment of the documents by subsequent editors. Was this cordial relationship and reciprocity between the two men nothing more than an invention of church officials or the creation of an over-zealous copyist? Indeed, the uncharacteristic credence of the Vizier may commend this scenario to some. While retaining the likelihood of editorial amendment, the following factors point in the direction of a broad historical reliability.

First, the subjects treated fall well within the spectrum of Muslim–Christian discourse of the period. Abū al-Qāsim's misgivings concerning the Christian Trinity, despite his proclivity to look favorably on Christians, suggest that he was subject to the prevailing view that Christians were polytheists or idolaters. Although this broad consistency with the Islamic polemical concern could easily be replicated by an enthusiastic editor, the more technical aspects of the debate may lend credence to authenticity. The use of *jawhar* for "substance" is of particular interest. The term had come under attack in Muslim polemic against Christianity as Christians asserted its legitimacy despite the lexical confusion caused for Muslims.[8] Iliyyā defended the use of the term but notably amended the term subsequent to his encounter with Abū

7. *Risāla fī waḥdāniyyat al-Khāliq wa-tathlīth aqānīmihi* ' رسالة في وحدانية الخالق وتثليث أقانيمه
8. Goddard, *History of Christian–Muslim Relations*, 61–62; Thomas, *Christian Doctrines*, 128.

al-Qāsim, suggesting that the Bishop observed the confusion caused by the term in the Islamic milieu and was willing to forego it.[9]

Landron points out two indicators of the historical reliability of the texts. First, the two texts contain varying details on the life of the two men yet they confirm what is generally known of them. For instance, the *Epistle* gives evidence of Abū al-Qāsim's precarious health and refers to Iliyyā's rebuttal of al-Jāhiẓ which appeared subsequently.[10]

Second, the dates recorded in the letter suggest that Iliyyā took care to reflect accurately the timing of the encounter. He recorded Abū al-Qāsim's arrival in Nisibis on Friday, 26 Jumada I in the year 417 (15 July 1026). The meeting took place the following day, Saturday 27. The dates cited by Iliyyā correspond precisely to the days of the week. At another point, Iliyyā recounts that the Vizier returned to Nisibis in the company of the Amīr Naṣr al-Dawla on Friday, 8 Dhū al-Qaʿda and remained there twenty-five days. Finally, there is a third visit of Abū al-Qāsim to Nisibis on Sunday, 17 Jumada I in the year 418/1027. The Vizier returned to Mayyāfāriqīn[11] after ten days and died four months later. Iliyyā records the date of his death as Sunday, 11 Ramadan 418 (15 October 1027).[12] The careful dating of *Sessions* suggests that Iliyyā was concerned to preserve the historic nature of the encounters.

Yet another factor is that Abū al-Qāsim concluded his final letter to Iliyyā requesting a written record of his means of expelling worry. The Vizier referred to the letter by the name "Removal of Sorrow and Expelling of Anxiety."[13] The work was published after the Vizier's death under the title *dafʿ al-hamm* (expelling worry). The fact that the errant name was allowed to stand in the *Epistle* may be an indicator that the copyist did not take the liberty to correct the text.

One final consideration commends itself from the documents. The texts preserve the integrity and dignity of both men and express respect for their respective religions. The whole encounter is surrounded by an air of dignity and honest inquiry that is seldom seen in the genre sometimes referred to as the "Monk in the Emir's *majlis*."[14]

---

9. I am indebted to Professor David Thomas who pointed this out in a personal conversation.

10. al-Niṣībīn, *Kitāb al-majālis* (Huntington 240), fols. 66r–66v.

11. This is the present-day city of Silvan in southeastern Turkey, situated on the banks of the Tigris. It is in the region of Diyārbakīr which was called "Amid" in the Assyrian period. From 983/372 it fell into the hands of the Kurdish Bād and then his nephew Abū ʿAlī Ḥasan Ibn Marwān who founded the Marwanid dynasty, which was replaced by the Seljuq dynasty in 1095 (Samir, "Entretien d'Elie de Nisibe," 52, fn 23).

12. Landron, *Chrétiens et musulmans en Irak*, 114–115.

13. Sbath, "Entry 1130:1," 19. *Izālat al-ḥuzn wa-dafʿ al-ghamm* إزالة الحزن ودفع الغامّ

14. Sidney Griffith has pointed out that this type of encounter became a literary genre in Muslim–Christian relations in the Middle Ages. However, the dialogue was often sharp with criticism and at times derogatory. Griffith aptly labels this encounter the "apogee of the genre." It is also noteworthy that though the monk was often summoned to the court of the Emir, Abū al-Qāsim is also portrayed as visiting Iliyyā

The skeptic may well counter these points with Abū al-Qāsim's uncharacteristic credulity, for which justification will be sought subsequently. While the historicity of the documentary evidence remains open to question, this chapter will analyze the documents as they have been preserved, seeking to avoid both naïveté and undue skepticism. While we make allowance for a degree of embellishment, the exchange nevertheless represents a high point in the church's affirmation of Trinitarian monotheism in the Islamic milieu.

3. Description and Interpretation

A biographical sketch of Iliyyā including the nature of his relationship with Abū al-Qāsim al-Ḥusayn ibn Alī al-Maghribī was provided in chapter 2, section 2.2.2. Therefore, I proceed to the documents which form the basis of this chapter.[15]

3.1 Epistle to the Vizier al-Kāmil Abī al-Qāsim al-Ḥusayn Ibn ʿĀlī (Epistle)

The historical conversations between Iliyyā and Abū al-Qāsim which came to be published in *The Book of the Sessions* (*Kitāb al-majālis*) took place between July 15 1026 (the date of Session 1) and the autumn of 1027. The first letter of the Vizier to the Bishop can be dated to the end of July 1027; Iliyyā's response may have been completed a month later; with the final response from the Vizier near the end of September.[16] At the end of Session 5, Abū al-Qāsim requests a written record of the helpful input he has received from the Bishop.[17] The *Epistle* is the extant version of the correspondence between the two men which also preserves the Vizier's request of a written record of the Sessions in addition to other resources Iliyyā had referred to during his visits to Iliyyā's residence.

---

in his *qallāya* – his cell or residence (see Sbath, "Entry 1130:1," 19). It seems the two men are on more friendly terms than the typical "monk in the Emir's *majlis*" (Griffith, "Monk in the Emir's Majlis").

15. See Samir's "Bibliographie" for important dates relative to Iliyyā as well as bibliographic sources (Caspar, Charfi, De Epalza, et al., "Bibliographie du dialogue islamo-chrétien").

16. Samir bases this date on the fact that the last personal meeting between the two men took place on 4 July 1027 and the Vizier died on 15 October 1027 (Samir, *Foi et culture en Irak*, 104–105). One internal problem concerning the dating is that the Vizier mentions his delayed response to the Bishop. This dating scheme conforms to what is known of the dates of the Vizier's death but also suggests the delay was not an extended one.

17. Martino Diez has produced a helpful introduction and translation of Session 5 containing the monotheistic confession of Iliyyā (Diez, "Profession of Monotheism").

This correspondence is preserved in an Aleppo manuscript held by the Fondation Georges et Mathilde Salem entitled Ar. 318 (Sbath 1131), folios 31a–71r.[18] Much of the correspondence has been preserved in a catalogue of the Sbath manuscript collection.[19]

3.1.1 Contents

3.1.1.1 Letter from Abū al-Qāsim to Iliyyā

After a lavish introduction and good wishes to the Bishop, Abū al-Qāsim praises Iliyyā's ability to remove all doubt and ambiguity from the "middle law,"[20] by which he means the law of the Christians. Other Christian scholars have been unable to provide clarity as might be expected since the matter of "making the one three and the three one" is of great complexity. Therefore, the Vizier requests Iliyyā to clarify the doctrine and remove his doubt concerning the unity (*al-tawḥīd*) of the Christian God, the union (*al-'ittiḥād*) of Christ as well as matters related to the Jews, infidels and astrology. He asks to receive the Bishop's response to al-Jāhiẓ and his work on "removing sorrow and expelling anxiety."[21]

3.1.1.2 Letter from Iliyyā to Abū al-Qāsim

As the letter is quite long (fols. 28r–67v), only those sections touching on the Christian Trinity and its relation to *tawḥīd* will be discussed though the entire letter has implications for Muslim–Christian relations of the period. Omitted sections are referenced in footnotes.

In the *Epistle*, Iliyyā indicates to the Vizier that he has been laboring to produce the written record requested, avoiding protracting its length. He begins with the subject of Christian *tawḥīd* (unity), assuring his reader in familiar Islamic language that for Christians, God is one.[22] This declaration is found in Session 5 where it is provided by Iliyyā in response to an accusation which the Vizier has heard from a judge named Abū ʿAlī.[23] The judge contends that Christians cannot affirm "one Lord" or that God has no associates.[24] After Iliyyā's composition and recitation of his response, the Vizier urges him to write a letter citing this confession both in the introduction and conclusion. Presumably, the *Epistle* is the initial attempt to reproduce Iliyyā's

18. al-Niṣībīn and al-Qasim, *Risāla ilā al-Wazīr*; Monferrer Sala, "Elias of Nisibis," 733.

19. Sbath, "Entry 1130:1," 10–19.

20. *al-sharī'a al-mutawassiṭa bayn al-qadīm wa-al-ḥadīth* الشريعة المتوسّطة بين القديم والحديث

21. *izālat al-ḥuzn wa- daf' al-ghamm* إزالة الحزن ودفع الغمّ

22. *ilāh wāḥid lā ilāh illā huwa* إله واحد لا إله إلا هو

23. The name of this judge varies among the manuscripts. Vat. Arabe 143 reads "Abī ʿAlī" (fo. 70r) whereas in Huntington 240 it appears to be اين يعلم which I presume to be a copyist's error that should be read "Abī ʿAlī" or perhaps "Abī Yaʿlā." Samir also deciphers it as one of the two preceding options (Caspar, Charfi and Samir, "Bibliographie du dialogue islamo-chrétien," 263).

24. Cheikho, "Majalis Iliyya mutran Nasibin," 270–272.

monotheistic confession. What follows is a rhetorically rich declaration of Christian *tawḥīd* in language to which Muslims would gladly assent:[25]

> He is one God. There is no God beside Him.
> He has no partner[26] in His lordship and no peer in His divinity.
> He has no equal in His eternality.
> No opponent can resist Him.
> No peer can contend with Him.
> He is non-corporeal, non-composite, not amalgamated,
> intangible, not localized, indivisible, uncontainable, not occupying space, immutable, not confined by place, not contained in time,
> eternal, without beginning, eternal without end,
> concealed in His essence, appearing in His actions,
> matchless in His power and perfection, peerless in grandeur and honor, source of all grace, spring of all wisdom,
> cause of all things from nothing,
> the fountainhead of all immaterial beings,
> Maker of all things by His command,
> the Creator of all created things by His word,
> Knower of all things before their existence,
> Discerner of mysteries before their concealment,
> living undying, unchanging never passing away,
> powerful, not deviating from justice, not oppressing,
> knowing not ignorant, forbearing not delaying bounty,
> gentle, unhurried, bounteous not begrudging, powerful not impotent,
> near to all, far from all,
> answering him who calls, aiding him who hopes for Him,
> sufficient for him who depends upon Him,
> a refuge for the one who takes refuge in Him,
> Purveyor of grace if it is accepted with thanks
> and remover of it if it is accepted with unbelief,
> near to the good, far from the infidels, receiver of the penitent,
> enemy of the recalcitrant, God of mercy, beneficent Lord, wise Creator who created the world for His will and as He willed.
> Then he commands resurrection and renewal and restoring life to those in tombs,

25. This translation is mine, based on the Arabic sources.
26. Arabic: *lā sharīk lahu* لا شريك له

He rewards the good by bringing them to His mercies and the evil by eternalizing their punishment,
the One who raises up, the one God, one Creator, one Lord,
who alone is worshiped, no god before Him and no Creator beside Him, no Lord other than Him and none to be adored but Him.[27]

After this substantial introduction, Iliyyā begins to explicate his doctrine of the Trinity, most of which will be omitted here as it is revisited in *Sessions*. The Bishop articulates the Islamic objection demonstrating his awareness of the difficulties Trinitarian thought poses. One example is: "there is no known substance that does not occupy space and is contingent and no hypostases who are not persons and no son who is not from marital relations."[28] The wording suggests God is limited, contingent and sexually procreative – each idea having strong currency at the Muslim–Christian interface of the medieval period. The word "persons" (*ashkhāṣ*) suggests a finite person though the use of the Syriac *aqānīm* (hypostases) is an attempt to avoid this undesirable miscommunication.

After displaying the Muslim objection to the Trinity in a most devastating form, the Bishop responds by confronting his Muslim interlocutor with a similar question from the Islamic point of view. If God has neither a body nor its limbs, why do you refer to his "two seeing eyes[29] or his two outstretched hands,[30] his two thighs which he reveals,[31] or his face[32] which he turns in all directions?" Such questions might lead those who do not know the beliefs of Islam into error and in fact there are sects which have gone the way of this errant belief. The Muslim responds that the qur'ānic usage of these words and their meaning is immaterial (metaphorical).[33] The Christian in like manner responds that the gospel uses these words for the three divine properties[34] and all who understand the three hypostases to mean three gods or three composite bodies[35] or three separate persons[36] have misconstrued its meaning: "The meaning of 'the Father

27. al-Niṣībīn, *Kitāb al-majālis* (Huntington 240), fols. 28r–29r; Sbath, "Entry 1130:1."
28. al-Niṣībīn, *Kitāb al-majālis* (Huntington 240), fol. 30r;
لم نشاهد جوهراً إلا ما شغل حيزاً وقبل عرضاً ولا الأقانيم إلا أشخاصاً ولا إبناً إلا من نكاح .
29. Q20:39; 52:48.
30. Q5:64; 48:10; 51:47; 20:36–39; 39:67.
31. Q68:42. The Saḥīḥ International Version translates the Arabic ساق as "shin."
32. Q2:115; 55:26–27.
33. *ghayr ẓāhir* غير ظاهر
34. *al-khawāṣṣ al-thalāth al-ilāhiyya* الخواص الثلاث الإلهية
35. *ajsām murakkaba* اجسام مركّبة
36. *ashkhās mutafarriqa* اشخاص متفرّقة

and Son' is not from fatherhood,[37] sonship,[38] marital relations,[39] biological descent,[40] intercourse,[41] conjoining[42] or birth from a wife.[43] Whoever says such, we prohibit him and curse him. Therefore if we commit idolatry[44] and anthropomorphization[45] because material language requires anthropomorphization and augmentation,[46] you also embody God[47] and anthropomorphize by saying God has two eyes, two hands, a face and two legs."[48]

The Bishop solemnly affirms Christian *tawḥīd* for his religious community (fols. 45r–46v) and, determined to refute any accusation of idolatry (*shirk*) on the part of his detractors, seals his innocence[49] as well as that of his religious community[50] of any sect that contravenes authentic *tawḥīd.* A recitation of sundry errant beliefs follows, including the belief that God would marry or have sexual relations. Finally, the Bishop articulates a solemn oath, extending for twenty-five lines, that anyone of his community who embraces such a defective faith will be accursed by God and his angels: "If the sceptic doubts or professes the delusion that our profession of divine unity is other than what we have professed and explicated in our belief, sect and law, I will produce yet a fourth aspect of proof which will not allow for any shadow of doubt. I hereby solemnly declare [*'uṭliq khitmatī*] my innocence and that of my entire denomination from any sect which contravenes authentic divine unity [*tawḥīd*]."[51]

---

37. *al-ubuwa* الأبوة

38. *bunuwa* بنوة

39. *nakāḥ* نكاح

40. *al-tanāsul* التناسل

41. *mubāḍa'* مباضع

42. *jamā'* جماع

43. *walāda min zawja* ولادة من زوجة

44. *al-shirk* الشرك

45. *al-tashbīh* التشبيه

46. *takthīr* تكثير

47. *al-tajassum* التجسّم

48. al-Niṣībīn, *Kitāb al-majālis* (Huntington 240), fols. 31r–31v. At this point in the text, Iliyyā proceeds to deal with the accusation of *shirk* on the basis that Jesus the man is said to be God. It includes the accusation made by Muslims that Jesus's birth of a virgin was similar to that of Adam who was born without father or mother (see Q3:59). The section labors to demonstrate Jesus's superiority to all other prophets. It also elaborates the nature of Christ's divinity as understood by the Nestorians, their view of Mary and biblical affirmations of God's unity from the Gospels and epistles. This discussion begins on fo. 31v and continues until 41r where the Bishop begins to adduce qur'ānic affirmations of Christian *tawḥīd* (al-Niṣībīn, *Kitāb al-majālis* [Huntington 240], fol. 31v–41r). This point will be discussed in chapter 6 on Christology.

49. *uṭliq khitmī bi-barā'atī* أطلق ختمي ببراءتي

50. *jamī' ahl millatī* جميع اهل ملّتي

51. Sbath, "Entry 1130:1," 14. This portion of the *Epistle* corresponds to the latter portions of S1 (verses 182–202 in Samir's version).

3.1.1.3 Delayed Response from Abū al-Qāsim

In this delayed response, the Vizier's praise for the Bishop is dominant. First, he praises Iliyyā for removing all doubt of Christian *tawḥīd* from his mind and heart as well as that of all Muslim monotheists.[52] The Bishop's elaboration of Christian doctrine will spare the Christians financial and social setbacks.[53] On the basis of what he has read, the Vizier states that the ongoing contempt of Christians will end as Christians and Muslims share the same understanding of God's unity.[54] Abū al-Qāsim makes the startling admission that Iliyyā's letter has caused the discrimination[55] of his heart and of all Muslims resulting from the Islamic conquests[56] to "grow cold." Prevention of harm done to Christians must now be understood as correct rather than a mistake.[57] Following this is a candid declaration from Abū al-Qāsim whereby he urges, even obliges, Muslim leaders to attend the prayers of Christians at their Christmas celebrations, stating that prayer behind them is equal to prayer behind many others.[58] The Vizier confesses to "flying with joy"[59] as a result of the Bishop's explication of "Trinitarian *tawḥīd*."[60]

The Vizier concludes by confessing two reasons for the delay in his response to the Bishop. The first is that he had lingered long over the meaning of Iliyyā's words.[61] The second reason for the delay was a "constriction of chest"[62] which served to further multiply his anxiety.[63] He recalled Iliyyā's speaking of a work on the expulsion of worries.[64] His final request of the Bishop is to put in writing the sayings of wisdom with which he was so impressed while he visited the Bishop.[65]

---

52. al-Niṣībīn, *Kitāb al-majālis* (Huntington 240), fol. 67r.

53. The text of the letter reads:
وآن وقت ضبط اليد عن أن يخطف شيء من مال من تقدّمهم أو التوصّل إلى إنحطاط رتبة من رتبهم والتعرّض
لسبب من أسبابهم ولعمري انّ بها وأقرانها يحتقن كثير من دماءهم
(al-Niṣībīn, *Kitāb al-majālis* [Huntington 240], 67v; Sbath, "Entry 1130:1," 18).

54. al-Niṣībīn, *Kitāb al-majālis* (Huntington 240), fol. 67v.

55. *tamyīz* تمييز

56. *al-ghazawāt* الغزوات

57. al-Niṣībīn, *Kitāb al-majālis* (Huntington 240), fol. 68r; Sbath, "Entry 1130:1," 18–19.

58. The Arabic is انّ صلاتهم خلفه ومعه تفي بعدة من خلف غيره The Vizier is urging his Muslim notables to attend the public prayers of the Christians, not merely as a formal gesture, but because prayer with the Christians is better than prayer with others.

59. *wa-kadtu aṭīr farahan wa-mariḥan* وكدتُ أطير فرحاً ومرحاً

60. Sbath, "Entry 1130:1," 19. *al-tawḥīd al-muthallath* التوحيد المثلث

61. *tawaqqufī li-'ajl al-fikr fī m'ānin awradahā* توقّفي لأجل الفكر في معان اوردها

62. *ḍīq al-ṣadr* ضيق الصدر

63. al-Niṣībīn, *Kitāb al-majālis* (Huntington 240), fol. 68r; Sbath, "Entry 1130:1," 19. *wa-ṣāra hamman ma' ghamm* وصار همّاً مع غم

64. Arabic: *Daf' al-hamm* دفع الهم

65. See al-Niṣībīn and al-Qasim, *Risāla ilā al-Wazīr.*

3.1.2 Interpretation and Analysis

The extended citation above as well as Iliyyā's extensive oath of divine unity exemplifies the Bishop's mastery of *tawḥīd* rhetoric. As the letter is read to the Muslim scholars in Mayyāfāriqīn, they are compelled to admire the beauty of Iliyyā's declaration. It serves as a forceful rejection of the charge of idolatry (*shirk*) in defense of his Christian community. For Iliyyā, as for Muslims, the unity of God leads to worship and exaltation.[66] Iliyyā's eloquent rhetoric is noticeably consistent with Islamic phraseology and, therefore, had persuasive power in the Islamic context, as demonstrated by Abū al-Qāsim's subsequent declaration that all doubt and ambiguity have been removed from his mind.[67] Moreover, in Session 5, the Bishop's recitation was able to secure an affirmation of Christian monotheism, with the only difference being what Christians believe concerning Muḥammad Ibn ʿAbd Allāh.[68] The fact that the confession was occasioned by a conversation of the Vizier with a judge indicates that the confession will serve as a legal reference for the Vizier in the Marwanid realm.

In his defense of the Trinity, Bishop Iliyyā is well aware that Christian terminology causes confusion for Muslims, as he asks hypothetically why the Christian chooses terms that lead hearers to misconstrue the meaning. Rather than amend the terminology (although he does offer amendments subsequently) his strategy is to confront his Muslim interlocutor with the fact that the Muslim's own use of qur'ānic language requires a measure of anthropomorphism. Therefore, it is unacceptable for the Christian to be accused of attributing human relationships (e.g. Father and Son) to divinity.[69] His list of negative connotations reveals his understanding of the Islamic abhorrence of the implications derived from the familial relations attributed to God but also his penchant to clarify that these implications are illegitimate and need not be inferred from Christian terminology. The Bishop rhetorically exhausts the negative meanings attributed to Christians by their Muslim counterparts and categorically denies them. What is more, he points out that the Muslim could be accused of a similar anthropomorphism if words are understood in a strictly literal sense.

Iliyyā is acting for the benefit of his religious community as a public representative of his church before the representative of the governing authority – the Vizier. Thus

66. In the following section, the author speaks of God's love of pardon (*'afū*) and charity (*iḥsān*), declaring this is why God is pleased with such qualities in his people. Those who pardon others who do them harm meet with God's approval. His people draw near to him asking his favor on their enemies and pardon for those who have sinned against them in order that they and all humans might receive his eternal mercies (Sbath, "Entry 1130:1," 13).

67. al-Niṣībīn and al-Qasim, *Risāla ilā al-Wazīr*, 68r.

68. Cheikho, "Majalis Iliyya Mutran Nasibin," 272.

69. Iliyyā adduces his qur'ānic evidence for Christian *tawḥīd* with the sūra *al-Zaghraf* (43:45): "And ask those We sent before you of Our messengers." S3 provides a number of qur'ānic proofs which will be discussed below.

the role of the Sessions in preserving peace and security for the Christians under the Bishop's charge comes clearly into view.[70] Iliyyā is exercising his role as the Bishop of his Christian community to clarify and defend Christian beliefs from false accusations which Abū al-Qāsim had stated explicitly in relating the accusation of the Judge Abū 'Alī. For the skeptic, the candid admission that Christians have been the object of misplaced resentment and social discrimination (section 3.1.1.3 above) which, in the light of Iliyyā's declaration, must be reviewed and corrected, strains credibility. Abū al-Qāsim's exhortation to Muslims to join Christians in their Christmas prayers, for example, appears out of harmony with the tone and tenor of Muslim–Christian relations in the medieval period. The charge of fabrication most easily falls on this latter part of the *Epistle*. Nevertheless, it is precisely here, in Abū al-Qāsim's explanation of his delayed response, that one finds a striking indication of the letter's authenticity. The Vizier has lingered long over the meanings in the Bishop's letter but he was also detained by a mysterious "constriction of chest" – a physical ailment brought on by considerable psychological trauma. Therefore, the Vizier closes his letter by requesting the Bishop's means of "expelling anxiety." In a matter of months, he meets his demise, dying before he receives the coveted writings of the Bishop. If the documentary evidence can be believed, one may imagine this Muslim statesman languishing in the throes of the illness which would soon take his life, reaching out through his letter to the pious Bishop whose reception and words of wisdom had brought him comfort. The fact of Abū al-Qāsim's death within weeks of writing his response to the Bishop gives the reader a sense that the plea is authentic and the relationship between the two men has transcended polemic to reach a life-giving and soul-enriching relationship.

3.2 Session 1: Unity and Trinity

Session 1 took place on July 15 1026. The Session is referenced using the shorthand S1. Father Samir Khalil Samir has provided a critical text, extended outline and textual apparatus based primarily on the three Vatican manuscripts which he deems

70. al-Niṣībīn, *Kitāb al-majālis* (Huntington 240), fols. 45r–46v; Sbath, "Entry 1130:1," 15–16. What follows is an extended section on the nature of Christian civil obedience to Muslim authorities and the obligation of Muslim overlords to protect their Christian constituents. It includes an argument that Muslims should defer judgment between two Christian complainants to their own religious community (*milla*) (fols. 47r–55v). This is followed by a discussion of "the best of Christians entering paradise" (*al-akhayār min al-naṣārā yadkhulūn al-janna*) in which the parameters of abrogation are discussed and an argument presented that only Christians and Muslims (not Jews or Sabeans) are those who believe in the resurrection and the day of judgment referred to in Q5:69 (56r–63r). Iliyyā then deals with the matter of astrology and its validity (63r–66r). He then turns to his rebuttal of al-Jāhiẓ (66r–66v) and the composition of his books *The Scales* (*al-Mawāzīn*), *The Expulsion of Worry* (*Daf' al-hamm*) (66v) and *Principles of Secretaries and Ordering of Oratories* (*Shurūṭ al-mukātibāt wa-tartīb al-mukhāṭibāt*) (66v–67r).

to be the most ancient and accurate renderings, as well as occasional reference to the Louis Cheikho edition.[71]

- *Vatican arabe 143, fols. 3r–29r* (twelfth to thirteenth centuries). This is understood by Samir to be the most ancient and unaltered version in its Nestorian form.[72]
- *Vatican arabe 180, fols. 70r–82r* (thirteenth century). This is Nestorian, albeit with evidence of Melkite editing.
- *Vatican arabe 645* (CE 1242). This is penned by Theophilos, the Melkite Metropolitan of Damascus. Samir notes numerous dogmatic and stylistic amendments as well as a prominent omission.
- *The edition of Louis Cheikho*[73] based on two later manuscripts of the eighteenth and nineteenth centuries. The Melkite work depends on *Vatican arabe 645*, thus one finds the same amendments and omissions.[74]

Samir's critical edition fosters a more detailed study of Iliyyā's Trinitarian thought as well as his unique contribution to Muslim–Christian discourse. The chapter divisions, titles and verse numbers are supplied by Samir and retained here as they are helpful in an analysis of the text.

3.2.1 Contents

3.2.1.1 Skepticism of Their Unbelief and Their Monotheism

The written session is composed as a report to one Abū al-ʻAlā' Ṣāʻid Ibn Sahl, a secretary who had expressed a desire to know the exact proceedings of the historic sessions.[75] After introductions and pleasantries,[76] the Vizier expresses his double skepticism toward the Christian faith: On the one hand he is skeptical of the widely held view that Christians are infidels and polytheists[77] due to a "wondrous sign" which had taken place among their sect. On the other hand, their beliefs confuse him

71. Samir, "Entretien d'Elie de Nisibe," 31. An additional manuscript from the Bodleian Library titled MS Huntington 240 also contains al-Niṣībīn's *Kitāb al-majālis* (1549). For an Arabic version of the remaining Sessions see Cheikho, "Majalis Iliyya mutran Nasibin." See also Bertaina, *Christian and Muslim Dialogues*, 231–234 for a summary of the seven Sessions.

72. Al-Niṣībīn, *Kitāb al-majālis* (Vat. Arabe 143).

73. Cheikho, "Majalis Iliyya mutran Nasibin."

74. Samir, "Entretien d'Elie de Nisibe," 33.

75. This secretary is otherwise unknown (Samir, 31, fn 4).

76. The Vizier expresses his desire that his meetings with the Bishop will become a regular occurrence. Samir surmises that the Vizier's ardent desire might have been owing to his relationship with Iliyyā's brother who for a time served as Abū al-Qāsim's personal physician. He was known by the honorific title Zāhid al-ʻUlamā' ("the most ascetic of the scholars") though his name was Abū Saʻīd Manṣūr ibn ʻĪsā (Samir, *Foi et culture en Irak*, 181).

77. *mushrikīn* مشركين

causing him to doubt their monotheism (verses 7–10). In response to Iliyyā's query, the Vizier proceeds to explain this "wondrous sign." While traveling, the Vizier had become ill to the degree that he was unable to take nourishment, speak or hear (21). As he began to despair of life due to his depleted state, he happened upon an unknown monastery called St Mary. A kindly monk insisted that he partake of pomegranates the healing qualities of which might restore Abū al-Qāsim. Indeed, the Vizier did eat the pomegranates and, though he had previously been unable to tolerate food and drink, the fruit was digested and restored his health. After partaking of a meal of lentils with the monks, the Vizier regained his strength completely. Abū al-Qāsim viewed this as a miracle – a "wondrous sign" – which prompted his skepticism of the widely held view that Christians are polytheists and infidels (11–29).

As for the Vizier's skepticism of Christian monotheism (*tawḥīd*), it is due to their belief in one substance and three hypostases, thus three gods as perceived by the Vizier. Additionally, they believe that the man Jesus was eternal and uncreated. Iliyyā replies stating that neither of these propositions is true. Christians do not believe in three lords, nor was Jesus the man eternal and uncreated. The Vizier responds by asking Iliyyā if Christians do not in fact believe that God is one substance and three hypostases – a Father, a Son and a Holy Spirit – and if they accept the declaration of the Council of Nicea, to which the Bishop replies in the affirmative. The Vizier responds that the belief in one substance and three hypostases is unbelief and polytheism, and that the Creed of Nicea declares that the man Jesus is Lord, uncreated and Creator (30–39).

At this point, Iliyyā asks his interlocutor if his intention is to gain a true knowledge of the Christian faith or merely to engage in polemics. If it is the latter, the Bishop requests that he pass on to other subjects unrelated to doctrine and religion. Abu al-Qāsim assures Iliyyā that he is seeking to vindicate Christianity of the charges raised against it. Furthermore, he reckons that the abhorrent external appearance of these charges may conceal a beautiful internal reality. He also assures Iliyyā of his personal delight in gaining a true knowledge of the latter's faith and that any monotheistic Christian is to be praised and rewarded even if he fails to acknowledge Muḥammad (pbuh). Furthermore, the pursuit of understanding[78] necessitates raising questions and objections and this must not be deemed anything more than honest inquiry. The Bishop expresses his gratitude for such a gracious response (40–46).

3.2.1.2 Christians Are Obliged to Say That God Occupies Space and Is Contingent

The Bishop introduces this section by outlining the Christian view of God's self-existence which, says the Bishop, Christians refer to as "substance" (47–52). Debate

78. *istifhām* إستفهام

over the term "substance" dominates the following sections of the Session. Abū al-Qāsim's first objection is that Christians are obliged to admit that God, if he is substance, is localized and contingent (liable to accidents) because every "substance" in the visible world is characterized by those two qualities (55–56). The Bishop responds by pointing out that Muslims refer to God as an existent without accident. In parallel fashion, no existent without accident can be found in the visible realm that is not localized and contingent.

The second objection of Abū al-Qāsim is that Christians are obliged to say that God is corporeal. He ties this assumption to Iliyyā's equating of substance to self-existence, stating there is no self-existent being in the visible realm who is not also corporeal (62–65). In the second response, Iliyyā invokes the Muslim belief that God is living, active, powerful and knowing. But there is no instance of a being in the created order who is living, active, powerful and knowing except by being corporeal. Therefore, if Christians are obliged to concede God's corporeality for their use of the term "substance," Muslims also are obliged to concede his corporeality by their use of the terms living, active, powerful and knowing (72–74).

In the third objection, Abū al-Qāsim states the Muslims are not obliged to use the word "substance"[79] both by reason of its definition (localized and contingent) and because it is not used in Islamic scripture. Iliyyā replies that Christians define the word differently (self-existent) and their books require them to use the word. In essence, Iliyyā is demonstrating to the Vizier that the debate is one of semantics while the meaning expressed by the different words used by Muslims and Christians is one and the same. Christians have chosen to use the word "substance" to express "self-existent" while Muslims use another term,[80] but the meaning is one and the same. Iliyyā suggests three plausible solutions but Abū al-Qāsim is content to allow the Christians to continue using "substance."

3.2.1.3 The Creator Is Living and Speaking

The Vizier asks what Christians mean by saying that the Creator is three hypostases. Iliyyā proceeds to explain through a series of deductive arguments based on the common premise that God is self-existent (93–94). If God is self-existent, he must be living, for a self-existent being cannot be other than living. He must also be speaking as he is the Creator of all speech and all speakers (95–106). Iliyyā qualifies that "speech"[81] for Christians is only attributed to intelligent beings, in contrast to Muslims who apply speech to non-intelligent beings as well (107–109). Furthermore, the fact that he is

79. Arabic: *jawhar* جوهر

80. Arabic: *qā'im bi nafsihi* قائم بنفسه

81. *Nuṭq* (speech) can be understood both as "articulation" and "rationality" or "intelligence."

living and speaking qualifies the Creator with the qualities of life and speech.[82] Iliyyā divides speech into two types. Speech of voice[83] is the mechanical ability of mortal beings to produce speech through the organs of speech. Speech of comprehension,[84] on the other hand, is the seat of rationality found in the soul of mortal beings as well as in God (110–117). Iliyyā summarizes by stating that God is substance, meaning that he is self-existent. He is living, not merely with animal life, but has a spirit.[85] He is speaking, meaning not merely that he produces sounds, but that he has a rational word (118–121).[86]

The Vizier objects saying that God having speech and life leads to polytheism, because it supposes two eternal entities in addition to God (122–124). Through a series of three responses, Iliyyā leads Abū al-Qāsim to see the rationale for his position. The second response points out that Sunnī Muslims believe that God is living, knowing, powerful, willing, articulating, hearing and seeing. If Christians are polytheists through their assertion that God is speaking and living, the Sunnīs must also be culpable of polytheism, only to a greater degree (130–134). His third response prepares the way for his assertion of the Trinity in the following section. In this response, Iliyyā states that the three meanings that have been developed thus far (self-existent, speaking, living) are three different meanings, each having its own connotation (135–139).

3.2.1.4 The Creator, His Word and His Spirit Are Three Hypostases, One Substance

In this section, Iliyyā begins by stating that the names given to the divine speech and life are "Word" and "Spirit." He demonstrates the invalidity of these two entities being accidents attributed to God or composed entities as God is liable neither to accidents nor to composition. He deduces that they must be equal to God's essence in substantiality and eternality (142–146). Furthermore, it is invalid to introduce accidents to these entities as they are not created beings. Explicitly, neither the essence,[87] nor the Word, nor the Spirit is an accident, nor are they contingent. Thus, basing his inference on Aristotle's *Categories*, they must be either a general substance or a particular hypostasis. It is not permissible that they be three substances; therefore, they must be three hypostases (147–153). The essence is the cause of both the generation of the

82. See Thomas, *Christian Doctrines*, 269, where ʿAbd al-Jabbār states his expectations that Christians will posit that God is living and speaking.

83. *nuṭq al-ṣawt* نطق الصوت

84. *nuṭq al-fahm* نطق الفهم

85. It was common among Church of the East fathers to portray life as that which is animated by spirit (Landron, *Chrétiens et musulmans en Irak*, 171).

86. In subsequent works, Iliyyā will substitute *ḥikma* (wisdom) for *nuṭq* (articulation). The similarity to the apostle John's doctrine of the *logos* is apparent.

87. Arabic: *al-dhāt* الذات

Son and the procession of the Spirit. Therefore, the essence[88] is named "a Father," the Word "a Son" and the life "a Spirit" (154–157). Finally, as the essence of the soul, its speech and its life are but one soul and the essence of the sun, its heat and its light are but one sun, so also the divine essence, the Word and the Spirit are but one God (158–159).

3.2.1.5 Anthropomorphism

In the following section, the Vizier expresses his objection to the Word and life of God being two hypostases. The Bishop insists that these two are neither accidents nor faculties and must be considered hypostases (161–165). In defense of his position the Bishop asserts that Muslim statements concerning the "hands of God" are also irrational and Muslims are at a loss to describe precisely what is meant by the expression (166–169). The Vizier remonstrates that the two hands of God are his grace and power, to which the Bishop responds that such could not be the case for there would be no point in specifying that Adam was created by the two hands of God – a specific reference to the qur'ānic account of creation – when all things were created by his grace and power. In effect, this renders God's hands as two unknown attributes. Therefore, Muslims should not reproach the Christian claim that God's life and Word are two known attributes (170–176).

The Vizier now comes to the crux of his objections, asking why Christians speak of the one God as three hypostases – Father, Son and Holy Spirit – as this leads the hearer to assume three persons, three gods or three parts. Moreover, this provokes the connotation that the Son was born of a sexual or reproductive union. Thus Christians bring upon themselves an accusation of which they are innocent (177–181).

The Bishop responds by querying why Muslims who hold that God is neither corporeal nor localized nevertheless refer to God's two eyes by which he sees, two hands which he extends, a leg which he reveals and a face which he turns in all directions, and that he comes in the shadow of the clouds.[89] Indeed, some have been led into error through such statements, though those who patiently examine their doctrine understand that Muslims are innocent of such anthropomorphism (182–187).

The Vizier's response is that Muslims use these terms in a non-literal fashion because the Qur'ān speaks thus, and whoever understands them to mean the embodiment of God or his confinement to a location is rightly cursed by Muslims for unbelief (188–191). Bishop Iliyyā responds in kind that Christians use the terms "Father," "Son" and "Holy Spirit" because the gospel uses them intending God, his Word and his life. Whoever holds that there are three gods, three bodies, three parts,

88. Further on, the correlation of "essence" (*al-dhāt*) with the Father will be discussed.

89. See footnotes 29–32 for qur'ānic references.

three accidents, or three composite faculties or other expressions which indicate polytheism, anthropomorphism, division or partition[90] is rejected. Those who consider the meaning of "the Father and the Son to be pro-generation, filiation, marriage, procreative reproduction, copulation or child-bearing[91] by a wife or bodies, angels or created things, such people are cursed, accused of impiety and anathematized by Christians." The Vizier then affirms that although the Bishop's formulation is open to debate from Muslims, nevertheless, what he has expressed is close to Abū al-Qāsim's understanding.[92]

3.2.2 Interpretation and Analysis

The Vizier's confession that he has experienced a miraculous healing at the hands of Christians must be considered in analyzing the Sessions. Abū al-Qāsim is existentially prepared for this encounter and eager to ask objective questions to which he has previously sought answers to no avail. The Bishop is reassured by Abū al-Qāsim's posture and proceeds to explain his Trinitarian views at length, including an explanation of why the attributes of life and wisdom do not imply eternal entities other than God. The Bishop draws from Islamic discussion of the seven attributes of God. Why, he reasons, does the Christian view of two essential attributes imply polytheism when Muslims freely speak of no fewer than seven attributes (130–134)? The Vizier's existential preparation will be considered more fully below.

It is incumbent to ask why the term "substance"[93] is so objectionable to the Vizier. The statement that God (*Allāh*) is substance leads Abū al-Qāsim to the conclusion that God is contained in a place and is contingent (S1 53). Iliyyā has already stated that he is using the word in a different way – to mean "self-existent."[94] The Vizier is not so

90. Polytheism (*ishrāk* إشراك), anthropomorphization (*tashbīh* تشبيه), division (*tajazzu'* تجزّئ), partition (*tab'īḍ* تبعيض).

91. Progeneration (*ubuwwa* أبوة), filiation (*bunuwwa* بنوة), marriage (*nakāḥ* نكاح) or procreative reproduction (*tanāsul mubāḍi'* تناسل مباضع), copulation (*jamā'* جماع), child-bearing (*wilāda* ولادة). This portion of S1 corresponds to *Epistle* (see section 3.1.1.2).

92. Samir, "Entretien d'Elie de Nisibe," 95–107. At this point in S1 (verse 203), the conversation moves from Trinitarian issues to christological issues. Therefore, we leave the discussion of S1 here in order to resume it in chapter 6 in connection with Iliyyā's christological formulation.

93. Arabic: *jawhar* جوهر

94. *Kalām* has defined *jawhar* as "a basic component of material objects that can be characterized by accidents" whereas the Christians use the definition from Greek philosophy "a self-subsistent entity." The Islamic assault on the Christian use of *jawhar* appears repeatedly in the Muslim–Christian discourse of the medieval period such as in Abū Bakr al-Bāqillānī's *al-Radd 'alā al-Naṣārā* found in his *Kitāb al-tamhīd* (Thomas, *Christian Doctrines*, 145). E. W. Lane's *Arabic Lexicon* reflects the complexity of the word: "in the conventional language of scholastic theology it signifies substance as opposed to accident" and it is "the constituent of a thing; the material part thereof" (Lane, *Arabic Lexicon*, 475). Al-Ash'ārī published more than a century before Iliyyā and clearly knew that Christians used the term depicting what is "self-existent." Furthermore, he records that the common understanding of the word is "that which is

easily convinced. He proceeds to explain the reason for his conviction: "Because every substance we have found in the created realm is localized[95] and contingent (liable to accidents)" (S1 54).[96] Here the Muslim perception of the word "substance" is perfectly clear. It is a localized entity – an identifiable body, solid, physical, material, confined in a space and contingent (liable to change). By stating that God is substance Christians have created lexical confusion for Muslims who do not understand the term to mean "self-existent." Iliyyā proceeds to apply the Muslim argument against Christianity to Islamic concepts, thereby demonstrating its fallacious nature. Muslims' use of "self-existent" might be understood to point to a localized God who is contingent (liable to accidents) because there is no "self-existent" being in the visible world that is not localized and liable to accidents. Consider Iliyyā's clever substitution of "substance" for "self-existent" in the following:

Objection of the Vizier[97]

He said your saying "God is a **<u>substance</u>**" leads to the statement that God is localized and liable to accidents because we have found no **<u>substance</u>** in the visible realm that is not localized and contingent.	a قال: قولكم "إنّ الله **<u>جوهراً</u>** b يؤدّي إلى القول بأنّ الله متحيّز وقابل للإعراض. c لانّنا لم نجد في الشاهد **<u>جوهراً</u>** d إلا متحيّزاً وقابلاً للأعراض.

Response of Iliyyā

a.' I said, then Muslims' statement that God is **<u>self-existent</u>** b.' leads to the statement that God is localized and liable to accidents c.' because we have found no **<u>self-existent</u>** [being] in the visible realm d.' that is not localized and contingent.	a' قلتُ: وقولُ المسلمين إذاً أنّ اللهَ **<u>قائم بنفسه</u>** b' يؤدّي إلى القول بأنّ الله متحيّز وقابل للإعراض c' لانّا لم نجد في الشاهد **<u>قائماً بنفسه</u>** d' إلا متحيّزاً وقابلاً للأعراض

liable to accidents" (i.e. contingent). He also records conflicting views on whether or not the *jawhar* can be a material body (al-Ashʿari, *Maqalat al-Islamiyiin*, 306–308).

95. Arabic: *mutaḥayyiz* متحيّز
96. This is a paraphrase of the Arabic for the sake of clarity:
لأنّنا لم نجد في الشاهد جوهراً إلى متحيّزاً وقابلاً للأعراض
97. Samir, "Entretien d'Elie de Nisibe," 67.

The argument is somewhat pedantic and, on the surface, it appears that Iliyyā is making the assertion that all self-existent beings are localized and contingent. However, another explanation is plausible. The formulation deals with observable phenomena – what is seen in the visible realm. Caution must be exercised when applying these descriptive terms (e.g. substance, self-existent) to the Divine as he is transcendent – beyond the visible realm. Words must, of necessity, take on a different meaning when attributed to God. The fallacy of the Vizier's argument does not lie in the conclusion (d, d'), but in the premise (c, c'). Iliyyā is not saying that self-existent beings are localized and liable to accidents. His point is that there is no self-existent being in the visible realm, for God exists outside the created order. Thus "substance" when applied to God takes on a different meaning.[98] The Vizier assumes his own definition of substance – that which is within the visible realm, localized and contingent. As there is no corollary to "self-existent" in the visible realm, so there is no corollary to the Christian's use of "substance" in the visible realm. The only corollary is God himself who exists outside the visible world. Muslims are giving a definition to "self-existent" in order to make it a useful term in speaking of God just as Christians are providing a definition for "substance."

This becomes even clearer in Session 1 verse 60. Iliyyā argues that if Muslims are not bound to confess that God is localized and liable to accidents, neither are Christians. Muslims state, "God is a non-contingent being."[99] According to Iliyyā, this very statement obliges Muslims to confess that God is localized and liable to accidents because "there is no non-contingent being in the visible realm."[100] The Muslim definition of God as self-existent cannot be found in the visible realm. It is, therefore, fallacious for Muslims to apply this criterion to the Christian formulation. Iliyyā, in essence, is pleading for equal consideration before the bar of judgment. Christians are doing nothing more than Muslims by selecting a term and giving it a meaning outside the visible realm. Christians use the term "substance" while Muslims use the term "self-existent" with precisely the same meaning. The different connotation arises from the Muslim use of the term "substance" to depict a material being, whereas Christians derive their meaning from Aristotelian thought and use the term to depict that which is self-existent.[101]

98. The point is similar to that made by al-Bāqillānī in his *kitāb al-tamhīd*: "Why do you claim . . . judgment about the unseen must simply follow the observable sphere, and that what exists in the unseen cannot differ from the kinds of things that exist in the observable sphere?" (Thomas, *Christian Doctrines*, 146–147).

99. *mawjūd laysa bi-'araḍ* موجود ليس بعرض

100. *idh laysa yūjad fī al-shāhid mawjūd laysa bi-'araḍ* إذ ليس يوجَد في الشاهد موجودٌ ليس بعرض

101. Despite his insistence on the use of the word *jawhar* in *The Sessions*, Iliyyā is prepared to abandon it in favor of the word *kiyān* in another treatise from his pen due to the ambiguity of the former term for Muslims (see Samir, "Un traité nouveau," 121). Samir highlights some phrases in the treatise

One might ask why Iliyyā was so insistent on the use of the word "substance." He has already stated that his Scripture uses the term.[102] Additionally, the fathers of the Eastern churches were committed to passing on their traditions unchanged as they received them from the apostles. Innovation was heresy. The test of Iliyyā's faithfulness as a bishop and shepherd of the church was his strict adherence to the Trinitarian formula as he had received it from the fathers of the Church of the East – Theodore of Mopsuestia, Diodore, Nestorius, Timothy I, and so on. Thus, given Iliyyā's role as a shepherd and bishop of the church, his reticence to alter the customary formulations of doctrine is better understood.[103] As will be demonstrated below, Iliyyā subsequently suggested an alternate term for "substance," indicating that he realized the problematic nature of the word for Muslims.

As the Bishop concludes his discussion of the Trinity, Abū al-Qāsim makes the noteworthy observation that Iliyyā's formulation is not far from the Vizier's previous understanding of the Christian tenet. This statement is one of several indicators that the Sessions were atypical of the genre called "the Monk in the Emir's *majlis*." The Vizier comes to the Bishop with a pre-existing commitment to grant Christians the benefit of the doubt, accepting them as fellow monotheists. His discussions with Iliyyā provide rational justification for and reinforcement of his growing conviction that Christians must not be deemed polytheists. This gracious stance gives the Bishop freedom to explicate the Christian doctrine drawing liberally on comparisons with Islamic formulations. This point upholds my contention that Iliyyā's success in the Sessions is due only secondarily to the Bishop's genius (although his formulations are robust) but primarily to the Vizier's existential preparation for the encounter.

3.3 Session 3

Session 3 (S3) portrays a distinct change of orientation. Iliyyā has elaborated the Christian formulation of the Trinity with the objective of demonstrating that Christians are indeed monotheists. However, in Session 3, Iliyyā will offer a new line of argumentation, drawn from the Qur'ān itself. Iliyyā's argumentation from the Qur'ān in Session 3 portends greater persuasive power in the Islamic milieu than the rational

---

that closely parallel the first session, where Iliyyā substitutes the word *kiyān* for *jawhar.*

102. Unfortunately, Iliyyā does not inform us which scriptural passage he has in mind. Modern versions (Boustanī-Van Dyck) use the word *jawhar* in Heb 1:3 stating that Christ is the "brightness of His glory and the express image of His person [*jawhar*]" – translating the Greek *hypostaseos.*

103. Griffith points out the catechetical value of the genre he labels "the Monk in the Emir's *majlis.*" Though *The Sessions* represents the record of the historical meeting between the two men, it also has catechetical value for the Christians of Iliyyā's community (Griffith, "Monk in the Emir's Majlis," 15).

arguments of Session 1 as he cites eight qur'ānic passages and refers to five qur'ānic exegetes in an attempt to demonstrate that the charge of idolatry must be dropped.

The description below is based upon Vatican Arabic 143, folios 1v–126v (twelfth to thirteenth centuries), Huntington 240, fols. 161r–190v[104] and Louis Cheikho.[105]

3.3.1 Contents

In Session 3, the Vizier asks Iliyyā about a qur'ānic verse that prohibits saying that God is "a third of three," found in Q5:73,[106] in addition to references in the Qur'ān accusing Christians of polytheism (*shirk*). Iliyyā immediately points out that he is not obligated to accept the Qur'ān but nevertheless will demonstrate to the Vizier from within the Qur'ān that Christians are monotheists. He begins by stating that the Qur'ān refers to Christians alternatively as adherents of monotheism (*al-tawḥīd*) and of polytheism (*al-shirk*). This being the case, the Qur'ān must either be contradictory or addressing different sects. He points to four sects that are heretical[107] but claims that the Nestorians, Melkites and Jacobites are all monotheists.[108] Thus, the only explanation of the Qur'ān's contradictory accusations is that it is accusing variant sects within the broad category of those called "Christians."[109]

He cites Q2:62[110] in support of Christian monotheism: "Indeed, those who believed and those who were Jews or Christians or Sabeans – those who believed in Allāh and the Last Day and did righteousness – will have their reward with their Lord, and no fear will there be concerning them, nor will they grieve." Abū al-Qāsim retorts that some exegetes understand this verse to have been abrogated by Q3:85[111] while others interpret it to mean that Christians, Jews and Sabeans deserve eternal reward only if they become Muslims.

---

104. al-Niṣībīn, *Kitāb al-majālis* (Huntington 240).

105. Cheikho, "Majalis Iliyya mutran Nasibin."

106. Cheikho lists it as verse 77. "They have certainly disbelieved who say, 'Allāh is the third of three.' And there is no god except one God. And if they do not desist from what they are saying, there will surely afflict the disbelievers among them a painful punishment."

107. The sects referred to are المرقيونية (Marcionites), الديصانية (Daysanites), المانوية (the Manacheans), الطريثونية (Tritheists, from the Latin *tritheismus*).

108. Cheikho, "Majalis Iliyya mutran Nasibin," 117–118. The comment is consistent with Landron's observation that the Nestorians rarely engaged in overt polemic against the other Christian ecclesial families. On the contrary, the tendency was to minimize the differences between them (Landron, *Chrétiens et musulmans en Irak*, 12). Nevertheless, chapter 6 will note that Iliyyā defined his Christology in distinction from that of the Byzantines.

109. Griffith refers to *The Sessions* as an example of a literary genre in early Muslim–Christian discourse wherein the "text of the Qur'ān is the preferred coinage of the arguments" (Griffith, "Monk in the Emir's Majlis," 222).

110. Cheikho lists it as verse 59.

111. Cheikho lists it as verse 79. "And whoever desires other than Islam as religion – never will it be accepted from him, and he, in the Hereafter, will be among the losers."

Iliyyā's reply is to recognize various divisions of speech: report, inquiry, request, warning and command.[112] It is obvious that "report" cannot be abrogated as that would be tantamount to falsification. In fact, the only division of speech which may be abrogated is "command." Iliyyā further divides "command" into two types: obligatory and non-obligatory.[113] Obligatory commands are further divided into two types: rational (e.g. belief in one God and obeying parents) and traditional (e.g. revering particular days and prohibiting foods).[114] It is the latter type – traditional obligations – which may be abrogated. Thus, Iliyyā effectively rules out the abrogation of Q2:62 as it is a report, not a command, and therefore not liable to abrogation. Furthermore, Q5:3 is an indication that the verse has not been abrogated: "This day I have perfected for you your religion and completed My favor upon you." After "completion" and "fulfillment" nothing further remains, according to Iliyyā.[115]

Next Iliyyā deals with the assertion that the verse applies only to those Christians, Jews and Sabeans who have become Muslims: "The Jews, Christians and Sabeans merit reward [in the hereafter] only if they become Muslims, not if they remain in their religion." He judges that the verse cannot sustain this meaning for it would be redundant[116] to speak first of "those who have believed" and then of the Christians, Jews and Sabeans if in fact these had believed in Islam. The Bishop reminds Abū al-Qāsim that "Muslims must not ascribe this (redundancy) to the Qur'ān." Furthermore, what would become of Hindus and Magians if only Christians, Jews and Sabeans receive a reward from the Lord after entering Islam? The particularization of the latter group would exclude the former from eternal reward for entering the fold of Islam. Iliyyā concludes that the verse promises an eternal reward for Christians, Jews and Sabeans who believe in Allāh and the final judgment and who perform good deeds and they must, therefore, be considered monotheists.[117] Iliyyā's next approach is to quote the venerable Abū Jaʿfar Muḥammad Ibn Jarīr al-Ṭabarī's commentary on the verse, concluding that the verse is speaking of Christians, Jews and Sabeans.[118]

He proceeds to Q2:221[119] that prohibits marriage to idolaters until they enter Islam. In contrast, Muslims are permitted to marry Christian women, even those

112. Report (*khabar* خبر), inquiry (*istikhbār* إستخبار), request (*ṭalab* طلب), warning (*indhār* إنذار) and command (*amr* أمر).

113. Obligatory (*farā'id* فرائض) and non-obligatory (*ghayr farā'id* غير فرائض).

114. Rational (*'aqlī* عقلي) and traditional (*sama'ī* سمعي).

115. Cheikho, "Majalis Iliyya mutran Nasibin," 119.

116. وهذا التكرير لا يفيد معنى "And this repetition is meaningless."

117. Cheikho, "Majalis Iliyya mutran Nasibin," 119–120.

118. This is Ibn Jaʿfar Muḥammad Ibn Jarīr Ibn Yazīd al-Ṭabarī, a renowned qur'ānic commentator and jurisprudent who died in Baghdad in 923/362 (Bosworth, "al-Ṭabarī," 11–15). This section does not appear in MS Huntington 240, suggesting the commentary of al-Ṭabarī was a later amendment.

119. Cheikho lists it as 220.

who remain in their Christian belief. Therefore, Christians must not be considered polytheists or idolaters.[120]

Furthermore, Q3:113 and 114 refer to the "People of the Scripture."[121] Iliyyā notes that the term may refer to sects of Jews or Christians. However, since the Qur'ān refers to the stringent enmity of the Jews toward Muslims, their hardness of heart and cunning, the "community standing" from among the "People of the Scripture" must be the Christians – those to whom the Qur'ān refers as "near in affection" (to Muslims) and "hastening to do good deeds." This also indicates that Christians are monotheists, not polytheists.

Q22:40[122] is also marshaled as evidence. If Christians are not monotheists, how, asks Iliyyā, does the Qur'ān refer to their reciting the name of God in churches in parallel fashion to the recitation of God's name in mosques? Indeed, verse 17[123] of the same sūra distinguishes between Christians and those who associate others with God. Such would not be the case, pleads Iliyyā, if Christians were deemed polytheists by the Qur'ān.

Further evidence is found in Q9:5[124] where Muslims are commanded to slay the polytheists whether or not they render the head tax (*al-jizya*). Iliyyā states that Muslims are enjoined to "spare the blood" of Christians, to partake of their sacrifices, to socialize with them and to guard them if they render the head tax.[125] As Muslims are required to behave in one way toward polytheists and a different way toward Christians, one must deduce that Christians are not polytheists.

---

120. al-Niṣībīn, *Kitāb al-majālis* (Huntington 240), 174r; Cheikho, "Majalis Iliyya mutran Nasibin," 220.

121. "They are not [all] the same; among the People of the Scripture is a community standing [in obedience], reciting the verses of Allāh during periods of the night and prostrating [in prayer]. They believe in Allāh and the Last Day, and they enjoin what is right and forbid what is wrong and hasten to good deeds. And those are among the righteous."

122. Cheikho lists it as 41. "And were it not that Allāh checks the people, some by means of others, there would have been demolished monasteries, churches, synagogues, and mosques in which the name of Allāh is much mentioned." Iliyyā suggests that the parallelism of mosques and churches along with the frequent mention of Allāh therein indicates a qur'ānic view of Christian monotheism.
ولو لا دَفعُ اللهِ الناسَ بعضَهم ببعض لَهُدمَت صوامعُ وبيعٌ وصلواتٌ ومساجدُ يُذكرُ فيها اسمُ اللهِ كثيراً ...

123. "Indeed, those who have believed and those who were Jews and the Sabeans and the Christians and the Magians and those who associated with Allāh – Allāh will judge between them on the Day of Resurrection. Indeed Allāh is, over all things, Witness" (Q22:17). The Arabic text indicates that the verse is found in the preceding sūra. This may indicate a copyist's error.

124. "Then kill the polytheists wherever you find them and capture them and besiege them."

125. "Spare the blood" (*ḥaqn dimā'* حقن دماء); partake of their sacrifices (*akl dhabā'iḥihim* أكل ذبائحهم); socialize with them (*mukhālaṭatihim* مخالطتهم); guard them (*ḥarāsatihim*حراستهم).

Referring to Q5:66[126] Iliyyā cites no fewer than four qur'ānic commentators (Mujāhid, Qatāda, al-Sanadī and Ibn Yazīd) who suggest that the phrase "a moderate community"[127] refers to the people of the Scripture, specifically those who faithfully observe the Word of God. Ibn Yazīd understands the verse to refer to those who revere the Tawrāt and the Injīl, which would only be true of Christians. Iliyyā infers that those faithful observers of the Word of God are Christians and, therefore, the Qur'ān considers them true monotheists.[128]

The Bishop returns to Q2:62 citing Abū Jaʿfar al-Ṭabarī's commentary which states that those who "believed Allāh and his Apostle" are Muslims while those who were rightly guided were the Jews and Christians. As for the Sabeans, they believed the prophet of Allāh, the day of judgment and the resurrection. Iliyyā sees that the Muslim commentator believes that these religious groups cited in Q2:62 will enjoy their reward in the afterlife, though he proceeds to castigate the Jews who "killed the prophets and apostles, resisted the commandment of God and corrupted his revelation."[129]

In response to the evidence, the Vizier responds that the Christians of his day are not the same as those referred to in the Qur'ān. Iliyyā replies that if contemporary Christians are not the same as those referred to in the Qur'ān, they should be exempt from the head tax which was applied to Christians in the early period of the Islamic empire. Also, the laws permitting marriage to Christian women would not be in force, nor would the laws permitting the eating of Christian sacrifices. In Iliyyā's view, Muslims' ongoing implementation of these laws indicates that Christians of his day must be the same as those referred to in the Qur'ān. Iliyyā cites Abū Jaʿfar al-Ṭabarī who clarifies that Muslims are permitted to partake of the sacrifices of Jews and Christians but prohibited from eating meats sacrificed by Arab idolaters who have no revealed book. He contends that Muslims are obliged to come to a consensus that Christians are the monotheists spoken of in the Qur'ān. Furthermore, the Christian belief in three hypostases does not contravene their belief in one God. Iliyyā further stresses his point by citing the judge Abū Bakr Muḥammad ibn al-Ṭayyib, also known as Ibn al-Bāqillānī, from his book *al-Ṭams* (presumably *al-Tamhīd – The Introduction*).

126. Cheikho cites it as verse 70. "And if only they upheld [the law of] the Torah, the Gospel, and what has been revealed to them from their Lord, they would have consumed [provision] from above them and from beneath their feet. Among them are a moderate community, but many of them – evil is that which they do."

127. Arabic: *al-ʿumma al-muqtaṣida* الأمة المقتصدة

128. Iliyyā also refers to Q5:82: "You will surely find the most intense of the people in animosity toward the believers [to be] the Jews and those who associate others with Allāh; and you will find the nearest of them in affection to the believers those who say, 'We are Christians.' That is because among them are priests and monks and because they are not arrogant." He also invokes Abū Jaʿfar al-Ṭabarī's commentary to buttress his argument.

129. al-Niṣībīn, *Kitāb al-majālis* (Huntington 240), 175r.

The author states that the Christian use of "substance" carries the meaning of self-existent although the term is unacceptable due to its not having been used by God himself. The author recognizes that the meaning understood by Christians is consistent with Islamic *tawḥīd*. Therefore, Christians must be deemed monotheists.[130]

The Vizier states his view that although al-Bāqillānī's tradition is not accepted, Iliyyā's other points have met with his approval.[131] Thus ends the third Session of Iliyyā with Abū al-Qasim.

3.3.2 Interpretation and Analysis

Iliyyā is attempting to make a very limited point – that Christians may not be accused of *shirk* and must be considered monotheists (*muwaḥḥidūn*). Unlike previous controversialists, he was seeking neither to prove a distinctly Christian tenet from the Qur'ān nor to discredit Muslim dogma. He was merely showing that those passages which seem to accuse the Christians of idolatry (e.g. *al-Ma'ida* Q5:73) cannot be understood to do so upon closer examination. He concedes that the Qur'ān does address some polytheists (*mushrikūn*) but manages to exclude his Christian community as well as the other major communities from this accusation. The promise of reward in the afterlife to Christians (and others) in Q2:62 is accompanied by a skillful attestation that the verse cannot have been abrogated. The Bishop shows his awareness of the text of the Qur'ān as well as of the complex issues surrounding its interpretation. He tackles the possibility that the verse is referring to Christians, Jews and Sabeans who have become Muslims. The Bishop adeptly shows that such an accusation also entails the charge of redundancy to the Qur'ān – an accusation with significant negative associations given the predominant Sunnī understanding that the Qur'ān is the uncreated word of Allāh. His discussion of Q2:221 draws on a well-known standard in Islamic law that Muslims are permitted to marry Christian women while marriage to idolaters is not permitted until they enter the fold of Islam. Manifestly, Christians must fall in a separate category from idolaters. Iliyyā's line of argument lands them in the category of *tawḥīd*.

130. Cheikho, "Majalis Iliyya mutran Nasibin," 122.

131. *fa-qad ḥasuna mawqi'uhā fī nafsī* فقد حسُنَ موقعها في نفسي

The "people standing"[132] of Q3:113 and 114 must refer to Christians and cannot refer to Jews.[133] The Christian churches[134] are set in parallel to mosques in Q22:40 as locales where the name of Allāh is recited. Q9:5 commands the slaying of polytheists which is never commanded in regard to Christians. The reader discerns Iliyyā's plea for the normalization of social interaction between the two religious communities as he points out that Muslims are allowed to have social intercourse with Christians.

The evidence of the two documents – *The Sessions* and the corroborating correspondence between Iliyyā and Abū al-Qāsim in the *Epistle* – suggests that the Bishop performed a valuable service to his Christian community. He was able to capitalize on Abū al-Qāsim's gracious predisposition toward Christians and present a solid qur'ānic rationale for Christians' inclusion in the category of monotheists (*muwaḥḥidūn*). The conclusion of Session 3 finds Abū al-Qasim acknowledging that though Iliyyā's use of al-Bāqillānī[135] is unacceptable, his other explanations have struck a resonating chord. *The Sessions* records that the Vizier was sufficiently persuaded to concede that the Christians should not be considered polytheists or idolaters. This was no small concession.

3.4 Additional Works

There are two other works of Iliyyā in my discussion. Their basic formulation of the Trinity does not vary greatly from what has been observed thus far. Therefore, they are introduced here without a detailed account of their contents, referring to salient points in the following analysis.

The first work is Iliyyā's treatise on *kiyān* (substance).[136] For the knowledge of this treatise I am indebted to Samir who has provided a critical edition of the only known manuscript located in Aleppo, Syria, at the Maronite Archbishopric.[137] The treatise consists of two sections. The first is a defense of Christian *tawḥīd* penned in response

---

132. *umma qā'ima* أمة قائمة

133. The reader may detect a bias against Judaism in this text as Iliyyā points out the qur'ānic view of the Jews as those who have a fierce enmity toward Muslims and whose hearts are hardened. Iliyyā and Abū al-Qāsim also discussed why the Greek texts of Scripture (presumably the Septuagint) were reliable whereas the Hebrew texts were not. It seems to have been Iliyyā's view that the Greek texts had been preserved from error while the Hebrew texts could not be considered free from corruption. It is unfortunate that no record of this discussion has reached us. The Bishop also undertook to rebut al-Jahiẓ who promoted the virtue of the Jews and censored the Christians (Sbath, "Entry 1130:1," 17).

134. *biya'* بيع

135. The *mufassir* is Abū Bakr Muḥammad Ibn al-Ṭayyib ibn Muḥammad ibn al-Bāqillānī (d. 1013). The Vizier rejects the Ash'ārī al-Bāqillānī as he is a Shī'ite Mu'tazilī (Thomas, "Al-Bāqillānī," 446–450).

136. The abbreviated title *Kiyān* is shorthand for this work as Iliyyā introduces the treatise as a response to his brother's inquiry concerning the meaning of this key word.

137. Samir, "Un traité nouveau."

to a question from the Bishop's brother Abū Saʿīd ʿĪsā Ibn Manṣūr.[138] Iliyyā indicates the desirability of using the word *kiyān* (substance) in place of the word *jawhar*. It is this aspect of the treatise which concerns our objective as it demonstrates that Iliyyā is aware of the problematic nature of *jawhar* and seeks to substitute a word which avoids undesirable connotations in his Islamic context.[139] Although the manuscript is of a late date (1630/1040), judging from lexical variants, it was composed after *The Sessions* and may be in the same time-frame as *Epistle 2* (i.e. 1029/420: see below).

Iliyyā informs his brother that Arabic linguists used the word *jawhar* to mean "self-existent." However, he also notes that language is determined by its association in the mind of the hearer and that *jawhar* has come to have quite a different meaning among Muslims. "If the objective of speech is to communicate what is in the soul of the speaker to the heart of the hearer in the language of the hearer, he should be addressed according to the demands of his own language" (*Kiyān* 37). Thus, it is technically correct to use the term *jawhar* but pragmatically it leads to an undesirable end (see 4.2.1 below for further discussion).

The second work is the *Epistle on the Oneness of the Creator and Threeness of His Hypostases*.[140] The oldest manuscript of the work – MS Huntington 240 – is found in the Bodleian Library and dates to 1549.[141] This manuscript has been consulted for the present work. Another manuscript exists in Aleppo at the Fondation Georges et Mathilde Salem; this has not been consulted.[142] I have also referred to Louis Cheikho's edition which is a reprint of L. Ma'lūf's edition in *Al-Mashriq 6* (1903).[143] I shall refer to this work using the shorthand *Epistle 2*.[144]

This brief letter was composed between 13 September and 12 October 1029 (Ramaḍān 420) in response to a request from a judge. It consists of an introduction and three chapters. The letter is significant in that Iliyyā amends his Trinitarian terminology vis-à-vis *The Sessions* evidently due to the ambiguity posed by some Trinitarian terms. He proposes an understanding of the attributes (*ṣifāt*) of essence and action. The letter demonstrates the author's involvement in the legal and social affairs of his era.

138. The familiarity evident in his correspondence with his brother allows Iliyyā to take a not-so-subtle jab at Arabic. Iliyyā states that there is no Arabic term to convey the meaning as there is in Syriac. He opts for a loan word from Syriac (*Kiyān* 38).

139. The second section deals with the question of calling Jesus the man, God. This section will be discussed in chapter 6 on Iliyyā's Christology.

140. *Risāla fī waḥdāniyyat al-Khāliq wa-tathlīth aqānīmihi* رسالة في وحدانية الخالق وتثليث أقانيمه

141. al-Ṭayyib, *Epistle on the Oneness of the Creator.*

142. Arabic 222; Sbath 1024: fols. 108r–126r.

143. al-Niṣībīn, "Risāla fī waḥdāniyyat al-Khāliq," 124–129.

144. Monferrer Sala, "Elias of Nisibis," 733–734.

In *Epistle 2*, the same proclivity to articulate the Trinitarian formulation avoiding the term *jawhar* is observed.[145] This work of Iliyyā delves more into the nature of the Trinitarian properties (*khawāṣṣ*) but also uses *kiyān* in place of *jawhar* with the meaning of "self-existent" (*qā'im bi-nafsihi*). The substitution is quite obvious as the judge's question refers to the *jawhar*, asking how Christians can refer to God as one *jawhar* and three hypostases (*Epistle 2* ¶1). Iliyyā's response – "God is one *kiyān* and three *aqānīm*" – is accompanied by an Islamic formula: "the Creator, exalted is his power, is one, [there is] no god but He" (*Epistle 2* ¶2).[146] Again in this work, Iliyyā takes the position that Arabs have no word other than *jawhar* to express the idea of self-existent and since they do not accept this meaning of the word, *kiyān* should be used (*Epistle 2* ¶12).

4. Analysis

4.1 Reciprocal Exchange

In our analysis of Iliyyā's works, it is the reciprocal nature of the exchange between the Bishop and Abū al-Qāsim that first arrests our attention. Abū al-Qāsim manifests an uncharacteristic predisposition toward accepting the formulations offered to him by Iliyyā. I am unaware of any other exchange in the medieval period where a Muslim interlocutor had such a positive leaning toward Christians or of any exchange where such a positive outcome was achieved.[147]

Initially, Iliyyā was reticent to speak forthrightly of his Christian faith. Even after the Vizier's personal exposé of his healing from a deathly illness, Iliyyā remains aloof and pleads that, if the Vizier's interest is debate and polemic,[148] he should pass on to other topics. This reticence on the part of Christians to enter the fray of polemics is consistent with Muslim–Christian relations of the period.[149] As Islamic *tawḥīd* had

145. al-Niṣībīn, "Risāla fī waḥdāniyyat al-Khāliq."

146. *lā ilāh illā huwa.* لا إله إلا هو

147. The renowned dialogue between the Caliph al-Mahdī and Timothy I could not claim such a positive result. "Although Mahdi asks but few questions, Timothy (in the absence of a direct knowledge of Islam) constantly finds himself on the defense and thus in a no-win situation" (Newman, "Dialogue of the Patriarch," 165–166).

148. *al-munāẓara wa-al-mujādala* المناظرة والمجادلة

149. Iliyyā's writings speak of his high regard for Muslims. He continually exclaims, "May God preserve them." Before writing a rebuttal of al-Jaḥiẓ, he states that he had "not intended to refute him given his knowledge, virtue and command of theology (*kalām*), but when I saw him advocating for the Jews and taking their place, blaming Christians, putting himself forward as someone skilled in theology and capable of rendering victorious whomever he willed, whether true or false, such as what he planned to do in his work *In Praise of the Blind and Preferring Fools to the Wise*, as well as his book *The Reduction of Medicine to Nothing*, I feared that his book *The Refutation of the Christians* might fall into the hands of someone who was unaware of al-Jaḥiẓ's objective in writing it and that he would feel that the Jews are

become the intellectual standard of debates in the *kalām* style, the Christian Trinity quickly became the primary point of attack.[150] Over centuries of Muslim political and economic dominance, Christians had largely withdrawn from the arena of public debate. There was too much to be lost and little to be gained. For Muslims, the Christian Trinity was now little more than "exhibit A" of inferior doctrine which was being progressively displaced by Islamic *tawḥīd*. Even when the Muslim–Christian engagement was carried out by high-ranking officials (e.g. the dialogue of Caliph al-Mahdī with Timothy I or Abū Qurra's exchange with the Caliph al-Ma'mūn),[151] goodwill or the willingness to see the other from his perspective was notably absent.[152]

The public debate (*munāẓara*) often carried with it implications that the loser of the debate would convert or at least concede the victory to his opponent. Griffith includes Iliyyā's Sessions in a list of five renowned sessions (*majālis*) conducted between Christians and Muslim state officials.[153] Christians increasingly realized the precarious nature of the debate and were reluctant to push the limits.[154] At times the debates were carried on before a state official with the implication that policy toward a religious community would be determined by the outcome. The *Epistle* gives evidence that this is indeed the nature of the Sessions, which may account for Iliyyā's hesitancy to engage. Against this backdrop of increasing polarization and retreat from the arena of debate, one may understand Iliyyā's reticence. Furthermore, the Vizier's willingness to view the plausibility of Christian doctrine from within the system of Christian thought is appreciated for its rarity. The outcome is unanticipated as Abū al-Qāsim perceives in Iliyyā's explication the possibility that Christians can avoid economic disadvantage.[155]

4.1.1 Abū al-Qāsim's Predisposition

Abū al-Qāsim initiates the dialogue by explaining that his previous persuasion concerning Christians was that they are infidels (*kuffār*) and idolators (*mushrikīn*) (verse 7). This opening sentence portends hope of Abū al-Qāsim's willingness to amend his view. It is plausible that the Vizier's opinion has already changed and

praiseworthy while Christians are to be blamed." Thus in his refutation of so eminent a figure as al-Jaḥiẓ, he manifests reticence to engage in debate and polemic. He is obliged to engage in the task rather than allow the truth he holds to be misconstrued (Samir, "Le Daf' al-hamm d'Elie de Nisibe," 112) (al-Niṣībīn, *Kitāb al-majālis* [Huntington 240], fols. 66r–66v).

150. Consider Aḥmad Ibn Ḥanbal (d. 240/855), Abū ʿĪsā al-Warrāq and Abū Bakr al-Bāqilānī who were discussed in chapter 2 (sections 5.1.1, 5.1.2, 5.2.2 and 5.2.3).

151. Griffith, "From Patriarch Timothy I," 76.

152. See Thomas, "Early Muslim Responses to Christianity," 231.

153. Griffith, "Monk in the Emir's Majlis," 14.

154. Keating, *Defending the "People of Truth,"* 26–27.

155. Sbath, "Entry 1130:1," 18.

his dialogue with Iliyyā is his seeking justification for the change. It is the Vizier's double skepticism – of both the Christians' monotheism as well as of their unbelief – that leads to this remarkable exchange. The story of Abū al-Qāsim's healing is told in some detail leaving the reader with the impression that it has prepared the Vizier existentially to view Christians in a new light. His announcement that he remains skeptical of the Christians' monotheism given their belief in one divine substance and three hypostases, despite his generally positive predisposition, enhances the credibility of the dialogue, suggesting that Abū al-Qāsim was in the throes of re-examining the prevailing attitude towards Christians (30).

The text of the first Session reveals yet more striking indicators of Abū al-Qāsim's uncharacteristic willingness to view the religious "other" from within his assumptions. He desires a true knowledge of the Christians' doctrine (42). He seeks vindication of the Christians of what is wrongfully attributed to them, the appearance of which may be abhorrent while its essence may, in fact, be beautiful. He expresses his great happiness in vindicating the Christians of polytheism (43). He already views the Christians who believe in God's oneness as "praised" and "victorious" (44). He expresses his joy in the discovery of what the Christians profess and even declares that this confirms his earlier impression of the Christians (201–202, 239). A mere surface familiarity with Muslim–Christian relations of the period suffices to demonstrate that Abū al-Qāsim's perspective is atypical.[156]

The *Epistle* provides further evidence of the Vizier's uncharacteristic open-mindedness. First he praises Iliyyā for removing all doubts of Christian *tawḥīd* from his mind and heart as well as from those of all Muslim monotheists. The Vizier confesses to "flying with joy" as a result of the Bishop's explication of the "Trinitarian *tawḥīd*"[157] – hardly an acceptable Islamic moniker. He lingers long over the Bishop's formulation grasping immediate social and economic implications for Christians in the realm.

Abū al-Qāsim's request for a written record of how to "chase away anxiety" suggests that he had derived existential comfort and solace from the Bishop's wisdom. *Daf' al-hamm* (*Dispelling Anxiety*) was the Bishop's response to Abū al-Qāsim's request although the work was presumably never seen by the Vizier. Samir records that around the end of September 1027, the Vizier made his request while being "weighed down with worry," a reference to the Vizier's candid admission that this infirmity had

156. David Thomas states that "the records that survive from the Muslim side of the encounter in the first four centuries of Islam show that far from being persuaded or even daunted by the arguments put forward by their Christian counterparts, Muslims were confident both of having truth and logic on their side and of being able to prove the superiority of their own beliefs with a finality that put Christians very much on the defensive" (Thomas, "Early Muslim Responses to Christianity," 231).

157. *Al-tawḥīd al-muthallith* التوحيد المثلث

added anxiety to worry.[158] Chapter 2 (section 2.2.2) observed Abū al-Qāsim's epitaph which pointed to a deepening of religious affections during the latter part of his life: "I have long traveled on the way of error and ignorance. It was time for me to arrive at the end of my journey. I have repented of my sins and this latter part of my journey will perhaps erase the first part. After forty-five years, I would have hoped for a longer respite had I not known that my Creditor is generous."[159]

The documents studied confirm a transformation of religious affections on the part of the Vizier – not a conversion, but rather an enlargement of heart and an inclusive view of Christians which is unparalleled in any other Muslim state official at this point in history, to our knowledge.

Due to the uncharacteristic response of Abū al-Qāsim in Muslim–Christian discourse of the period, I venture to speculate as to what factors contributed to his positive acceptance of Christian *tawḥīd.* Our texts make no allusion to Abū al-Qāsim's former distress at the hands of the Fāṭimid Caliph in Cairo, al-Ḥākim bi-Amr Allāh (d. 1021/412), nor to the fact that he was a political refugee who sought protection under the Marwanid Amīr Naṣr al-Dawla. Abū al-Qāsim had attempted to overthrow al-Ḥākim, ostensibly in revenge for his father's execution at the hands of the Caliph (his uncle and two brothers were also executed). It should be borne in mind that al-Ḥākim's antics included the destruction of many churches and the implementation of fierce measures of discrimination which were atypical of the Fāṭimid Caliphs. When the attempted coup failed, Abū al-Qāsim made his way to Iraq where he served the Dailemite sovereign Musharraf al-Dawla, becoming for a time the Vizier of Baghdad. After his implication in still further intrigue and disapprobation of sovereigns, Abū al-Qāsim was forced to flee to Naṣr al-Dawla Ibn Marwān in 1025/415.[160] While in Mayyāfāriqīn he made the acquaintance of Iliyyā. Given this history of his father's execution and his own persecution and flight from the Fāṭimid Caliph of Egypt, the question whether or not this turbulent past may have contributed to the Vizier's positive inclination toward Christians is appropriate. It appears plausible, based on the preceding circumstantial evidence, that his having been the object of a Muslim ruler's wrath and persecution afforded him a reflexive empathy toward those who were under threat of such persecution. The Vizier's uncharacteristic empathy toward Christians was due in part to his own suffering at the hands of a Caliph who was renowned for destroying churches and inflicting suffering on Christians and others in his oversight.

The Vizier's personal experience of loving care and healing at the hands of the monks had reoriented his perception of Christians and his encounter with Iliyyā

158. Samir, "Le Daf' al-hamm d'Elie de Nisibe," 116; Sbath, "Entry 1130:1," 19.

159. Landron, *Chrétiens et musulmans en Irak*, 114.

160. Khallikan, *Ibn Khallikan's Biographical Dictionary*, 450–456.

provided an intellectual basis for his goodwill toward Christians. He desires to believe the best of Christians and humbly implores the assistance of one who is able to interpret the Christian faith to him. The texts portray a Muslim official who had a life-altering encounter with Iliyyā, having been profoundly impressed by the piety and wisdom of the latter, so much so that he requested a written record of their interaction shortly before his death and while he was passing through extreme personal difficulties. Furthermore, Iliyyā's willingness to alter some lexical aspects of his Trinitarian formulation issued from this genuine and reciprocal encounter with Abū al-Qāsim.

In a sense, Abū al-Qāsim al-Ḥusayn ibn ʿAlī al-Maghribī may be considered the protagonist of *The Sessions*.[161] His willingness to enter the dialogue for the purpose of learning and for the objective of clearing the Christians of any wrongdoing or wrong belief falsely attributed to them is admirable. Abū al-Qāsim's penchant to listen empathetically to Iliyyā allowed the Bishop to speak unguardedly, and the reader of *The Sessions* is indebted to Abū al-Qāsim for this specimen of the Bishop's thought.

4.1.2 Outcomes of the Exchange

4.1.2.1 Personal Impact on the Vizier Abū al-Qāsim

We may better understand Abū al-Qāsim's pleasure in Iliyyā's apt explication given that he had made previous attempts to gain understanding of Christian belief. He praises Iliyyā for removing the source of contempt toward Christians and states that Muslims, by study of Iliyyā's *Epistle*, will be convinced of the equality of Muslim *tawḥīd* with that of the Christians.[162] Thus, the Bishop's correspondence has left absolutely no doubt in the heart and mind of the Vizier that Christians share *tawḥīd* with Muslims.

In *The Sessions*, the end result is similar, but the long process of the Vizier's arrival at his conviction suggests the process was not as straightforward as the *Epistle* indicates. In *The Sessions*, the Vizier wishes to engage in honest questioning (*istifhām*) of the Christian tenet. The report of the Sessions with the Bishop records no fewer than five substantial objections to the Bishop's explanation of the Trinity. The objections provide the opportunity for the Bishop to clarify the Christian meaning which Abū al-Qāsim implicitly accepts as the Sessions continue to unfold. Nevertheless, the

161. See Samir's Bibliographie for a brief synopsis of Abū al-Qāsim's life including his seven literary works, among which were a biography of the Prophet and a book of poetry (Caspar, Charfi, De Epalza, et al., "Bibliographie du dialogue islamo-chrétien" [1977], 259).

162. "And by contemplating this letter in their hearts, the precise unity of the Muslim is made equal to the verified unity of the Christian."
وساوى في قلوبهم بالوقوف على هذه الرسالة بين توحيد المسلم المدقّق والنصراني المحقّق

ideas are not easily digested by the Muslim, Vizier nor does he heap praise upon the Bishop as is the case in the *Epistle*.

Concerning the use of *jawhar* for "substance," Iliyyā takes considerable time and effort to establish that the intended meaning of the Christians when using this term is "self-existent" (*qā'im bi-nafsihi*). Again, the variance in reaction portrayed in the two documents is noteworthy. In Session 1, the Vizier allows the use of *jawhar* when presented by the Bishop with three options. However, this is only after he has remonstrated that the problematic expression includes the meaning of corporeality. It is clear that the Vizier is accommodating the Bishop's lexical variants with difficulty even though he finally concedes that the Christians may use *jawhar* (substance) to mean "self-existent." Quite distinctly from Session 1, as has been observed, the *Epistle* gives a ringing endorsement of Christian *tawḥīd* with no mention from Abū al-Qāsim of the troublesome nature of the term *jawhar.*

The Sessions also records the Vizier's concession that Christians are indeed monotheists though they differ in their view of Muḥammad. However, the Bishop's lengthy correspondence with Abu al-Qāsim more fully persuaded Abū al-Qāsim. In the description of the *Epistle* presented above, the exposé of Iliyyā's *tawḥīd* (also found in Session 5) bears many similarities to the Islamic formulation. The Vizier had the document read before Muslim scholars who lavished praise upon its author. It is plausible that Iliyyā's statement of *tawḥīd* in his correspondence with the Vizier was of sufficient clarity and poignancy that both the Vizier and the Muslim scholars attending his court were satisfied of the Bishop's true adherence to *tawḥīd.* Thus Iliyyā's command of rhetoric and specifically his mastery of Islamic monotheistic phraseology drew forth the approbation of Abū al-Qāsim as well as of the Muslim scholars who attended the reading of the *Epistle*.

4.1.2.2 Societal Impact of The Sessions

The *Epistle* provides a fuller understanding of the socio-political implications that the historical Sessions might have had. As has been observed, the monotheistic confession of Iliyyā was occasioned by the accusation of a Muslim judge reported by the Vizier. Abū al-Qāsim praises the Bishop for dispelling Muslim contempt[163] of Christians. The Bishop's elaboration of Christian doctrine will spare the Christians financial and social setbacks.[164] Presumably, the Vizier envisions a relaxation of the head tax (*jizya*) or of some other economic sanction that would have been imposed on Christians due to their failure to embrace *tawḥīd.* Perhaps most startling is Abū al-Qāsim's

163. *Istirdhāl* إسترذال

164. The text of the letter reads: ...وآن وقت ضبط اليد عن أن يخطف شيء من مال من تقدّمهم أو التوصّل إلى إنحطاط رتبة من رتبهم والتعرّض لسبب من أسبابهم ولعمري انّ بها وأقرانها يحتقن كثير من دماءهم (Sbath, "Entry 1130:1," 18).

admission that, in light of Iliyyā's letter, the distinction made in the Islamic invasions (*al-ghazawāt*) must now "grow cold" and prevention of harm done to Christians must now be understood as the right course of action rather than a mistake.[165] This brief statement provides a glimpse into the reality of medieval Islamic jurisprudence which was discussed in chapter 2 (section 3.2.3).[166]

While it is difficult to measure the extent of the social and political impact brought about by *The Sessions*, the documents indicate that at least one Muslim ruler was prepared to dispense with the juridical distinction between Muslims and Christians on the basis of shared *tawḥīd.* Bertaina suggests that the Kurdish Marwanid dynasty provided a brief renaissance for relations between the Syriac Christians and their Muslim overlords.[167] It is doubtful that Abū al-Qāsim lived long enough to bring his goodwill toward Christians to fruition in social and political realms. He died only a few short months after writing his "ringing endorsement" of Christian *tawḥīd* to Iliyyā. If nothing else, the correspondence between the two men reveals that the stakes of the Sessions were high. The entire religious community could be impacted through the success or failure of a participant to persuade his counterpart. The documentary evidence suggests that Iliyyā succeeded and that Abū al-Qāsim's skepticism of Christian *tawḥīd* was negated while his skepticism of their unbelief (*kufr*) was confirmed.

4.2 Lexical and Theological Amendments

4.2.1 *Jawhar* and *Kiyān*: God's Self-Existence

In *Kiyān* and *Epistle 2*, Iliyyā's realization that the word *jawhar* is misunderstood at the Muslim–Christian interface becomes apparent. His willingness to concede the term suggests that Iliyyā may have been impacted positively by the Vizier's honest and inquiring spirit. Though he was initially intransigent regarding the term *jawhar*, Iliyyā yields to other terms for the advantage of clear communication in the Islamic milieu. The shift suggests that the impact of the two men was reciprocal, with both making adjustments in the aftermath of the Sessions. In addition, given that *jawhar* was entrenched in the Christian formulation, the amendment may be counted as one

165. Khallikan, *Ibn Khallikan's Biographical Dictionary*, 453; Sbath, "Entry 1130:1," 18–19.

166. Levy-Rubin argues, based on the implementation of a legal code by Ibn Tulūn who ruled Palestine from 878 to 884, that the silence of the sources regarding the intermittent application of the *Shurūṭ 'Umar* should not be interpreted as to suggest they were never or rarely implemented (Levy-Rubin, *Non-Muslims in the Early Islamic Empire*, 109–110). Thomas also points out that "Muslim attitudes towards Christians . . . remained governed by the so-called 'Pact of 'Umar' though it is unclear how far its stipulations were applied beyond the exaction of the *jizya*" (Thomas, "Muslim Regard for Christians," 15).

167. Bertaina, "Salvation and Monotheism," 1.

factor pointing us toward the historicity of the exchange. Though not an absolute proof, the shift in terminology must be considered an argument in favor of authenticity.

Although Iliyyā appeals to Arabic linguists to vindicate the Christian use of the term, his penchant is to adopt a different word which, he contends, should not cause lexical confusion for Muslims – the Syriac *kiyān*. Although Iliyyā contends the word should not be problematic, the very fact that it is Syriac in origin raises questions. Furthermore, the formulation that God is one *kiyān* (substance) and three *aqānīm* (hypostases) is merely a word substitution from the problematic formulation including *jawhar*. Iliyyā was attempting to make his Trinitarian conception more accessible to Muslims despite the fact that the debate had become passé by the eleventh century. His formulation, however, was not a significant departure from that which Christians had affirmed for centuries, nor could it have been, for Iliyyā's objective was not to convince Muslims so much as to preserve and maintain the faith handed down to him by his forebears in the Church of the East.[168] His encounter with the Vizier must have demonstrated the need for some lexical amendments to the formulation; however, the content of the Trinitarian doctrine would not change and would continue to be the object of assault by Muslims.

4.2.2 God's Eternal Word (*ḥikma* and *nuṭq*)

Another indicator that Iliyyā is choosing terminology that clarifies the Christian doctrine in the Islamic context is his use of the word *ḥikma* (wisdom, rationality) for the hypostasis of the Son. In Session 1, Iliyyā consistently uses *nuṭq* (speech, articulation) while specifying that what is intended is not merely the physical faculty of making sounds through the organs of speech, but rationality.[169] In Iliyyā's estimation, this use of the word is different from its common use among Muslims. However, in *Kiyān* and *Epistle 2*, he opts for the word *ḥikma* (wisdom) which clarifies the rational aspect of speech (*Kiyān* 13 & 14). The *ḥikma* of God is one of his essential attributes. God cannot be "unwise" as he is the fountain of wisdom and Creator of the wise (*Kiyān* 14).

Iliyyā's use of *ḥikma* is not surprising given the *logos* doctrine of the apostle John. The Jacobite Yaḥyā Ibn ʿAdī developed his Trinitarian formula around a triad of rationality – Intelligence, Intelligent One and Intelligible (*'aql*, *'āqil* and *ma'qūl*).[170]

168. Samir is more enthusiastic about this change in vocabulary declaring it to be a "veritable mental revolution operating in the mind of the Bishop" (Samir, "Un traité nouveau," 130). The change from the problematic *jawhar* to the Syriac *kiyān* shows an increasing awareness of the problematic nature of the former, but little more.

169. *nuṭq al-fahm* نطق الفهم

170. It is likely that Yaḥya drew on his own teacher al-Farābī and the roots of the triad may go back to Aristotle (R. Haddad, *La Trinité divine*, 229–230; Samir, *Maqāla fī al-tawḥīd*, 129).

Iliyyā's lexical adjustment from *nuṭq* to *ḥikma* reflects his own perception of a misunderstanding of the word in the Islamic context and a need to find a word that more closely approximates the *logos* doctrine.

4.2.3 The Hypostases (*al-aqānīm*)

It is noteworthy that Iliyyā does not introduce the hypostases by name until verse 151 of Session 1 and only supplies the names of "Father," "Son" and "Spirit" in verse 159 – quite late in Session 1. The first 150 verses of Session 1 may be seen as a patient laying of the theoretical foundation for the Trinity in an Islamic intellectual milieu before unveiling the offensive familial names of "Father," "Son" and "Spirit." Iliyyā labors to demonstrate that God's articulation and life cannot be considered accidents but must be considered hypostases – belonging to the substance. In a somewhat unusual twist, Iliyyā now reverts to the word *dhāt* (essence)[171] as a corollary of *qa'im bi-nafsihi* (self-existent) and uses this word no fewer than twelve times from section 139 to 159, anticipating the hypostasis of the Father. "Our saying 'self-existent, speaking, living' expresses three meanings which are the essence [*al-dhāt*], the speech and the life."[172] He regularly links the word *dhāt* to the source of these entities – their cause (*'illa*). The substance (*jawhar*) is defined by being self-existent. This meaning is represented by the *dhāt* (essence) and becomes the logical (not sequential) "first" entity of the triad "self-existence, speech, life" (S1 139).

Similar to his contemporary Ibn al-Ṭayyib, Iliyyā's response to the question why Christians limit the entities to three is found in a division of the attributes of God into attributes of essence and attributes of action. *Epistle 2* provides Iliyyā's most comprehensive development of this concept. There are two factors that separate these properties of God. The first factor is that the attributes of action derive from God's acts. Here Iliyyā uses the moniker "attributes" (*ṣifāt*). As God creates, he is the Creator (*al-khāliq*). He shows mercy and therefore is the Merciful (*al-raḥīm*). He gives generously and is therefore the Magnanimous (*al-jawād*). Iliyyā sees a distinction between these attributes of act (*ṣifāt al-fi'l*) and self-existence, life and wisdom, which are entities innate to the being (*kiyān*) of God.

Second, the attributes of act extend to the creation. There is an object of God's creation – a created being – as there are recipients of his mercy, generosity, clemency,[173]

171. *Al-dhāt* is a common and accessible term used by Muslims as well as some Christian theologians for the divine "essence." Interestingly, Iliyyā has avoided its use until this point in the Sessions. Rather than use it for the divine essence, he uses "substance" (*jawhar*) and only reverts to the use of *al-dhāt* as a corollary for the hypostasis of the Father.

172. *fa-qawlunā 'al-qā'im bi-nafsihi, al-nātiq, al-ḥayy' yafīdunā thalātha ma'ānin hiyya al-dhāt wa-al-nuṭq wa-al-ḥayā.* فقولُنا "القائم بنفسه، الناطق، الحي" يفيدنا ثلاثة معان، هي الذات والنطق والحياة

173. *ḥilm* حلم

hearing and sight. In Iliyyā's conception of divinity, the properties of God's self-existence, wisdom and life do not extend to the creation but remain innate to the being of God. Iliyyā refers to those "communicable attributes" as attributes of act (*ṣifāt al-fi'l*) while he maintains a different designation for those which remain innate to the being of God – properties of the essence (*khawāṣṣ dhātiyya*) (*Epistle 2* ¶6).

The conception of Iliyyā is not unlike that of Ibn al-Ṭayyib but with a few important distinctions. The latter was content to use *ṣifāt* as the broad category for all of God's attributes, both those of essence and those of act, similar to the Muslim rational theologians (*al-mutakallimūn*). Ibn al-Ṭayyib benefited from the Islamic concept of the attributes to explicate the Christian Trinity. Iliyyā preserved the designation "properties"[174] for the Trinitarian persons. Ibn al-Ṭayyib felt the need to limit the attributes of essence to three on the basis of revelation alone. Iliyyā attempted to demonstrate a linguistic separation – the "attributes of act" derived from verbs depicting God's actions in and upon his creation. Both men perceived the attributes of act to have objects/recipients in creation.

4.3 A Christian Interprets the Qur'ān

We note that the Sessions themselves are somewhat understated in their approval of Iliyyā's qur'ānic exegesis whereas Abū al-Qāsim's correspondence with Iliyyā indicates a much greater degree of esteem on the part of the Vizier. This suggests that if Iliyyā's record of the Sessions reveals any discrepancy with the historical reality, it is that Iliyyā himself understated the level of the Vizier's approbation of his qur'ānic statements. The correspondence reveals that the content of *The Sessions* was read before Islamic scholars in Mayyāfāriqīn who praised the Bishop's ability in appropriating Muslim exegetical literature (*tafsīr*). Abū al-Qāsim intimates that this new understanding may spare the Christians in the Marwanid Emirate financial hardship, enhancing their social status.[175] At the least, the reader is given the distinct impression that the Sessions, the objective of which was often to secure a definitive interpretation of religious views before a state official, were a crowning success for the Bishop, securing favor for his Christian community and near religious parity with Muslims under Marwanid rule.[176]

Iliyyā used the Qur'ān skillfully in ways that set him apart from his Christian forebears. Early Christian apologists make use of the Qur'ān but in a different vein. An unknown monk provides answers for a sheikh (possibly ninth or tenth century)

174. *khawāṣṣ* خواصّ

175. Sbath, "Entry 1130:1," 18–19.

176. Landron, *Chrétiens et musulmans en Irak*, 9.

but interpreting qur'ānic passages so as to confirm Christian claims.[177] Al-Kindī (d. ca. 870) sought to discredit Muḥammad's prophethood through qur'ānic proof texts.[178] Abū Qurra (early ninth century) uses qur'ānic concepts (e.g. God's session on a throne) to convey that Muslims and Christians share foundational concepts such as God's immanence and forgiveness. He also seeks to establish that Christians were the "people of the Scriptures" before the advent of Islam.[179] Abū Rā'iṭa quotes from the Qur'ān extensively in an attempt to demonstrate his Christian meanings from Islamic scriptures.[180] ʿAmmār al-Basrī also references the Qur'ān, attempting to explain how particular passages normally understood to contravene Christian belief (God's begetting a Son) need not be understood that way.[181]

Iliyyā takes a different approach in his qur'ānic referencing. Though he is clear that he is not bound by the Qur'ān, he uses the authoritative texts of Islam to establish the fact that Christians are and must be treated as believers in only one God. His limited use of the Qur'ān may in part be owing to unsuccessful attempts of his Christian predecessors to use the Muslim scriptures in debate. More positively, he buttresses his view with reputable qur'ānic exegetes, plausible examples from Islamic jurisprudence and careful nuancing of qur'ānic accusations of idolatry or polytheism (*shirk*) so as to exclude his Christian community as well as the other major Christian communities. In addition, the Bishop skillfully elicits current themes in Islamic discourse (e.g. the impossibility of redundancy and contradiction in the Qur'ān, and qur'ānic anthropomorphisms debated among Muslim scholars) to lead his hearers toward his conclusions. If the testimony of the scholars of Mayyāfāriqīn is to be accepted, the Bishop succeeded.

5. Conclusion: Transcending Polemic

The word "polemic" derives from the Greek *polemos*, meaning "war." The medieval polemicists on either side of the Muslim–Christian divide waged a war of words. They were skilled in their craft employing the intricacies of Greek philosophy and *kalām* to buttress their views, ever relying on their own presuppositions as the proper starting point for evaluating the theological claims of the other. Our study of the historical

177. Griffith, "Answers for the Shaykh," 290–297.

178. Griffith, "Monk in the Emir's Majlis," 211–212; Newman, "Al-Kindi's Apology," 358. Examples include Q93:6–7 to show that the Prophet was in error and then guided to the truth; 33:37 to show the questionable marriage of Muḥammad to Zaynab; 17:61 to show that Muḥammad was given no miraculous sign (Newman, 426, 433, 439).

179. Beaumont, *Christology in Dialogue with Muslims*, 30; Griffith, "Monk in the Emir's Majlis," 223–233.

180. Beaumont, 50–53; Husseini, *Early Christian–Muslim Debate*, 101.

181. Beaumont, 68–69.

sessions of Bishop Iliyyā of Nisibis and his Muslim counterpart Abū al-Qāsim al-Ḥusayn Ibn ʻAlī al-Maghribī demonstrates that the two men surpassed many of their forebears in their ability to transcend polemics.

From a documentary and historical perspective, embellishment must have tainted the evidence to some degree. Nevertheless, when considering it as a whole, through the narrative of the relationship and mutual appreciation between the two men, the reader emerges with a sense that what was achieved in the Sessions was indeed remarkable. The Vizier's posture as a sincere skeptic searching for honest answers belies the medieval period in which he lived and begs for explanation. I have sought that explanation in the Vizier's existential preparation for his encounter with Iliyyā including both his claim to have experienced a miraculous healing and the severity with which his family had been treated by the Faṭimid elite. For the Vizier – a cultured and well-traveled Muslim statesman – we may assume that his joy in reading Iliyyā's correspondence was owing not only to his determination to pursue understanding but also to the Bishop's unique grasp of Islamic scruples coupled with his erudite responses to the Vizier's queries about Christianity – a combination which impressed the Vizier deeply. Iliyyā's reticence to engage, his patient explication of his doctrine, his respectful and responsible use of Islamic scriptures – all unveil a sage who merits our respect even centuries later. It may not be mere honorific exaggeration for the office of bishop that the copyist of *Kiyān* refers to Iliyyā as "the saint, the pure, the inestimable."[182] Indeed, though the story may have been embellished, the exchange so preserves the dignity of both Muslim and Christian that it continues to stand as a testament to the reciprocal relationship shared by the two men and as a ray of hope for more irenic relations between the two faiths.

182. Samir, "Un traité nouveau," 133.

5

Christological Reverberations in the Muslim Milieu

The Union of Human and Divine in Ibn al-Ṭayyib's Christology

1. Introduction

After the contest over the nature of God (Trinity or unity), the next great controversy at the Muslim–Christian interface concerned the nature of Christ. The topic had already been debated in the early church councils, but the Chalcedon formula was unable to mend the rift in the ancient churches of the Middle East. It was along the fault lines of christological dissension that the ecclesial families self-identified in one of three broad groups: Byzantine Orthodox (Melkite, Chalcedonian), Oriental Orthodox (Jacobite, miaphysite) and Church of the East (dyophysite). Broadly speaking, these were the three ecclesial families that encountered Islam in the lands of the Middle East. Whereas the Byzantine Melkites were the political adversaries of Muslims, the Church of the East had deep roots in the lands that had come under Muslim sovereignty. Their doctrine of Christ set them apart from the other ecclesial families and gave them a unique claim to parity with Muslims in asserting *tawḥīd* – the unity of divinity. The theologians of the Church of the East proffered the argument that their formulation most carefully shielded the divine nature of Christ from human contingencies. Furthermore, their nomenclature upheld the distinction between the humanity and the deity. Their concern was to defend their ecclesial family from the charge of *shirk* – association of divinity with creation. The charge was theological in nature but also carried social and financial implications for their Christian constituency.

In this chapter, I provide an overview of the christological controversy especially as it related to the Church of the East. My concern is how the Church of the East arrived at its understanding of the relation of the humanity and divinity of Christ. The lexical, political and geographic factors that contributed to this formulation are briefly considered. The purpose of the survey is to provide a critical background for understanding the Church of the East Christology before examining Ibn al-Ṭayyib's particular contribution to the issues that continued to surface in his Islamic milieu. There is only one independent text of Ibn al-Ṭayyib on Christology that remains extant: "The Union," discussed in section 3.1. Therein, the author provides his own version of the definition of "one" which had been a common theme at the Muslim–Christian interface. He also locates the motivation for the incarnation in God's magnanimous character in his interactions with humanity. The other texts have been preserved in the collection of the Copt Mu'taman al-Dawla Ibn al-ʿAssāl entitled the *Summa of Religious Principles*.[1] The encyclopedic collection has preserved extensive sections of Ibn al-Ṭayyib's treatises and testifies to the polymath's high esteem among other ecclesial families. I have selected four texts attributed to Ibn al-Ṭayyib by Ibn al-ʿAssāl, each of which reveals critical aspects of his christological formulation. These include locating the union in the property of filiation, separation of the divine and human hypostases to maintain the non-contingency of the divinity, the means of transfer of miraculous power to the humanity, and scriptural justification for Trinitarian and christological terminology including "Father" and "Son."

Each text is described in detail as I attempt to stay as close as possible to the wording of the texts. After the description, I proceed to interpret and analyze the texts paying particular attention to their resonance with Muslim–Christian discourse of the period. The conclusion pulls together the threads of Ibn al-Ṭayyib's christological formulation as a coherent Christian response shaped by the Muslim milieu.

2. Controversy over Christ

2.1 Church Councils Define Christology

The Council of Chalcedon (451 CE) confirmed the Christological definitions of Nicea and Constantinople. It determined that Christ is both fully divine and fully human: "like us in all things apart from sin. He is acknowledged in two natures,[2] without

---

1. The full Arabic title is *Majmūʿ uṣūl al-dīn wa-masmūʿ maḥṣūl al-yaqīn*
مجموع أصول الدين ومسموع محصول اليقين

2. *physeis* φυσεις.

confusion, without change, without division, without separation; the difference of the natures being in no way abolished by the union, but rather the characteristics of each nature being preserved, and concurring into one Person[3] and one hypostasis (υποστασις)."[4] This union is referred to as the hypostatic union – the union of two natures in one person.

The Chalcedon definition opposed four heresies. "Christ is fully God (against Arius) and fully man (against Apollinarius), indivisibly one (against Nestorius) and without confusion (against Eutyches)."[5] The monophysite (one nature only) view espoused by Eutyches (378–454 CE) rejected the consubstantiality of Christ's humanity with that of other men.[6] The Chalcedon definition was also deemed incompatible with Cyril of Alexandria's formulation more accurately described by Brock as "henophysitism" or by others as "miaphysitism."[7] This led to the dissension of the Oriental Orthodox churches from the Chalcedon definition. The concern of this study is the dissension of the Church of the East, sometimes referred to as "dyophysitism" (meaning "two *physeis*" or "substances" or "natures"). The moniker is inadequate as the Chalcedon formula also upheld the duality of the *physeis*. The Church of the East's Christology insisted that two *qnoma* accompanied the two natures of Christ, as will be observed. As *qnome* translates the Greek "hypostasis," it is more correct to designate the Church of the East christological position as "dyohypostatism," though this moniker, as well, is inadequate as the Church of the East understood *qnome* differently from how their Greek-speaking counterparts understood "hypostasis."[8]

2.2 Dyohypostatic Dissension

2.2.1 *Theotokos*

While he was Bishop of Constantinople, Nestorius applied the dyohypostatic Christology of Theodore of Mopsuestia to the controversy concerning the honorific title of the Virgin Mary – *Theotokos* (God-bearer or "Mother of God").[9] Others favored

---

3. *prosōpon* προσωπον.

4. Parry, *Blackwell Companion*, 171; Rissanen, *Theological Encounter*, 164.

5. Lane, "Christology Beyond Chalcedon," 261.

6. Rissanen, *Theological Encounter*, 164.

7. The distinction between the monikers "monophysite" and "miaphysite" maintains a distinction between Eutychian thought – one nature only – and the official position of the Oriental Orthodox churches. See Brock, "The 'Nestorian' Church," 26.

8. Naming theological concepts inevitably betrays a predisposition or bias. To be absolutely true to the intention of the Church of the East, we should call their position "dyo-qnomism." I opt for "dyohypostatism" simply because the Syriac word *qnoma* is unknown to the average English reader.

9. For a discussion of historical developments in the study of Nestorius, see Grillmeier, *Christ in Christian Tradition*, 492–495.

anthropotokos ("Mother of man") but Nestorius suggested a compromise in a sermon in 429 CE "that she should be called mother of Christ, a term which represented both the divinity and the humanity, as it is used in the gospels."[10] However, his refusal to admit the moniker *Theotokos* resulted in his exile in 436 CE after the Council of Ephesus in 431 CE determined that Mary should indeed be given the title "Mother of God." The prevailing perception is that the Church of the East followed Nestorius in refraining from saying *yaldath Alaha* (Syriac for *theotokos* "God-bearer") in reference to Mary, preferring the title *Yaldath M'shikah* – "Christ-bearer."[11] The truer picture, however, is that the moniker *yaldath Alaha* had never gained traction in the well-established liturgies of the Church of the East.[12] This is largely due to the East Syrian understanding of salvation which emphasizes the full humanity of Christ: "the *homo assumptus*, which is raised to glory as a pledge of the salvation of all humanity."[13] The Church of the East never conceived of Mary as the mother of divinity, but ever the mother of Christ's humanity. One ancient confession penned by Ishu-Yahb (585 CE) stipulates that Christ was "begotten in his Godhead eternally of the Father, without Mother . . . born in His manhood of a mother without Father."[14] Brock maintains that the association of the Church of the East with Nestorianism was, in fact, a "smear" campaign by theological opponents effected by the stigma of applying a moniker of one who has been publicly declared a heretic.[15] In point of fact, Church of the East fathers often self-designated as "Nestorian." Nevertheless, because the title invokes a

10. Grillmeier, 451, citing from F. Loofs, *Nestoriana* (Halle, 1905), 185; Winkler, *First Thousand Years*, 195–196.

11. Atiya, *History of Eastern Christianity*, 254.

12. Interestingly, Babai the Great did allow the use of the term *theotokos* if the meaning was properly guarded so as to communicate "Mother of God, in that He was united to His manhood from the first moment of its conception; and it is His temple eternally, and He is God and Man unitedly, one Son, one Christ" (Wigram, *History of the Assyrian Church*, 289).

13. Brock, "The 'Nestorian' Church: A Lamentable Misnomer," 31. Brock uncovers the assumption of Church of the East Christology that Christ "having lowered himself to humility in order to raise up our fallen state to the exalted rank of his divinity, and in the person of the 'hostage' he took from us (i.e. his humanity), he associated us in the glory of his majesty" (Brock, 31, quoted from "Christ 'the Hostage': A Theme in the East Syriac Liturgical Tradition and Its Origins," in *Logos: Festschrift für Luise Abramowski*, ed. H. C. Brenneke, E. L. Grasmuck and C. Markshies [Beihefte zur *Zeitschrift fur die neutestamentiche Wissenschaft*], 1993, 67, 472–485, quote found on 485.)

14. Wigram, *History of the Assyrian Church*, 276.

15. Brock, "The 'Nestorian' Church," 29. Brock makes the case that the Church of the East would be described more accurately as "Theodoran" (owing to the dominant influence of Theodore of Mopsuestia) as opposed to "Nestorian." Furthermore, the church's understanding of Nestorius's doctrine appears to be piecemeal and vague. Only one of Nestorius's actual writings remains extant – the *Bazaar of Heracleides*, which indicates that Nestorius's views were aligned with those who opposed Eutyches the monophysite. The work was translated into Syriac in 539–540 CE. Nestorius's doctrine was not widespread in the Church of the East until at least a half century after the Church was said to have followed Nestorius based on Church of the East Councils held in 484 CE and 486 CE (Brock, 29–30). Having said this, I note that Iliyyā often self-identified as "Nestorian" though Ibn al-Ṭayyib thought the moniker was wrongly applied

connotation of heresy and because recent spokesmen of the Church of the East have repudiated it, I opt for the more acceptable moniker "Church of the East."[16]

2.2.2 *Communicatio Idiomatum* and Theopaschitism

Related to the conflict over *Theotokos* was the understanding of the *communicatio idiomatum*. By this is meant, in Christology, the attribution of human attributes in Christ to the divine nature and vice versa, such that one can legitimately speak of the "suffering God" or even "the death of God" in Christ.[17] The concept grew from roots in Ignatius of Antioch and received impetus from the doctrine of the hypostatic union but was unacceptable to the Church of the East as indeed it was for other ecclesial families of the Antiochene tradition. Grillmeier has noted that the tenet of *communicatio idiomatum* was still being clarified in the time of Nestorius, such that his reaction may be appreciated as a safeguard against the excesses of Apollinarianism and Arianism.[18] Nestorius's second letter to Cyril deals with the impassibility of Christ's divinity:

> Examine what was said more closely, and you will discover that the divine chorus of the Fathers did not say that the coessential Godhead is passible or that the Godhead which is coeternal with the Father has only just been born, or that he who has raised up the temple which was destroyed has [himself] risen.
>
> To attribute also to him, in the name of this association, the characteristics of the flesh that has been conjoined with him – I mean birth and suffering and death – is, my brother, either the work of a mind which truly errs in the fashion of the Greeks or that of a mind diseased with the insane heresy of Arius and Apollinarius and the others.[19]

This determination to guard against the passibility of Christ's divine nature gave impetus to Nestorius's insistence on the separation of the divine and human natures in Christ. The issue of "theopaschitism" arose later in Constantinople when Scythian monks, including John Maxentius, employed the formula "one of the Trinity suffered." The formula, initially rejected by the Patriarch of Constantinople, was later viewed as orthodox by the Emperor Justinian who won the support of Pope John

---

to the Christians of the East. Therefore, it is somewhat difficult to conceive of the moniker as merely a "smear campaign" though I acknowledge it to have been an inaccurate label at best.

16. In 1976, Mar Dinkha, then Catholicos of the Assyrian Church of the East, stated that Nestorius had nothing to do with his Church as he was a Greek (Brock, "The 'Nestorian' Church," 35).

17. Grillmeier refers to the "suffering God" (*Deus passus*) as the evolution of the church's *kerygma* at that time which Nestorious felt needed to be corrected. He sees Nestorius's error as attempting to halt a necessary evolution of the *kerygma* (Grillmeier, *Christ in Christian Tradition*, 370).

18. Grillmeier, 376.

19. Norris, *Christological Controversy*, 136, 139.

II. The Chalcedonians understood suffering to be attributable to the Logos through the hypostatic union though contingency was not attributable to the divine nature. *Communicatio idiomatum* provides the conceptual framework for this understanding of theopaschitism.[20] The repudiation of human suffering or pain from the divinity of Christ is consistent in early Antiochene Christology.[21] Nevertheless, the Church of the East theologians were enabled to brandish the tenet more forcefully due to their dyohypostatic Christology.[22] The repudiation of theopaschitism became critical for the Church of the East theologians in the Muslim milieu.

2.2.3 Factors Contributing to the Church of the East's Dissent

The Church of the East dissented, at least in part, from the Chalcedon formula.[23] However, this was not due to the influence of Nestorius as is often assumed.[24] Sebastian Brock has clarified the issues surrounding the Church of the East's dissent from Chalcedon in the matter of Christology. He analyzes the dissension under four aspects: geographical, political, linguistic and the variety of positions within the christological spectrum.[25]

2.2.3.1 Geography

The Nestorian Church of the East, lying outside the Byzantine domain, was represented neither at Chalcedon nor at any of the imperially convened councils. Nothing prevented its retroactive acceptance of the conciliar definition, as happened in the case of Nicea (325 CE) some eighty-five years afterwards at the Synod at Selecuia-Ktesiphon in 410 CE.[26] Only twenty years prior to Chalcedon, the Church of the East had dissented from the Council of Ephesus in 431 CE as its irregular proceedings declared Nestorius a heretic.[27] It must be remembered that from the point of view of the Church of the

20. "The Definition of Chalcedon"; Parry et al., *Blackwell Dictionary*, 485; "Theopaschites."

21. The Chalcedonian Abū Qurra confessed that "the divinity abides in the Incarnate Word not subject to any limitation, suffering or death which belong to the human nature." Abū Rā'iṭa the Jacobite also said, "when the sun's rays light up the ground the sun is not limited to that spot, so the body is not a limiting factor for the word" (Beaumont, *Christology in Dialogue with Muslims*, 32, 53).

22. Pelikan, *Spirit of Eastern Christendom*, 70–71.

23. Wigram discusses the manuscript *Synodicon Orientale* at Mosul which accepts Chalcedon albeit with slight emendation of significant terms. *Theotokos* is rendered "mother of Christ" and "one hypostasis" is rendered "two *qnumi*." Wigram suspects the latter to be a copyist amendment as the phrase was not adopted until two generations after the synod (Wigram, *History of the Assyrian Church*, 296).

24. Grillmeier notes that Nestorius's intentions were closer to Chalcedon than those of Cyril as he looked for "the unity and diversity of Christ on two different levels." Thus the natures (*physeis*) were distinct but existed in one person (*prosopon*) (Grillmeier, *Christ in Christian Tradition*, 364).

25. Brock, "Christology of the Church," 129–132.

26. Brock, 126.

27. Faultless, "Two Recensions," 183.

East, "these councils were far from being truly ecumenical seeing that they were only of direct concern to those living within the Roman *oikkoumene*." The geographic isolation of the Church of the East from developments in the Byzantine world meant that it was not privy to discussions of a theological nature taking place in the Greek-speaking world though these discussions were mediated to the Church of the East by the schools of Edessa (closed in 489 CE) and then Nisibis.[28]

2.2.3.2 Politics

The adoption of Christianity as the official religion of the Byzantines provoked persecution in the realm of the Sassanians, the homelands of the Church of the East. Any outbreak of hostilities intensified the persecution as Christians were considered collaborators of the hated Romans. Brock suggests the possibility that one of the reasons for the dissent from the Chalcedon formula was the desire to disassociate the Church of the East from the official christological position of the Roman Empire. Indeed, this tendency will appear in Bishop Iliyyā's Christology in chapter 6.

2.2.3.3 Language

As the linguistic factors in the Church of the East's dissent have been elucidated fully in the literature, a basic summary is provided here illustrated by quotations from Church of the East representatives. The Greek terms *ousia* (οὐσια: essence), *physis* (φυσις: nature), *hypostasis* (ὑποστασις) and *prosopon* (προσωπον: person) did not have precise equivalents in Syriac, the language of the Church of the East.[29] Aside from the fact that these terms were not regularly used in the credal formulations of the Church of the East, the semantic range of the various words differed in Syriac and Greek.[30] This was further complicated by the fact that, although some refinements had taken place in Syriac translation techniques from the late fifth to early seventh centuries, these were confined largely to the West Syrian Church which lay in the eastern provinces of the Roman Empire. Thus, the Church of the East in the Sassanian Empire remained largely impervious to them.[31] As Arabic became the *lingua franca* of the Church of the East, the linguistic disarray became more pronounced. The division

28. Brock, "Christology of the Church," 130.

29. Wigram has likened Syriac theologians laboring in Greek to David wearing Saul's armor. Many intellectuals of the Church of the East labored with ease in both languages. Therefore it is more correct to see a diverse lexical evolution of Greek terms in separate geographic regions (Wigram, *History of the Assyrian Church*, 266).

30. Brock, "Christology of the Church," 28.

31. Brock, 130.

of the Arabic-speaking churches as well as derivation of a theological lexicon from both Greek and Syriac led to an inevitable hybridity of terminology.[32]

It was the phrase "one hypostasis" (μια ὑποστασις) which did not accord with the Church of the East's understanding of Christology. The Syriac word *qnoma* translated the Greek *hypostasis* in the Nicene Creed which the Church of the East had accepted in 410 CE.[33] For the Church of the East, the two natures implied two *qnome.* Accordingly the Church of the East, when speaking of the two natures, referred to the two natures and their *qnome*, where *qnoma* denotes "something like 'individual manifestation': a *qnoma* is an individual instance or example of a *kyana* ('nature' translating the Greek *physis*)."[34] Wigram clarifies the distinction: "hypostasis is the inward reality which underlies the outward appearance; the word looks, as it were, from outward to inward. *Qnuma* is the specialization of that which is common to many; it looks from the abstract to the concrete."[35] Christ was understood to have two *kyane* ("natures") – the divine and the human. The *qnoma* of divinity is God the Word while the *qnoma* of the humanity is the man Jesus.[36]

Although the Church of the East naturally referred to two *qnome* in the incarnate Christ, this does not equate to two *hypostases* because the word *hypostasis* (ὑποστασις) in Greek has the sense of "self-existence." Whereas two *hypostaseis* (Greek) is an untenable concept, two *qnome* (Syriac) is requisite given the presence of the two natures.[37] The *qnoma*, then, is the requisite instantiation of the *kyana* such that, to the mind of the Church of the East theologians, the *kyana* cannot be conceived of apart from its *qnoma.* The doctrine of two natures with but one hypostasis appeared illogical to the Church of the East.[38]

The traditional formula for understanding the conflicting christological positions is accurate insofar as it goes:

32. Faultless, "Prologue to John," 149.

33. Wigram, *History of the Assyrian Church*, 268.

34. Brock, "The 'Nestorian' Church," 28.

35. Wigram, *History of the Assyrian Church*, 283.

36. Brock, "Christology of the Church," 131.

37. Brock points to a document that originated with the Church of the East during an interregnum in 612. In the preamble, one passage demonstrates the difference between the Church of the East's understanding of *qnome* and the prevailing understanding of hypostasis in a christological context: "It is clearly apparent that Christ is perfect God and perfect Man. Now he is said to be God, being perfect in the nature and *qnoma* of divinity, and he is then said to be perfect Man, being perfect in the nature and *qnoma* of humanity. And just as it is made known, from the opposition (expressed in) the words just used, that Christ is two natures and two *qnome*, so too, from the fact that they refer to the one Christ, Son of God, it is made known that Christ is one – not in a oneness (*hdanayut*) of nature and of *qnoma*, but in an the [*sic*] single *prosopon* of Sonhip [*sic*] and the single (source of) authority and single governance and single power and single lordship" (Brock, "Christology of the Church," 142).

38. Brock, "The 'Nestorian' Church," 24.

- Chalcedon: two *physeis*, one *hypostasis*, one *prosōpon* (in two natures, one hypostasis and one person)
- Oriental Orthodox: one *physis*, one *hypostasis*, one *prosōpon* (one incarnate nature of God the Word)
- Church of the East: two *kyāne*, two *qnōme*, one *parsufā* (union of two natures and their *qnōme* in one person).[39]

However, the complexities of the linguistic variants are not represented in such a depiction. A more nuanced view is provided by Brock who shows that all views (except that of Eutyches) held that Christ was consubstantial in both humanity and divinity, though Antiochene Christology rejected theopaschite language and was, therefore, wary of *communicatio idiomatum*.[40]

2.3 The Church of the East's Christology in Its Own Words

It is helpful at this point to hear the christological formulations of the Church of the East as expressed by her own spokespersons.

A statement issued from the Synod of Seleucia-Ctesiphon, held under the Catholicos Adadios in 486 CE, represents the first credal statement issued by the Church of the East subsequent to the Councils of Ephesus and Chalcedon. Brock has noted that while the statement reflects Antiochene Christology, "it can in no way be described as openly 'Nestorian,'" meaning "two persons in Christ."[41] The statement shows evidence of a partial embrace of the Chalcedon formula while stipulating a repudiation of theopaschite language:

> Further, let our faith in the dispensation of Christ be in the confession of the two natures, of the divinity and of the humanity, while none of us shall dare to introduce mixture, mingling or confusion into the differences of these two natures; rather while the divinity remains

39. Atiya, *History of Eastern Christianity*, 254, fn 254. Faultless, "Two Recensions," 186. Wigram points out that this formula was adopted in 612 AD by an assembly of Church of the East bishops (Wigram, *History of the Assyrian Church*, 278).

40. Brock, "The 'Nestorian' Church," 27.

41. Brock, "Christology of the Church," 126; Brock, "The 'Nestorian' Church," 28. With the hindsight of history, it appears doubtful that even Nestorius was "Nestorian" according to this definition, though some of his followers would have understood him in this way: "they [the Orthodox side] find in Nestorius a denial of the true unity of God and man in Christ, i.e. a teaching of two persons. But as far as Nestorius in fact sees the difference or distinction in Christ on the level of the natures, he cannot be accused of teaching such a doctrine of two persons in the strict sense, not as he himself intends it. 'I did not say that the Son was one (person) and God the Word another; I said that God the Word was by nature one and the temple by nature another, one Son by conjunction'" (Grillmeier, *Christ in Christian Tradition*, 455. Nestorius's quote is from F. Loofs, *Nestoriana* [Halle, 1905], 308).

> preserved in what belongs to it, and the humanity in what belongs to it, it is to a single Lordship and to a single (object of) worship that we gather together the exemplars of these two natures, because of the perfect and inseparable conjunction that has occurred for the divinity with respect to the humanity. And if someone considers or teaches others that suffering and change have attached to the divinity of our Lord, and he does not preserve, with respect to the union of the *prosopon* of our Saviour, a confession of perfect God and perfect Man, let such a person be anathema.[42]

Furthermore, the synod of 576 CE held under Catholicos Ezekiel, in its preamble to the canons, makes some noteworthy christological references: "Christ who is in the flesh, who is known and confessed in two natures, God and Man, a single Son . . ." Brock discerns that this statement as well as the profession of faith issuing from the synod in 585 CE echoes the Chalcedon formula.[43]

The Christology of Mar Babai the Great (d. 628) – abbot of the Monastery of Mount Izala (569–628) – is considered the apogee of Nestorian thought. His succinct definition of Church of the East Christology is as follows:[44]

> One is Christ the Son of God, worshipped by all in two natures. In his godhead begotten of the Father without beginning before all time: in his manhood born of Mary, in the fullness of time, in a united body. Neither his godhead was of the nature of the mother, nor his manhood of the nature of the Father. The natures are preserved in their *qnume* (Syriac with Arabic equivalent *aqnūm* and normally translated *hypostases*) in one person of one sonship.[45]

Another quotation from Mar Babai highlights the Church of the East's understanding of "hypostasis":

> Every nature is known and revealed in the hypostases which are beneath it, and every hypostasis is a demonstrator and upholder of the nature from which it is. And every prosopon in the hypostasis is fixed and made distinct (as to what) it is. And no nature can be known without an hypostasis and no hypostasis can stand without a nature, and no prosopon can be distinguished without the hypostasis. Take the

42. Brock, "Christology of the Church," 133–134.

43. Brock, 127.

44. See also G. Chediath for an extensive analysis of Mar Babai's Christology (Chediath, *Christology of Mar Babai*). Babai's influence was profound on other Church of the East theologians such as ʿAmmār al-Baṣrī (Hayek, "ʿAmmār al Baṣrī," 82).

45. Atiya, *History of Eastern Christianity*, 254.

> hypostasis [away] and show us the prosopon! Take away the nature and show us the hypostasis! Because nature is common and invisible, it is known in its own hypostases. And just as the nature of the Trinity is common to the three hypostases, so the nature of men is common to all the hypostases of men. And if we say of the two natures that they were united in one prosopon, not declaring expressly two hypostases with them, we are saying that the whole nature of the Trinity was united, Father, Son and Holy Spirit, and that the whole nature of men was united, Jesus, Judas and Simon. This is (a matter) of wickedness and blasphemy, in that prosopon cannot be the same as nature, because it (sc. nature) is common; but it (the prosopon) is fixed and distinguished in hypostasis, as in the visible, so in the known (things), so that the Father is not the Son, nor is Gabriel Michael, nor Peter John. For the difference between these is in prosopa, not in hypostases, and not in the equality of the natures.
>
> . . . And see, Mary did not bear the common nature without hypostasis, nor many hypostases, but she bore one hypostasis, the man Jesus, he who is also Son of the most high in the union of the one prosopon. Therefore it is known and evident that it is impossible for us to say that the two natures were united to one prosopon without our confessing and declaring with them two hypostases. . . . But as we say two natures from the testimonies of the scriptures, so also, two hypostases from the same natures have we learnt, as we have shown above. And therefore everybody who does not declare and confess two natures preserving their properties, which are their hypostases, in one prosopon of Christ, the Son of God, he is foreign to the church and denies the truth.[46]

The Church of the East did not hold to "two persons" in Christ, but to two natures in Christ – the divine and the human. It is clear that the word *qnuma* should not be understood as "person." Rather it is roughly synonymous with the *kyana* or nature of a being. The preferred translation of the *qnuma* may well be "subsistence."[47]

46. Abramowski and Goodman, *Nestorian Collection*, 123–125.

47. Wigram notes that Mar Babai commented extensively on Heb 1:3: *και χαρακτηρ της υποστασεως* ("the exact representation of his person"). The Peshitta renders *hypostasis* as *ithutha* (essence). In five of eleven quotations from this passage, Mar Babai substitutes *qnoma* for *ithutha*. Wigram infers that the two are used nearly synonymously with *ithutha* meaning "essence" and *qnuma* meaning "subsistence" (Wigram, *History of the Assyrian Church*, 284).

2.4 Conclusion

Although there were significant variations in christological thought across the ecclesial families of the Middle East, it is not accurate to depict the Church of the East as a "Nestorian Church" if what is meant by that term is a belief that Christ was two persons. Rather, the view which dominated in the Church of the East drew from Theodore of Mopsuestia and was enshrined in the liturgy of the Church of the East.[48] It sought to preserve the human aspect of the man Jesus as a prerequisite to his accomplishment of salvation on behalf of humanity. This was accomplished by insistence on the duality of substance and hypostasis and the union in the one *prosopon* (person) of Christ. Furthermore, it sought to safeguard divinity from theopaschitism, reflexively understanding pain, suffering and other human contingencies as not attributable to the divinity.[49] Though this was true of other ecclesial families in the East, the Christology of the Church of the East emphasized the impassibility of the divine nature by its consistent rejection of the hypostatic union. Ironically, this permitted the Church of the East to make a more plausible argument for the divine nature of Christ in the Islamic milieu. As stated in chapter 2, Muslims were not inclined to give Christ a share of divinity under any aspect. However, the intentional exclusion of the divinity from the evils of suffering encountered by the reality of Christ's incarnation had more conceptual appeal in the Islamic milieu than the hypostatic union proffered by the adherents of Chalcedon.

3. Christological Formulation of Ibn al-Ṭayyib

In the following I pull together the strands of Ibn al-Ṭayyib's Christology. As observed in his Trinitarian formulations, the author seldom makes explicit reference to Islam. However, as a responsive theologian in an Islamic milieu, he responds implicitly to Islamic thought. Accordingly, this chapter is entitled "Christological Reverberations in the Muslim Milieu" as the themes of Ibn al-Ṭayyib's Christology reverberate with the themes of Muslim–Christian discourse of the period. I will observe some areas of continuity from his Trinitarian formulation although my primary interest is to probe

---

48. Theodore's Christology spoke clearly of the two natures (divinity and humanity) in the one person of Christ (Mingana, *Commentary of Theodore*, 37–39). Theodore saw in the phrase "the only begotten Son" and "the firstborn of all creation" a reference to the two natures of Christ. The only begotten Son was the divine nature with no peer or equal, consubstantial with the Father. The "firstborn of all creation" was the human nature which was assumed.

49. An ancient confession of the Church of the East Assembly of Bishops of 612 declares, "It is not possible that Godhead should be converted into Manhood, or Manhood into Godhead, for essential being is not capable of change or suffering; and if Godhead be changed, it is not a revelation, but an alteration of Godhead; and if Manhood be taken out of its nature, it is not the redemption, but the destruction of Manhood" (Wigram, *History of the Assyrian Church*, 278).

Ibn al-Ṭayyib for correspondence with Islamic thought. Five examples of the author's christological formulation are examined. It is necessary to provide a substantial description of the works in question, adhering as closely as possible to the wording of the texts, before passing on to interpret and analyze each in turn.

3.1 "The Union" by Ibn al-Ṭayyib:

Ibn al-Ṭayyib's treatise "The Union" (*al-ittiḥād*) is preserved in two manuscripts:

- Huntington 240 (sixteenth century), Bodleian, Oxford; folios 104r8–105r21. It follows the author's third Trinitarian treatise.[50]
- Vatican Arabe 145 (thirteenth to fourteenth century), folios 67v1–71v4.[51]

Gérard Troupeau has produced a critical Arabic edition with French translation based on the two manuscripts listed above.[52]

3.1.1 Description

The paucity of christological material from Ibn al-Ṭayyib's pen is compensated by citations gathered in Ibn al-ʿAssāl's collection discussed below. Unfortunately, the one extant treatise titled "The Union" (*al-ittiḥād*) appears incomplete as the author mentions "many proofs" for his dyohypostatic Christology but lists only one proof before the treatise comes to an abrupt end.[53] Here I present a brief description of the treatise, adhering closely to the wording of the text.

The treatise divides into three sections, with the author stating his intention to summarize three items: (1) What is "the union"? (2) What is "the one"? (3) Under how many aspects is "the one" an apt descriptor? The first two points are dispensed with quickly and succinctly. The union is defined as: "two or more things becoming one." The definition of "the one" is "a being in whom no 'other' exists."[54]

The author presents twelve divisions of "the one" (his response to the question of point 3 above) taking pains to show that "one" in ordinary speech carries various

50. al-Ṭayyib, *al-Kalām fī al-ittiḥād.*

51. Caspar et al., "Bibliographie du dialogue islamo-chrétien," 207.

52. Troupeau, "Le traité sur l'union."

53. Other proofs are preserved in al-Mu'taman Ibn 'Assāl and will be treated below.

54. موجود ما لا يوجد فيه غيره من حيث هو ذلك الواحد The definition is nearly identical to the definition provided by ibn Yumn – a student of Yaḥyā Ibn 'Adī who defined "the one" in the court of 'Aḍud al-Dawla, the Buyid Amīr فالواحد هو موجودٌ ما، لا يوجد فيه غيره من حيث هو ذلك الموجود (Samir, *Maqāla fī al-tawḥīd*, 142). A similar definition is found in Yaḥyā's *Epistle of Unity* (*risāla al-tawḥīd*) (Samir, *Maqāla fī al-tawḥīd*). Thus, Yaḥyā Ibn 'Adī is understood to be the source of much of Ibn al-Ṭayyib's thinking on the matter. Yaḥyā's definition إنّ الواحد هو موجودٌ ما، لا يوجد فيه غيرية (او غيره)، من حيث هو واحد .

meanings.[55] There is "the one" of species (*jins*) as is spoken of among animals, the "one" of type (*naw'*) as in types of people, and the "one" of subject, such as blackness and whiteness which can be spoken of as "one" when their subject is one and the same. The fourth is the "one" of limitation (*ḥadd*) as including all persons within the limitation of their type (e.g. humanity). The fifth division is the "one" of number (*'adad*) such as Zayd and 'Umar who are one in number. Then comes the "one" of connection as a surface connects to a line, the "one" of indivisibility such as the "one" point, the "one" of essence and the "one" of accident such as the assembled army (presumably, "assembled" is the accident of which the army is the "essence"). The tenth is the "one" of potentiality, said of things that become one. The eleventh is the "one" of action, as this person and this person in action. Lastly is the "one" of relationship, when, for example, two fathers are "one" by the common relationship of fatherhood.

The second section treats the necessity of the union – specifically the union of the Eternal One with what is caused. This derives from the generosity of the Creator. He created the world due to no necessity laid upon him, but by the magnanimity of his grace. Such a generous one is not prone to give once and then cease to give. Rather he cares for what he has graciously given and provides for it such that his goodness is not cut off. After creating man – the noblest of his creatures – in his likeness and blessing him with intelligence and discernment, God commanded that his actions be oriented toward virtue, eschewing vice. When humanity failed in obeying the commandment, God had mercy on them by sending prophets. It was to no avail as man descended to the depths of covetousness. Because God would not cut off his kindness, the One whose name is honored desired to save humanity from its fallen state. This would not happen by the hand of man as the prophetic warnings went unheeded. Therefore, God undertook to save them himself, so that the overflow of his goodness would not cease. Because God is not of tangible objects, nor does he have a body, he took a person and united to him and appeared by means of him to the world.[56] Thus, the necessity of the union is apparent, and it remains to explain by what aspect the Eternal One united with the created and why the union took place with the hypostasis of the Son and not with the other hypostases.[57]

In response to this question, one Christian ecclesial family – the Jacobites – claims that the created (the person taken from Mary) united with the Eternal in both substance and hypostasis. This means that the eternal substance of the Son and the

55. The description of "the one" is repeated virtually identically in Ibn al-'Assāl's collection (Ibn al-'Assāl, *Majmū' usūl al-dīn*, 351–352, chap 26, paras 25–27).

56. لانّه ليس من الأشياء المحسوسة وليس بجسم إتّخذ شخصاً وإتّحدّ به وظهر بتوسّطه للعالم

57. This latter question is dealt with extensively in section 3.5 below.

person taken from Mary became one substance and their two hypostases also became one. Therefore, they speak of Christ as one substance and one hypostasis.

Another ecclesial family – the Melkites – claim that the union happened in the hypostasis such that the person taken from Mary and the eternal Son became one hypostasis. Their substances, however, remained as they were.

A third ecclesial family – the Nestorians – claim that the union between the eternal and the created was a union of property (*khāṣṣa*)[58] only, meaning the property of filiation. As for the two substances – the eternal Son and the human being – they remained as they were as did the two hypostases.

We should occupy ourselves with proving the truth of this last group and its verification will also demonstrate the error of the other two groups. We will demonstrate this through many proofs.

The first is as follows: everything which is characterized by a necessary property, as long as it remains stable in form, the property also remains necessary to it. The hypostasis of the eternal Son and the person taken from Mary are characterized before the union as two substances and two hypostases. So it is established that, after the union, they remain two substances and two hypostases. [At this point, the copyist of Huntington 240 adds, "This is what is extant of it."][59]

3.1.2 Interpretation and Analysis

This exposition of the meaning of "one" is not unique to Ibn al-Ṭayyib as it is influenced by Aristotelian thought and can already be perceived in Abū Rā'iṭa, who defines God as "one in species" which he also equates to the meaning of "one in substance."[60] The Melkite Nazīf Ibn Yumn (d. after 982) distinguished seven divisions of "the one," six of which are included in Ibn al-Ṭayyib's twelve divisions.[61] Ibn Yumn was a student of Yaḥyā Ibn ʿAdī who spoke of six divisions (*aqsām*) of "the one" in his "Treatise on Unity" as well as six aspects (*jihāt*). In Yaḥyā's response to Abū Yūsuf Yaʿqūb Ibn Isḥāq Al-Kindī (ca. 800–870 CE) he lists eight divisions of "the one." In the latter, Yaḥyā was clearly dealing with Islamic objections to his

58. The word denotes a unique property or exclusive characteristic.

59. al-Mu'tamin Ibn al-ʿAssāl in chapter 8 of his *Majmūʿ uṣūl al-dīn* enumerates fully thirty proofs of the Nestorians. Furthermore, Metropolitan Daʿūd in his *Kitāb al-kamāl* refers to Ibn al-Ṭayyib citing ten proofs of Nestorian Christology (Caspar et al., "Bibliographie du dialogue islamo-chrétien," 207–208). Thus, the proofs of Ibn al-Ṭayyib appear to have survived though they must be salvaged from secondary sources.

60. Husseini, *Early Christian–Muslim Debate*, 176–177. Abū Rā'iṭa suggested three categories for "the one": one in genus, species and number. One in genus would imply God's containing different species, thus implying compositeness within God, while one in number would negate God's uniqueness as "one" is a divisible number and the beginning of a series of numbers. Therefore, God's oneness is best expressed as oneness of species (Husseini, 176).

61. Samir, *Maqāla fī al-tawḥīd*, 142.

Christian faith.[62] Though Ibn al-Ṭayyib shows no evidence of explicit interaction with Islamic thought, his extensive definition of "the one" flows out of the precedent Muslim–Christian exchange of ideas where the concept of "oneness" was shown to carry multiple meanings.

Samir has pointed out that Ibn al-Ṭayyib may not have fully assimilated Yaḥyā's definitions. First, he did not note that the "one of number" contains within it three divisions – the "one" of "connection, boundary and indivisibility." Second, Ibn al-Ṭayyib did not maintain Yaḥyā's categorization of "the one" into six divisions (*aqsām*) and six aspects (*jihāt*).[63] It is clear that Ibn al-Ṭayyib has taken his twelve divisions from Yaḥyā. However, Samir is overstating the case to say that he has "mixed up" the categories. It is possible that Ibn al-Ṭayyib simply found the categorization confusing. Yaḥya mentions the "one of boundary" in both his divisions and aspects. Indeed, it is difficult to understand why the "one of boundary" and the "one of connection" are considered "one in number" (*fī al-ʻadad*) while the "one of species," "one of type" and "one of relation" are not. Samir reckons that Ibn al-Ṭayyib has overlooked (*sahā ʻan*) the repetition of the "one of boundary" in both the divisions and the aspects. It is unlikely that an intellectual of Ibn al-Ṭayyib's stature would inadequately represent Yaḥyā's thought especially as Yaḥyā is quite organized in his presentation even if his rationale is difficult to penetrate, as Samir readily acknowledges.[64] It is at least plausible that Ibn al-Ṭayyib found Yaḥyā's categories unwieldy or unhelpful and simply dropped them in favor of a straightforward enumeration of the twelve categories.

Moreover, while Yaḥyā refers to his definition of the "one" when writing on the unity (*al-tawḥīd*) of God, Ibn al-Ṭayyib is writing on the union (*al-ittiḥād*) – the becoming one of the Eternal and the created. In plainer terms, the former is treating theology while the latter, Christology.

Ibn al-Ṭayyib's explication of Christology from God's magnanimous nature merits consideration. The necessity of the incarnation is not rationally deduced but arises from the plight of fallen humanity and the indefatigable generosity of God. It is here that the reader can discern an implicit and subtle response to Islamic currents of thought. The notable forerunner in this type of argumentation is ʻAmmār al-Baṣrī (early to mid-ninth century), a Church of the East forebear of Ibn al-Ṭayyib. In his *Book of Proof* (*kitāb al-burhān*), he proposes a theology of history moving from God's

62. R. Haddad, *La Trinité divine*, 160.

63. Samir, *Maqāla fī al-tawḥīd*, 146–147.

64. See Samir's treatment and critical text of Yaḥyā's *Epistle of Unity* (*Risāla al-Tawḥīd*) (Samir, *Maqāla fī al-tawḥīd*, 196–207). Samir acknowledges that Yaḥyā's treatise is the most difficult Arabic text he has ever grappled with. Understanding Yaḥyā requires a thorough knowledge of Aristotle and medieval philosophy (Samir, 21).

initial gestures of grace to their climax in the incarnation.[65] Thus, it was fitting that the Divine would fulfil his gracious interaction with mankind by taking human nature. For ʿAmmār, the incarnation of divinity in Christ is shrouded in mystery which only the divine mind can comprehend.[66] Likewise, Abū Rā'iṭa (fl. 810–830/194–215), the Jacobite, appealed to the divine prerogative in revealing his righteousness, goodness and grace to mankind as the theological basis for the incarnation.[67] Both ʿAmmār and Ibn al-Ṭayyib sought to demonstrate that the essential framework for understanding the incarnation was not mere rationality but theology. By understanding the nature of God and his gracious disposition toward mankind, one is brought to an understanding of the reasonableness of the incarnation. The incarnation is, in fact, the pinnacle of God's gracious self-manifestation to humanity.

Landron has noted that for Church of the East theologians, the point of emphasis in Christology is God's self-manifestation rather than redemption. The reality of sin attaches to mankind but is only secondarily portrayed as having a causative role in the necessity of the incarnation.[68] For Ibn al-Ṭayyib, the bounteous nature of God hovers over the fallen nature of humanity to necessitate the incarnation. He refers to God having undertaken "to save human beings from the fall in which they were implicated."[69] Although the expression does not bear directly on the crucifixion as a means of salvation, the author views mankind's moral dilemma as irresolvable apart from the union of the divine and human in Christ. It is not merely God's self-manifestation that is featured in Ibn al-Ṭayyib's Christology, but also God's saving intentions toward humanity.

It is noteworthy that Ibn al-Ṭayyib highlights the inefficacy of the prophetic warning to rectify man's alienation from God. The Islamic solution to mankind's waywardness was "guidance" (*hudā*) as no original sin prevented one being rightly guided. The descended revelation (*tanzīl*) was deemed sufficient to lead human beings to repentance. Conversely, for Ibn al-Ṭayyib, the failure of the prophetic warnings to effect change in the human predicament led to God's dramatic solution in the incarnation. As was observed in the study of Ibn al-Ṭayyib's Trinity, he does not eschew a rational explication – the "how" of the incarnation (taken from Ibn ʿAdī and also proffered in his exposition of the Church of the East view below). Still, the

65. ʿAmmār also reveals a sophisticated anthropology whereby humanity participates in both the material nature of the cosmos from which they are taken and the spiritual nature by virtue of their soul (Griffith, "ʿAmmar al Basri's *Kitab al-burhan*," 175; Hayek, "ʿAmmār al Baṣrī").

66. Hayek, *Apologie et Controverses*, 62.

67. Keating, *Defending the "People of Truth,"* 120; Mikhail, "ʿAmmār al-Basrī's Kitāb al-Burhān," 218.

68. Landron, *Chrétiens et musulmans en Irak*, 206.

69. أحب إنقاذ البشريين من السقطة التي حصلوا فيها (Troupeau, "Le traité sur l'union," 149).

true rationale of the incarnation derives from the nature of God – theology proper. It is ascertained by understanding the gracious disposition of God toward humanity. Rational constructs are useful in aiding understanding, but the reality of the Christian dogma must be discovered through the revelation of the nature of God. Christ is incarnate deity because the incessantly giving nature of the Creator demands the salvation of mankind.

3.2 Ibn al-Ṭayyib's "Enumeration of People's Views of the Union"

This work of Ibn al-Ṭayyib is preserved only in the *Summa of Religious Principles*[70] by Abū Isḥāq Mu'taman al-Dawla Ibn al-ʿAssāl (hereafter, Ibn al-ʿAssāl). Therein it is described as the eleventh chapter of his "Enumeration of People's Views of the Union and Their Proofs."[71] Indeed, the remainder of Ibn al-Ṭayyib's contribution to Christology is preserved only by the Coptic encyclopedist Ibn al-ʿAssāl.[72] The work is mostly a description of opposing views of Christology (which may well be part of the lost treatise "The Union" described above). It is introduced by a brief but noteworthy description of Church of the East Christology. The description, though not a literal translation, adheres closely to the wording of the author, attempting to render his thought accessible in contemporary English.

3.2.1 Description

(129)[73] In introducing the issue, Ibn al-Ṭayyib points out that the moniker "Nestorian" is inaccurate for the Christians of the East (*naṣārā al-mashriq*) who received their creed from Saint Addaī Salīḥ[74] and Saint Thomas. The descriptor "Nestorian" overtook

70. The Arabic title is *Majmūʿ uṣūl al-dīn wa-masmūʿ maḥṣūl al-yaqīn*
مجموع أصول الدين ومسموع محصول اليقين

71. Ibn al-ʿAssāl, *Majmūʿ usūl al-dīn*, 192–193, bāb 8. The Arabic title supplied by al-Mu'taman is *taʿdīd arāʾ al-nās fī al-ittiḥād wa-ḥujajihim* تعديد اراء الناس في الإتحاد وحججهم

72. Ibn al-ʿAssāl and his two brothers, Ṣafī al-Dawla and al-Asʿad al-Shahīrayn, contributed to a renaissance of Christian Arabic literature in what has been called the "golden age" of the Coptic Church. Ibn al-ʿAssāl compiled his work prior to 1260. It is notable for its breadth of theological interest and accessibility. Many of Ibn al-Ṭayyib's writings are preserved only in this collection of Ibn al-ʿAssāl (Samir, "Ṣafaḥāt min maqāla," 247–248).

73. The numbers correspond to the paragraph numbers in Ibn al-ʿAssāl's *Summa: Majmū' usūl al-dīn.*

74. The tradition of the founding of the Church of the East is preserved in Eusebius's *Ecclesiastical History* (produced between 311 and 325 CE). Mar Addai (anglicized as "Thaddeus") is thought to have been one of Christ's seventy (or seventy-two) disciples commissioned in Luke 10. In Church of the East thought, it was Mar Addai who healed King Agbar of Edessa which led to his fruitful evangelism of the city and the spread of the Church in northern Mesopotamia. In addition to Addai, Mari and Aggai were also thought to have played a role in the founding of the Church of the East. The three were purported to be included in the seventy disciples (Baum & Winkler, *Church of the East*, 12–13). This traditional

them due to the assistance they offered to Nestorius, the Patriarch of Constantinople. This group believes that the substances remain the same (*'alā ṭabā'ihimā*) as do the hypostases. The union takes place in the property (*khāṣṣa*) of filiation which is the Creator's self-knowledge. The rightly guided person from Mary (*al-sayyida*) participated in this property with God. Through this property he became one Christ and one Son, but not one substance or one hypostasis.

The proofs of Church of the East Christology follow. It is noteworthy that these may well be a copy of the proofs which were mentioned although not discussed in "The Union" treated above. (132) First, the union of the substances would spoil the natures of both substances. It would render Christ neither man nor God. Because he is both man and God the two substances must remain unchanged as well as the two hypostases. Thus, the union is a union in the property of filiation.

(133) By the same token, the created substance cannot unite with the eternal one or else we are left with a substance that is neither created nor eternal. Christ is both created and eternal; therefore, both substances remain. (134) If the two substances mixed (*'ikhtalaṭa*) the result would be neither man nor God. However, Christ was both man and God.

(135) If the two substances mixed to become one, this would require a "mixer" (*khāliṭ*) and the Creator is exalted beyond being acted upon. (136) If the two mixed so as to become one substance and one hypostasis, a despicable tenet would result: the creature (*al-kā'in*) would be eternal and the eternal, a creature. That (divine) essence is exalted beyond being deposed to the level of earthly beings (*al-kawniyyāt*). (137) Even if the two substances and the two hypostases were one, the result could not be described as "God and man."

(138) The view that the two substances and hypostases remain after the union removes them from the realm of composites (*al-murakkabāt*) and mixtures (*al-muzājiyyāt*). Neither does it detract from their union concerning what is correctly attributed to the union – the filiation – by which the person taken from Mary worked miracles and innovation of the Law (*ibdā' al-sunna*). (139) According to the (other) view, humanity (which is corporeal) and divinity (which is non-corporeal) became one nature by mixing (*al-mizāj*). The non-corporeal became corporeal. The corporeal became non-corporeal. So it is necessary to maintain both (the substance and the hypostasis) according to their nature. That being the case, the coming together of the two (*al-mujtama'*) is described as two substances and two hypostases.

(140) This view – that Christ is two substances and two hypostases, one Son – eliminates all repulsive tenets. It eliminates the eternal being created, mixture of the

understanding is rejected by Wilmshurst who thinks it more likely that Christianity first took root in the Jewish communities of Mesopotamia. He suggests that early Jewish attendees of Pentecost returned to the kingdom of Parthia (see Acts 2:9) and became its first Christians (Wilmshurst, *Martyred Church*, 1, 5).

two and the sovereign one being acted upon. (141) Either the two substances remained in their states after the union or they were reciprocally corrupted. If they remained in their states, their coming together must be described as two substances. If they were reciprocally corrupted, both deity and humanity are lost, such that Christ cannot be described as either God or man. Christian law rejects such a view.

(142) The proclamation to Mary is known: "Our master [*sayyidunā*] is with you, O blessed among women." This does not refer to God, but to the man. Necessarily, the one taken from her was not united with him, so they are two substances, not one. (143) The meaning of birth, crucifixion and other acts requires that he was acted upon and this could not be true of him who is never acted upon. So Christ is two natures: the divine nature that is not acted upon and the human nature that is acted upon.

(144) From Christ's saying "I ascend to my Father and your Father, to my God and your God" it is known that he has an essence other than the essence of the Creator for God cannot ascend to God. So Christ is two substances and two hypostases, the one ascending (to God) and the other ascended to him.

(145) Christ ate and drank and was crucified for our salvation. These are attributes of humanity but not of divinity. (146) It is unfitting to depict something as acted upon when it is not. (147) If the two substances are preserved unspoiled, so are the hypostases. If the hypostases are not preserved, neither can be the substances. (148) Receiving baptism (*al-ṣabgha*) from John and Christ's being elevated on the cross exclude Christ from being one in substance and hypostasis. (149) In calling himself the "Son of man" and also saying that he and the Father are one, it is clear that he describes himself as both human and divine after the union.

(150) If every two substances that meet become one substance, there could be no composite entities (*baṭalat sā'ir al-murakkabāt*). Mankind is both soul and body. The body is a different substance from the soul. So if two substances coming together form one substance, then the soul must be the body and the body the soul.

(151) It is known that the Master shared in all that is of our nature – eating, drinking, dying and rising again. He differed from us in the nature which is not appropriate to us, which is the working of signs and miracles.

(152) These proofs demonstrate that Christ, after the union, is two substances and two hypostases, one Son. So the union is in filiation, (neither in)[75] substance nor in hypostasis. This does not require that the substances be spoiled or that the divine substance overturn the human or vice versa. These are the proofs of the people of the East that Christ, after the union, is God and man.

---

75. Al-Mu'taman omits the negation here. It is supplied not because of manuscript evidence, but in keeping with context as Ibn al-Ṭayyib has stated repeatedly that the union is not in the substance.

From this point, Ibn al-Ṭayyib begins to explicate the Melkite view. Interestingly, he begins by providing a Church of the East view (156–158) and proceeds to supply his version of how the Melkites would refute the position. (159–165) He does the same for the miaphysite view attributing it to Kīrilus, Patriarch of Alexandria, as well as Ya'qūb al-Sarūjī (from whom the West Syrian Jacobite Church derives its name) (166–167). The description is admirable for its objectivity and lack of Nestorian bias. His summary paragraph (178) supplies a laudable ecumenical tone to the christological debate: "Those are the proofs of the three ecclesial families concerning their denominations' claims. However, they are in agreement that Christ is both God and man, substance of God and substance of man, hypostasis of God and hypostasis of man. Their disagreement concerns how they describe the coming together [*al-mujtama'*] of the divine and the human. After the coming together, does he remain in his state? Is he one substance or two? One hypostasis or two?"[76]

3.2.2 Interpretation and Analysis

The Church of the East and other ecclesial families shared with Islam a view of God's impassibility – that he could not suffer pain, death or human vicissitudes. Though Christ was of the divine substance, it remained distinct from the human substance. Furthermore, and as stated previously, for the Church of the East, the hypostasis (*al-uqnūm*) could not be understood separately from the substance. There is no possibility of a hypostatic union while the two substances remained divine and human. This presupposition becomes evident in Ibn al-Ṭayyib's proofs above (e.g. "If the two substances are preserved unspoiled, so are the hypostases. If the hypostases are not preserved, neither can be the substances"). This separation of the divine and human in both substance and hypostasis allowed Ibn al-Ṭayyib and other Church of the East theologians to demarcate the acts of Christ, attributing some to the human substance and others to the divine. He enumerates the acts of the human substance: eating, drinking, baptism and crucifixion. These are all acts and attributes common to human substance but improper to attribute to the divine substance. On the other hand, certain acts of Christ are clearly attributable to his divine substance and must not be attributed to his humanity. The primary example is miraculous signs. Furthermore, the mixing or blending of the substances was inconceivable for Ibn al-Ṭayyib for it implied the spoiling of the two natures to produce a third.

76. Ibn al-'Assāl, *Majmū' usūl al-dīn*, 202, bāb 8. Further along, Ibn al-Ṭayyib undertakes a painstaking examination of how the various Christian sects refute one another's Christology. He begins with the Nestorian refutation of Jacobite Christology (paras 193–225) and then provides the Jacobite refutation of Nestorian Christology (paras 227–237). Finally, he discusses how the Jacobites contradict the Melkites (paras 239–248) and how the Melkites respond (paras 250ff.) (Ibn al-'Assāl, *Majmū' usūl al-dīn*, 205–220, vol. 8).

In an interesting exposition of the angelic announcement to Mary, Ibn al-Ṭayyib uses the translation *sayyidunā* – our master – to describe the person who was "with Mary." Given his dyohypostatic assumptions, it appears obvious that it is the man Jesus who is with Mary, not the divine Spirit. The one born of the woman was acted upon (*infa'ala*). The substance of the eternal God could not be acted upon. Therefore, the birth to the Virgin had to be understood as the birth of the human substance, not united to the divine substance.[77] Nor could the divine substance be said to "ascend to my God." Rather the human substance ascends to God where the divine substance is. The author's citing of the most-often referenced biblical passage at the Muslim–Christian interface to refute the union may not be merely coincidental.[78] The author finds further justification for his view in the diverse sayings of Jesus – "I and the Father are one" (referring to the divine substance) and the "Son of man" (the human substance).

Islamic polemicists had long argued that divinity could not be subject to human contingencies (e.g. to be born, eat, drink, suffer, die). Abū ʿĪsā al-Warrāq (d. after 864/250) was one of the most adroit Muslim polemicists who belabored the incongruity of Christ's human characteristics with his claimed divine substance. *The Refutation of the Three Christian Sects*[79] takes pains to point out the impossibility of Christ's divinity given the changes he underwent through gestation, birth and his early years. His death and burial are also portrayed as incongruent with a claim to divinity.[80] He holds to his Muʿtazilī assumptions unswervingly, insisting on the complete separation of divinity from creaturely characteristics. Abū ʿĪsā was determined to show the irrationality of the intermingling of the human with the divine, as were other Muslim polemicists such as Nāshi' al-Akbar (d. 906/293) and Abū Bakr Muḥammad al-Bāqillānī (d. 1013/403).

As stated previously, the Church of the East theologians held to the separation of the substances and hypostases, preferring to see the union in the attribute or property of filiation. They eschewed imagery that portrayed "mixture" and upheld images that stressed the duality of the substances and hypostases illustrated by the distinction between body and soul.[81] Although this tendency preceded Islam, the dominance

77. This is not intended to be a statement of the moment of the union. For most Church of the East theologians, the union took place at conception (Landron, *Chrétiens et musulmans en Irak*, 204). I do not understand Ibn al-Ṭayyib's statement to counter that tenet. Rather, he is affirming that the birth of Christ belongs to the human substance, not the divine. Thus, though the union had presumably already taken place, the divine substance was not subject to the pain and change implicated in human birth.

78. Accad, "Ultimate Proof-Text," 200.

79. الرد على الثلاث فراق من النصارى *al-Radd 'alā al-thalāth firaq min al-Naṣārā*.

80. Thomas, *Early Muslim Polemic*, 64.

81. Landron, "Apologétique, polémique et attitudes Nestoriennes," 359. ʿAmmār had pointed out that "properties of the soul, when united to the body become actions of the body by virtue of borrowing." Eating and drinking were perceived as bodily properties while life and speech are attributes of the soul. Through the union of body and soul "they become attributes of the body without the soul being emptied of them" (Mikhail, "ʿAmmār al-Basrī's Kitāb al-burhān," 233).

of *tawḥīd* applied pressure on Christians to further define the union of the divine and human substances of Christ. Their separation of divine and human actions and attributes allowed them to argue that they were not contravening *tawḥīd* and were, therefore, not guilty of *shirk* (associating the creature with the Creator). Indeed, one detects an Islamic-like repulsion[82] vis-à-vis the claim that the eternal God was born, suffered, died, and so on. In this vein, it is noteworthy that Ibn al-Ṭayyib avoided engaging in internecine polemics. He explicated the other christological views without denigrating them though he clearly held a dyohypostatic Christology.

Though Ibn al-Ṭayyib was not engaging in polemical argument, his theological concerns demonstrate that he was aware of the perennial issues at the Muslim–Christian interface. While upholding the Christology of his forebears in the Church of the East in eleventh-century Baghdad, he also attempted to strengthen his church's theological resolve in the Islamic milieu. He drew from the theological heritage of the Church of the East to respond to the mounting polemical attack of Islam. As a responsive theologian in such a context, he distinguished human actions from divine, attributing each to its proper substance. He demonstrated the consistency of his church's Christology with John 20:17 (the most often-quoted biblical text at the Muslim–Christian interface). While it is entirely possible that his christological formulation was never considered seriously by Muslim *mutakallimūn*, I contend that, at the very least, it gave his Church of the East parishioners a handle by which to grasp the union of the divine and the human in Christ and provided greater plausibility for its doctrine in the Arabic Muslim context in which he lived and worked.

3.3 "Treatise Composed of Fourteen Chapters"

Only parts of this work are preserved by Ibn al-ʿAssāl in his *Summa of Religious Principles* (*faṣl* 8, bāb 11, paras 92–101). Graf supposed it is part of the lost work mentioned previously, "Enumeration of Peoples' Views on the Union and Their Proofs,"[83] although Samir is reluctant to accept that opinion. I retain the title given by Ibn al-ʿAssāl, "Treatise Composed of Fourteen Chapters."[84] Ibn al-Ṭayyib deals with Christology in one of the two preserved sections.[85] Samir has also prepared a critical edition which is based on three manuscripts.[86] The paraphrased description

82. Portrayed in Ibn al-Ṭayyib's work through words such as شناعة ("hideousness") and قبيح ("repugnant").

83. *Ta'dīd 'arā' al-nās fī al-ittiḥād wa-hujajihim* تعديد اراء الناس في الإتّحاد وحججهم

84. *Maqāla 'adaduhā arba'ta 'ashara bāban* مقالة عددها اربعة عشرة باباً

85. Ibn al-ʿAssāl, *Majmū' usūl al-dīn*, 275–277.

86. Samir, "Ṣafaḥāt min maqāla." The three manuscripts are Paris Arabic 200 (95v–96v, 137v–138v), Paris Arabic 201 (162r–163v and 232r–233v) and Vatican Arabe 103 (139v–140v and 205v–207r).

below adheres to the author's wording, seeking to render it in accessible English. The latter section included in Samir's critical edition (*aṣl* 6, bāb 19 of Ibn al-ʿAssāl) will not be examined as its content has been explored in other works by Ibn al-Ṭayyib.

3.3.1 Description

(92)[87] The author gives a brief glossary of terms: substance (*jawhar*), hypostasis (*aqnūm*), person (*farṣūf*), unity (*tawḥīd*), Trinity (*tathlīth*), attributes (*ṣifāt*) and union (*ittiḥād*). (93) The substance of every essence (*dhāt*) denotes the expression of the character (*muṭlaq al-ṭibāʿ*) of the thing, such as the character of humanity which is expressed in its persons and fire which is also expressed in its manifestations (*ashkhāsihā*). (94) Now if the essence is particularized by an attribute, it is named according to its particularity as a hypostasis. If the attribute is instantiated (*taʿayyanat*) it is named a person (*farṣūf wa-shakhs*). If its descriptors are portrayed from one aspect as many and from a different aspect as but one, then it is but one substance though it has many descriptors.

(95) The essence of the Creator has three descriptors, neither more nor less: paternity, filiation and procession. So the essence of the Creator, in a sense, is one. In the sense of its descriptors, as they adhere in the essence, he is many. "Father" is different from "Son" which is different from "Spirit." So the essence of the Creator is one although the descriptors are many. So (the essence) is many from the vantage point of the descriptors, not from the vantage point of the essence. (96) Socrates is an example of a person who is one although he is a philosopher, white and a geometrician. So he is many in reference to his descriptors. If those descriptors are added to him, it is said "he is a philosopher, white and a geometrician."

(97) "Union" (*al-ittiḥād*) is the becoming one of two or more joined things. The result is either the spoiling of both, producing a third entity (e.g. water and fire), or they remain in their state with each thing transmitting to the other its attribute (*ṣifa*). (98) An example is provided of Socrates and the color white. Although their natures are not the same, Socrates can be described as white, and white as Socrates, as the attribute of each is transferred to the other. (99) However, if the union is one of mixture (*al-mazj*), the essence of each is negated and the description refers to the composite, not the parts, as the parts have now lost their nature. (100) As the essence of the Creator united and connected with the man born of Mary, there was no spoiling (of the nature) nor transformation (*istiḥāla*). Their natures remained unaltered and the attribute of each was transferred to the other. So we say of the humanity of Christ "he is God" and we lawfully describe God as man. (101) However, the prohibition of that (describing God as man) is evident as the objective of the union is the ennobling of

87. These are paragraph numbers in Ibn al-ʿAssāl.

the human nature, not the debasement of the divine nature.[88] For this reason, we do not transfer the human attribute to God, but the divine attribute to man. So we say of the humanity (*al-nāsūt*) "it is the divine attribute; it performs miracles by transfer (of the divine attribute)" because the performer (of the miracles) is God by mediation.[89]

3.3.2 Interpretation and Analysis

In this passage as well as the previous one (see 3.2.1) one finds the author's clearest definition of the union. The fact that he took pains to define what was meant by the Church of the East's view of the union should not pass unnoticed. ʿAmmār provided a defense of the union but did not define the doctrine. Mikhail has concluded that this may indicate that ʿAmmār was writing with a Muslim readership in mind. His focus was to clear the Christian view of slanderous accusations.[90] Ibn al-Ṭayyib, on the contrary, is explicit in defining the union which indicates that he writes for his Christian constituency.

The author's discussion of the transfer of the attribute (*ṣifa*) is noteworthy. For Ibn al-Ṭayyib, it was the union of the divine and human in the property of filiation that allowed the transfer of the divine attribute to the human Jesus. This "one-way" *communicatio idiomatum* – communication of the attributes – took place as the divine power was transferred to the human Jesus through the property of filiation effecting miraculous works. It is not entirely clear how Ibn al-Ṭayyib avoids locating the union in the hypostasis. In his Trinitarian treatises, he has defined the hypostasis as any one of the attributes of essence (paternity, filiation and procession) when taken with the essence. If, therefore, the author is suggesting the transfer of the divine attribute of essence to humanity, it is difficult to understand how this is not a "hypostatic union." Nevertheless, I grant the author the benefit of the doubt in that he nowhere specifically states that the attribute of essence (*al-bunūwa*) is "transferred" to the man born of Mary. He does indicate that the property of filiation is the locus of the union – that it is held in common by both the eternal Word and the man born of Mary. It is through the agency of this commonality that the attribute of miraculous power (not an attribute of essence but an attribute of act) is granted to the human substance. Both substances hold the property of filiation in common such that the divine power of the miraculous is transferred. The careful demarcation of the attribute (*ṣifa*) from the property (*khāṣṣa*) is consistent with Ibn al-Ṭayyib's dyohypostatic Christology. The attribute of essence – filiation – is not transferred to Christ's humanity. Rather

88. In paragraph 182 of Ibn al-ʿAssāl, bāb 8, the author describes how the union does not result in the mutual corruption of the two, but in their coming together (*'ijtimā'uhumā*) such that the more noble of the two completes the baser, raising it to its character.

89. Ibn al-ʿAssāl, *Majmūʿ usūl al-dīn*, 275–277, bāb 11, para 92–101.

90. Mikhail, "ʿAmmār al-Basrī's Kitāb al-Burhān," 202.

the attribute of act is transferred. The deity of Christ in the hypostasis of the Son (defined as the divine essence taken with the attribute of filiation) remains separate from the humanity. If this reading of Ibn al-Ṭayyib's Christology is pedantic for the modern reader, it must have been inaccessible for the medieval Muslim. Though Ibn al-Ṭayyib is speaking in the Muslim milieu, he is seeking to define his doctrine in ways that are helpful to his Christian constituency. Thoughtful Muslims would have found his subtleties confusing and charged him with contradiction.

The penchant of Ibn al-Ṭayyib's Christology, as of the Church of the East generally, is to preserve the divine essence from comingling with the human. Thus, though it is lawful to speak of the transfer of the human attribute to divinity, such is not desirable for it would be tantamount to denigrating the Divine. Church of the East theologians were careful to avoid attributing human suffering to the divine substance – theopaschitism. This outworking of dyohypostatic Christology predated the advent of Islam although the strident monotheism of the *mutakallimūn* may have incentivized the Christians to feature this aspect of their Christology more prominently in their formulation. The incarnation issues in the elevation of humanity by virtue of the transfer of the divine attribute as portrayed in Christ's miracles, not the degradation of the divine substance. It is consistent with the theological thrust of Church of the East Christology: the incarnation issues in the elevation of humanity to participate in the divine.

It is doubtful that Ibn al-Ṭayyib's Christology would have had persuasive power in Muslim–Christian relations where the miraculous would be seen not as an indicator of a divine attribute (whether of essence or of act) but as a capacity conferred by God on his messengers. Nevertheless, Christ's miracles had been a constant reference point at the Muslim–Christian interface. Given the Christian claim that Christ's miracles far surpassed those of other prophets, it is not surprising that they would see his miraculous powers as a transfer of the divine attribute. Though Muslims may have paid scant attention to the miracle accounts in the Gospels, it is clear that Christians such as Abū Qurra, Abū Rā'iṭa and ʿAmmār al-Baṣrī found the preponderance and spontaneity of Christ's miracles to be a weighty argument for his divinity. Ibn al-Ṭayyib joins his voice to theirs.

3.4 Ibn al-Ṭayyib's Textual Referents for Christ

It is noteworthy that Ibn al-Ṭayyib presented textual support for the persons of the Trinity. As seen in chapter 3 section 2.3.2, Ibn al-Ṭayyib was convinced that the Trinitarian nature of God as well as the names of the Trinity could not be ascertained from the created order but had to be revealed. Thus, it is not surprising that he seeks referents to "the Son" not only in the New Testament Gospels but also in the prophecies of the Old Testament.

The preservation of his formulation is found in Ibn al-'Assāl's *Summa of Religious Principles*, bāb 19.[91] The citation preserves much of Ibn al-Ṭayyib's Trinitarian formulation in paragraphs 29 to 43. Significant textual references to crucial titles of Christ are found in paragraphs 41 to 47.

3.4.1 Description

(41) Ibn al-Ṭayyib defends the term "Son" citing the scriptural use of the term by Old Testament prophets Jeremiah[92] and Hosea (1:10) in reference to Israel. If it is legitimate for this moniker to be applied to Israel, how much more to Christ. (42) Nebuchadnezzar perceives a fourth being in the flames of fire who was "like a son of the gods" (Dan 3:25). (43) Ibn al-Ṭayyib notes that God is called the "father of orphans" in the Psalms (68:5), and if he is called thus, how much more fitting for him to be called the Father of Christ?[93] Malachi (1:6) asks, "If I am your father, why do you not honor me?" The Wisdom of Solomon exclaims, "As for your rule, O Father, you administer all."[94]

(44) The titles "son" and "word" are treated as synonyms. The author cites Exodus 4:22, referring to it as the "second book" which declares the children of Israel to be the divine son. Again, if the title is apt for Israel, it is even more fitting that Christ should be thus designated. The "word" of God is said to have "dwelt upon" (*ḥallat 'alā*) the patriarch Abraham. Though only this passing reference is given, it is noteworthy that Ibn al-Ṭayyib discerned a reference to the second of the Trinitarian persons through Abraham's encounters with the Word of YHWH.[95]

(45) Ibn al-Ṭayyib also refers to various psalms: "You are my Son; today I have begotten you" (Ps 2:7). "By the word of the LORD, the heavens were made" (Ps 33:6, referred to by the author as Ps 32). "He sent out his word and healed them" (Ps 107:20). "Your word is a lamp" (Ps 119:105). (46) Isaiah is quoted twice: "The virgin shall conceive and bear a son, and shall call his name Immanuel" (Isa 7:14). "To us a

91. Ibn al-'Assāl, *Majmū' usūl al-dīn*, 409–413.

92. It is unclear which biblical reference Ibn al-Ṭayyib has in mind. The most plausible suggestion is Jer 3:20–22 which contains both a reference to a treacherous wife who leaves her husband and the call to the faithless "sons" to return to the Lord.

93. Ibn al-Ṭayyib refers to him as the "cause of the caused" (علة المعلول) which is a reference to the Father as the cause of the Son, as was seen previously in his Trinitarian formulation.

94. A reference to the apocryphal book Wisdom of Solomon 14:3: "But thy providence, O Father, governeth it; for thou hast made a way in the sea, and a safe path in the waves" (www.kingjamesbibleonline.org).

95. I am not certain which encounter Ibn al-Ṭayyib has in mind, Gen 15:1 and 4 speak of the word of Yahweh (*davar Yahweh*) coming to Abraham.

child is born, to us a son is given and his authority shall be upon his shoulders and his name is 'wonderful'" (Isa 9:6[96]). (47) Solomon asked, "Who has ascended to heaven and descended? Who has established the earth? Who has gathered the wind in his fist? What is his name and what is his son's name if you know?" (Prov 30:4[97]). Ibn al-Ṭayyib refers to the Wisdom of Solomon: "He said of the Egyptians: 'Pharaoh and his hosts because of enchantment did not believe the plagues that struck them. In the demise of the first-born, they confessed that the people are his son.'"[98]

3.4.2 Interpretation and Analysis

Ibn al-Ṭayyib goes to some length to establish the scriptural precedent of the monikers "Son" and "word" (in addition to "Father" and "Spirit"). As noted in the treatment of his Trinitarian formulation, he was insistent that the knowledge of these essential attributes (paternity, filiation and procession) cannot be inferred from creation but must be revealed. Thanks to Ibn al-ʿAssāl's preservation of the polymath's thought, we have this exposition of the revelation of the divine attributes.

What then is the role this exposition was intended to play at the Muslim–Christian interface of the medieval period? The lack of reference to Islam leads to the conclusion that the author is not writing for a Muslim readership. Indeed, much of the exposition corresponds with the demands of Jewish–Christian interaction as well. Nevertheless, his insistence on the legitimacy of the familial terms (Son, Father) suggests that Ibn al-Ṭayyib had an eye to the Islamic context in which his Church of the East co-religionists lived and interacted. The perennial argument of the Muslim polemicists was the illegitimacy of these familial terms when applied to divinity because God neither "begets nor is He begotten" (Q112:3). Al-Qāsim Ibn Ibrahīm as well as ʿAlī Ibn Rabbān al-Ṭabarī had voiced opposition to the familial terms employed for the Trinity.[99] ʿAmmār al-Baṣrī had defended the familial terms based on the teaching of Christ in the New Testament and also offered three Old Testament passages to lend credence to the terms.[100] Ibn al-Ṭayyib called on other Old Testament scriptures to demonstrate the legitimacy of familial terms being applied to Christ, which may indicate that he was cognizant of the Jewish presence in Baghdad. Though any explicit

96. Translated from Ibn al-Tayyib.

97. Translated from Ibn al-Tayyib.

98. A likely reference to the apocryphal book Wisdom of Solomon 18:13: "For whereas they would not believe any thing by reason of the enchantments; upon the destruction of the firstborn, they acknowledged this people to be the sons of God" (www.kingjamesbibleonline.org).

99. Al-Qāsim asked if these names were of the essence of God or merely accidental. His objection insisted that if the Father bore his name after begetting the Son, then the name must be accidental rather than of the essence. He stresses his point that these names are not of the substance of God (Mikhail, "ʿAmmār al-Basrī's Kitāb al-Burhān," 195).

100. Mikhail, 187–188, 238.

reference to Islam is absent, the nature of Ibn al-Ṭayyib's defense of the familial terms falls well within the parameters of topics discussed at the Muslim–Christian interface. His reference to Old Testament terminology is his own contribution.

If Ibn al-Ṭayyib is writing only in the context of sectarian Christian debates, why does he go to great lengths to establish the legitimacy of the biblical monikers? Such is hardly necessary when one is speaking to other Christians, regardless of their affiliation. What is at stake in this expression of his argument is the legitimacy of the biblical terminology. To establish this fact, he turns to the prophetic precedents to discover the use of the terms in the Old Testament. While his intended audience may not be Muslims, his formulation is keenly attuned to the theological rhetoric at the Muslim–Christian interface.

As mentioned previously, there may have been reason to avoid explicit mention of Islam in the resurgent Ashʿārī context of early eleventh-century Baghdad. What seems clear is that he is keen to establish the legitimacy of the biblical monikers in an Islamic context where they are under assault. In fact, one of the monikers of Christ – "Son" – is under attack while the other – "Word" – is affirmed in the Islamic milieu. His appeal to the Jewish and Christian Scriptures may have had minimal persuasive power vis-à-vis the growing consensus of scriptural corruption (*taḥrīf*) in the Islamic context. Nevertheless, the fact that Ibn al-Ṭayyib sought to establish the legitimacy of problematic terminology must indicate that he was aware of Islamic polemic and sought to establish a solid textual foundation for his church's confession.

3.5 Response of Ibn al-Ṭayyib to a Christological Question

Yet another quotation of Ibn al-Ṭayyib is found in Ibn al-ʿAssāl's *Summa of Religious Principles*, bāb 27, paragraphs 12 and 13.[101]

3.5.1 Description

The question concerns why the union happened with the hypostasis of the Son but not with that of the Father or Spirit. Ibn al-ʿAssāl lists this as a question raised by Abū ʿĪsā al-Warrāq. It is found in the first section of his *Refutation of the Uniting*.[102] A twofold response from Ibn ʿAdī is provided, after which comes Ibn al-Ṭayyib's response that the union took place with the hypostasis of the Son and not with the other hypostases (of the Trinity) because the Eternal can have contact (*waṣla*) with the created in that hypostasis only. He further explains that the hypostasis of the Father is the essence of the Creator with the property of paternity which is the entity (*maʿnā*) of intellect

101. Ibn al-ʿAssāl, *Majmūʿ uṣūl al-dīn*, 77–78.

102. Thomas, *Early Muslim Polemic*, 97.

(borrowing Ibn ʿAdī's terminology). It is impossible for the essence of the person born of Mary to be pure intellect. Furthermore, the hypostasis of the Spirit is the essence of the Creator with the entity of procession which is the Creator's self-intellection. It is also impossible for the person born of Mary to be the Creator's essence in self-intellection.[103] However, it is not aberrant that God have a person who knows him as he knows himself.[104] This is the property of filiation by which the Son is characterized so that he alone might be the Son.[105]

3.5.2 Interpretation and Analysis

Ibn al-ʿAssāl calls on the author for an explication of Ibn ʿAdī's response to Abū ʿĪsā al-Warrāq which precedes it. Ibn ʿAdī reckons that both Father and Spirit are prohibited from uniting with another hypostasis because the Father is pure intellect[106] while the Spirit is the object of pure intellect.[107] The Son, by contrast, is he who knows pure intellect.[108] Therefore, it is not prohibited for this knowing one to unite with another hypostasis. This is the argument of Ibn ʿAdī the Jacobite who understands the union differently from Ibn al-Ṭayyib.

Ibn al-Ṭayyib will carefully avoid claiming a union in the hypostases of the divine and human. Although one cannot be sure to what degree the miaphysite Ibn al-ʿAssāl might have edited Ibn al-Ṭayyib's formulation, enough remains of the work to see that the author carefully guards against a hypostatic union, urging that the union takes place in the property of filiation. He uses the term *waṣla* (connection), not *ittiḥād* (union), to depict what takes place between the divine hypostasis and the created one. He returns to his carefully crafted definition of the hypostasis as the essence of God taken with one of three properties (he has also used the term "attributes" in other writings) – paternity for the Father, procession for the Spirit and filiation for the Son. He agrees with Ibn ʿAdī that the person taken from Mary may be neither pure intellect (Father) nor self-intellection (Spirit). The formulation seen above – "it is not aberrant that God have a person who knows him as he knows himself" – raises a question as to why Ibn al-Ṭayyib here refers to the property of filiation as a "person." The author is referring to the human person taken from Mary. It is this person who has united with the Divine in the property of filiation.

103. ومحال ان يكون الشخص المأخوذ من مريم ذات البارئ معقولة نفسها...
Wa-maḥāl an yakūn al-shakhṣ al-ma'khūdh min Maryam dhāt al-bāri' ma'qūla nafsahā.

104. وليس بقبيح أن يوجد لله شخص عالم به كما هو عالم بنفسه
Wa laysa bi-qabīḥ an yūjad li-lāh shakhs 'ālim bi-hi kamā huwa 'ālim bi-nafsihi.

105. Ibn al-ʿAssāl, *Majmūʿ usūl al-dīn*, 77–78.

106. *al-'aql al-mujarrad* العقل المجرّد

107. *al-ma'qūl 'aqlan mujarradan* المعقول عقلًا مجردًا

108. *al-'āqil 'aqlan mujarradan* العاقل عقلًا مجردًا

Ibn al-Ṭayyib borrows from his predecessor in *Bayt al-Ḥikma* ("the House of Wisdom"), Ibn ʿAdī, to explicate the union while adding his own particular dyohypostatic understanding. The union does not take place in the hypostasis as Ibn ʿAdī suggested but in the property of filiation which is rightly attributed to both the human Jesus and the eternal Son. It is noteworthy that Ibn al-ʿAssāl calls on Ibn al-Ṭayyib to respond to one of the burning questions at the Muslim–Christian interface posed by the very able Muslim polemicist Abū ʿĪsā. I suggest that the compiler (Ibn al-ʿAssāl) saw the utility of Ibn al-Ṭayyib's theological formulation even if the latter made no explicit mention of Islam.

4. Conclusion: Ibn al-Ṭayyib: A Responsive Theologian in the Islamic Milieu

Throughout this research, I have sought to allow the theologians of the eleventh-century Church of the East to speak in their own terms. In terms of Christology there is no explicit evidence that Ibn al-Ṭayyib is seeking to engage a Muslim audience in his writing. However, his formulation bears the marks of an astute theologian attuned to the challenges of his context. As noted in chapter 3 regarding his Trinitarian formulation, his Christology reverberates with the Muslim milieu in which he lives and works. A string of an instrument, though unplucked, will assimilate sound waves, resonating at the same frequency of a played note from another instrument. Similarly, the theologian reverberates in his Islamic milieu and responds to the pertinent issues raised therein. As the most prominent philosopher/theologian of the renowned *Bayt al-Ḥikma* of Baghdad, he is not isolated from the intellectual currents of his day. He writes not as a polemicist but as a Christian intellectual and pastor, with an eye to reinforcing the tradition handed to him through the Eastern fathers, derived from his sacred scriptures. As his formulation reverberates in the sectarian milieu of Baghdad, Ibn al-Ṭayyib is not unaware of conversions and migrations that are impacting his ecclesial community.[109] He writes to reinforce his Christian confession in an Islamic milieu which has already begun to witness the defection of many from the Church of the East.

This contextual reverberation is discerned in several aspects of Ibn al-Ṭayyib's formulation. First, he locates the motivation for the incarnation in the magnanimous character of God. Although the doctrine is rationally defensible, the necessity of the incarnation is not derived through human reason, but by understanding the desperate plight of mankind and the magnanimous nature of God who acts to secure salvation for his creation. In this, the author is attuned to his Church of the East forebear

109. Wilmshurst, *Martyred Church*, 190.

and apologist ʿAmmār al-Baṣrī, who also viewed the incarnation as the pinnacle of God's gracious interaction with mankind. The prophetic message was ineffectual to secure such salvation. The assertion comes from the biblical record but also carries an implicit critique of Islam's offer of a new revelation which is nothing more than a prophetic word. The incarnation proffers a reconciliation or union of humanity with their Creator. God graciously initiates the union of the eternal Word with the man born of Mary to heal the alienation caused by rebellion.

A second note reverberated by Ibn al-Ṭayyib is his careful avoidance of theopaschitism – the attribution of human suffering and pain to the divine substance. The shielding of the divine substance and hypostasis from the vicissitudes of humanity established this claim. The Church of the East's avoidance of theopaschitism, though unconvincing for Muslim polemicists, was nevertheless a substantive defense against the charge of associating the created with the Creator (*al-shirk*). Adherents of Chalcedon holding to a hypostatic union of the divine and human in Christ could not make as strong an argument for the deity's disassociation from all human contingencies. Ibn al-Ṭayyib's contemporary Iliyyā of Nisibis would wield it effectively to secure his monotheist confession before a Muslim Vizier. Accordingly, Ibn al-Ṭayyib admits the legitimacy of the transfer of attributes but will only consent to the transfer of the divine attribute to the human substance. It is a one-way *communicatio idiomatum* the purpose of which must never trespass into the denigration of the divine but must remain in the realm of the elevation of humanity.

Related to this concept is the location of the union, not in the hypostasis, but in the property of filiation. The distinction, pedantic perhaps to modern ears, allows the author to avoid the attribution of human pain to the divine substance. The imagination need not be overly pressed to perceive that a clear statement of the absence of suffering and pain in the divine substance must have served the Church of the East constituency well in an Islamic milieu where *tawḥīd* had become the intellectual standard-bearer. To speak of the suffering or even death of God in such a milieu would entail disastrous consequences of a religious, social and economic nature. Beaumont has suggested of ʿAmmār al-Baṣrī that one may almost detect a note of thanks to Islam for the opportunity to vindicate his anathematized Nestorian Christology. He appealed to Muslims to substantiate his claim that only the Church of the East had rightly understood the nature of the union.[110] This was not mere theological pragmatism as the Church of the East theologians were seeking to fend off the charge of *shirk*. Indeed, the plant of dyohypostatic Christology had germinated for centuries prior to the advent of Islam in the Antiochene theological tradition. Still, the strident *tawḥīd* of Islam reacted

110. Beaumont, "ʿAmmar al-Basri on the Incarnation," 58; *Christology in Dialogue with Muslims*, 102.

against the doctrine of a divine–human Christ, provoking a more careful definition of dyohypostatic Christology. The theologians felt their Christology did not contravene *tawḥīd*, unlike both Jacobite miaphysitism and the hypostatic union of Chalcedon.

A third resonating note is Ibn al-Ṭayyib's discerning of Christian monikers for the Trinitarian persons in the Scriptures of the Old Testament. He labors to demonstrate that both "word" and "Son" – the former embraced by Islam and the latter eschewed – have a long history of textual legitimacy. In doing so, he is building upon the foundation laid by his Church of the East predecessor ʿAmmār al-Basrī. In the Islamic milieu, where the Qur'ān claims to confirm the precedent revelation, the author is placing a protective hedge around his Christian flock. Indeed, the period under consideration was characterized by the rising tide of the charge of textual corruption. To overthrow Christ's filiation and displace the doctrine enshrined in the Church of the East's formulation, Muslims must demonstrate the fallacy of the entire Judeo-Christian tradition. Ibn al-Ṭayyib's formulation, though not a polemical *tour de force*, was nonetheless a stabilizing force for his Christian constituency.

Finally, Ibn al-Ṭayyib joined his voice to others at the Muslim–Christian interface who had sought a more inclusive understanding of *tawḥīd*. His enumeration of Ibn ʿAdī's twelve categories of "the one" was an appeal to broaden the prevailing monadic rigidity of the *tawḥīd* concept as formulated by the *mutakallimūn*. That God was one in view of his substance, and plural in view of his attributes, demonstrated that the Christian formulation adhered to the formal rules of logic. Ibn al-Ṭayyib's enumeration of the twelve categories precedes his description of the union of humanity and divinity in Christ. The fact of God's being one did not preclude his union with the man born of Mary as a union in the property of filiation.

The resonance of a stringed instrument provides a means of understanding Ibn al-Ṭayyib's role vis-à-vis the Islamic context. A second analogy, that of moorings, provides another angle of consideration. The author rarely gives indication of entering polemics. The absence of direct references to Islam is somewhat surprising given the prevalence of Islam in eleventh-century Baghdad. On the other hand, the fruitless outcome of endless disputation may have led him to eschew polemic engagement.[111] He sought to secure his Church of the East constituency by clarifying the terms of the union, by demonstrating the rationale of its doctrine and by featuring the distinctive view of God (theology proper) as passed down to him by his theological forebears. The past debates of the early centuries of Muslim–Christian interaction in the Abbasid period had become a gathering storm that had significantly beaten down the Syriac and Arabic-speaking Christians of the East. Ibn al-Ṭayyib's abjuring of polemics

111. See the argument that Christian intellectuals of Baghdad were declining to enter the fray of public polemical debate in chapter 3, section 4.2.3.

is understandable, even pragmatic, given the acerbic nature of past exchanges. His penchant is to strengthen the Christian consensus around its distinct doctrine. He wishes to secure the moorings of the Church of the East in the midst of the rising storm incited by the *mutakallimūn* and evidenced by the intellectual, political and social dominance of Islam. Where *tawḥīd* has become the only plausible understanding of deity, Ibn al-Ṭayyib is seeking to secure the confession of his church before a tumultuous Muslim–Christian interface.

I conclude that Ibn al-Ṭayyib formulates his Christology as a responsive theologian laboring in an Islamic milieu. His burden is not to prove Christ's divinity to a Muslim readership but to reinforce the doctrine within his ecclesial family as it has come under polemical bombardment from without. He wants to show potential deserters to Islam that the Christian doctrine is rational. His formulation aligns carefully with his Church of the East forebears. Although he seeks to prove his dyohypostatic position over against Chalcedon and Jacobite Christology, he also carefully delineates the nature of the difference between them as being only in the manner of the union, not the fact of it. The union of the divine and human in Christ is limited to the property of filiation and does not extend to the substance or hypostasis of the divinity or humanity. In this way, a curtain is drawn between the divine substance and the experience of human contingencies – pain, suffering and the like. In the concluding chapter, I will have more to say about the plausibility of this imposed veil between the human and the divine in dyohypostatic Christology, but in this present chapter, I have attempted to highlight the role and value of Ibn al-Ṭayyib's formulation in his Islamic milieu.

6

Unblemished Deity Incarnate

The Christological Formulation of Iliyyā of Nisibis

1. Introduction

In his *Sessions*, the Church of the East Bishop Iliyyā of Nisibis enters into dialogue with Abū al-Qāsim al-Maghribī, a Vizier of the Marwanid dynasty of Diyārbakīr (eastern Turkey and western Syria today).[1] In *The Sessions*, the Bishop responds directly to Abū al-Qasim's objections in the area of Christology. Iliyyā's profound understanding of Islamic thought enables him to present his christological views avoiding the sting of the Islamic accusation of *shirk* (the association of the created with the Divine – idolatry) which was being pressed upon Christians by Muslim polemicists. The question of the belief in one God without association with created beings was vital theologically but also entailed practical implications in the social and economic realms. Iliyyā espouses *tawḥīd* (the unity of deity) on behalf of his Christian community while distancing himself from the accusation of *shirk*.

Iliyyā adhered to the Church of the East dyohypostatic[2] christological formulation while extending its application to its outermost boundary to create common ground with

1. Concerning questions on the historicity of Abū al-Qāsim and *The Sessions*, see chapter 4, 2.2. For biographical information on Abū al-Qāsim, see chapter 2, 2.2.2.

2. The normal nomenclature is "dyophysite" but this term does not adequately capture the distinctive doctrine of the Church of the East. Both the Byzantines and the Church of the East held to a duality of natures (*physeis*) in Christ. Only the Church of the East held to a duality of hypostases, thus "dyohypostatic." See the discussion of the dissension of the Church of the East in matters of Christology in chapter 5, section 2.2.

his Muslim interlocutor. His formulation is a Christian theological response uniquely shaped by the surrounding Muslim milieu – an attempt to preserve an unblemished deity in the incarnate Christ while adapting to the prevailing intellectual environment molded by *tawḥīd*. This chapter examines evidence for this claim in recurrent aspects of Iliyyā's formulation, including (1) the Bishop's christological nomenclature which aligned with the non-communication of the attributes between Christ's deity and humanity; (2) Iliyyā's dyohypostatic analogies of the "indwelling" and the "union"; (3) the Bishop's implicit plea for social inclusion of his Christian constituency in the fold of *tawḥīd*; (4) his rhetorical strategy; and (5) Iliyyā's identifying the locus of the union in the divine will (as opposed to the substance or hypostasis).

I will examine four documentary sources which form the corpus of Iliyyā's Christology. Each will be described and analyzed in the attempt to understand the content (what does the author espouse?) and motivation (why does the author focus on particular aspects?).

2. Session 1

2.1 Session 1: Documents

Iliyyā deals with Abū al-Qāsim's understanding of Christology briefly in Session 1 and more extensively in Session 2 (S1 and S2). Samir's critical edition[3] will serve as the basis of my analysis of Session 1 although the manuscripts Vatican Arabe 143[4] and Huntington 240[5] have been consulted for corroboration of the critical edition. The paraphrased description below adheres closely to the logical flow of the Session, quoting sections which I deem to be critical. The numbers correspond to Samir's edition.

2.2 Session 1: Description

The entirety of Session 1 has been taken up with the question of the Trinity – the Vizier's first objection in the Sessions. Near the end of Session 1, the Vizier returns to the second of his reasons for skepticism of Christian *tawḥīd*: "the man born of Mary is an eternal Lord, Creator, uncreated, begotten of God before the ages" (204). The two objections were introduced in verses 31 and 32, and after a lengthy exchange on the first objection, the Vizier now recalls the second. Abū al-Qāsim will pursue his questions relative to Christology in Session 2; therefore, this treatment of Session 1

3. Samir, "Entretien d'Elie de Nisibe," 203–238.
4. al-Niṣībīn, *Kitāb al-majālis* (Vat. Arabe 143).
5. al-Niṣībīn, *Kitāb al-majālis* (Huntington 240).

is a general introduction to Iliyyā's Christology with further elaboration coming in the following Session.

2.2.1 Christological Nomenclature

The Bishop denies Abū al-Qāsim's assertion: "We do not believe, may God support the Vizier, that the man born of Mary was eternal, Creator, uncreated, nor that he was begotten of God before the ages. Rather we believe him to be created, caused, indistinguishable from other people in relation to substance, except that he knew no sin" (205–206). In response, the Vizier queries the Bishop concerning his adherence to the Nicene Creed, referring to it as the "pledge of the three hundred and eighteen."[6] Iliyyā is able to affirm, "we accept it as we accept the gospel" (208). The Vizier's confusion is evident as he cites the precise wording of the creed: "We believe . . . in one Lord Īshūʿ al-Masīḥ the only Son of God, the firstborn of all creation, begotten of his Father before the ages, uncreated, very God of very God, the son of his Father's substance" (210–211). The Bishop solemnly affirms his community's adherence to the creed, which exacerbates the Vizier's confusion: "then you are obliged to affirm that Īshūʿ (who for you is the man born of Mary) is the true and eternal God, begotten of his Father before the ages, uncreated" (213–214). The Bishop protests that he is under no such obligation.

The following paragraphs lay out the Bishop's semantic clarification around the titles given to Christ. Iliyyā's sharp distinction between the "man born of Mary" (whom he refers to as "Jesus" [*Īshūʿ*]) and the "Lord" preserves the distinction of the hypostases. The human name *Īshūʿ* attaches to the human hypostasis – the man born of Mary. By contrast, the divine moniker "Lord" is the eternal and uncreated one. Iliyyā acknowledges that some degree of interchange between the two titles cannot be avoided due to the nature of the union (218). Nevertheless, in his theological lexicon, "Jesus" connotes the human hypostasis while "Lord" connotes the Divine. "Christ" connotes the two meanings together (219). Accordingly, the descriptors of divinity cited above in the Nicene Creed follow and modify "Lord" but not "Jesus," according to the Bishop (222–225).[7]

6. The Council of Nicea is referred to as "the pledge [*amāna*] written and recorded by the three hundred and eighteen," a reference to the number of bishops in attendance at Nicea.

7. While this may appear clear to the Bishop, the Arab Muslim reader can be forgiven for not seeing it so clearly. The moniker "Christ" (*al-masīḥ*) follows the given name "Jesus" (*yasūʿ*) and thus stands in proximity to the following descriptors: "the only Son of God, born of the Father from all eternity, God of God, light of light, true God of true God, begotten not made."

إبن الله الوحيد. المولود من الآب قبل كل الدهور إله من إله. نور من نور. إله حق من إله حق. مولود غير مخلوق. ذو جوهر واحد مع الآب

(Grudem, *bi-mātha yufakir al-injīliyūn*, 282).

2.2.2 Guarding the Beatific Vision

Iliyyā supports his point by referring to the official Church of the East ruling relative to the beatific vision – the possibility of seeing the divine either in the mind or by physical vision. The synod was convened in response to a schism that arose during the time of Harūn al-Rashīd. The Catholicos Timothy gathered sixteen metropolitans, more than thirty bishops and many monks and scholars for the occasion. In this council the church anathematized anyone who claimed that the man Jesus had seen the "Lord" (who is the eternal Word) whether by physical vision or mental perception (229–231). To be precise, the prohibition of the beatific vision was not a claim that Jesus the man had not seen the Father, although doubtless that would be true in the Bishop's conception. Rather, the synod ruled that the eternal Word who was united with the human Jesus had never been seen by him. In this way, Iliyyā states that the assembly "upheld adherence to the divine law and the non-mitigation[8] of divinity [that would result from] association [*yushrikahu*] of his attributes of essence [*ṣifātihi al-dhātiyya*] with created beings" (232–233).

Iliyyā stresses that though Christians view the human Jesus as the most honorable of creation, nevertheless he is not given license to have seen the divine substance although united with him. This synodical declaration upholds Iliyyā's contention of the "non-mitigation [*tanzīh*] of the divine substance, may his name [*dhikruhu*] be exalted!" (236). Having now established the unassailable divine unity of his community, Iliyyā rhetorically asks, "How then do they accuse them of associating[9] with the divine substance some other substance, equal to it in substantiality?" (237). Indeed, if this were the only proof that Christians hold to divine unity, it would be sufficient (238).

The Session concludes as the call to prayer sounds. The Vizier dismisses his interlocutor stating that he would like to summon him again when his duties permit.

2.3 *Session 1: Analysis*

In this section of Session 1 the reader is treated to Iliyyā's understanding of his church's christological implications at the Muslim–Christian interface. Iliyyā refuses to describe the humanity of Christ with the attributes of divinity, aligning with the historic restraint to speak of the *communicatio idiomatum* in the Church of the East.[10] This non-reciprocity of the communication of the attributes was observed in Ibn

8. *Tanzīh* تنزيه
9. *Yushrikū* يشركوا
10. Grillmeier, *Christ in Christian Tradition*, 370.

al-Ṭayyib's Christology, although there, reciprocity was technically correct but not desirable as it led to the denigration of divinity.[11]

Iliyyā's insistence on the non-mitigation of the divinity of Christ was upheld by his theological forebears who had come to apply divine traits to the divinity of Christ and human traits to the humanity only as upheld by the synodical declaration. By using a human title for Christ and applying divine descriptors thereto, Abū al-Qāsim has displayed a misunderstanding of the Christian tenet as adhered to by the Church of the East. The Bishop patiently unveils the Church of the East's christological nomenclature,[12] seizing upon the Vizier's question regarding Christian adherence to the Nicene formulation. The christological nomenclature leads the argument into the non-communication of the attributes which Iliyyā seals with his discussion of the synodical prohibition of ascribing the beatific vision to the man Jesus. The entire discussion is meant to buttress the claim of Christian *tawḥīd* against a backdrop of Islamic insistence on God's unicity as the proper standard for theology (*kalām*).

Iliyyā was not the first to put forward this understanding of the beatific vision. ʿAmmār al-Baṣrī had declared nearly two centuries earlier that no human could see the divine essence, though he also understood the incarnation to be God's response to the human need to see the divine, making himself visible in the human person Jesus.[13] Iliyyā went further by substantiating the claim through an official declaration of the Church.[14] The Church of the East had gradually developed the reflex of attributing human attributes to the man Jesus while divine attributes would be attributed to the eternal Word. Iliyyā's penchant to draw a defined line between the two hypostases was consistent with the Church of the East's thought although his association of it with specific titles of Christ is unexpected for his interlocutor.[15]

Islam had its own debate around the issue of the beatific vision flowing from qur'ānic declarations such as Q75:22–23[16] and Q6:103.[17] The Ashʿarī view of the beatific vision diverges from the Muʿtazilī view. Al-Ashʿarī himself insisted that in the

---

11. The tendency can also be observed in the Church of the East apologist ʿAmmār al-Baṣrī (Hayek, "ʿAmmār al Baṣrī," 81). When theologians of the East spoke of the communication of the attributes, it was defined differently as the close moral union between Christ and God (Maas, "Communicatio Idiomatum").

12. Timothy I provides a detailed list of the titles of Christ with their meanings: "'God' refers to divine nature, 'Word' to divine hypostasis, 'Son' to person, 'man' to soul and body, 'flesh' to union of potential elements, 'Christ' not to nature and hypostasis but to the operations of natures, 'Jesus' to human nature, 'Immanuel' and 'Son of man' to both divinity and humanity" (Rissanen, *Theological Encounter*, 191).

13. Landron, *Chrétiens et musulmans en Irak*, 208.

14. Mikhail, "ʿAmmār al-Basrī's Kitāb al-Burhān," 249.

15. Landron, *Chrétiens et musulmans en Irak*, 201–202.

16. "[Some] faces, that Day, will be radiant, looking at their Lord" (Q75:22–23).

17. "Vision perceives Him not, but He perceives [all] vision, and He is the Subtle, the Acquainted" (Q6:103).

afterlife, God will be seen by the resurrected faithful "as the moon is seen on the night when it is full."[18] A Ḥanbalī creed is of the same opinion.[19] The Muʿtazilīs, holding staunchly to God's transcendence, viewed all anthropomorphisms as metaphorical. God's hand, eyes, and so on, depict his attributes but must never be understood in a corporeal sense. By the same token, God cannot be seen as he is not materially composed.[20] The Shīʿites also held that the vision of God was only metaphorical, not literal.[21] Iliyyā was wading into an inter-Muslim debate, creating commonality with his Shīʿite interlocutor by demonstrating that Christians were of the same persuasion. By preserving the distinction of the hypostases expressed in the non-communication of the attributes, Iliyyā is convinced that he is avoiding the unpardonable transgression of Islam (*shirk*) while maintaining a cardinal tenet for both Muslims and Christians – the transcendence (*al-tanzīh*) of the Divine substance. The shielding of Jesus from the beatific vision demonstrates the Bishop's tenacity in holding to the absolute transcendence of the eternal Word although claiming that it united with the human Jesus. The substance of the eternal Word remains in its state of *tanzīh* – literally, "unblemished." Iliyyā concludes by forcefully rejecting the accusation of *shirk*, revealing his determination to maintain *tawḥīd* status for his Christian constituency.

The motivation behind the Bishop's argument can be perceived from the Islamic vocabulary which reveals Iliyyā's awareness of his Muslim milieu. Throughout the Abbasid period, Muslims were increasingly taking the Christian doctrines of the Trinity and Christ's divinity as prime examples of the violation of Islamic *tawḥīd*.[22] Though primitive Islam had granted the status of *ahl al-kitāb* (people of the book) to both Jews and Christians, the anti-Christian polemic of the Abbasid period had become deeply entrenched such that renowned Muslim apologists tended to place Christian dogma in the category of *kufr* (unbelief).[23] Accordingly, Christian theologians were now

18. Watt, *Islamic Creeds*, 43; Wensinck, *Muslim Creed*, 88–89.

19. Renard, *Islamic Theological Themes*, 109.

20. Gimaret, "Mu'tazila," 788–789.

21. Gimaret, "Ru'yat Allāh," 649; Mikhail, "ʿAmmār al-Basrī's Kitāb al-Burhān," 226–227. Verses referring to the vision of deity in the Qur'ān are normally understood not to refer to the direct vision of God, but to beholding his reward. E.g. Q75:22–23, "Faces on that day shall be bright, gazing on their Lord," is understood to mean "(the faces) will be lighted up (*mushriqa*), looking at their Lord's reward" (Fyzee, *Shi'ite Creed*, 28).

22. I have alluded to the fact that Abū al-Qāsim's ready assent to Christian *tawḥīd* suggests to some that the documents are a fabrication and cannot represent a historical meeting between the two men. In chapter 4, 2.2, I have offered aspects of the exchange which suggest the historical reliability of *The Sessions.* The exchange is indeed uncharacteristic of medieval Muslim–Christian relations; nevertheless the looming topic of the Sessions – *tawḥīd* – is the standard for true speech of God (*kalām*) throughout the medieval period.

23. Note that this is Abū al-Qāsim's dilemma with which he opens the Sessions. He has come to doubt the unbelief (*kufr*) of the Christians due to a wondrous sign which took place (Samir, "Entretien d'Elie de Nisibe," 51). I infer that Abū Qāsim's doubt was troubling him, due to the growing consensus

hard pressed to validate their monotheism. The Bishop is attempting to authenticate the *tawḥīd* of his Christian constituency, referring repeatedly to the "non-mitigation" (*tanzīh*) of divinity as well as to the aversion to "associating" (*shirk*) created beings with the uncreated Lord. His defense of Christian *tawḥīd* is laden with key references to Muslim lexical elements which together build an impregnable bulwark against the charge of *shirk*.

The growing contention of the polemicists was reason enough for Iliyyā to vigorously assert Christian monotheism.[24] However, the Sessions served equally important purposes for his Christian community. They fit into the genre which has been named "the Monk in the Emir's *majlis*."[25] From the Christian side, the *majālis* (sessions) were meant to inform and entertain. Christian spokesmen were often depicted as being in command of the situation, possessing an unanticipated level of knowledge and skill to outwit their Muslim overlords although the questions sometimes originated from Christian editors of these dialogues rather than Muslim officials. Nevertheless, the Christians' insightful responses served to validate the community's existence, strengthening its confessional resolve, despite the spread of Islam in regions that were once dominated by the Christian faith. This high-level dialogue was also a formal representation of the Christian community to the Muslim governing official which could issue in social and legal implications for the Christian community. *The Sessions* includes indicators that such issues were at stake, but a further exploration of the content of Session 2 is necessary before returning to this question in the conclusion below.

3. Session 2

3.1 Session 2: Documents

As Louis Cheikho's version of Session 2[26] is incomplete, I refer to the manuscripts Huntington 240 and Vatican Arabe 143 which contain two lengthy sections omitted by Cheikho. It is the latter of the two sections which adds significant elaboration to Iliyyā's understanding of Nestorian Christology. This section is found on folios 42r4

---

of *kufr* attributed to the Christians.

24. In the Muslim–Christian discourse of the period, the debate over the communication of the human attribute to the divine crystallized around the title "servant" as applied to Christ. The Caliph Al-Mahdī (781/165) could not understand why Christ was referred to as a "servant" if he was in fact divine. In response, the Church of the East Catholicos Timothy I likened Christ's divine nature to the royal aspect of the Caliph's own son, fully royal and yet awaiting the full expression of his glory in his eventual coronation.

25. Griffith, "Monk in the Emir's Majlis."

26. Cheikho, "Majalis Iliyya mutran Nasibin," 112–117.

to 49r7[27] of Vatican Arabe 143[28] and folios 170v13 to 172v5 of Huntington 240.[29] The numbering of the following description of Session 2 corresponds to the folio numbers of Vatican Arabe 143 by reason of its anteriority to Huntington 240.

While only the final section of Session 1 deals with Christology, the entirety of Session 2 is dedicated to Abū al-Qāsim's significant questions on the issue of "the indwelling" and "the union," by which is meant the union of the divine and human in Christ. Due to the length of this Session, my description below must include some summarization though I adhere closely to the flow of the argument with translations of key words and phrases.

3.2 Session 2: Description

3.2.1 The Objection of Abū al-Qāsim

After cordial greetings, the Vizier began to inquire about a lingering doubt concerning the unity (*tawḥīd*) of the Christians as a result of his ruminations on the previous dialogue. He asks Iliyyā if it is correct that Christians speak of the indwelling.[30] The Bishop replies that the Nestorians do so, whereas the Jacobites and Melkites deny it. The Vizier's concern is the Christian claim that God Most High indwells[31] the man born of Mary, a tenet which contradicts *tawḥīd*. The Christians must know that God cannot indwell him as an accident[32] indwells a substance, for that would render God an accident. Nor can he indwell him as a body within a body, for that implies God is a material body. Both concepts are blatant unbelief.[33] Similarly, "if the entirety of the substance indwelt the man born of Mary then God was contained. If only a part of God indwelt him, then God was divided and both concepts are blatant unbelief" (29r4–30v1).

3.2.2 Definition of "the Indwelling" (*al-ḥulūl*)

In response, Iliyyā assures the Vizier that none of the views he has suggested are acceptable to Christians for precisely the reasons he has stated. Rather the indwelling

27. The folio number is followed by "r" or "v" (recto or verso) and the number that follows is the line on which the section begins or ends.

28. al-Niṣībīn, *Kitāb al-majālis* (Vat. Arabe 143).

29. al-Niṣībīn, *Kitāb al-majālis* (Huntington 240). Paris Arabe 206 also contains S2 and was consulted for this research, though Vatican Arabe 143 was deemed to be more reliable (al-Niṣībīn, *al-majlis al-thānī*).

30. *ḥulūl* حلول

31. *ḥall fī* حلّ في

32. *'arḍ* عرض

33. *Kufr* كُفر

of God in Christ is one of dignity, assent and will[34] and not the indwelling of the essence and substance. The claim is illustrated by the fact that God's essence and substance are omnipresent but are said to indwell some individuals and places but not others through the indwelling of "dignity, assent and will" (30v1–31r7).

Abū al-Qāsim's reply points to a perceived weakness in the Bishop's response: "If the Creator indwelt the man [Jesus] by means of dignity, assent and will as he also indwelt the rightly guided prophets, there is nothing that distinguishes him from other prophets. Therefore, there is no difference between them and no reason to prefer him over the other prophets" (31r7–31v4).

3.2.2.1 A Semantic Clarification

The Bishop contends that the word "indwell" is a general word that can apply to different classes of things just as the word "existent" can be used of the Creator, human beings, the earth, fire, stone and other existent things. The word "animal" applies to man, ox and donkey. As human beings do not rival God for their having the same descriptor as him (existent), so the other prophets cannot rival Christ for their having the same descriptor as him (indwelling). A further illustration indicates that both Christ and his disciples were called "prophets" yet the latter were not equal to the former. Christ declared he was "ascending to my Father and your Father, to my God and your God. Yet the disciples are not equal to him in filiation. In the same way, it is said that Allāh indwelt him as he indwelt the prophets without rendering him equal to the prophets in indwelling" (31v4–33r3).

3.2.2.2 Reasons for the Superiority of Christ's Indwelling

Continuing his argument, Iliyyā enumerates reasons for the non-equality of the indwelling of prophets with that of Christ. First, the "eternal Son," who is the Word, united with him to become one "Christ"[35] (as Christians designate him) or "Word of God" (as Muslims designate him). No other prophet among Christians or Muslims is referred to by this title, demonstrating the uniqueness of Christ's indwelling. Second, he was not born through physical procreation[36] nor did he physically procreate. Third, he performed miracles which no other prophet performed. Fourth, God raised him to paradise[37] and he is alive there today, which is not true of any other prophet. Fifth, he knew no sin whether in thought, word or deed, and the Scripture does not testify to the sinlessness of any other prophet (33r3–34r3).

---

34. Dignity (*waqār* وقار), assent (*riḍā* رضا) and will (*mashī'a* مشيئة).

35. أنّ الإبن الأزلي الذي هو الكلمة اتّحدّ معه فصار ومسيحاً واحداً *anna al-ibn al-azalī aladhī huwwa al-kalima ittaḥda ma'hu fa-ṣāra masīḥan wāḥidan.*

36. *al-jamā'* الجماع

37. *al-samā'* السماء

3.2.2.3 Abu al-Qāsim Objects

Abū al-Qāsim objects that these descriptors are found in all the prophets. Furthermore, Muslims refer to Christ as "the Word of God because he was created by a command of God as was true of the creation of all things: He said to it, 'be,' and it was." The Bishop's claim that Christ was born without physical procreation is also true of Adam. The assertion that Christ did not experience sexual relations is also true of Yaḥyā Ibn Zakariyyā (John the Baptist). With regard to Christ's miraculous signs, Abū al-Qāsim replies that Christ performed no miraculous sign that Moses did not also perform. Christ's being raised to paradise was also true of Idrīs (Enoch). "He knew no sin, but other prophets were also immune to sin."[38] For the Vizier, these considerations indicate the equality of the aforementioned prophets with Christ in their being indwelt, and therefore Christ is not to be preferred above them (34r3–35r3).

3.2.2.4 Iliyyā Explicates Christ's Superior Indwelling

Iliyyā exploits the Vizier's assertions, taking the same prophets to display Christ's uniqueness and superiority over each one. Whereas each of these prophets was given a particular virtue, Christ gathers all the virtues of Adam, Yaḥyā, Moses and Idrīs into one person. The Bishop suggests this fact alone indicates that the indwelling of God in Christ is complete whereas it is incomplete in other prophets (35r3–36r1).

The Bishop proceeds to the issue of Christ's title "Word of God," stating that if the meaning is merely that he was created by God's command then no distinction is afforded Christ, as all things, animate and inanimate, were created by the divine command. But the title is given to Christ and none other before or after. Therefore, it must imply a unique distinction whereby the eternal Word united with Christ, "as the body is referred to as 'speaking' by virtue of its unity with the speaking soul" (36r2–36v3).

Iliyyā returns to Abū al-Qāsim's assertion of Christ's equality with other prophets. Adam's creation without sexual union is in no way superior to the birth of the first donkey, horse or bull. Adam was created when there were neither male nor female parents available to give birth. Christ's being born of Mary, on the contrary, happened at a time when human procreation was ubiquitous, indicating the superior nature of his indwelling. Adam transgressed God's command and was banished from the garden whereas Christ was raised to heaven. Adam was promised toil, suffering, hunger and fatigue, ultimately returning to the dust. The man born of Mary was honored and exalted. He was given the most honorable names and his followers were promised the blessings of paradise. Iliyyā concludes that, given this evidence, Christ must not be made equal to Adam though they are of the same human substance (36v4–38r7).

---

38. *ma'ṣūmīn* معصومين

The Bishop proceeds to the assertion that Yaḥyā Ibn Zakariyyā (John the Baptist) is equal to Christ in indwelling as both prophets abstained from sexual relations. He concedes that many have abstained for reasons of religion and nature. Nevertheless, Christ is unique among the prophets by combining both Adam's particularity – birth without human parentage – and Yaḥyā's – abstaining from sexual relations (38v1–39r3). Furthermore, Moses's equality is invalid as none of his predecessors prophesied his coming. Moreover, his miracles before Pharaoh were not spontaneous but given by God's command or as a result of intercession. His sin near the end of his life resulted in his being prohibited from entering the land of promise despite his pleading and penance. Christ, on the other hand, was prophesied of two thousand years prior to his coming, being designated "the coming one," "the sovereign one" and "the hope of the nations." His miraculous signs were given spontaneously and with serene composure. The dead he resurrected. The bowed-down he made upright. The leper he cleansed. The sick he healed. To the blind he restored sight. Satan was cast out of men. The tempest was calmed. Even the qur'ānic miracles find their way into the Bishop's litany: speaking while still an infant in the cradle and giving life to clay birds formed by his own hand by breathing on them (Q5:110). How then, the Bishop asks, do Muslims compare Christ's miraculous works with those of Moses (39r4–40v1)?

Idrīs (Enoch) must not be made equal to Christ. The gospel does not indicate that he is in paradise[39] and the Qur'ān only states that he is in an elevated place (Q19:57). Christ, on the other hand, was raised to the most elevated place[40] as the Qur'ān also testifies: "[Mention] when Allāh said, 'O Jesus, indeed I will take you[41] and raise you to Myself and purify you from those who disbelieve and make those who follow you [in submission to Allāh alone] superior to those who disbelieve until the Day of Resurrection'" (Q3:55). This indicates that Christ was raised to the highest elevation and exaltation, demonstrating that he must not be compared with Idrīs (40v2–41v7).

The Bishop points out that sins of omission or commission[42] can be committed in thought, word or deed and the Scriptures do not testify that the former prophets were free of such sins (he has already demonstrated the sin of Moses and Adam). Christ, on the other hand, was free from sin in thought, word and deed as the gospel indicates, as did the prophets who foresaw his coming. In conclusion, the Bishop attests that "the man born of Mary united with the eternal Son who is the Word and

39. Gen 5:24 states cryptically: "Enoch walked with God, and he was not, for God took him." Heb 11:5 adds: "By faith Enoch was taken up so that he should not see death, and he was not found, because God had taken him. Now before he was taken he was commended as having pleased God."

40. Acts 2:33; 5:31; Eph 1:20; Phil 2:9; 1 Pet 3:22.

41. *Mutawaffīka* متوفيك

42. Omission: *sahū* سهو and commission: *ghalaṭ* غلط

became the one Christ which is not true of other prophets and saints. Moreover, the virtue of [his] indwelling is distinct from theirs" (41v1–42v4).[43]

3.2.2.5 Christ's Indwelling: Divine Will Apart from Essence

The Vizier interjects a new question: "How is your claim reasonable that the will of God apart from his essence indwelt the man [Jesus]? And how is it correct that the will acts apart from the essence?" Iliyyā responds: "And how is the statement of all jurisprudents reasonable: that God created the world by [his] will without movement of the essence?" That would be to say that the act of creation was executed through the divine will without reference to the essence. In the same way, by saying that God indwelt the man born of Mary, Christians realized that the indwelling was accomplished by the divine will and not the divine essence. The Vizier contends that the Christian tenet of the indwelling of Christ by dignity, assent and will has misled hearers into the belief of indwelling of the divine substance in the human body such that a proper belief has been transformed into a reprehensible one. The Bishop rejoins that the Muslim tenet of God's indivisibility[44] risks being misconstrued due to the qur'ānic affirmation that God is "seated on a throne." God's essence is not limited to a particular place though the hearers may indeed understand God to be seated as a human being. The Vizier replies that such expressions in the Qur'ān must be understood metaphorically[45] and are intended to magnify the throne from which God's commands are given. The Bishop, in turn, replies that Christians who speak of Christ's indwelling by divinity must be understood to mean the indwelling of dignity, assent and will. If Christians are obliged to hold to the literal understanding of the indwelling (i.e. that God's essence indwells a human body), Muslims also must adhere to God's corporeality and limitation to a particular place (42r5–45v2).

3.2.3 Jacobite and Melkite Views of "the Indwelling" (*al-ḥulūl*)

At the end of the Bishop's lengthy exposition of Christ's superiority, the Vizier returns to ask why the other Christian sects do not have the same view of the indwelling. Iliyyā's response is that they have a different belief concerning Christ. The Melkites perceive two substances and one hypostasis, while the Jacobites hold to one substance and hypostasis. This obliges them to adhere to a natural union[46] like that of the "soul and body" and a composite union[47] like that of iron and wood in the composition of

43. This is where Cheikho's version of S2 ends (Cheikho, "Majalis Iliyya mutran Nasibin"). It omits significant sections found in Huntington 240 and Vatican Arabe 143.

44. *lā yatajazzā wa-la yataba''aḍ* لا يتجزّى ولا يتبعّض

45. *ghayr ẓāhir* غير ظاهر

46. *ittiḥād ṭabī'ī* إتّحاد طبيعي

47. *al-tarkīb* التركيب

a door or chair, or the union of mixture or intermingling.[48] According to the Bishop, this leads the Melkites and Jacobites into disbelief of the indwelling. Their position is impossible to hold rationally and impractical in terms of jurisprudence (45v2–46r7).

3.2.4 Definition of "the Union" (*al-ittiḥād*)

The other major section of Session 2 defines and clarifies "the union" through three key terms: "The Word united with the man born of Mary in will, cleaving and aspect so as to become one Christ and one Son." The Bishop provides one illustration of each term with little further elucidation. The union of will is perceived by the union of two or more individuals in will though they are differentiated in essence and personhood. The union of will is illustrated by the early Christians of the book of Acts who were of one soul and will. "Cleaving"[49] is the second clarifying concept provided by Iliyyā regarding the concept of the union. The biblical mandate for marriage – "cleave to his wife such that the two become one flesh" (Gen 2:24)[50] – provides a paradigm of the union of the divine and human in Christ. The third and final clarification of the union is that of "aspect."[51] The illustration of this dimension of the union is drawn from a king and his delegate. As the two are in union, the king's delegate carries the king's authority in decree, prohibition, opinion and management.[52] "By these aspects the eternal Son united with the man born of Mary and became one Son, one Christ by will, cleaving and aspect, not in substantiality or personhood. For this reason, we affirm that Christ is two substances and two hypostases, one Son." The Bishop further clarifies that "two substances and two hypostases" is like ʿAmr and Zayd being two men or a man and his wife being two persons or the king and his delegate being two. Moreover, declaring that "the Word and the man are one Son" is like the one will of ʿAmr and Zayd or the one flesh of a man and his wife or the one command of a king and his delegate. The name of Christ is used of both the Word and the man born of Mary just as the name of a city designates both its people and its buildings though its people are different from its buildings in essence and attributes. Likewise, the word "Christ" designates both the Word and the man born of Mary though the one differs from the other in essence and substantiality since the Word is a divine hypostasis[53]

48. Mixture: *al-mumāzaja* الممازجة; intermingling *al-ikhtilāṭ* الإختلاط

49. *al-ittiṣāl* الإتّصال

50. Also cited in Matt 19:5; Mark 10:7; 1 Cor 6:16; Eph 5:31.

51. *Wajhiyya* وجهية

52. Huntington 240 occasionally uses the dual form *wajhayn* (two aspects) rather than the word I have translated "aspect" – *wajhiyya*. This may help the reader understand that the author intends that the two aspects of a king and his delegate represent but one authority.

53. *qanūm lāhūtī* قنوم لاهوتي

from the divine substance, eternal, ancient, Creator, and the man is a human hypostasis[54] of human substance, caused and created. Just as one can speak of a city, referring either to its inhabitants or to its structures, so when we speak of Christ raising the dead and working astonishing miracles we refer to the Word which is the divine power. If we say that Christ ate, drank, was tired and died, we are referring to the man born of Mary (46v1–49r2).[55]

At the conclusion of Session 2, Abū al-Qāsim asks the Bishop, "Do you not say that Mary gave birth to God?" The Bishop replies "No." The Vizier asks if some among the Christians do affirm the statement. Iliyyā replies that the Melkites and Jacobites speak in this way. The Session ends with the surprising affirmation of the Vizier: "I had not verified that the Nestorians were as you describe them but now the truth of your divine unity [*tawḥīd*] is established" (49r2–7).

3.3 Session 2: Analysis

In this Session, Iliyyā has provided terminology and analogy to clarify his Christology in the Muslim milieu. The dialogue represents an adroit adherence to the christological understanding of Iliyyā's Church of the East, while simultaneously pushing its allowances to their outer boundaries to create plausibility for Christian inclusion in Islamic *tawḥīd.* Before embarking on my analysis, it is helpful to envision the structure of Session 2. The Session addresses two primary questions: What is meant by the indwelling? And what is meant by the union? A final question concerning Mary's giving birth to God concludes the Session. In response to the first question, the Bishop defines the indwelling, which leads to a prolonged discussion of Christ's superiority over the other prophets, proving the superior nature of his "indwelling." This section concludes with a brief exposé of the christological views of the Jacobites and the Melkites. The second section is shorter and concerns the union of divinity and humanity in Christ. Here Iliyyā uses four christological analogies to preserve the separation of the divine and human hypostases. This overall structure can be schematized as follows with subtopics (indicated by indention) following the primary questions:

Introduction: Greetings

Question on the indwelling (folios 29–46)

Exposition on indwelling: dignity, assent and will (not essence and substance)

Christ's superior indwelling: titles, birth, miracles and resurrection

54. *qanūm nasūtī* قنوم نسوتي

55. al-Niṣībīn, *Kitāb al-majālis* (Huntington 240), fol. 72a.

- Christ combines and excels the virtues of Adam, Yaḥyā, Moses and Idrīs
- Christ was immune to sin in thought, word and deed

Further exposition: indwelling of will not essence

Jacobite and Melkite views of the indwelling

Question on the union (folios 46v7–49)

Union in will, cleaving and aspect

- Analogy of will: early Jerusalem believers
- Analogy of cleaving: man cleaves to his wife
- Analogy of aspect: king and delegate
- Analogy of 'Amr and Zayd
- Proper use of titles: Christ, Son and the man born of Mary

Question on Mary giving birth to God

Though the Session divides neatly into two major sections ("the indwelling" and "the union"), the crux of the issue throughout is to preserve the divine essence from mixing or intermingling with the human essence. Thus in both sections Iliyyā is intent on clarifying what is meant by his theological jargon in such a way as to demonstrate to his Muslim counterpart that his Christian community is not violating *tawḥīd.* By avoiding both hypostatic union (Byzantine-Melkite) and union of the divine and human substances (monophysitism), Iliyyā is able to build a credible case that his Church of the East cannot be accused of *shirk* (associating the divine with the created).

3.3.1 Analysis: Question on the Indwelling

3.3.1.1 The Indwelling as Understood by the Church of the East

Iliyyā's vocation as a Bishop of the Church of the East requires that he preserve the tradition as it was handed down by the fathers. Thus it is no surprise to find him drawing from his church's dyohypostatic roots in Theodore of Mopsuestia who used each of the three descriptors Iliyyā has enumerated: dignity,[56] assent and will.The influence of ʿAmmār al-Baṣrī is also evident in the Sessions. Though Iliyyā does not define the term "dignity," his predecessors referred to the honor conferred upon humanity by the union as dominion over creation was restored to humanity. The honor

56. ʿAbdishoʿ of Nisibis (d. 1318/718) illustrates the intention of the term *waqār* (dignity) by speaking of the unity of the word of God with the book called the Bible. Because the two are in union, the two receive reciprocal honor (Landron, *Chrétiens et musulmans en Irak*, 200). The same author illustrates the incarnation through the marriage of a royal to a woman of another nation. The son born of the union bears the honor of royalty but also enjoys the brotherhood of his mother's native nation. In like manner, Christ is born of a human mother and has become a brother to mankind. Nevertheless, he fully bears the royal pedigree of the Divine (Landron, 209).

and dignity of Christ is conferred to humans as he is their brother and of their race.[57] Further assistance in ascertaining its meaning at the Muslim–Christian interface is found in the letter of ʿAbd al-Masīḥ Ibn Isḥāq al-Kindī to ʿAbd Allāh Ibn Isma‘īl al-Hāshimī (813–843/197–228):

> God honoured the human kind in that the creative word was incarnated in him, united to him and conferred upon him lordship, divinity, dominion and power which he possessed. As a result, the angels prostrated before him, sanctifying his name and praising him as an equal of God . . . Until in a supreme act of grace, he was given to sit at the right hand of the Almighty for the honour of this body taken from among us and descended from our father Adam. For he is like us and our brother according to nature as well as our Creator and our God because of the authentic union of the creative word with him.[58]

The second descriptor, "assent" (*riḍā*), translates Theodore of Mopsuestia's Greek (*eudoκia*, ευδοκια) and was also used by ʿAmmār al-Baṣrī.[59] In the union of "assent," the author is expressing the pleasure found by the Divine in the union with the man born of Mary.[60]

The third descriptor of the indwelling is the "will." The Church of the East understood Christ to possess only one will despite the duality of the substance and hypostasis. God took human nature and through it expressed his divine will in acts.[61] It was common in the Church of the East to speak of the "one will" of Christ as the divine will which dominated the human will. For Iliyyā, the indwelling by means of the "will" is an expression of Christ's human nature as a vessel for the works of God wrought through Christ. I will return to the discussion of the will below in the analysis of the union.

3.3.1.2 The Indwelling in Muslim–Christian Discourse

Muslim polemicists such as the Mu'tazalī Nāshī' al-Akbar (293/905–906) had discussed the issue of the "indwelling" and even provided an accurate account of the Nestorian view.[62] Abū ʿIsā al-Warrāq also mentioned that some Christians claimed that

57. Mikhail, "ʿAmmār al-Basrī's Kitāb al-Burhān," 235–236.

58. Quoted in Landron, *Chrétiens et musulmans en Irak*, 210.

59. Mikhail, "ʿAmmār al-Basrī's Kitāb al-Burhān," 235–236.

60. The noun form derives from the verb *eudokeo* which means "to be content or well-pleased." It also includes the connotation of "satisfaction" or "delight" (Liddell and Scott, *Greek–English Lexicon*, 710).

61. Landron, *Chrétiens et musulmans en Irak*, 200.

62. Thomas, *Early Muslim Polemic*, 42.

deity indwelt Christ.[63] Muslims had defined "indwelling" as either partial or complete. In either case, the indwelling of deity in creatures was ruled out. The former would indicate a division in God while the latter assumed two eternal entities. It was not only Christians who held to such a view, but Sufīs as well.[64] Abū al-Qāsim's understanding of indwelling reflects the common Muslim perception and plainly violates *tawḥīd.* It can only be categorized as "unbelief" (*kufr*). Thus, the Bishop proceeds to explicate his view of the indwelling, taking pains to demonstrate that the indwelling is not one of essence or substantiality.

The Bishop introduces his discussion of the indwelling by providing a semantic clarification. The word "indwelling" can be used with different meanings. Diverse entities fall under the category of "existent," yet these entities are not all equal, nor does the donkey equal the man though both fall under the category of "animals." Jesus, speaking to Mary Magdalene, refers to God as "my Father and your Father, my God and your God." As was observed in the discussion of Ibn al-Ṭayyib, it is unlikely that the Bishop's reference to the most extensively used Gospel verse in Muslim–Christian relations, John 20:17, is mere coincidence.[65] The verse was a well-worn target of Muslim polemicists who saw in it a candid admission of Jesus's equality with others and a metaphorical understanding of his filial relationship to God. The Bishop preempts the argument stating that though Christ applies the same paternal relationship to himself and Mary, the relationship is not of the same quality and degree. Rather, Christ's indwelling is one of inseparable "union." His citing of this verse forestalls the normal Muslim objection and lays the groundwork for his argument that Christ's indwelling is superior to that of other prophets.

3.3.1.3 Reasons for the Uniqueness of Christ's Indwelling

The issue of the indwelling leads to a comparison of Jesus with other prophets in which the Bishop explicates five reasons why Jesus's indwelling is unique.

The first reason given by the Bishop is that the "eternal Word united with him and he became one Christ." Iliyyā perceptively adds that for this reason he is called Christ by Christians and the "Word of God" by Muslims. Thus, the indwelling is indicated by the lofty titles ascribed to Christ. In Church of the East thought, it was Christ – the divine Son – who alone enabled human beings to participate in divine filiation.[66] By the Son's incarnation, an ontological unity of the eternal Word with

63. Thomas, 88–89.

64. Massignon and Anawati, "Ḥulūl," 570–571.

65. Accad, "Ultimate Proof-Text," 200.

66. Landron points out that had the Spirit or Father been the object of the incarnation, mankind would have theoretically been enabled to become the Spirit or Father of God – an impossible concept (Landron, *Chrétiens et musulmans en Irak*, 204).

the man born of Mary is inaugurated, opening the way for mankind to enter into a state of sonship. However, for Abū al-Qāsim, participation in filiation of God was as inconceivable as participation in the Spirit or Father. It was rejected by the Qur'ān and Muslim theologians as an outrageous example of *shirk*. Iliyyā's use of the qur'ānic title attributed to Christ, "a Word from God," obviates reference to Christ's filiation, despite his previous reference to John 20:17. Though Abū al-Qāsim will later object that the title gives no unique standing to Christ vis-à-vis any other prophet, Iliyyā effectively rejoins that the title cannot simply mean that Christ was "created by a command of God" – recognizable as the qur'ānic view (Q3:47) – for all things were created by God's command. The Bishop overplays his hand by claiming that the only possible meaning is that he was indwelt by the eternal Word much as the speaking body was indwelt by the soul.[67]

The second reason supplied by the Bishop is that Christ was neither born of physical procreation nor did he engage therein. The Qur'ān also declares the conception of Christ through divine fiat without human procreation (see Q19:20). Iliyyā is quick to add that this descriptor is true of no other human being. Later, when the Vizier counters that Adam was born without human parentage, the Bishop presses his argument, effectively stating that Adam was brought forth as the first human being and, therefore, had no possibility of having human parentage. Christ, on the other hand, was born at a time in history when it was manifestly possible for him to be born of human parentage (36v3–38v1). For Iliyyā, this is an adequate indicator of the indwelling of the Word in the man born of Mary.

Not only is the doctrine of the virgin birth of Christ shared with his Muslim counterpart but Iliyyā effectively highlights the uniqueness of this fact. It is said of no other prophet, and though Iliyyā does not refer to Muḥammad's birth or make any direct comparison, it cannot be far from the reader's mind that the Bishop is displaying his view of Christ's supremacy among the prophets with relish. Though Abū al-Qāsim has contended that Christ is equal to Adam (born without parentage) and John the Baptist (in terms of chastity), the Bishop has demonstrated that in combining the qualities of both, Christ is superior (38v1–39r4).[68]

67. The analogy of the human soul indwelling the human body also had historical precedent among Church of the East theologians and was often used to shed light on the doctrine of the incarnation (Landron, 191).

68. Landron, *Chrétiens et musulmans en Irak*, 211.

على هذا الحال فليس ينبغي أن يُقاس البشري المأخوذ من مريم بآدم وإن تساويا في الجوهرية والبشرية

Louis Cheikho points to this sentence as an indication of Iliyyā's Nestorianism which Cheikho finds defective. In Cheikho's view, this sentence indicates Iliyyā's equating Christ and Adam in humanity and substantiality such that Christ was not co-substantial with the divine substance (Cheikho, "Majalis Iliyya mutran Nasibin," 115, fn 2).

The third reason given by the Bishop is Jesus's ability to perform miraculous signs spontaneously and without intermediary.[69] Abū al-Qāsim's understanding that other prophets had performed signs equal to those of Jesus is reflected by Muslim polemicists.[70] The comparison with Moses, Elijah and other biblical prophets had been discussed in the polemical literature by al-Maturīdī (d. ca. 944/333), Ḥasan Ibn Ayyūb (fl. tenth/fourth century), al-Bāqillānī (1013/403), ʿAbd al-Jabbār (1025/415), to name but a few. The Christian convert to Islam ʿAlī Ibn al-Rabbān al-Ṭabarī (d. ca. 855/241), who impugned the claim of Christ's divinity due to miracles, cited other prophets through whom miracles were performed. Adam was born without father and mother. Moses fed multitudes and parted the Red Sea. Elijah raised the dead. Both Elijah and Enoch were raised up to heaven.[71] Indeed, the Session presents some of the stock arguments of Muslim polemics. The recitation will suggest to some that the text has been amended to permit the erudite Bishop to answer the most common Muslim objections. The plausible alternative is that Abū al-Qāsim, a well-instructed Muslim, had heard or read these objections and was eager to hear the Bishop's response. Whatever the case, the reader is treated to Iliyyā's understanding of Christ's superiority over other prophets in the Muslim milieu. Indeed, the Bishop's apologetic is rational and scripturally informed, invoking both the Christian and Muslim scriptures. The Vizier offers no resistance as the argument unfolds.

Some Muslims (e.g. al-Māturīdī d. ca. 944/333) had argued that Christ's miracles required his imploring God, as was evidenced by his Gethsemane prayer.[72] Iliyyā highlights the immediacy of Christ's miracles in counter-distinction to the common Muslim understanding that Christ performed his signs by the leave of Allāh (Q3:49; 5:110). His long recitation of Christ's mighty works – raising the dead, healing the lame, lepers and blind, casting out demons, stilling the sea – reveals a determination to prove his point: Christ was not obliged to obtain divine permission for his miraculous

69. Others in the Church of the East have gone so far as to attribute creation to Jesus as he healed blind eyes by his saliva which was infused with the divine Spirit to bring healing (Landron, *Chrétiens et musulmans en Irak*, 211).

70. Note that al-Jahiz in his *al-Radd ʿalā al-Nasārā* (*Refutation of Christians*) held that Adam is more worthy than Christ to be called the "son of God" because neither a man nor a woman was involved in his generation (Rissanen, *Theological Encounter*, 172). The same view appears at the end of the ninth/third century in a letter written pseudonymously by a Muslim to a Christian, purportedly by the Caliph ʿUmar II to the Basileus Leo III (Gaudeul, "Correspondence between Leo and ʿUmar," 145–146, paras 49–51; Thomas, "Miracles of Jesus," 225).

71. Thomas, 222.

72. Thomas, 227. In the Letter of al-Kindī to al-Hāshimī (9th cent.) (al-Hāshimī and al-Kindī, "Ḥiwār Dīnī," 168–169), the Patriarch Iliyyā and Abu al-Ḥasan Ibn al-Atradī cite Christ's ability to perform miraculous powers at will with no need of a divine command (Landron, *Chrétiens et musulmans en Irak*, 211). See also Thomas for a discussion of miracles at the Muslim–Christian interface of the period (Thomas, "Miracles of Jesus").

signs. Iliyyā includes two of Christ's qur'ānic miracles, the latter of which originates from the apocryphal Infancy Gospel of Thomas.[73] It is given prominence by the Bishop as indicating Jesus's power to perform miracles spontaneously and without an intermediary. The Bishop is on shaky ground here as Muslims had been quick to point out that this miracle was done by the leave of Allāh (Q3:49).

The Bishop responds to Abū al-Qāsim's contention that Moses worked miracles similar to those of Christ (39r4–40v2) in a threefold response that demonstrates a stark contrast between Moses and Christ: Moses's prophetic career was not prophesied by those who preceded him; his miracles were commanded of him by God; and he committed a tragic error in his striking of the rock, an act which prohibited his entrance into the promised land though he sought forgiveness. Christ is presented as the ideal counterpart to Moses in these three concerns. It is noteworthy that the Bishop refers to the prophetic announcement of Christ's advent and immunity from sin two thousand years in advance. Additionally, he was to be the "hope of the nations" and "the sovereign one."

Iliyyā draws no explicit comparison of Muḥammad and Christ. Though Muslims claimed that miracles were accomplished by Muḥammad, the Qur'ān itself indicates that he was given no sign other than the revelation he brought (Q2:145; 6:37; 13:7). Certainly, for Iliyyā, the scale and immediacy of the miracles performed by Christ left no room for comparison with any other prophet.

Christ's being raised is the Bishop's fourth reason for the uniqueness of his indwelling. The Muslim convert from Christianity ʿAlī Ibn al-Rabbān al-Ṭabarī cited Enoch's ascension as well as Elijah's to indicate that Christ was not superior.[74] The story of the nocturnal voyage of Muḥammad[75] portrays him as seeing Christ in only the second of seven heavens.[76] Iliyyā cites Q3:55 to demonstrate that Christ has been raised to the very presence of God. Thus both the Qur'ān and the Bible indicate that Christ was raised to a place of ultimate honor and exaltation, unlike Enoch.

Christ's immunity from sin is the Bishop's fifth reason. While he makes no explicit reference to Islam, the concept of prophetic immunity[77] of all prophets had been a controversial topic in Islam. In a very general sense, a consensus

73. The Infancy Gospel of Thomas exists in thirteen late antique and medieval languages. This likely indicates it was a popular source of information on Jesus's early life. The Greek manuscripts are later in origin (14th and 15th centuries). Other translations include Syriac, Latin, Georgian and Ethiopic. There are many variants to the manuscripts and it is notoriously difficult to establish an original version of this apocryphal Gospel. The story of Jesus's giving life to birds formed out of clay is found in chapter 2 of the Gospel (Ehrman, *Apocryphal Gospels*, 3–7, 10–11).

74. Thomas, "Miracles of Jesus," 222.

75. *al-isrā' wa-al-mi'rāj* الإسراء والمعراج

76. Robinson, "Miʿradj," 99.

77. *'iṣma* عصمة

was developing concerning prophetic immunity from major sins after a prophet received his prophetic mission from God. There were exceptions (including Iliyyā's contemporary al-Bāqillānī) as the doctrine of immunity seemed to controvert a literal reading of the Qur'ān. Sins of inadvertence (*sahū*) were generally excluded from this immunity.[78] Iliyyā forcefully holds forth the sinlessness of Christ in distinction to all other prophets. The Muslim claim that Muḥammad was the seal of the prophets had, for all practical purposes, eclipsed Christ as well as the other biblical prophets. By claiming a unique divine indwelling for Christ, the Bishop is asserting Christ's superiority over Muḥammad in veiled language.

Iliyyā does not miss the opportunity to remind his interlocutor that Christ's sinless perfection was prophesied by the ancients. Although Muslim scholars had given attention to the precedent scriptures to identify prophetic indicators of Muḥammad's advent, their findings had been less than persuasive for Christians. This failure to identify prophecies of Muḥammad may have contributed to the rapidly forming consensus of Muslim scholars that the Jewish and Christian scriptures had been subject to textual corruption (*taḥrīf*). Indeed, it was precisely during the eleventh century that the accusation of textual corruption was crystallizing in both East and West through the likes of ʿAbd al-Jabbār and Ibn Ḥazm.[79] It is in this milieu that Iliyyā is intent upon demonstrating that Christ was the object of prophetic predictions long before his advent.

3.3.1.4 Concluding Questions

Abū al-Qāsim questions the Bishop as to how the divine will could indwell Jesus without mitigating the divine essence. Iliyyā calls on his understanding of Islamic thought to establish parity with the Christian concept. God's act of creation was exercised through the will without disturbing the divine essence according to Muslim scholars. Christians say a similar thing in reference to the indwelling: Jesus was indwelt by the divine will, not the divine essence. Iliyyā presses the Vizier to consider the Christian tenet from within its own assumptions as he does for the Islamic tenet. When viewed in this way, the Christian tenet is, in fact, rational and coherent. The Vizier discerns that the Christian terminology of "indwelling" has caused ill-instructed adherents of the religion to assume a deviant view. Iliyyā's masterful rejoinder is reminiscent of Session 1 as he obliges the Vizier to concede that theological language, of necessity, entails metaphorical meanings. The divine indwelling of Christ is no more liable to misinterpretation than Muslims' speaking of God's session on a throne. Speaking in this anthropomorphic vein, whether by Muslims or Christians,

78. Tyan, "ʿisma," 182–184.

79. Accad, "Gospels in the Muslim Discourse," 72; Reynolds, *Muslim Theologian.*

entails the risk of misunderstanding. Once again, we see Iliyyā skillfully assisting his interlocutor to make similar allowances for Christian terminology as he intuitively does for Muslims.

It is not entirely clear why he does not attribute the doctrine of the indwelling to Jacobites or Melkites. Abū Qurra the Melkite had used the term.[80] However, other terms such as "became flesh" and "became human"[81] were being preferred when speaking of the incarnation. I will analyze Iliyyā's representation of Melkite and Jacobite views in reference to Christology in the discussion of *Proof of the True Faith* (section 4 below).

3.3.2 Analysis: Question on the Union

The Vizier's line of questioning turns from the "indwelling" to another lexical feature of Christian theology: the "union" of the divine with the human in Christ. Conceptually the discussion remains in the realm of Christology with *tawḥīd* being the central point of interest. The indwelling considered the outworking of the divine through the human in acts of power. The union defines the interrelations of the divinity and humanity of Christ. My analysis of this section of Session 2 will focus on the Bishop's christological analogies which I deem to be problematic in terms of the ontological unity of Christ's two natures.

3.3.2.1 Session 2 and Christian Predecessors

Considering Iliyyā's predecessors in the Church of the East who worked at the Muslim–Christian interface demonstrates how Iliyyā amended his formulation. Timothy I's analogies to convey the unity of Christ while maintaining the duality of natures included the body and soul,[82] the rays issuing from the sun and the word from the soul.[83] Each analogy carefully maintains an ontological unity. In response to al-Mahdī's assertion that the divine and human natures of Christ demanded two distinct beings, Timothy retorts, "Christ is not two beings, O King, nor two Sons, but Son and Christ are one . . . we do not deny the duality of natures, O King, nor their mutual relations, but we profess that both of them constitute one Christ and Son."[84]

80. Beaumont, *Christology in Dialogue with Muslims*, 35.

81. Became flesh: *tajassada* تجسّد ; became human: *ta'annasa* تأنّس

82. Iliyyā also referred to the metaphor in his discussion of the title "Word of God" though he did not elaborate it in his exposition of the "indwelling" or the "union." "If it is established that he was not called 'the Word of God' because he was created by the command of God, it is also established that he is given that title due to his union with the eternal Word just as the body is called 'speaking' due to its union with the speaking self [*al-nafs al-nāṭiqa*]" (al-Niṣībīn, *Kitāb al-Burhān al-Ṣaḥīḥ*, 36r1–36v2).

83. Putnam, *L'église et l'islam sous Timothée I*, 218–219.

84. Mingana, "Apology of Timothy the Patriarch," 153, 155; Putman, 218.

ʿAmmār al-Baṣrī treats the notion of the union effected in the incarnation in the first twenty-five questions of Part 4 of the *Book of Questions and Answers*, where he insists on the unity of the divine and human in Christ, finding the locus of the union in filiation as did Ibn al-Ṭayyib.[85] Response to Question 1: "the eternal Word and the temporal created human being became one Messiah . . . who is the union of two natures."[86] Response to Question 3: "The two natures are united." ʿAmmār holds to the duality of the hypostases and substances to ensure that his interlocutor does not presume a third entity different from the other two resulting from the union.[87] ʿAmmār spoke of the coal and the flame, an analogy that shows a distinction in nature but also a profound unity. The "body and soul" metaphor was also referenced by ʿAmmār.[88] Though hypostatic duality is apparent, the unity of person is equally emphasized.

3.3.2.2 Iliyyā's Dyohypostatic Analogies: Union in Will, Cleaving and Aspect

The first descriptor of the union is "will." In speaking of the union of will, the Church of the East was echoing monothelitism which had been rejected in the Sixth Ecumenical Council (680 CE) in Constantinople.[89] The union of will expressed a sense of agreement between distinct persons which had precedence in the Church of the East as used by Babai. They would also find subsequent use by ʿAbd Īshū.[90] Arabic facilitated the concept by supplying distinct terms. The two wills (*irāda*) were seen to unite into the one will (*mashī'a*).[91] Thus, the union is not one of essence or substance but will. In this union, it is the divine will that predominates as the divine substance takes a human person to accomplish his acts. Predictably, the tenet of the union of the will was criticized by Islamic polemicists. The trenchant ʿAbd al-Jabbār critiqued the view on the basis that Christ's miracles were of no different quality from

85. In his response to the first question, ʿAmmār states: "They [the two substances] are united in the aspect of filiation and relationship to the Father, described as the essence of fatherhood" بل إتحدا في جهة البنوة والنسبة إلى الاب الموصوف بذات الابوة (al-Basri, *Kitab al-Burhan*, 178).

86. al-Basri, *Kitab al-burhan*, 179; Beaumont, *Christology in Dialogue with Muslims*, 74. *Jawharain* جوهرَين

87. al-Basri, *Kitab al-burhan*, 180–181.

88. Mikhail, "ʿAmmār al-Basrī's Kitāb al-Burhān," 393.

89. The controversy was an ill-conceived attempt to foster reunion with the Monophysites. The union of the will, it was thought, would suffice as an impetus to return the Monophysites to agreement with Chalcedon. Such would not be the case as Maximus the Confessor led the charge to reject the doctrine of the one will. He argued that the will belongs to the substance. As Christ is both human and divine substance, it follows that he has two wills (Khalifeh, "The Maronites," 281). It appears that the Council's ruling was made without reference to the Antiochene Church which had long insisted on the unity of the will in Christ.

90. Landron, *Chrétiens et musulmans en Irak*, 192. ʿAbd Isho of Nisibis follows Iliyyā in explaining the union of will by drawing on the account of the Acts of the Apostles where the believers are said to have been united in heart and soul (Landron, 200).

91. Landron, 198.

those of any other prophet. Accordingly, he suggested that Christians apply the union of the will to all prophets.[92]

Iliyyā illustrates the union of the will through a well-known description of the early Christians in the book of Acts where they are said to have been of one "soul and will." The analogy refers to a plurality of persons who were united by a common will, thus upholding the separation of the hypostases.

The analogy of the union of "cleaving" follows. This cleaving is not a dissolving of the duality into oneness, but a preservation of the two. It was Theodore of Mopsuestia who had originally spoken of the union in these marital terms.[93] He had opted for the Greek word "conjoining" (συναφεια) rather than "union" (ενοωσις).[94] Iliyyā's explication is faithful to his Theodoran theological heritage and well suited for the Islamic milieu. Though one could legitimately speak of the two as one, the union envisioned by Iliyyā preserved an ontological distinction of the two persons – husband and wife – and thus fell short of a true ontological union.

The union of "aspect" is illustrated by the union of the king and his delegate in every facet of the king's rule. Once again, there is no question of merging the essences of the two persons; rather the one dominant person carries out his royal decrees through the function of the subordinate person. The Arabic word is derived from *wajh* meaning "face" or presentation. The Greek, *prosopon*, had been used in Trinitarian discourse and is likely the source that Iliyyā draws from. It is the delegate who bears the king's authority through its being conferred upon him. Seeing or hearing the delegate who acts as the king's image is tantamount to seeing or hearing the king. This illustration had also been used by Babai in his *Book of the Union*.[95] Clearly, the duality of the essence and personhood is maintained through the use of this illustration as well. The human nature acts as the *wajh* or the presentation of the eternal Word, bearing his authority.

Perhaps the Bishop senses that the ontological unity of the Son has been undermined by his analogies. He recapitulates his exposé by restating that there are "two substances and two hypostases" illustrated by the duality of 'Amr and Zayd, man and wife, king and delegate. There is also "one Son" illustrated by the one will of 'Amr and Zayd, the one flesh of man and wife and the one command of king and delegate. The name "Christ" envelops the humanity and divinity just as the name of a city includes both its inhabitants and its buildings, yet another analogy employed

92. Thomas, "Miracles of Jesus," 234.

93. Mingana, *Commentary of Theodore*, 90.

94. Bishoy, "Councils of Ephesus and Chalcedon," 195.

95. Landron, *Chrétiens et musulmans en Irak*, 192.

by Babai.[96] Though the Bishop's intent is to reaffirm the union, he again refers to entities that are ontologically discrete: a city and its inhabitants.

Iliyyā's analogies position him well for a defense against the charge of *shirk* in that they emphasize the duality of the hypostases; however, they fall short of upholding the ontological unity of the person of Christ. His analogies have some precedence among his Church of the East forebears, but Iliyyā notably avoids analogies that provide balance to establish the ontological unity of the one Christ (e.g. the fire in the iron, the body and soul). Iliyyā has moved beyond Timothy I and ʿAmmār while seeking to adhere to the dyohypostatic formulation. Iliyyā's Christology allowed him to innovate through analogy in ways that drove the divine and human hypostases further apart with no counter analogies that would also uphold the union of the divine and human in the one person of Christ. Indeed, the accusation of "two persons in Christ" leveled against Nestorianism appears justified in Iliyyā's analogies. His analogies upholding duality or plurality are an apologetic defense against *shirk* but belie his refrain of "one Christ, one Son."

3.3.2.3 Other Ecclesial Families

It is noteworthy that the Bishop attributes the union of soul and body to other ecclesial families, implying it is a substandard view. Church of the East predecessors such as Timothy I had spoken of Christ's taking a body. In response to the Vizier's assertion that "Word of God" meant nothing more than Jesus's creation by divine command, the Bishop explicated the title "Word of God" through the metaphor of a "speaking body" by virtue of its union with the "speaking soul" (fol. 36v). Iliyyā does not elaborate further on this analogy nor return to it later when he is explicating the union. ʿAmmār al-Baṣrī elaborated the analogy, answering the question how human actions can be attributed to the incarnate God. "The properties of the soul when united to the body become the actions of the body by virtue of 'borrowing.'"[97] The Bishop's attribution of the analogy to other ecclesial families who held a different view of Christ raises the question: Was the Bishop no longer willing to portray the union as a union of soul and body? It is important to notice that Iliyyā reveals his disapproval of the metaphor of soul and body to express "the union." I will continue this discussion of Iliyyā's view of the other ecclesial families below.

96. Landron, 192.

97. Mikhail, "ʿAmmār al-Basrī's Kitāb al-Burhān," 233.

4. Additional Documents

4.1 Proof of the True Faith

Iliyyā's work entitled *Proof of the True Faith*[98] adds to our understanding of his Christological formulation. It is an extensive treatise (eighty-eight folios) preserved in the manuscript Vatican Arabe 180.[99] It contains four chapters, the first of which addresses concerns at the Muslim–Christian interface (fols. 131r–134r). The precise date of the document is unknown though the date of Iliyyā's death provides the latest possible date of composition as 1046/437. To date, there is no critical edition of the Arabic text.[100] A detailed account of *Proof of the True Faith* is not necessary as my purpose is to demonstrate the Bishop's determination to distance his church from the two other ecclesial families.

4.1.1 Christological Significance

Although most of the work is not addressed to a Muslim audience *per se*, it provides an understanding of Iliyyā's Christology and his defense of Christian *tawḥīd.*[101] Much of the work is an apologetic for the dyohypostatic views of the Church of the East citing reasons why the corrupted Jacobite and Melkite expressions prospered. Of particular interest is his determination to demarcate his own Church of the East from the Byzantines and Jacobites. Indeed, an entire section of chapter 2 is devoted to "establishing proof that the Jacobites and Melkites are two deviating divisions."[102] A few of these statements merit closer examination as they buttress the argument that Iliyyā was defending his dyohypostatic Christology as concurring with *tawḥīd* while other ecclesial families fell short.

The Bishop contends that both Jacobites and Melkites hold an inferior understanding of Christ that led to impugning God's aseity:

---

98. *Kitāb al-burhān 'alā ṣaḥīḥ al-īmān* كتاب البُرهان على صحيح الإيمان

99. al-Niṣībīn, *Kitāb al-burhān al-ṣaḥīḥ.*

100. Monferrer Sala, "Elias of Nisibis," 738.

101. In reference to the Trinity, Iliyyā refers to the Father as the "cause" of both wisdom and life. "Wisdom" is "Son" because he is existent from the essence and begotten from it as "light is born from the sun and pronunciation from the soul." This transpires without separation in time whether priority or anteriority (al-Niṣībīn, *Kitāb al-Burhān al-Ṣaḥīḥ*, fol. 131r6–8). He is insistent that the three hypostases are "properties" not persons (*khawāṣṣ lā ashkhās*). Thus the hypostases are properties of the essence and cannot be construed to violate God's unity. The important word *shirk* (association of the divine with created beings) is mentioned explicitly in the text. The Bishop draws a distinction between God's essence, wisdom and life which are hypostases, meaning properties (*khawāṣṣ*) (fol. 132b). Like his contemporary Ibn al-Ṭayyib, Iliyyā demonstrates that the monikers "Son," "Word of God" and "Spirit" can be found throughout the Scriptures of the Old and New Testaments rendering them legitimate.

102. al-Niṣībīn, *Kitāb al-burhān al-ṣaḥīḥ*, fol. 144r7–8. *firqatān muḥdithatān* فرقتان محدثتان

> And the Jacobites said that it is a union of nature and union of intermingling[103] as the two substances and two hypostases intermingled. So there generated from it one substance and one hypostasis. This is the most pernicious of confessions.[104] And the Melkites confess something like this except that the two substances remained as they were and the two hypostases united to become one hypostasis. And both confessions lead to transformation and change. They violate rationality and destroy the origin of belief that God most high is neither transformed nor does he change.[105]

The Bishop censures the belief that Mary gave birth to God as it "contradicts what is required by the substance of humanity and its holiness among us."[106] He proceeds to rebut both Jacobite and Melkite thought at length. "Melkism and Jacobism became enemies of the truth as we have explained and demonstrated from their conditions [that they were] deviating divisions because of what came into their faith of corruption and change which we have elucidated."[107] It is apparent that Bishop Iliyyā firmly held that his own dyohypostatic Christology adhered to *tawḥīd,* while that of the Melkites and Jacobites violated divine aseity and suggested change in God. *Proof of the True Faith* accords with Iliyyā's determination to establish his church as a community of Christian *tawḥīd* in the Islamic milieu. Furthermore, it reveals the Bishop's contention that the other ecclesial families have failed to measure up to a correct monotheistic formulation. In the conclusion below, I will further evaluate the Bishop's impassioned defense of Christian *tawḥīd* in the Muslim milieu.

4.2 Treatise on Kiyān (Substance)

One final extant document from the pen of the Bishop will further define the contours of his Christology.[108] The treatise expounds Iliyyā's justification for Christians applying the moniker "a God"[109] to Jesus, the man born of Mary. The Bishop works through various descriptors (living, wise, lord, etc.) which may be applied to different kinds of beings in various roles. "Lord" may be applied both to the master of a slave and

---

103. *ittiḥād al-ikhtilāṭ* إتّحاد والإختلاط

104. The Arabic text appears to be: وهذه أسبَح المقالات وأشنعها The meaning of *asbaḥ* is unclear although *ashna'* leaves no room for doubt that Iliyyā is castigating the christological formulation of the Jacobites and Melkites.

105. al-Niṣībīn, *Kitāb al-burhān al-ṣaḥīḥ*, fol. 140r11–140v3.

106. al-Niṣībīn, fol. 155b1–2.

107. al-Niṣībīn, fol. 159r7–10.

108. For bibliographic information on *Kiyān* (*Substance*), see chapter 4, 3.4.

109. *Ilāh* إله

the Lord of the universe. The title "Allāh" may also be applied by Jews and Christians to the king, a nobleman, the governor and the man born of Mary. However, no fault may be found for the practice because Christians and Jews do not apply the essential attributes of divinity to these entities who are described as "gods": "They are indeed deserving of reproach if they describe a man or the king as they describe the exalted Creator with the essential attributes belonging to him or if they describe God with the essential attributes of a man or the king."[110] Accordingly, Iliyyā finds no fault in the Christian attribution of the title "God" to Jesus provided the essential attributes of divinity are only attributed to the divinity and not to the "man born of Mary." Thus, in the Bishop's view, the title "God" applied to Jesus's humanity is of no more significance than the application of the same title to a human sovereign, king or noble.

The argument highlights the dyohypostatic tendency which we observe in Iliyyā's Christology. The Bishop's focus is on the distinction of the two hypostases and their non-communication. In the final analysis, the Bishop's defense falls short of the ontological unity of Christ's divinity and humanity in the one Christ. Moreover, it serves to highlight the necessity of defining and affirming divine unity in the sectarian milieu.

5. Iliyyā's Christology in the Islamic Milieu: Adherence to *Tawḥīd*

Iliyyā's Christology is an extension of Theodore of Mopsuestia's, not a departure.[111] He is not reshaping Christology so much as pushing it to its outer limits in order to create plausibility for Christian adherence to *tawḥīd* in the Islamic milieu. The dyohypostatic Christology of the Church of the East served as the springboard from which Iliyyā (and others before him) launched into the Muslim–Christian interface. The theological standard of *tawḥīd* and the intellectual, fiscal and legal implications for failing to adhere to it led Christians toward a definitive separation of the hypostases. This delineation of the hypostases is observable in Iliyyā's shielding of the divine hypostasis from human blemishes, identifying nomenclature and analogy for the divine and human hypostases, and finding the locus of the unity in the will, evading the accusation of *shirk*.

110. Samir, "Un traité nouveau," 147, vs. 62–63.

111. Much of Theodore's theology is no longer extant. Perhaps the best example of his Christology is found in his commentary on the Nicene Creed. There it is clear that Theodore was a strong advocate of the duality of Christ's natures and the unity of his person. ". . . they [the 318 Fathers of Nicea] followed the Sacred books which speak differently of natures while referring (them) to one *prosopon* on account of the close union that took place between them, so that they might not be believed that they were separating the perfect union between the man who was assumed and the one who assumed" (Mingana, *Commentary of Theodore*, 64–64).

5.1 Christological Nomenclature and the Non-Communication of the Attributes

Iliyyā's bifurcated nomenclature facilitated a distinction between the divine and human attributes. Distinct monikers of Christ were not a new phenomenon among Church of the East theologians,[112] but the Bishop eagerly asserts them at the Muslim–Christian interface to show that the attributes of divinity cannot be attributed to the humanity of Christ. The synod he mentions was convened by Timothy I and may have been motivated apologetically by the predominance of *tawḥīd* as an intellectual standard in the early Abbasid Empire. The synodical ruling that Jesus himself could not claim to have seen the divine substance[113] buttresses his argument that despite the Christian doctrine of the incarnation, Christians under his charge do not associate (*shirk*) what is created with what is uncreated and eternal. The entire point is to avoid the charge of *shirk* by affirming *tawḥīd* as integral to his theology and Christology. Through this separation of the hypostases, Iliyyā insists that the divine hypostasis remains in its state of *tanzīh* (literally, "unblemished"). In a theological sense, the term implies the elimination of anthropomorphic elements from divinity and can be translated as "transcendence." For Iliyyā, God's transcendent impassibility was not compromised by his indwelling the man born of Mary or by his union with him.

Iliyyā's bifurcation of the monikers "Jesus, the man born of Mary" and "Lord," though cogent in the dyohypostatic frame of reference, must have been confusing for a Muslim reader steeped in Islamic *tawḥīd.* In fact, Muslims such as Abū ʿIsā al-Warrāq had already entertained the suggestion that the two substances in Christ allowed his divinity to remain impassible and had summarily dismissed it: "For if any of this happened to either of the two substances, and either of the two substances alone was not the Messiah, then the one who was crucified, killed and buried would not actually have been the Messiah."[114] Additionally, the Bishop's shielding of the man Jesus from the beatific vision would have been the norm for Muslims who held Jesus to be a prophet but nothing more.

But this raises the question: How did Iliyyā manage to obtain a positive reaction from Abū al-Qāsim? Abū al-Qāsim's acceptance of Iliyyā's formulation may well

112. See footnote 12 above.

113. Samir theorizes that this denial that Jesus had seen God was not a prominent aspect of Church of the East thought until Timothy I who convened the synod which would condemn Messalianism. This is the same Timothy who held a two-day dialogue with the third Abbasid Caliph al-Mahdī. Samir, therefore, theorizes that the synod may have arrived at its position for apologetic reasons (in addition to scriptural and philosophic reasons). That is to say, the denial of Jesus's having seen the divine substance may have served to strengthen the claim of *tawḥīd* on the part of Christians in the Islamic milieu. Samir also suggests that Iliyyā's reference to the synod in an apologetic vein lends credence to the apologetic nature of the synodical declaration (Samir, "Entretien d'Elie de Nisibe," 39).

114. Thomas, *Early Muslim Polemic*, 133–115.

have been owing to the warm and reciprocal relationship enjoyed by the two men. As mentioned previously, one of the contributing factors to this relationship was the existential preparation of Abū al-Qāsim including his healing in a Christian monastery and his family's persecution at the hands of the Faṭimid Caliph al-Ḥakim. Nevertheless, the cordial relationship enjoyed by the two interlocutors and the positive results of their dialogue do not seem to translate to subsequent Muslim–Christian relations. The Marwanid dynasty was short-lived and its irenic Vizier Abū al-Qāsim passed away before *The Sessions* was published. *The Sessions*, though it may have been a trophy of the Church of the East, made little headway in amending the predominant themes of the Muslim–Christian interface of the period. There is no noticeable turning of the tide such that Muslims could now reconcile the Christian view of Christ with their understanding of *tawḥīd.* Muslim polemicists during the lifetime of Iliyyā (e.g. ʿAbd al-Jabbār [d. 1025/416]) and subsequent to him (e.g. al-Shahrastānī [d. 1153/458] and Ibn al-Jawzī [d. 1200/596]) would continue to charge Christians with delusion and corruption of the true revelation of God.

5.2 Dyohypostatic Analogies

The use of analogy to depict the complexities of Christian doctrine had been well established in the Church of the East by luminaries such as Timothy I and ʿAmmār al-Baṣrī. It has been demonstrated that Iliyyā's defense of the union relied on analogies which preserved the separation of the hypostases – the man and wife, the king and his delegate, the city and its inhabitants, ʻAmr and Zayd and the early Christians of the Jerusalem church. This is not surprising as these analogies can be found in precedent theologians. What does surprise is the lack of analogies that portray the unity of the person of Christ to provide a counterbalance. Justification for this lack of counterbalance may be found in the prevalence of Islamic *tawḥīd* and its pre-eminence as an intellectual and theological construct to which all should adhere. Other Church of the East theologians who labored at the Muslim–Christian interface provide this counterbalance, preserving the unity of the person beyond the separation of the hypostases.

Iliyyā adhered to Church of the East Christology. He was not reshaping the *kerygma* of his church. This is borne out by the fact that Ibn al-Ṭayyib, secretary to the Catholicos, read and heartily commended Iliyyā's formulation. Nevertheless, Iliyyā chose analogies that could only be understood to represent the duality of the hypostases. They did not adequately depict the union of the human and divine in the person of Christ and, therefore, fell short of preserving a uniquely Christian monotheism, this despite the fact that the Bishop repeatedly spoke of the "one Christ." For this reason, I observe both the utility of the analogies in the sectarian milieu and their inadequacy to portray the unity of Christ's person. Considering that Iliyyā was writing in the Muslim milieu for Islamic consumption, there is no need to impugn his view of the union. His analogies served his purpose of defending Christian monotheism. Nevertheless, while these images served the Bishop well in the Sessions, their lack of balance had the potential for negative ramifications, especially given the dominance of Islamic *tawḥīd* as an intellectual construct coupled with the complexity of the Christian view. It is striking that the Bishop offered no explicit critique of Islamic *tawḥīd*. Presumably a critique would have drawn the ire of Muslims and, therefore, was undesirable. The Bishop is adamant that his community adheres to *tawḥīd* but he fails to make a significant distinction, at least in his analogies of "the union," between Christian *tawḥīd* and that espoused by Muslims.

5.3 The Motivation of Social and Religious Status

In the sectarian milieu where Christ's divinity had become "exhibit A" of defective *tawḥīd*, the social and jurisprudential implications for Iliyyā's Christian community in the Marwanid dynasty must not be passed over. The *Kitāb al-Umm*, a legal compendium considered authoritative by the Shāfiʿī school of jurisprudence, contains a version of the Pact of ʿUmar prohibiting the proclamation of "polytheism" on the part of Christians: "You may not display crosses in Muslim cities, nor proclaim polytheism, nor build churches for meeting-places for your prayers, nor strike clappers, nor proclaim your polytheistic beliefs on the subject of Jesus, son of Miriam, or any other to a Muslim."[115] Though Christians, as well as Jews, were esteemed as "People of the Book" since the inception of Islam, the acrimonious nature of the Muslim–Christian interface brought the Christian doctrines of the Trinity and Christ's divinity increasingly under scrutiny until they were finally ascribed to infidelity (*al-kufr*).

The social and fiscal implications of the Sessions emerge at various points in the literature, such as Abū al-Qāsim's declaration near the end of Session 2: "I had not ascertained that the Nestorians were as you describe them. I now see your monotheism as correct and your right is established."[116] It is even more explicit in the *Epistle*,[117] the correspondence between the two men which took place between the historical encounter and the writing of *The Sessions*. Therein, the Vizier acknowledges that, based on Iliyyā's affirmation of Christian *tawḥīd*, his community will avoid financial setbacks. Abū al-Qāsim's brief reply to Iliyyā in the *Epistle* states: "the time has arrived to restrain the financial withholding of their advancement, the diminishment of their

115. Levy-Rubin, *Non-Muslims in the Early Islamic Empire*, 175; Tritton, *The Caliphs and Their Non-Muslim Subjects*, 14.

116. The Arabic is: ما كنت اتحقق مذهب النسطور على ما وصفت والآن فقد صحّ لي توحيدكم ووجب حقّكم

117. See the discussion of the *Epistle* in chapter 4, section 3.1.

remuneration [and] objection to their means of subsistence. By my life, in these ways, much of their blood is spared."[118] Though the possibility of editorial amendments to the *Epistle* must not be discounted, if taken at face value the document indicates that the Sessions had social and jurisprudential implications for Iliyyā's Christian community.

As discussed in chapter 2, non-Muslim peoples living in lands conquered by Muslims were accorded certain public and private rights through a convention known as *dhimma.* The *dhimmī* pact provided the non-Muslim with the protection of a Muslim *Amīr* in exchange for the payment of a poll tax. In addition to taxation, the *dhimmī* was subject to social segregation embodied in dress, social status and building codes. The implementation of such laws varied across epochs owing largely to the severity or lenience of the *Amīr*. Indeed, the Marwanid dynasty was known for its leniency. So what was the rationale for the Bishop's protracted argument for the *tawḥīd* of his Christian community? Was he seeking amelioration of their status in the *dhimmī* convention or perhaps at minimum a preservation of the status of "People of the Book"? The suggestion is plausible. A more appealing alternative is that the Bishop was pleading for disassociation from the "house of war *par excellence*" – the Byzantines.[119] Iliyyā's favorable contrast of his Christology with that of other ecclesial families commends this line of argument.[120] The *Proof of the True Faith* is an extended apologetic against the Jacobite and Melkite formulations of the union. He describes the Melkite union as one of "composition, mixture and intermixing."[121] The Chalcedon formula prohibits a union of "intermixing."[122] Iliyyā suggests that the very stipulation laid down by Chalcedon has been transgressed by the Melkites. The union they espouse is one of intermingling. The Melkite and Jacobite formulae, according to Iliyyā, are impossible to implement in jurisprudence and are untenable intellectually. By contrast, the Christology of the Church of the East is compliant with Islamic *tawhīd.* Though the roots of the Church of the East's Christology predate

118. al-Niṣībīn, *Kitāb al-majālis* (Huntington 240), 67v; Sbath, "Entry 1130:1," 18. The Arabic reads as follows:

...وآن وقت ضبط اليد عن أن يخطف شيء من مال من تقدّمهم أو التوصّل إلى إنحطاط رتبة من رتبهم والتعرّض لسبب من أسبابهم ولعمري انّ بها وأقرانها يحتقن كثير من دماءهم...

119. Bernard Lewis speaks of Europe as the "*jihād* par excellence" in the later history of Islam. I have borrowed his idea and applied it to the Byzantines in the Abbasid period (Lewis, *Islam and the West*, 10).

120. Iliyyā is unwilling to ascribe a belief in the indwelling to Melkites and Jacobites although at least one Melkite, Abū Qurra, states, "It would be astonishing for anyone to deny the residence of God [*hulūl Allāh*] in the human body which we have shown is the most perfectly suited aspect of his creation." Also, "the eternal Son . . . indwelt the womb of Mary the immaculate virgin by the Holy Spirit" (Beaumont, *Christology in Dialogue with Muslims*, 35, 39). It is clear that the Melkites adhered to some understanding of the indwelling.

121. Composition: *tarkīb* تركيب ; mixture: *al-mumāzaja* الممازجة ; intermixing: *al-ikhtilāt* الإختلاط

122. The Chalcedon formula also includes the following alpha privatives: "without confusion [*bilā ikhtilāṭ*], without change [*wa-lā taḥawwul*], without division [*wa-lā inqisām*], without separation [*wa-lā infiṣāl*]." While the latter two descriptors were seen to address the error of Nestorianism, the former two addressed the error of monophysitism.

Islam, it is striking that the Bishop felt his Christology enabled his church to adhere to the Islamic understanding of divine unicity.

While Christians under Islamic rule were considered *dhimmīs*, Christians outside the "house of Islam" were considered the "house of war." The Byzantines were the perennial enemies of Muslims and posed an ever-present threat to the Marwanid Emirate. Iliyyā has an incentive, therefore, to draw a clear line of demarcation between himself and the Melkite Byzantines. Iliyyā's extensive argument which hovers over the first three Sessions – that Christians are people of *tawḥīd* – establishes this line between the Church of the East and the Byzantines before the Muslim Vizier. Iliyyā presses the leniency of the Marwanid dynasty[123] and more specifically the irenic disposition of Abū al-Qāsim to secure a favorable social and religious status for his Christian community – *tawḥīd*.

5.4 Iliyyā's Rhetorical Strategy

A common rhetorical strategy of Iliyyā is to identify concepts in Islamic thought which parallel his own Christian formulation. He then turns the question back on his Muslim interlocutor. Consider Iliyyā's response to the Vizier's inquiry concerning the risk of speaking of the "indwelling." Abū al-Qāsim perceives that this language will surely lead less-instructed Christians into the error of thinking that the divine essence was united with humanity as a body within a body. Iliyyā refers to a well-known and often-debated aspect of Islamic *kalām*: anthropomorphisms – the attribution of human attributes to God. The Qur'ān itself describes Allāh's session on a throne (Q7:54; 25:59) which begs the question as to whether the essence of God is taking a seat or whether this is a reference to an attribute of divinity (e.g. sovereignty) such that a literal session need not be invoked. The Vizier explains, as Iliyyā has anticipated, that the verse must not be understood literally to indicate that God is contained in space. The majestic essence of God is not taking a seat. In much the same way, Christians use the language of "indwelling" to refer to the relationship of the divine and the human born of Mary. Though there is inherent risk, it is an acceptable way of speaking. The technique is used masterfully by Iliyyā to help his Muslim counterpart realize that Muslims speak in much the same way as Christians when describing God.

A second example occurs when the Vizier discerns a difficulty in Iliyyā's doctrine of the "indwelling." If the divine will is operative, must not the essence of divinity be indwelling the human Jesus? Iliyyā states that Islamic jurisprudents had declared that God created the world without change to his essence or properties as it was the will which acted in creation. This aspect of Islamic *kalām* (theological disputation)

123. See chapter 2, section 4 for a discussion of the Marwanid dynasty of the eleventh century.

allows Iliyyā to find a commonality with his understanding of the indwelling of the divine in Christ. It is the dominant divine will that exerts itself through the subservient human born of Mary. The essence need not be invoked for actions such as miracles and sublime teaching. Thus, the essence is not compromised by the indwelling and Christians are preserved from the accusation of *shirk*. It was a masterful apologetic move in the Islamic milieu, though it certainly did not convince all (e.g. ʿAbd al-Jabbār).[124] There is, however, more to question in this approach than its strategic value apologetically. Was it a robust formulation in terms of the ontological unity which all Christians espoused? The formula by which the Church of the East came to be known was "two *kyāne*, two *qnōme*, one *parsufā*" (union of two natures and their *qnōme* in one person).[125] The formulation of Iliyyā conforms with the first two qualifiers – "two *kyāne*, two *qnōme*" – but begs the question of the "one person." Does a united will constitute a unity of persons? If the Bishop's analogies are entered as evidence, the answer is "no." Although the Bishop's analogies alone may be inadequate to form a final verdict on his Christology, the unity of the will does little to redress the implication. Though the Bishop was a brilliant logician, his compromised analogies portended implications he might have wished to avoid.

In summary, as was observed in the discussion of Iliyyā's Trinitarian formulation, the Bishop exploits his knowledge of Islamic thought to expand the plausibility of his Christian doctrine. The defects which Muslims find in the Christian way of describing Christ's divinity are not unlike those in the ways Muslims speak of God. The complexity of theological language results in a certain amount of ambiguity whether the speaker is Muslim or Christian. Iliyyā's patient exposition urges his Muslim counterpart to lay aside any thought of *shirk* in reference to his Christian community.

6. Conclusion

Theology in an Islamic milieu is, of necessity, a response to Islam and Iliyyā is clearly a responsive theologian in the Islamic context. The intellectual currents of the day had established *tawḥīd* as the standard bearer for theological accuracy. Iliyyā's Theodoran doctrine provided a solid foundation on which the Bishop was able to build a credible case for monotheism. Yet one must respectfully ask if Iliyyā's zeal for *tawḥīd* blurred distinctions between his church and the Islamic society which surrounded it. Would his co-religionists or their progeny misconstrue his formulation as a concession to Islam, an attempt to dissolve the barriers erected in the sectarian environment? Iliyyā assumes that the *tawḥīd* construct as framed by the *mutakallimūn* (Muslim theologians) can

124. Thomas, "Miracles of Jesus," 234.

125. Atiya, *History of Eastern Christianity*, 254, fn 254; Faultless, "Two Recensions," 186.

fully bear the weight of the incarnation. Was *tawḥīd* a sufficient construct to contain the doctrine of the unity of humanity and divinity in Christ? Would the Bishop's plea to be included within the fold of *tawḥīd* carry ramifications he might not have considered? Would his Christology have any effect on the flow of conversions from the Church of the East, either to stem it or, inadvertently, to facilitate it?[126] If Christians and Muslims alike are monotheists,[127] what prohibits merging the two communities? Such questions, though of interest, carry us beyond the pale of this research. Nevertheless, the union of deity and humanity in Christ has been the defining characteristic of the Christian faith. Given the numerical decline of the Church of the East in subsequent centuries, a critical reading of *The Sessions* in light of such questions is warranted.

On the one hand, Iliyyā provides an outstanding example of *apologia* from a responsive theologian in the Muslim milieu. His knowledge of Islam, his familiarity with and fidelity to his ecclesial heritage, his patient use of analogy and his reciprocal relationship with Abū al-Qāsim all serve to create an opportune moment for the polymath Bishop at the Muslim–Christian interface. Nevertheless, the Bishop emphasizes his dyohypostatic Christology to the detriment of the unity of the divine and human in the person of Christ. His analogies push the boundaries established by his predecessors in the direction of the Islamic conception while his exposition provides few correctives. The contemporary reader of Iliyyā must not forget that the stakes were high. Theology was not merely a matter of academic interest. Muslim polemicists had forcefully excluded Christians from *tawḥīd.* Complicating matters was the fact that the Byzantines were the perennial enemies of Muslims and were distinguished from the Church of the East only by a complex discrimination of doctrine. By demonstrating that his Christian community was indeed monotheistic, Iliyyā would preserve a favored social status for his community for future generations. He was faithful to his theological heritage in that he worked out of the dyohypostatic christological framework. He used analogies and nomenclature to shield the divine hypostasis from any blemish which might be presumed on the part of Muslims through union with humanity. The driving force behind Iliyyā's Christology is an impassioned plea for *tawḥīd* status for his Christian community.

126. See chapter 2, sections 3.2.2 and 3.2.3 for a discussion of demographic and political issues facing the Church of the East.

127. *Muwahhidūn* موحّدون

7

Defending Divine Unity

From Medieval to Postmodern

1. Introduction

This concluding chapter first pauses to look back at the eleventh-century theologians, the objects of the research. I attempt to isolate the contributions of these Arabic-speaking theologians in the Muslim milieu in which they lived. In this section, I "zoom in" to try to identify narrowly their contributions (section 2). Second, I take in the broader horizons of Muslim–Christian discourse of the medieval period. This section describes how this research informs a scholarly understanding of the period and specifically of the two theologians in question (section 3). Finally, I take a brief look at the Muslim–Christian interface in the contemporary era. To what degree is the defense of Christian divine unity pertinent to contemporary issues? Has the divisive doctrine now been circumvented by more promising areas of dialogue? Finally, are there lines of connection between the eleventh-century theologians and those who labor today at the Muslim–Christian interface? To that end, the boundaries of this study will extend beyond the Arab Muslim context to the worldwide dialogue in which Islam and Christianity as the two largest world religions participate daily (section 4).

2. Concluding Findings of this Research

2.1 Ibn al-Ṭayyib's Definition of the Hypostases

I have contended that Ibn al-Ṭayyib made a noteworthy contribution to Muslim–Christian discourse of his era. The formulations of his theological treatises are brief, precise and dense. They bring to mind the Arabic adage "*mā qall wa dall*," meaning the economic use of words for maximum impact and effectiveness. The elaborate and lengthy deliberations of Yaḥyā Ibn ʿAdī are distilled to produce succinct and clear statements of Trinitarian unity in the Muslim milieu. In distilling Ibn ʿAdī, the author is not merely summarizing. Rather Ibn al-Ṭayyib manifests his peculiar genius in lucidity and scriptural reasoning. It is the work of a pastoral theologian aware of the pressures exerted on his ecclesial community by the dominance of Islamic *tawḥīd* and seeking to clarify the Christian doctrine of divine unity for the sake of his flock.

His most prominent contribution is his clear and compelling definition of the Trinitarian persons (the hypostases) as the three essential attributes of the one God taken with the essence. The features of the definition reveal a responsive theological statement in the Muslim milieu. First, the attributes divide into those that are of the essence and those that are non-essential, communicated to beings in creation. The division reflects Ashʿārī thought which also divided the attributes into those of essence and act. Furthermore, the philosopher-theologian recognized, as did others before him, that the Ashʿārī definition of the attributes (*al-ṣifāt*) could embrace a Trinitarian understanding of the hypostases. Al-Ashʿārī himself "used to say, 'The word of God (exalted is He) is a pre-eternal *ṣifa* [attribute] belonging to Him, eternally subsisting in His essence.'"[1] It remained to determine on what basis the attributes of essence were distinguished from the non-essential attributes. In response, Ibn al-Ṭayyib did not draw on the common understanding that the attributes of essence were those attributes without which God would not be God. Rather, he insisted that because the attributes were of the essence and not revealed in the created order, humanity was dependent on divine revelation to ascertain them. Their names – paternity, filiation and procession – were revealed in Scripture and, therefore, subject to neither debate nor variation in number. In response to the prevalent Islamic rejection of familial terms for divinity, he took refuge in scriptural authority, even as Muslims had done to justify their view of the attributes.[2] Finally, the attribution of action to the essence of God (MM II) as opposed to the hypostases preserved the unity of the divine essence.

This research, therefore, advocates for a re-examination of Ibn al-Ṭayyib as a theologian who labored intentionally at the Muslim–Christian interface of his

1. *inna kalām Allāh taʿālā ṣifa lahu qadīma lam yazal qāʾim bi-dhātihi.*
إنّ كلام الله تعالى صفة له قديمة لم يزل قائم بذاته
(Translation from Cumming, "Ṣifāt al-dhāt," 34; original: Ibn Furak, *Mujarrad Maqālāt*, 40, 59).

2. In chapter 3 we noted that Ibn al-Ṭayyib also linked these three attributes of the essence to Ibn ʿAdī's triad of knowledge. In the Muslim milieu the formulation had traction as it related to Ibn Sīnā's thought. Therefore, it is understandable that Ibn al-Ṭayyib would incorporate it. However, as discussed, Ibn al-Ṭayyib recognized that the association made his formulation vulnerable to the criticism that God's knowledge was not purely an attribute of the essence, but one of act. In response, he amended his formulation slightly (M3 VI) to say that this attribute referred to God's perfect self-knowledge, not the imperfect human knowledge of God (see chapter 3, section 2.4.2).

era.[3] My argument has relied on demonstrating clear lines of connection to Islamic thought as well as identifying the key themes of Ibn al-Ṭayyib's Trinitarian treatises as they animated the Muslim–Christian discourse of his day. These themes include the unity of the divine essence, the definition of the hypostases and their relation to the doctrine of the attributes, and the attribution of divine action to the essence through the hypostases. It may be asserted that Ibn al-Ṭayyib, though only obliquely referring to his Islamic counterparts, spoke directly to their theological concerns, as did Bishop Iliyyā.[4]

2.2 Divine Impassibility

Ibn al-Ṭayyib also defended the divine unity espoused by Christians in his christological formulations. The first line of defense was to ground the incarnation theologically in the magnanimity of God. God who so graciously created and sustains mankind was unwilling to leave them as a prey to sin and deception. In order to rescue them from the plight brought on by sin, the eternal Word emptied himself to take on humanity. The incarnation was the climactic expression of God's love for humanity and the only means whereby man's salvation could be effected.

Given the dyohypostatic Christology of the Church of the East, it is not surprising that Ibn al-Ṭayyib not only associates the hypostasis (*al-uqnūm*) with the substance but also rejects the hypostatic union as it would equate to the spoiling of the divine perfections. What emerges in the texts is the author's concern to shield the divine hypostasis from human pain (theopaschitism) as well as from events common to humanity which portray contingency – birth, eating, drinking, and so on – the very point on which Muslim polemicists, such as Abū ʿĪsā, had interrogated Christians relentlessly.[5] There could be no comingling of divinity and humanity. Thus the locus of the union was the property (*khāṣṣa*) of filiation.[6] In effect, the author explicitly stated a one-way communication of the attributes. The divine hypostasis elevated the human

3. Samir's excellent article on Ibn al-Ṭayyib's contribution to Arab thought recognizes his noteworthy contributions in science, medicine, philosophy, translation and scriptural commentary. However, the article does not consider the polymath's contribution to the Muslim–Christian interface (see Samir, "La place d'Ibn at-Ṭayyib dans la pensée arabe"). Samir does suggest that parts of Ibn al-Ṭayyib's Introduction to the *Commentary on the Psalms* may relate to Islam (Faultless, "Ibn al-Ṭayyib," 675). Faultless has noted that "the lack of explicit mention of Islam or Muslims by Ibn al-Ṭayyib's works" is remarkable for an "intellectual living in Baghdad who must have thought daily about the position of Christians within the Islamic context" (Faultless, 670).

4. See the introduction to M2 where Ibn al-Ṭayyib refers to other religions. See chapter 3, section 2.3.2.

5. See Thomas, *Early Muslim Polemic.*

6. I have noted the inherent discrepancy between this formulation and Ibn al-Ṭayyib's definition of the hypostasis as "the attribute of essence taken with the essence" (chapter 5, 2.3.2).

hypostasis but the human did not denigrate the divine. The transfer of divine power to the humanity of Christ enabled the working of miracles which Ibn al-Ṭayyib and other Christians saw as a proof of the union of deity and humanity in the one Christ.

Finally, Ibn al-Ṭayyib labored to defend the legitimacy of Trinitarian terminology including the problematic familial monikers – Son and Father. He sought to establish the Old Testament background of these referents beyond those that ʿAmmār al-Baṣrī had suggested. In summary, Ibn al-Ṭayyib's theological treatises reverberated in the Islamic milieu – picking up themes of the discourse and echoing a uniquely Christian apologetic while preserving the orthodoxy of his Christian confession.

An examination of Ibn al-Ṭayyib's responsive theology in the Muslim milieu raises some questions. I have not criticized his reluctance to engage in public polemics (though others might) for reasons given in this research. However, I offer a criticism in that Ibn al-Ṭayyib, like other intellectuals of his era, was confined by his own adherence to Greek thought, particularly to the concept of "essence" and its elaboration of and application to the concept of divinity. His categories of thought, inherited from the Greek intellectual heritage, colored his reading of Scripture. Significantly, he gave more attention to Scripture than did others of his time (e.g. Yaḥyā Ibn ʿAdī) but he nevertheless read the text through the lens of Greek philosophical concepts. This proclivity was owing to generations of theologians who had integrated Platonic and Aristotelian thought with their theology to commend it intellectually. Accordingly, he is unable to countenance the thought of the divinity's exposure to human contingencies in the one Christ. His theology labors to shield the deity from the normal human experiences of pain and privation, the point of attack of Islamic polemic. He therefore rejects the reciprocal communication of the attributes, effectively widening the gap between the divine and human hypostases in Christ. In point of fact, that rejection is not unique to Ibn al-Ṭayyib but the norm for medieval Christians. Herein lies the criticism: Ibn al-Ṭayyib did not seek to redefine the parameters of Muslim–Christian discourse. His inclination was to uphold the boundaries rather than question their legitimacy, though his definition of "the one" may be considered a beginning in this direction. He claimed inclusion in the fold of *tawḥīd* as opposed to questioning its validity as a theological construct as defined by Muslim theologians. He was unable to transcend the strictures of his era to offer a new understanding of Christology. That transcendence would wait for another era when the grip of Greek philosophical categories would be loosened and theology would be cast in another mold.

2.3 Iliyyā's Uncharacteristic Impact

Though Iliyyā's Sessions with Abū al-Qāsim fit well in the genre of "the Monk in the Emir's *majlis*," this research has highlighted one uncharacteristic aspect in the nature of Iliyyā's success. The common perception of "success" in the *majālis* (sessions) was a thorough routing of the opponent. Iliyyā's success has the greater appeal in that he persuades his interlocutor respectfully. Abū al-Qāsim is brought to confess that Christians are indeed monotheists based on the Bishop's defense of divine unity. The point is quite easily demonstrated from the text, but begs the question as to what factors contributed to Iliyyā's success. Was it his rhetorical skills? The monotheistic confession (found in *Epistle* and Session 5), when read before the scholars of Mayyāfāriqīn, elicited their approval and paved the way for the Vizier's welcome of Iliyyā into the fold of monotheism. Therein, Iliyyā reveals his awareness of Islamic sensitivities and his skill in the Arabic medium, specifically the rhetoric of divine unity (*tawḥīd*).

Did Iliyyā's analogies play a role in illuminating his dyohypostatic Christology such that the Vizier was persuaded? We have seen that Iliyyā moved beyond his Church of the East forebears to suggest analogies which failed to uphold an ontological unity of divinity and humanity. Was this innovation sufficient to convince the Vizier that divinity was not mitigated by the union?

Was it the Bishop's skillful exegesis of the Qur'ān, a measured and careful usage? As a Christian, he averred that he was not bound by the Qur'ān's dictates but wished to demonstrate from the revealed Islamic scripture that Christians are indeed worshippers of the one God (*muwaḥḥidūn*). His use of deductive reasoning and reliance on reputable qur'ānic exegetes demonstrated that the Islamic scripture placed Christians of the Prophet's time in the fold of *tawḥīd*. He accomplished the task so ably that the Muslim scholars of Abū al-Qāsim's court affirmed his correct interpretation of their holy book as read to them from the *Epistle*.

No doubt, each of these aspects of the great Bishop's defense of divine unity played a role in the success of the Sessions. Nevertheless, the documents also reveal a relational dynamic between the two men which elicits the reader's appreciation. The account of Abū al-Qāsim's healing in a monastery, long before meeting Iliyyā, made a lasting impression on him, indicated by the fact that he relates it in some detail to Iliyyā and thereby introduces his double skepticism. His candid admission of skepticism of Christian belief in one God (*tawḥīd*), on the one hand, and of idolatry (*kufr*), on the other, is refreshingly honest and disarming. The text paints Abū al-Qāsim as a sincere and objective inquirer who has previously sought explanation of the Christian faith from less able spokesmen. He assures Iliyyā repeatedly that his intention is not to castigate but to rightly ascertain what must be the hidden beauty of the Christian faith.

As if this were not enough as a portent of a fruitful dialogue, there is also the intriguing extra-textual narrative of the Vizier's failing health and demise. In an ironic twist, the brother of Iliyyā, himself a renowned physician, is charged with the care of the Vizier but withdraws due to a strange dream indicating that the Vizier will in fact die.[7] The *Epistle* reveals the Vizier's wish to obtain a written copy of Iliyyā's words of wisdom in order to "chase away anxiety." The correspondence takes place in the months preceding the Vizier's death, while he is in the throes of a demoralizing illness. Alas, the Vizier breathes his last while awaiting the coveted writings of the Bishop. Finally, his self-composed epitaph conveys a deepening of his religious sensitivities in his latter years. All of this takes place against the backdrop of the Vizier's flight, years prior to the Sessions, from Faṭimid Cairo after the Caliph al-Ḥākim bi-Amr Allāh had put his father and brothers to death.

The attendant circumstances of the narrative, on the one hand, strain credibility. They cause the reader to wonder if such an uncommon preparation for dialogue is conceivable. I have considered the possibility of editorial amendment to *Sessions* without dismissing it. Nevertheless, the dialogue also bears notable marks of authenticity (chapter 4, 2.2) prompting a respect for a baseline textual integrity and an objective reading. This attentive reading of the *Epistle* in tandem with *Sessions* suggests that at least one key ingredient which allowed the two men to transcend the polemical acerbity of their era was the Vizier's uncharacteristic existential preparation for the encounter. Iliyyā's arguments are robust and substantive; however, they are not novel at the Muslim–Christian interface of the period. We cannot identify the sole reason for Abū al-Qāsim's persuasion in the strength of the arguments presented. There appears to be more transpiring. A warm bond exists between the two men which is portrayed in the Vizier's openness and willingness to entertain Iliyyā's explications. Therefore, I suggest that the uniqueness of *The Sessions* is due, in large part, to the existential preparation of the dialogue partner – Abū al-Qāsim, the Shīʿite Vizier of the Marwanid dynasty.

3. Impact on the Field of Muslim–Christian Discourse

At this point, I broaden the horizon of our study to Muslim–Christian relations in the medieval period, specifically the Abbasid period (750–1258/132–656). What impact does this research have on this field of study? The textual evidence of the period offers little in terms of reciprocal and respectful religious interchange. The texts testify to innate assumptions on both sides of the religious divide. Christians viewed the Prophet of Islam as an impostor at worst, or an emissary who might serve to prepare

7. Might this element be nothing more than a framing of the story by subsequent editors and redactors? While it is indeed possible, we also note that Iliyyā's brother, Abū Saʿīd Manṣūr Ibn ʿĪsā, was a historical person and a distinguished doctor in the capital of the Marwanid dynasty – the personal physician of Amīr Naṣr al-Dawla Ibn Marwan. It is not beyond credibility that he was the doctor who treated Abū al-Qāsim (see chapter 2, 2.2) (Samir, *Foi et culture en Irak*, 175–177).

his Arab people for the more advanced truth of the Christian gospel.[8] Muslims, on the other hand, assumed that Christians had misunderstood the revealed faith or willfully subverted it, and should recognize that Islam was a course-correction.[9] The discourse reveals an indifference to the totality of Christian truth claims, focusing only on those doctrinal issues where Christianity was seen to contravene Islam's cardinal doctrine of *tawḥīd* – the absolute unity of divinity. As Thomas summarizes: "Through the course of the shared history of the faiths these . . . attitudes have led to widespread misunderstanding, to the mistaken point that each faith has represented the other in its own terms, to a reduction of the other down to the stature of a subsidiary form of itself, and then to demonization, enmity and the sanction of bloodshed."[10]

3.1 The Exceptional Sessions

We have noted that Iliyyā's *Sessions* is regarded as the apogee of the literary genre entitled "Monk in the Emir's *majlis*."[11] However, I suggest that Iliyyā's *Sessions* was, at least in some respects, exceptional. In order to highlight the points of distinction between *Sessions* and comparable works, it will be useful to survey a few salient points and outcomes of the other four historical *majālis* (sessions) of Griffith's study. The account of the monk Michael the Sabaïte depicts Michael as a skilled debater before the Caliph ʿAbd al-Malik. However, his views on Muḥammad's prophethood and Islamic inducements to conversion result in his exposure to fiery coals and fatal poison. In the end, the monk is beheaded by caliphal fiat and venerated by the Christian community.[12]

A second *majlis* is that of Abraham of Tiberias who appears before a parade of Muslim scholars in the court of the Amīr ʿAbd al-Raḥmān al-Hāshimī, overcoming them in debate to show the superiority of his Christian faith. The Amīr himself, somewhat ill-informed regarding the Christian faith, is infatuated by a slave girl whom Abraham cures of demonic oppression. The debate features both Muslim converts from Christianity and Jewish participants. At the conclusion of the debate, the monk

8. Timothy I's assessment of Muḥammad has been described as the most positive assessment coming from a Christian and yet it is innocuous at best. "He walked in the path of the prophets, and trod in the tracks of the lovers of God" (Mingana, "Apology of Timothy the Patriarch," 197; Putman, *L'église et l'islam sous Timothée I*, 248).

9. Consider ʿAbd al-Jabbār's reconstruction of early Christian history contending that the apostle Paul rewrote the gospel while the original gospel of Christ made its way into Arabia to prepare a few followers for the coming of Muḥammad (see Kuhn, "Early Islamic Perspectives"; Reynolds and Samir, *Abd al-Jabbar*).

10. Thomas, "Past and the Future," 39.

11. Griffith, "Monk in the Emir's Majlis," 53.

12. Griffith, 19–21.

consumes poison with no deleterious effects, performs an exorcism and places his hand in fire with no harm. The result is that the Jewish and Muslim participants in the debate profess Christianity and are beheaded. Abraham himself is imprisoned but later released.[13]

The third debate is that of Abū Qurra in the court of the Caliph al-Ma'mūn, where the extant texts reveal the Melkite bishop defending the veracity of his faith by basing his responses on qur'ānic texts. Abū Qurra puts his religious rivals to flight in debate and obtains the Caliph's approbation. His pointed polemical attack against Islam goes so far as to supply a Christian meaning to the *Fātiḥa* – the opening sūra of the Qur'ān which figures prominently in Muslim canonical prayers. "Those toward whom God has been gracious" are the Christians while "those going astray" are the very ones offering the prayer – Muslims. He asks other polemically loaded questions, such as who will be the spouses of Muslim women after their men have chosen the *ḥūrīs*[14] in paradise.[15]

The fifth and final dialogue in the genre of "the Monk in the Emir's *majlis*" is the Arabic account of the debate between the monk George and three Muslim scholars of Aleppo in the *majlis* of the Amīr al-Malik al-Mushammar. The dialogue features the spiritual interests of the Christians vis-à-vis the carnal pleasures which appeal to their Muslim interlocutors. The monk George, after being encouraged to speak his mind freely and assured that no harm will befall him, expostulates on the base nature of inducements to Islam even suggesting that the Prophet's motivation was dominance rather than bringing his followers to a true knowledge of God. Nevertheless, the monk's arguments meet with the Amīr's approval as the latter has confided to George that he himself was born of a Christian mother. Another day of debate ensues in which the Christian monk continues to adduce proofs for the superiority of his faith. The event concludes with a series of challenges to the participants, none of which are agreeable. Thereupon the monk is rewarded by the Amīr with a provision of fish and a mule to ride upon for his return to the monastery.[16]

I am now in a position to make some observations relative to these examples of medieval Muslim–Christian dialogue in tandem with *The Sessions* of Iliyyā. In *The Sessions*, we note the absence of the acrimonious tone which characterizes the other four dialogues. Iliyyā quite often speaks of Muslims in honorific terms – "may God

13. Griffith, 26–29.

14. The meaning of the qur'ānic phrase *ḥūr 'īn* (حور عين) is debated but probably describes the gazelle-like eyes of the heavenly companions. The term is often understood to mean the pure female companions who are among the rewards of paradise. See Q52:20 and 56:22–23.

15. Griffith, "Monk in the Emir's Majlis," 44–47.

16. Griffith, 55–60.

preserve them."[17] He manifests proper decorum toward the Muslim official (as did Abū Qurra to the Caliph), often requesting that God might lengthen his days. However, the mutual respect goes deeper as Iliyyā carefully crafts an extensive letter recording their exchange and sends it to the Vizier for his perusal and approval. The Vizier praises the Bishop in response and urges him to complete the written record and to supply him with his means of "banishing anxiety." It is also noteworthy that the Sessions preserve the integrity of both men. Certainly, Iliyyā's skill in debate fulfills the educational and entertainment role which marks the *majālis*, but never at the expense of Abū al-Qāsim. The latter is portrayed as neither ignorant nor buffoonish, unlike in other *majālis.* Most noteworthy is the fact that Abū al-Qāsim readily confesses the Christian bishop's monotheism and makes reference to the implications of this fact. This is understated in *Sessions* but is evident in the *Epistle.* In the *majālis* mentioned above, the Christian spokesmen enjoy success in that they outmaneuver and outwit their opponents. As stated above, Iliyyā's *Sessions* reveals a success of a different nature. The reader is treated to a rare public declaration on the part of the Vizier that the Christian community is granted monotheistic status[18] in the Marwanid realm. The victory has potentially far-reaching implications legally, socially and fiscally. For this reason, the Sessions of Iliyyā of Nisibis with Abū al-Qāsim Ibn ʿAlī al-Maghribī are uncharacteristic of the Abbasid medieval period. They represent a small but significant breakthrough in the impasse of Muslim–Christian relations of the era.

In a plea to move beyond the acrid polemics of the Middle Ages, Thomas has suggested a way forward for participants of the two faiths as they interact, whether in formal dialogue or life. This way forward is characterized as "respectful, agnostic inquisitiveness." "By this is meant an attitude of open inquiry into the religion of the other that puts preconditions about its truthfulness or its divine origins to one side and attempts, as far as is possible for an outsider, to discover its core beliefs and diversity of expressions with respect and attentiveness."[19] Abū al-Qāsim was an early example of "respectful, agnostic inquisitiveness." He was willing to lay aside preconceived notions of his Christian counterparts and entertain the notion that Christians are indeed worshippers of the one God. Though he was skeptical of both Christian unbelief and monotheism (*tawḥīd*), he was willing to suspend judgment in order to carefully listen to and actively cross-examine his Christian counterpart for

17. We note that Timothy I's dialogue with the Caliph al-Mahdī also contains this note of public decorum and respect, which is to be expected as Timothy was in the royal court of the Caliph (see Putman, *L'église et l'islam sous Timothée I*). Thus terms of respect proliferate in the dialogue. The Sessions, however, seem to go beyond the mere public preservation of decorum to a personal and reciprocal respect between the two men.

18. *Muwahhidūn* موحّدون

19. Thomas, "Past and the Future," 41.

the purpose of understanding.[20] He is delighted to have discovered in Bishop Iliyyā a knowledgeable Christian who is competent to fill in the gaps in his understanding. It may even be argued that the Vizier's expressions of joy in his new discovery take him beyond the domain of mere inquisitiveness. It is indeed possible that he saw himself as something of an advocate for the large Christian constituency in the Marwanid realm. For these reasons, *Sessions*, coupled with the *Epistle*, signifies not only a classic example of "the Monk in the Emir's *majlis*," but also an exceptional species of medieval Muslim–Christian relations, contravening the acrid and dismissive tone which had come to dominate the discourse.

3.2 A Note of Irony

Though praise for *Sessions* and its protagonists is the dominant note of this research, there is also a note of irony as I contemplate the implications of Iliyyā's dyohypostatic analogies for the future of his ecclesial community. I have belaboured the fact that his analogies failed to uphold the ontological unity of divinity and humanity in Christ. Moreover, his proclivity to define his Christology over against that of the other ecclesial families that encountered Islam in the medieval period is striking. By claiming that his view of Christ was different from that of the Melkites and the Jacobites, Iliyyā was seeking to establish parity in *tawḥīd* for his ecclesial community. Was the Bishop's accommodation to Islamic *tawḥīd* and his insistence that Christians adhere to it a salutary move for the Church of the East? It held great promise of social and religious parity in the short-term but would there be a high price to pay in subsequent decades? Did the insistence on Christian adherence to *tawḥīd* contribute to a dissolution of the distinctive religious character of the Church of the East? Did it ultimately contribute to its demise? Questions such as these must be traced through centuries of theological development in the Church of the East. Though these matters extend well beyond the limitations of this research, my considered opinion is that such a critical reading of Iliyyā's Christology is warranted by the analogies themselves and must figure in the historical study of the Church of the East in its increasingly Islamic milieu.

3.3 Forging a Link

There are other angles through which this study might impact the field of medieval Muslim–Christian relations. First of all, Ibn al-Ṭayyib's active engagement at the Muslim–Christian interface of his era is sustained by this study. His contribution in

---

20. *Istifhām* إستفهام

providing a robust and succinct definition of the Trinitarian persons in the Muslim milieu cannot be overlooked.

Ironically, Ibn al-Ṭayyib labored in the pre-eminent Muslim city of the period – Baghdad – and yet never explicitly mentioned the presence of Muslims in his writings. Other students of his work have noticed this fact.[21] A minor correction has been provided by this research in that Ibn al-Ṭayyib did speak of the religious other in his second Trinitarian treatise (M2; see chapter 3, 3.2). This observation does not suffice to answer the question why Ibn al-Ṭayyib's theological formulations responded only implicitly to Islam (never explicitly). A more satisfying answer, though admittedly incomplete, lies in the fact that the tone of the Muslim–Christian interface considered with the possible social implications of losing the contest may have deterred Christians from entering the fray of public debate. Christian sentiment may be represented by the Arabic proverb: "he who is burned by the soup, blows on the yogurt." We have highlighted ʿAbd al-Jabbār's revealing comment about the Christians of Baghdad: "after him was Yaḥyā b. ʿAdī from whom came the heretics who are in your area, the sect that does not engage in debate."[22] Whether or not the statement can apply directly to Ibn al-Ṭayyib is immaterial. In fact, it reveals a reticence among the Christian intellectuals of Baghdad to engage in public debate – an aspect which the Muslim polemicist duly notes. The point is not without importance in this research. Ibn al-Ṭayyib's theological formulations clearly addressed concerns at the Muslim–Christian interface. Yet he avoided an explicit engagement with and direct challenge to Muslim polemical attacks. His theological method combined a sophisticated knowledge of Islamic thought with unflinching fidelity to his theological heritage in the Church of the East. Indeed, Ibn al-Ṭayyib's use of Islamic terms and concepts in tandem with his strict observance of Church of the East doctrines suggests he was more engaged in his Muslim milieu than has been assumed. He demonstrates a meticulous observance of theological propriety as a responsive theologian laboring in the Islamic milieu seeking to enhance the rational credibility of his confession in an environment where *tawḥīd* has become the intellectual standard bearer.[23]

This research is, then, an argument for the value of theology as engagement. Though Ibn al-Ṭayyib hesitates to announce his engagement with Islam, it is nonetheless present and poignant. Factors beyond our detection may have given rise

21. See footnote 3.

22. Reynolds, *Muslim Theologian*, 211, from "Tathbit," 92, 11.8–10. See chapter 3, section 4.2.3, fn 139. This translation of ʿAbd al-Jabbār differs from that of Reynolds and Samir. We believe this to be a more accurate rendering and it upholds our contention that the Christian intellectuals of Baghdad had withdrawn from the field of public debate.

23. Consider Ibn al-Ṭayyib's excoriation of his co-religionist bishops because of their love of material reward, found in the introduction to his *Commentary on the Gospels* (Faultless, "Ibn al-Ṭayyib," 677; Samir, "La place d'Ibn at-Ṭayyib dans la pensée arabe," 191).

to his reticence but that does not minimize the value of his theological response in the Islamic context. Fruitful avenues for future research include both his exegetical work and his canon law considered from the vantage point of Muslim–Christian engagement. Indeed, Ibn al-Ṭayyib's engagement with Islam is an incentive to examine other Christian theologians in the Muslim milieu for their implicit theological response to Islamic thought.

The reticence of Christians to engage in public debate is also reflected in Iliyyā's *Sessions*. This curt phrase reported in Session 1 is revealing: "If his [the Vizier's] objective is debate and polemics, I request him to spare me this and pass on to subjects that do not concern sect and religion."[24] It was only the Vizier's continued reassurance that his objective was to understand the Christian faith and to vindicate it from false and abhorrent accusations that fostered the Bishop's collaboration.

"Reading between the lines" of the eleventh-century Muslim–Christian interface points to a uniting factor between our two characters. The acrid atmosphere of the sectarian milieu had resulted in Christians' partial retreat from public debate. There was too much to be lost and little to be gained. In this period, Iliyyā's *Sessions* emerges as an exception to the rule, demonstrating that reciprocal and thoughtful interchange can still take place as participants transcend the bitter sectarian atmosphere and come to their task with the proper mindset. No doubt the explicit nature of the *Sessions* is due to a prevailing leniency of the Marwanid Emirate which finds expression in the Vizier's "respectful, agnostic inquisitiveness." Ibn al-Ṭayyib, on the other hand, is understood as a responsive theologian who labors under the scourge of the sectarian climate but does so as a positive participant, exploiting the prevalent intellectual debates to commend his Christian formulations. Indeed, the one literary link which exists between the two men expresses Ibn al-Ṭayyib's endorsement of Iliyyā's explicit defense of the faith before Abū al-Qāsim: "I have read it and prayed for the life of its composer and for the continuation of his prayers for the world. The letter is extremely beautiful, orthodox and in harmony with the ecclesial books. It is impossible for him who loves the truth to reject a single word thereof."[25]

In summary, I have surveyed two theologians of the Church of the East and their engagement with Islamic thought. Both react to the strained atmosphere of polemical attack, not by withdrawal from the contest, but by using their unique intellectual gifts to defend a Christian and Trinitarian view of divine unity in the Muslim milieu. Ibn al-Ṭayyib's implicit engagement supplies a robust understanding of the Trinitarian persons as well as of the impassibility of the divinity in Christology, adopting compliant Muslim terminology and concepts. Bishop Iliyyā has the good

24. Samir, "Entretien d'Elie de Nisibe," 61 (my translation).

25. Delly, *La théologie d'Elie bar-Senaya*, 16.

fortune to encounter a uniquely prepared Muslim interlocutor whose "respectful, agnostic inquisitiveness" reveals an island of Muslim–Christian reciprocity amidst the turbulent waters of medieval Muslim–Christian relations.

4. Divine Unity and Incarnation in Today's Muslim Milieu

The reason for my interest in the defense of divine unity in the Muslim milieu is largely owing to my vocation. I have worked twenty-five years in the Muslim milieu and acquired a non-native fluency in Arabic. I have benefited from Arab Christians who were willing to explain the complexities of their context to me. Equally valuable has been my interaction with Islam in the medium of Arabic whether through the printed text or through many acquaintances and teachers who have broadened the horizons of my understanding. I have a profound respect for Islam. Nevertheless, I am a Christian and an aspiring theologian, having come to the Middle East to participate in the life of the church and assist it, in small measure, to reflect on and embrace the life of the Trinity in a society where Islam is the majority faith. I have observed something of the progression of events, already well underway in the medieval period, as Christians of the Middle East migrate to lands they perceive, rightly or wrongly, will accommodate their religious beliefs or improve their economic status. In some ways, this research has served to further and deepen my participation in the life of the church of the Middle East – seeking to resurface an aspect of its ancient testimony in the Muslim context and question the possible reasons for its long and slow decline.

4.1 Defense of Divine Unity in Contemporary Muslim–Christian Discourse

The defense of divine unity has not abated in the Arab Muslim context. A cursory survey reveals a plethora of Arab writers, largely unknown outside the Arab world, who continue to assert that their Trinitarian views correspond to monotheistic faith. Among these are the Eastern Orthodox Metropolitan of Mount Lebanon Georges Khodr (b. 1923) and the Lebanese intellectual and Greek Catholic (Melkite) Priest Father Mushīr Bāṣīl ʿAwwun.[26] A series of collaborative works by Muslim and Christian scholars to explicate the meaning of the Christian Scriptures in the Muslim milieu is also noteworthy. The two titles are *The Candid Report of Christ's Disciples*

26. Heidi Hirvonen treats the Christian–Muslim dialogue of Khodr and ʿAwwun (Hirvonen, *Christian–Muslim Dialogue*).

and *The True Meaning of Christ's Gospel.*[27] Two examples of Arab intellectuals who now carry the mantle of Iliyyā of Nisibis and Ibn al-Ṭayyib are the Egyptian ʿAwwaḍ Simʿān and the Protestant ʿImād Shaḥāda.[28]

4.1.1 ʿAwwaḍ Simʿān

Perhaps no one at the contemporary Muslim–Christian interface has wielded a more winsome and robust apologetic of Christian divine unity than the Egyptian ʿAwwaḍ Simʿān. His three major works, combined and published in one volume, are titled *Allah in Philosophy and Christianity*, *Allah: His Essence and the Type of His Unity* and *Allah: The Means of His Self-Revelation.*[29] The title of the collection is *Allāh in Christianity.*[30] A careful analysis of Simʿān's work would require additional chapters but even a cursory overview will suffice to show how this Arab thinker is carrying the discussion of divine unity forward in the Arab Muslim milieu.

Simʿān argues for a conception of divine unity that is distinct from any other unity in the visible world. First, he defines the concept of substance. The medieval Christian theologians defined it as "self-existent." Simʿān accepts this definition while pointing out that finite substances are discovered by their accidents. The divine substance, on the contrary, is free of accident. Here he refers to Aquinas who states that the divine substance is sufficient to itself.[31] Therefore the divine substance is free of accident, a significant clarification to the discussion of the substance among medieval theologians.

In his discussion of the divine attributes Simʿān eschews the idea that the divine attributes were active only in potentiality (effectively idle) until creation. The attributes were eternally present and eternally active within the divine essence and they were active among intelligent beings. Unlike Ibn al-Ṭayyib, Simʿān does not conceptualize the Trinitarian persons as the "attributes of essence when perceived with the essence." He does, however, demonstrate that philosophers from all religious persuasions, including Islam, hold to some understanding of relationality in the divine being. God

27. Abīd, *al-Bayān al-ṣarīḥ*; Jaṭlāwī, *al-Ma'nā al-ṣaḥīḥ*. *al-Bayān al-ṣarīḥ li-ḥawārīy al-masīḥ* البيان الصريح لحواري المسيح and *al-Ma'nā al-ṣaḥīḥ li-injīl al-masīḥ* المعنى الصحيح لإنجيل المسيح
The works have copious introductory articles treating many of the theological impasses in Muslim–Christian discourse such as "The Relationship of Christ to the Father," "The Meaning of 'Son of God'" and "The Word of God among the Divine Attributes."

28. Shaḥāda's recent monograph addresses many pressing issues in the defense of Trinitarian monotheism in the Muslim milieu (Shaḥāda, *Al-āb wa-al-ibn*).

29. His titles include *God: His Essence and the Type of His Unity* (*Allāh: Dhātahu wa-naw' waḥdāniyyatihi* الله: ذاته ونوع وحدانيته), *God: The Unity of the Trinity and the Trinity of the Unity* (*Allāh: waḥdāniyyat thālūthihi wa-thālūth waḥdāniyyatihi* الله: وحدانية ثالوثه وثالوث وحدانيته) and *God between Philosophy and Christianity* (*Allāh: bayn al-falsafa wa-al-masīḥiyya* الله: بين الفلسفة والمسيحية) (Simʿān, *Allāh bayn al-falsafa*).

30. Simʿān, *Allāh fī al-masīḥiyya.*

31. *Mustaghnā* مستغنى

was eternally loving and beloved, hearing and speaking, knowing and known, seeing and seen, wanting and wanted. For Simʿān, an absolute unity would negate the act of creation. A god who had no relationality would seek no relations.[32] Simʿān quotes Avicenna (Ibn Sīna) who perceives that God is love, lover and beloved[33] or knowledge, knower and known one.[34] Ibn ʿArabī's reference to the interiority and exteriority[35] of the divine essence provides further corroboration. Other Muslim intellectuals are marshaled as evidence that many Muslims have recognized relationality in the divine essence.[36]

As was the case with his Christian predecessors in the Muslim milieu, Simʿān recognizes the need for lexical amendments to the Trinitarian conception for divine unity. He coins an Arabic word which can be translated as "instantiation"[37] or "particularization" for the Trinitarian persons. Simʿān attempts to move beyond the importation of the Syriac word *aqnum* to provide a more satisfying definition of the Trinity in the Arab Muslim context. The word "person" is inaccurate for Simʿān as it denotes a person separate from other persons with different characteristics. Such is not the case for the Trinitarian persons. These instantiations are not divine essences, but particularizations of the one divine essence. The Trinitarian instantiations are God revealed in attributes and essence.

Simʿān arrives at a definition of divine unity which he describes as a unity of "communion and exclusion" or "internalized relationality."[38] Though the phrase is difficult to translate into lucid English, the concept is uniquely poignant in the Muslim milieu. Simʿān holds that God's relationality was within his divine essence, relying on no external other and no composite parts. It is a divine unity, unlike the unity of the human being or any other created thing, a unity exclusive unto itself, existing in perfect harmony within the particularizations of the divine being. Such would be the case if the divine attributes were eternally present and active within the divine being. These attributes of love, knowledge, power, wisdom, and so on, were interacting among the divine persons. This avoids the posturing of the Ashʿārīs who said the attributes were neither Allāh nor other than Allāh, as well as the Muʿtazilīs who claimed the attributes were Allāh himself.[39] For Simʿān, the Christian Trinity resolves the conundrum of

32. Simʿān, *Allāh fī al-masīḥiyya*, 106.

33. *'isq*, *'āshiq* and *ma'shūq* عشق، عاشق ومعشوق

34. Simʿān attributes to Avicenna both forms that have been discussed in previous chapters: *'ilm*, *'ālim* and *ma'lūm* علم وعالم ومعلوم and *'aql*, *'āqil* and *ma'qūl* عقل وعاقل ومعقول

35. *bāṭiniyya* باطنية and *ẓāhiriyya* ظاهرية

36. Simʿān, *Allāh fī al-masīḥiyya*, 106.

37. *ta'ayyun* تعيّن

38. *waḥdāniyya jāmi'a māni'a* وحدانية جامعة مانعة

39. Simʿān, *Allāh fī al-masīḥiyya*, 62.

how the attributes relate to the divine essence and how one avoids a co-eternal being when considering the attributes. This is precisely the question that Ibn al-Ṭayyib was compelled to answer in the medieval Muslim milieu. Reading Simʿān in light of Ibn al-Ṭayyib, one may perceive that the Trinitarian persons are the instantiation of God's attributes of essence (fatherhood, filiation and procession) as perceived in relation to the divine essence.

4.1.2 Imad Shehadeh

Professor Imad Shehadeh, the current president of the Jordan Evangelical Theological Seminary, has also made a significant contribution to the defense of divine unity in the Muslim milieu. Shehadeh has become the foremost interpreter of Simʿān, especially the concept of the eternal activity of the attributes among the Trinitarian persons. In addition to his elaboration of Simʿān, Shehadeh has introduced clarifying concepts and provided significant biblical support for the Trinitarian conception. His seminal work is titled *The Necessity of Plurality in the Divine Unity.*[40] A thorough analysis of Shehadeh's contribution is beyond the scope of this book though a modest overview of his work will demonstrate its significance.

Shehadeh engages with the Islamic conception of divine unity stating that the will of God is predominant. In his discussion of the attributes, drawn from the ninety-nine divine names, the author points out that God's attributes function in submission to his will and are not understood to be a revelation of his nature or character which are unfathomable to human beings. God has mercy on whom he chooses to have mercy and he loves those who love him. Furthermore, the attributes of God span the spectrum of his action such that opposite actions are revealed in the ninety-nine divine names. God is both life-giver and the one who puts to death.[41] He brings down but also exalts.[42] He is the revealed one, but also the concealed one,[43] the one who harms but also the benefactor.[44] In Shehadeh's understanding, the binary nature of the attributes portrays the range of God's action but not the nature of his character. In this way, the attributes reveal a God whose will is unconstrained by his nature. The will of God contains the attributes and not vice versa.[45] Though a credible Muslim would engage Shehadeh in this critique, it is nonetheless a poignant Christian critique of Muslim divine unity.

40. Shehadeh, *Al-āb wa-al-ibn. ḍarūriyyat al-ta'addūdiyya fī al-waḥdāniyya al-ilāhiyya* ضرورية التعدّدية في الوحدانية الإلهية

41. *Al-muḥīy wa-al-bā'th: al-mumīt* المحيي والباعث وأيضاً: المميت

42. *Al-khafīḍ wa-al-mudhil: al-rāfi' wa-al-mu'iz* الخفيض والمذلّ وأيضاً الرافع والمعزّ

43. *Al-ẓāhir wa-al-bāṭin* الظاهر والباطن

44. *Al-ḍārr wa-al-nāfi'* الضارّ وايضًا النافع

45. Shehadeh, *Al-āb wa-al-ibn*, 119.

Like Simʿān, Shehadeh underscores the conundrum of the attributes in the formulation of absolute unity. He provides a succinct review of salient aspects of the Muʿtazilī and Ashʿārī conceptions. The former refused to supply the article to the divine attributes for fear that such would connote a co-eternal existent. The moral attributes, for the Muʿtazilīs, were created while anthropomorphisms must be interpreted metaphorically. The Ashʿārīs, in strict adherence to the Qur'ān, acknowledged the attributes of act but insisted that these did not reveal the essence of God which was unknowable. The Ashʿārīs stated that the attributes were not Allāh, nor were they other than he, and famously insisted on human inability to answer the question "how" in relation to God's attributes. Any effort to define God or know his essence was tantamount to limiting God to human perception and was therefore prohibited.[46]

Shehadeh provides helpful diagrams that portray the points of demarcation he is drawing. Often the Christian conception and that of Islam are juxtaposed.

Absolute oneness	**Trinitarian oneness**
No relationality in the divine essence	Eternal relationality in the divine essence
God's attributes flow from his will	God's attributes flow from his nature
God's power controls his other attributes	All of God's attributes are harmonious
God's nature is unknown	God's nature is known and unchanging
God cannot be known nor his attributes known with certainty	God can be known and his attributes can be known with certainty

Shehadeh does excellent work in providing a biblical foundation for the Trinitarian formulation. While the medieval theologians referred to the Old Testament to find the Trinitarian nomenclature, Shehadeh underscores six elements of the Old Testament revelation that reveal relationality in the divine essence: (1) revelation of a unique kind of oneness; (2) the revelation of the angel of the Lord; (3) the names of the Lord; (4) the use of human analogies as an expression of mankind's creation in the divine image; (5) divine speech; (6) the revelation of the Holy Spirit.[47] Throughout, Shehadeh is careful not to claim a fully elaborated Trinitarian conception from the Old Testament. His point is that the Old Testament reveals a God of plurality, a God in whom relationality is expected. Thus the fuller revelation of the Trinity in the New Testament is consistent with the Hebrew scriptures. The author arrives at three important conclusions from his exegesis of the Old Testament: (1) God desires to

46. Shehadeh, 124.

47. Shehadeh, 141.

reveal himself; (2) God is entirely trustworthy; (3) God is portrayed as plurality within unity. Therefore, the attributes are a trustworthy revelation of the nature of God. They are not mere expressions of the inscrutable will which may appear capricious from a human point of view.

Shehadeh also provides a helpful elucidation of Simʿān's descriptor of divine unity as "communion and exclusion." Concerning "communion," "God, in his divine being, draws together all that is requisite for the eternal efficacy of the attributes." In other words, God contains within himself both the subject and the predicate of his divine attributes. He is love, but also beloved, knowledge, but also the known one. Concerning "exclusion" as a descriptor of divine unity, Shehadeh provides several concepts to fill out the picture. God, within his divine being, is the sole necessary being, unique in his attributes, exclusive of other eternal substances, excluding compositeness and dependency. Furthermore, each of the Trinitarian persons possesses all of the divine attributes.[48]

Finally, Shehadeh finds *perichoresis* to be a useful descriptor of the Trinitarian conception. He cites his Eastern forebear John of Damascus as an elaborator of the concept which he defines as the "mutual indwelling and inter-penetration"[49] of the Trinitarian persons. Shehadeh demonstrates that he writes with his Christian constituency in mind as he provides extensive biblical support for the idea of *perichoresis*. In fact, Shehadeh's work in the Christian Scriptures commends it as a unique contribution to the defense of divine unity in the Muslim Arab milieu.

An analysis and comparison of these contemporary theologians with those of the Church of the East yields many commonalities and significant points of divergence. The theologians of the eleventh century serve as points of reference for the contemporary Arab theologian. They were men of culture, contributing to public life in multiple domains. Though somewhat tethered by the predominance of Islam as a political and theological system, they used their intellectual gifts to make a strong case for the rational coherence of their Christian confession, employing lexical and notional elements drawn from their Islamic milieu. Even if their Muslim counterparts were slow to listen, the two theologians served to reinforce their Christian confession in an environment increasingly dominated by Islam. Intellectuals such as Simʿān and Shehadeh are forging a contemporary defense of Christian divine unity in the Muslim milieu. They are one horizon of this defense and their theological rootedness, intellectual acuity and awareness of Islam place them squarely in the tradition of Iliyyā of Nisibis and Ibn al-Ṭayyib.

48. Shehadeh, 154–155.

49. *Al-sukn wa-al-taghalghul al-mutabādil* السكن والتغلغل المتبادل

4.1.3 New Horizons at the Muslim–Christian Interface

The robust contributions of contemporary Arab theologians such as Simʿān and Shehadeh are joined by new voices arising as theologians of today's Muslim–Christian interface scan the global theological horizon for poignant and credible responses in the Muslim milieu. For the medieval theologians, the defense of the ineffable divine substance against any mitigation brought about by the incarnation was the defining issue. However, the Greek philosophical heritage which formed the intellectual atmosphere around both Christian and Muslim conceptions in medieval times has receded in the postmodern period. Indeed, the "Muslim milieu" is not so narrowly defined in the era of mass migration of peoples and heterogeneity. Therefore, it is not surprising that non-Arab contributions to the conceptualization of divinity in the Muslim milieu will come increasingly into play.

"A Common Word," the irenic initiative of 138 Muslim scholars to call Christian leaders to dialogue around the two great commandments of Jesus – love of God and neighbor – has ignited renewed interest in the definition and defense of Christian divine unity.[50] The Croatian theologian Miroslav Volf has edited a significant response to "A Common Word," not to mention his erudite work *Allāh: A Christian Response*.[51] The former Archbishop of Canterbury, Rowan Williams, penned a lengthy and gracious response to "A Common Word" and delivered an address at Al-Azhār, the renowned Islamic University of Cairo.[52] He finds "A Common Word" to be a useful *point de départ* for further elaborations of Trinitarian unity, addressing his Muslim readers with awareness and skill. A lesser-known theologian is Joseph Cumming. Cumming merits mention here as one who labored extensively in the Arab Muslim milieu with awareness of the historical debate and the Arabic lexicon.[53]

As one reads these authors, it becomes clear that the debate has shifted at least a few degrees in both tone and content. In terms of tone, the contention of *shirk* (association of deity with created beings) still underlies the debate. Christians are eager to define their understanding of monotheism even as perceptive Muslims increasingly recognize they are not guilty of *shirk*. Accordingly, the rigidity of the debate has receded as prominent Muslims express a willingness to listen to Christians and consider their views. The interpenetration of ideas and peoples coupled with a diminishing of the prominence of empires of religion (despite the recent reassertion and subsequent dissolution of a "Caliphate") has created a more suitable climate where both Muslims and Christians are prepared to express their truth claims. This welcome

50. "A Common Word between Us and You."

51. Volf, "Common Word for a Common Future"; *Allah: A Christian Response*.

52. Williams, "Archbishop's Address"; "Response by the Archbishop of Canterbury."

53. Cumming, "Meaning of the Expression"; "Problem of Divine Unity"; "What Do We Mean?"

détente in the conversation concerning divine unity is observed in "A Common Word" and the flurry of responses offered by academic theologians.

Nevertheless, the playing field in the Arab world and much of the Muslim world is not level. The political and social dominance of Islam in many countries of the Middle and Near East continues and expresses itself through the repression of dissenting ideas. Recent research bears out the reality that religious identity has legal, social and fiscal implications.[54] Although these are different in nature from the implications we observed in medieval times, the net result remains a reticence to engage one another at a grassroots level due to a threatening social and religious environment. The proliferation of communication media adds a significant layer to an already complex situation. The Internet and satellite television provide forums where the exchange of ideas goes forward in regions where social mores would normally dictate reserve.[55] In today's Muslim world, the entertainment and educational role which Christians derived from formal debates such as the Sessions is filled largely by satellite broadcasts. Television personalities such as the Coptic Priest Father Zacharia Boutros and Brother Rashid (program title: *Daring Questions*) are able to cast caution aside and directly engage their Muslim audience in live dialogue. The result is a shift from dialogue to polemic as Christians question Muslim tenets overtly.

If the tone of the debate has evolved vis-à-vis medieval times, the content also shows noteworthy differences. Intellectuals such as Simʿān and Shehadeh continue to discuss the definition of the hypostases and the relationship of the attributes to the divine essence.[56] However, they also bring new dimensions in their critique of the absolute unity of divinity in the Muslim conception.[57] Christians appear more comfortable highlighting the distinctive nature of their Trinitarian concept, moving away from restrictive Islamic terminology. Their preferred nomenclature for "unity" is *waḥdāniyya* rather than the Islamic *tawḥīd.* They speak with ease of "self-giving love"

---

54. Jon Andrews documents the plight of non-Muslim religious minorities in several Islamic countries (see Andrews, *Identity Crisis*).

55. It is also recognized that these media foment acerbity and aggressive polemical engagement though there are notable examples of "respectful, agnostic inquisitiveness."

56. ʿAwwaḍ Simʿān states that numbering or defining the attributes of God is beyond human rationality. He is content to list a few of the divine attributes with brief definitions: necessary being (*wujūb al-wujūd*), power (*al-qudra*), knowledge (*al-ʿilm*), will (*al-irāda*), sight (*al-baṣr*), hearing (*al-samʿ*), speech (*al-kalām*), unchangeableness (*al-thabāt*) and life (*al-ḥayāt*). He does not divide the attributes into those of essence and act (Simʿān, *Allāh bayn al-falsafa*, 8–9). Interestingly, *al-Bayān al-ṣarīḥ li-ḥawārīy al-masīḥ* (*The Candid Report of Christ's Disciples*) discusses the Ashʿarī tenet of the attributes suggesting it has conceptual affinity with the Christian Trinity. The discussion is drawn largely from Joseph Cumming's work (Abīd, *al-Bayān al-ṣarīḥ*, 74–80; Cumming, "Ṣifāt al-dhāt," 53).

57. ʿAwwun refers to Islamic thought as a "theology of sovereignty" (*lāhūt al-siyāda*) and the Christian conception as "theology of fatherhood" (*lāhūt al-ubuwwa*) (Hirvonen, *Christian–Muslim Dialogue*, 179–180). Shehadeh also engages in a critique of absolute unity.

or the "circulation of love" at the heart of the Trinity.[58] The love-relatedness of the Trinitarian persons is a point of distinction and preference for contemporary Christian theologians. This relational dynamic eclipses the rational constructs which dominated the dialogue of the past. God does not merely show love or give love, but his essence is love. The Trinitarian persons exist in an interpenetrating relationship such that all the persons of the Trinity are present in any other. Moreover, the appearance or visible role of any one in relation to creation, often referred to as the "economic Trinity," is an expression of the self-denying or other-promoting love that lies at the heart of the Trinitarian God (the immanent or ontological Trinity). The Son glorifies the Father. The Father honors the Son. The Spirit reveals the Son and Father.

4.2 Implications of Christian Theology in the Contemporary Muslim World

Adherents of both Islam and Christianity view their faiths as universal with core missional imperatives. In the contemporary period, it is incumbent on Christians not only to ask how their Trinitarian faith is truly a theology of divine unity but also what an incarnate deity offers the Muslim milieu. No doubt it is also fitting that Muslims ask what *tawḥīd* offers societies that are not predominantly Muslim. Given that this book has examined the defense of Christian divine unity in the Muslim milieu, the concluding question is: Does this apologetic have contemporary implications for the people of the Middle East? Or is it a relic of history, laid to rest in the rubble of medieval polemics?

I have observed the concern of the theologians to shield the deity from any shadow of human contingency. Their insistence drew from the concept of God's impassibility which Christians and Muslims embraced and worked out in their respective theological discourses.[59] The conceptual separation of the divine and human hypostases in Christ allowed the Church of the East theologians to fend off the charge of *shirk* – associating the Creator with creation. The formulation was accompanied by the separation of deity from the experience of human contingencies, whether pain or pleasure. The conception moves away from divine immanence and toward divine transcendence.

58. Hirvonen, *Christian–Muslim Dialogue*, 167–171, 179–180.

59. The Greek *apathēs* was applied by the Greek philosophers to mean that God was beyond both pain and pleasure as this would disturb his state of tranquillity (Stott, *Cross of Christ*, 330). For a discussion of the influence of Aristotelian thought on Islam, see Peters, *Aristotle and the Arabs*.

The past century in the Arab–Muslim experience has been summed up by one scholar in the question "What went wrong?"[60] The anguish of disillusionment echoed through the Middle East after the First World War as the once-proud Ottoman Empire fell to Western hegemony and was divided up into nation states for imperialistic interests. The recent effort to resurrect the Caliphate is due to its demise in that period. The end of the Second World War also gave the Arab world a bitter cup to drink as Palestinians were removed from their ancestral lands which were awarded to Jewish immigrants. The anger became palpable through the Arab–Israeli wars and *intifadas* and the fires of rage still burn today. Wars in Sudan, Afghanistan, Iraq, Yemen and Syria have left the region vulnerable to despotic regimes claiming divine right for their atrocities. The upheaval reached fever pitch in the Arab Spring, also known as the Arab Awakening.

If Christian theology has any service to render to the contemporary Middle East, it must be precisely at the point of the existential angst that grips the region and its people. Reflecting on human suffering from Auschwitz to Hiroshima, some contemporary theologians have embraced the idea of a suffering God, finding in the incarnation not only an identification with human suffering but also hope for its elimination through Christ's resurrection.[61] The theologian who most thoroughly elaborates the implications of divine suffering, integrating it into both Trinitarian and christological formulation, is Jürgen Moltmann. Picking up on Chalcedon language, he notes: "if the *homousios* does not merely identify Christ with God, but identifies God with Christ as well, then the divine unity can no longer be interpreted monadically." For Moltmann, Islam's monotheistic concept cannot be squeezed into the mold of orthodox Christology:

> Strict monotheism has to be theocratically conceived and implemented as Islam proves. But once it is introduced into the doctrine and worship of the Christian church, faith in Christ is threatened: Christ must either recede into the series of the prophets, giving way to the One God, or he must disappear into the One God as one of his manifestations. The strict notion of the One God really makes theological Christology impossible, for the One can neither be parted nor imparted. It is ineffable.[62]

---

60. Bernard Lewis, the Princeton Islamic historian, gave this title to one of his books discussing the perennial disillusionment that Muslim societies have experienced in recent years which fed into the terrorist attacks of 9/11 (Lewis, *What Went Wrong?*).

61. Richard Bauckham points to the Japanese theologian Kazoh Kitamori, the black theologian James Cone, and the Germans Karl Barth, Emil Brunner and Deitrich Bonhoeffer. Jürgen Moltmann has brought the suffering of God to the forefront of theological discussion in *The Crucified God* and *The Trinity and the Kingdom of God* (Baukham, "Only the Suffering God Can Help," 6–7). John Stott also eloquently defends the suffering of deity in Christ (Stott, *Cross of Christ*, 329–337).

62. Moltmann, *Trinity and the Kingdom*, loc. 1978 and 1938.

Moltmann, like Shehadeh, refers to another Eastern father, John of Damascus, whose doctrine of the eternal *perichoresis* or "circumincession" of the Trinitarian persons explicates the "circulatory character of the eternal divine life." Therefore, one does not arrive at a Trinitarian faith by beginning with an ineffable substance. The persons of the Trinity must be conceived of in their internal relations which, as Ibn al-Ṭayyib affirmed, are revealed in Scripture. It is the internal relations that define the persons but not in exclusion of the divine substance. The substance is the premise upon which the personhood is perceived. "The unity of the triunity lies in the eternal perichoresis of the trinitarian persons."[63]

If one could anachronistically place Moltmann into the eleventh-century world of Iliyyā and Ibn al-Ṭayyib, he would have advised them to give up the fight for inclusion in the fold of *tawḥīd* as it was premised on the ineffable substance. Perhaps he would have warned them that by persisting they risked giving up essential elements of their Christian confession. No doubt they would have found Moltmann's embrace of a suffering deity totally out of step with their reality. The imaginary dialogue is useful if only to highlight that doctrine, like human perception of the divinity, shifts over time and across contexts. As horizons fuse new possibilities open. The unthinkable medieval tenet of divine suffering has gained appeal in the modern period as the impassibility of the divine substance is eclipsed by the reality of existential pain.[64] Given the wave of displacement and devastation currently sweeping over the Muslim world, the moment is ripe to revisit the hope of the God-man union that Christians espouse. "Though he was in the form of God, [he] did not count equality with God a thing to be grasped, but emptied himself, by taking the form of a servant . . ."[65] – the form of God (μορφή θεου) and the form of a servant (μορφή δουλου) are together, raised in one united person before whom every knee should bow and every tongue confess his Lordship. The deity, through the union, becomes liable to human contingencies voluntarily. Nevertheless, the dominant theme is the absorption and vanquishing of human vulnerability through union with the divine nature portrayed in the resurrection.

Dietrich Bonhoeffer's maxim "only a suffering God can help"[66] may supply a uniquely Christian theological response to Lewis's socio-political question "What went wrong?" The assertion that God is love must lead to the costliness of love and its vulnerability. God is not far removed from the cries of suffering in the Arab or any other context. He is present in the pain of a father who finds the body of his six-year-old son washed up on the shores of Greece. He attends to the tears of the Yazidi

63. Moltmann, loc. 1978 and 1938.

64. Admittedly, there are many contemporary theologians who react against this movement toward divine passibility (see Weinandy, "Does God Suffer?").

65. Phil 2:6–7.

66. Cited in Stott, *Cross of Christ*, 332.

woman whose honor has been decimated by the jihadist who considers the slaking of his debauched lust to be the just reward of his religious fervor. A ten-year-old boy in Aleppo moans in abject desolation, "*ya rabbī*" ("my Lord") as he stoops over the corpse of his older brother. The shocking reality of a God who suffers the agonies of the cross can point to meaning beyond the senseless pain of these tragedies. Their cries ascend, not to the impervious will of a divine dictator, but to a "Lamb as though slain."

Abū al-Qāsim's existential preparation for his encounter with Iliyyā may offer a paradigm for the future of theological encounter in today's Middle East. There are yet more like him who, irrespective of their religious affiliation and in response to insuperable life experiences, are prepared to hear and reconsider their perception of God. The practice of theology itself can be an exercise in Trinitarian and incarnational life. It must be active engagement, not only listening to but actively serving the other. It is an "other-promoting" exercise such that even when the theologian (or the believer) speaks, the purpose is not to dominate or outmaneuver but to serve and elevate, to reconcile and heal. Admittedly, this Trinitarian, communal model of engagement is embraced by religious adherents only at their finest moments. The Muslim scholars of "A Common Word" have modeled it for Christians by inviting them to engage dialogically. Still, if other-promoting love is at the heart of deity, and if humans are created in that Trinitarian image, Christians may also hold to the hope that their presence embodies good news in the Arab and Muslim milieu. Indeed, they may hope that they embody Christ even as they speak of themselves as his "body."

I have suggested that intellectuals of the stature of Ibn al-Ṭayyib and Bishop Iliyyā could not have been unaware of some level of defection from their church to Islam. A search for their progeny in today's Middle East reveals the unabated diminishing of their ecclesial family such that one writer refers to the Church of the East as "the martyred church."[67] The hope of their Scripture is that "unless a grain of wheat falls into the earth and dies, it remains alone; but if it dies, it bears much fruit."[68] The belief in a condescending God, a God who is as near as "word become flesh," whom John says "we have seen with our eyes . . . and have touched with our hands,"[69] is difficult to reconcile with Islamic *tawḥīd* as articulated by its medieval theologians. Yet the vision of a suffering Lamb of God portends hope for the Muslim world. Despite all appearances to the contrary, the twenty-first century may be an auspicious moment for the grain of wheat to live again.

67. Wilmshurst, *Martyred Church.*

68. John 12:24.

69. 1 John 1:1.

Appendix 1

Glossary of Theological Terms

1. Arabic Terms

Transliteration	Arabic	Definition
ahl al-kitāb	اهل الكتاب	"People of the Book," a qur'ānic title given to religious groups who had received a divine revelation prior to the Qur'ān. In later Islamic tradition it refers to Jews and Christians.
'araḍ, pl. *a'rāḍ*	عرض ج أعراض	"Accident" as used in philosophy: a property which has no necessary connection to the essence of the thing being described.
al-bāri'	البارئ	The Creator
al-bay'a	البيعة	The church
al-bay'iyyūn	البيعيون	Theologians of the church
bayān shar'ī	بيان شرعي	Scriptural proof or a proof from the text of God's law
bayān 'aqlī	بيان عقلي	Rational proof
al-bunūwa	البنوة	Filiation, sonship. Ibn al-Ṭayyib held that it was one of the three attributes of essence.
al-dhāt	الذات	The divine essence – the true nature of a being
halla	حلّ	Verb "to indwell"
al-ḥulūl	الحلول	The indwelling of the divine in the human Christ

al-inbi'āth	الإنبعاث	Procession, as in the procession of the Spirit from the Father. It was one of the three attributes of essence according to Ibn al-Ṭayyib.
al-irāda	الإرادة	The will; a synonym of *al-mashī'a* although in Christ the human and divine *irādas* united in one *mash'īa* (according to Bishop Iliyyā).
al-'iṣma	العصمة	Infallibility, immunity of divinely inspired prophets from sin
al-ittiḥād	الإتّحاد	The union of the divine and human in Christ
al-jawhar	الجوهر	The divine substance (used synonymously with *dhāt* by Ibn al-Ṭayyib; Iliyyā defines the term as "self-existent")
al-jizya	الجزية	Tribute (Q9:29): a head tax exacted by Muslim leaders in exchange for protection of religious minorities
al-kalām	الكلام	Theological deductive reasoning (Islamic)
al-khāṣṣa	الخاصّة	Property of a being
al-kufr	الكُفر	Unbelief, disbelief in God, blasphemy
majlis, pl. *majālis*	مجلس ج مجالس	Session. Said of two people or parties "sitting down" for a dialogue. It is the title given to Iliyyā's Sessions with Abū al-Qāsim.
al-ma'nā, pl. *al-ma'āni*	المعنى ج. المعان	Often used with its common definition "meaning" but at times takes on a more technical meaning and can be translated as "innate entity."
al-mashī'a	المشيئة	"Will." Bishop Iliyyā held that the union of divinity and humanity was through a united will.
al-maṣlaḥa	المصلحة	Beneficence or magnanimity. Ibn al-Ṭayyib asserts that God's creation was motivated by his beneficence.

ma'ṣūm	معصوم	(Derived from *al-'isma* above.) Infallible; immune to sin; Islam holds to the infallibility of all prophets after they received their prophetic call.
al-mufassir	المفسّر	Exegete of the Qur'ān or other monotheistic texts
mutakallim, pl. *mutakallimūn*	متكلّم ج متكلّمون	Muslim theologians
Mu'tazilī	معتزلي	An adherent of Muʿtazilism, known for the denial of the eternality of the Qur'ān as well as for emphasizing divine unity and justice. It was an intellectual movement within Islam that flourished from the eighth to tenth centuries in Baṣra and Baghdad. It was devoted to the rational defense of Islam against any other intellectual or religious claim.
mushrik, pl. *mushrikūn*	مُشرِك	One who associates what is created with the Creator. An idolater or polytheist.
muwaḥḥid	موحّد	A monotheist. One who holds to the unity of divinity.
naṣrānī, pl. *naṣārā*	نصراني ج نصارى	Christians. It is the commonly used term for the Church of the East and is often used in the Qur'ān for Christians generally.
qā'im bi-nafsihi	قائم بنفسه	Self-existent; said of God as God is a non-contingent being
al-shāhid	الشاهد	The visible realm ("the seen") meaning the visible, material realm
al-sharī'a, pl. *al-sharā'i'*	الشريعة ج الشرائع	The law: the term refers to religious scriptures.
al-shirk	الشرك	Association of created beings with uncreated divinity, polytheism. It is blasphemy in Islamic thought.
ṣifa, pl. *ṣifāt*	صفة ج صفات	Attribute (often of divinity): for Ashʿārīs, the meaning goes beyond the English translation to take on the meaning of an eternal entity within the divine essence.

al-sunna al-'atīqa	السنة العتيقة	The Old Testament
al-sunna al-jadīda	السنة الجديدة	The New Testament
ta'annasa	تأنس	To become human (as in the incarnation)
al-taḥrīf	التحريف	The corruption of a divine scripture whether dissimulating its meaning or altering the written text
tajassada	تجسّد	To become flesh (as in the incarnation)
al-tanzīh	التنزيه	The removing of all anthropomorphic elements from the divine conception; preserving God's transcendence
al-tanzīl	التنزيل	Literally "the coming down"; in Islam, used for the monotheistic scriptures which were made to "descend" from Allāh
al-tashbīh	التشبيه	Anthropomorphization: ascribing human characteristics to God
al-tathlīth	التثليث	Trinity
al-tawḥīd	التوحيد	The doctrine of God's oneness, unicity
al-tawqīf	التوقيف	Assurance of belief by means of revelation
al-ubuwwa	الأبوة	Paternity, fatherhood (an attribute of essence according to Ibn al-Ṭayyib)
uqnūm, pl. *aqānīm*	أقنوم ج اقانيم	The hypostases of the divine Trinity. The persons of the Trinity (a loan word from Syriac – *qnome*).

2. English and Other Terms

Anthropomorphism: Assigning human characteristics or attributes to God (e.g. "the hand of God").

Anthropotokos: Mother of man or "man-bearer." The moniker was proposed as an alternate to *theotokos* – mother of God – as applied to the Virgin Mary.

Catholicos: Title of the highest-ranking archbishop of the Church of the East and therefore considered the Patriarch of the Church.

Communication of the Properties (Latin: *communicatio idiomatum*): In Christology, the attribution of human attributes in Christ to the divine nature and vice versa, such that human contingencies can be legitimately attributed to deity (e.g. the "suffering God").

Dyohypostate: The belief that Christ's two natures requires that he be understood as having two hypostases or two instantiations of his person – one divine and the other human. (In this book we use this expression to express the Church of the East's unique understanding of Christology. The Church of the East is usually referred to as "dyophysite" but this does little to distinguish it from the Chalcedon churches who also believed in a duality of natures.)

Dyophysite: The belief that Christ is two natures (*physeis*) (divine and human) in one person.

Economic Trinity: The consideration of the Trinitarian persons (hypostases) through the lens of their roles in relation to creation and redemption. The word "economic" is from the Greek *oikonomikos* denoting the arrangement of functions.

Hypostasis: For Greeks, the word meant "self-existence" and, as such, was close to the meaning of "essence." For the Syriac tradition, the word indicated "the instantiation of a person." Ibn al-Ṭayyib defines it as an attribute of the essence when taken together with the essence. Thus the hypostasis of the "Father" is the attribute of "paternity" when taken with the divine essence. The word is translated by the Arabic *aqnūm* or Syriac *qnume* (see chapter 5, section 2.2.3).

Impassibility: The theological tenet that God does not experience pain or pleasure resulting from the actions of another being.

Kyana (Syriac): The nature of a being.

Melkism (Melkite): The Byzantine Church which was loyal to the Roman Emperor. The word derives from the Arabic *malak* meaning "king." The Byzantines were loyal to the Roman king.

Messalianism: A heresy that originated in Mesopotamia claiming that the sacraments of the church were not necessary to give grace, but that spiritual power was conferred through constant prayer. Messalians believed they could see God with their physical eyes. The teaching was anathematized by the Third Ecumenical Council of Ephesus in 431.

Miaphysite: The belief that Christ is of one nature (*physis*) divine-human, as opposed to the two natures (divine and human) in one person.

Ontological Trinity: The consideration of the relation of the Trinitarian persons through the lens of their eternal being and equality.

Oriental Orthodox: The Eastern Churches which recognized the first three Ecumenical Councils but dissented from Chalcedon dyophysitism holding that Christ was "one nature of God, the incarnate *Logos*."

Ousia (Greek): The divine essence.

Perichoresis (Greek): The triune relation of the Trinitarian persons one to another; co-indwelling, co-inhering, mutual interpenetration. A "community of being" allowing each Trinitarian person to maintain a unique personhood while sharing in the life of the other persons. The concept implies that while each Trinitarian person (hypostasis) is distinct, the persons never act in isolation from one another.

Physis (Greek): Nature; in philosophy, the nature of a being. Syriac: *kyana.*

Prosopon (Greek): Literally "face"; in philosophy, "person." Syriac: *farṣūf.*

Qnoma (pl. ***Qnome***) (Syriac): The individual manifestation of a being.

Theopaschitism: The belief that deity can experience human contingencies such as pain and pleasure.

Theotokos (Greek): God-bearer or Mother of God. The title was used for the Virgin Mary by the Chalcedonians but resisted by the Church of the East in favor of Christotokos (*Yaldath M'shikah*) – Mother of Christ.

Appendix 2[1]

A Treatise on the Divine Attributes

by

Abū al Faraj 'Abd Allāh Ibn al-Ṭayyib

Introduction

Abū al-Faraj 'Abd Allāh Ibn al-Ṭayyib (d. 1043) wrote three extant treatises dealing with questions of God's unity and Trinity at the Muslim–Christian interface.[2] The polymath uses conceptual language adopted from his Christian predecessors, amending it to propose a Trinitarian formulation grounded in both rationality and scripture. He explains the Trinitarian hypostases (Father, Son and Spirit) in their relation to the divine essence to uphold the Christian belief in the divine unity, a critical issue at the Muslim–Christian interface because of polemical accusations of *shirk* – associating the uncreated God with created things. This appendix is an Arabic edition with English translation of one of the three treatises.

1. This appendix was previously published in the journal *Islam and Christian–Muslim Relations* (Kuhn, "Third Treatise"). *ICMR* also published an article drawn from this study relating to Ibn al-Ṭayyib's contribution to Muslim–Christian relations in his Trinitarian treatises (Kuhn, "Ibn al-Ṭayyib's Trinitarian Formulation").

2. A fourth work, generically titled "Work in Fourteen Chapters," is preserved in Ibn al-'Assāl's *Majmū' uṣūl al-dīn*. See Faultless, "Ibn al-Ṭayyib," 686; Samir, "Ṣafaḥāt min maqāla."

Chronology of the Treatises

Manuscripts Huntington 240 (a seventeenth-century Coptic manuscript)[3] and Vatican Arabic 145[4] preserve the treatises. The copyist of Huntington 240 (fols. 95v, 99v) refers to two of these as "the second" and "third treatise" respectively. In this article, the shorthand "M2" and "M3" (M = *maqāla* – treatise) is used. A third treatise is titled "A Brief Treatise" (*Maqāla mukhtaṣara*) and is referred to as "mm." The treatise translated below is M3.

The following considerations assist in establishing a tentative chronology for the three treatises.

1. M3 adds definitions and concepts as well as responding to objections that are not raised in M2 and it therefore represents a more developed expression of Ibn al-Ṭayyib's Trinitarian thought.
2. The introduction to M3 presents in summary form the argument laid out in M2, so it is reasonable to assume that M3 is a further elucidation of Ibn al-Ṭayyib's thought on the doctrine of the Trinity.
3. MM appears to be a further clarification of section 5 of M3. It argues that the actions must be attributed to the essence and not to the attributes.
4. M3 section 8 refers to the author's commentary on the book of John, but uses the future tense, suggesting that the commentary had not yet been completed but was in process.
5. The copyists of Huntington 240 called M2 "the second treatise" and M3 "the third treatise." Although it is impossible to know if these titles were carried over from an earlier copy, these manuscripts may preserve an early witness to the priority of M2.

Given these considerations, one may infer a sequential order of the three treatises as follows: M2, M3, MM. Faultless shows that the final composition date of the commentary on John was 409/1018.[5] Therefore, both M2 and M3 must have been written before 409/1018. M3 may be dated in the latter years of the second decade of the eleventh century, roughly 406–409/1015–1018. MM may have been written soon thereafter but certainly before 434/1043 (the date of Ibn al-Ṭayyib's death).

---

3. MS Oxford, Bodleian Library, Huntington 240, *Al-maqāla al-thālitha li-al-shaykh Abū al-Faraj ʿAbd Allāh Ibn al-Ṭayyib fī al-tathlīth wa-al-tawḥīd*, 1549, fols. 99v–104r. Beeston ("Important Christian Arabic Manuscript," 200) provides an overview of the manuscript's contents and estimates on the basis of a colophon (fol. 160v) that the original contents were copied in 1550.

4. MS Vatican, Arabic 145, *Maqālat al-shaykh Abū al-Faraj ʿAbd Allāh Ibn al-Ṭayyib fī al-tathlīth wa-al-tawḥīd*, fols. 48v–69v.

5. Faultless, "Ibn al-Ṭayyib," 676.

Contents of the Second Treatise (M2)

M2 begins with a general introduction presenting the superiority of the Christian Trinity over rival religious formulations, and exhorting the reader not to be troubled by the proliferation of the false. This is as close as Ibn al-Ṭayyib comes to an explicit mention of Islam. The author presents a rational argument for God's Trinitarian nature derived from Ibn ʿAdī. The Trinity is likened to "knowledge, knower and known One." A basic definition of the hypostases follows with clarification of what is meant by certain Christian terms (e.g. "properties" as opposed to the more common "attributes"). The attributes are divided into two types: attributes of essence and of action. While the former are limited to three, the latter have no specified number. The attributes of essence must be revealed to humanity while those of action may be discerned by human beings as they extend beyond the essence to the created order. The Christian Scripture has provided the names of the attributes of essence and therefore they cannot be disputed.[6]

Introduction to Ibn al-Ṭayyib's Third Trinitarian Treatise (M3)

The treatise entitled "The Third Treatise of Shaykh Abū al-Faraj ʿAbd Allāh Ibn al-Ṭayyib concerning Trinity and Unity"[7] is translated below. There are significant variations in vocabulary between M2 and M3; notably, M3 does not use the specific words "Trinity" and "unity," despite the title given by the manuscript copyists. This is accomplished by the use instead of expressions such as "three hypostases" or "three attributes" or "the essence of the Creator is perceived in three ways" or "one essence." The presumed earlier treatise, M2, uses both words liberally, like MM. The absence of these terms raises the question of whether Ibn al-Ṭayyib may have intentionally avoided using them and, if so, why? We also note the avoidance of the specific term "attributes of action" (*ṣifāt al-fiʿl*), again referred to through circumlocutions such as "an attribute that extends beyond the essence to created things."

Ibn al-Ṭayyib begins by stating his concept of divine unity, that God is one substance with three attributes of essence and three hypostases. The hypostases are the attributes of essence (paternity, filiation and procession) when taken with the substance, which is to be understood as the essence. Further explication of the

6. See editions of M2 presented by Samir (Arabic) and Troupeau (Arabic-French) (K. Samir, "maqāla fī al-tahlīth li-abū l-faraj ʿabd allāh ibn al-Ṭayyib al-mutawaffā sanat 1043"; Troupeau, "Le traité sur l'unité").

7. *Al-maqāla al-thālitha li-al-shaykh Abī al-Faraj ʿAbd Allāh Ibn al-Ṭayyib fī al-tathlīth wa-al-tawḥīd* المقالة الثالثة للشيخ ابي فرج عبد الله بن الطيّب في التثليث والتوحيد

rational and legal proofs of God's Trinitarian nature is followed by a response to five possible objections. The author also takes up a defense of the Christian view against that of the philosophers concerning the real existence of the attributes of essence as opposed to their supposed existence as the means by which inadequate minds grasp divine realities.

Although Ibn al-Ṭayyib makes no explicit reference to Islam in the treatise, the topics he discusses are prominent in the Muslim–Christian discourse of the period. His division of God's attributes into those of essence and action finds a parallel in Ash'arī formulations of the period. He provides a unique Christian perspective by arguing that the attributes of essence cannot be known through creation, but only through revelation. For him, revelation is the final court of appeal, as is also the case in Ash'arī *kalām.* These attributes, according to Ibn al-Ṭayyib, are precisely three – paternity, filiation and procession. Their names are designated by revelation and therefore cannot be disputed. These three eternal attributes, when conceptualized with the divine essence, yield the three persons of the Holy Trinity – the Father, Son and Holy Spirit. Ibn al-Ṭayyib skillfully exploits the inter-Islamic discussion of the divine attributes to commend his formulation of the Christian Trinity.

Gérard Troupeau has provided an Arabic edition with French translation of M2 and M3.[8] Troupeau's titles reflect the copyist of Huntington 240 but lead to confusion because of how similar they are. A more apt title would be "A Treatise on the Trinitarian Hypostases: Their Relation to the Divine Essence and the Attributes of Essence." Nevertheless, as the following is a translation, it retains the manuscript copyist's title. I have maintained Troupeau's section divisions while providing verse numbers to aid further analysis of the text. Variations from Huntington 240 and Vatican Arabic 145 appear in footnotes. Some adjustments in the Arabic text are made to render the text more accessible to the contemporary Arabic reader. Huntington 240 folio numbers are indicated in the Arabic text (e.g. 99v|100r indicates the division between the back of fol. 99 and the front of fol. 100).

8. Troupeau, "Le traité sur l'unité"; "Le traité sur la Trinité."

1. Definition of the Substance and the Hypostases

1. He said: the church believes that the Creator is one substance described by three attributes.
2. It also believes that he is described by three hypostases.
3. It is necessary to examine these words and contemplate the implications of these expressions. Afterwards, we will proceed to demonstrate what we deem needful.
4. By "substance" is meant the essence of the exalted Creator which is plainly one.
5. "Attributes" refers to entities in this essence not self-existent essences. These three are paternity, filiation and procession.
6. By "hypostasis" is meant the ensemble of the essence with each of the attributes. If the essence is taken with the meaning of paternity, the ensemble is referred to as "Father." If it is taken with the meaning of filiation, the ensemble is referred to as "Son." If it is taken with the meaning of procession, the ensemble is referred to as "Holy Spirit."
7. The essence of the Creator may be seen as having three aspects: with regard to its essence the clear evidence indicates that it is one; with regard to its attributes, three.[9] (We will demonstrate they are three, no more, no less.) With regard to joining of two together, the perception indicates three hypostases because the hypostasis is no more than the joining of the essence with the attribute.
8. Given that the attributes are three, if the essence is taken with each one, that is a hypostasis. So the exalted Creator is one and many – one with regard to his essence and many with regard to his hypostases.
9. An example of this found in the observable sphere is Zayd who is one in number, having three states – whiteness, writing and geometry.
10. The essence is one which is the person known by these states, and his attributes, found in him, are three.

9. Note that Troupeau's edition omitted "three" though it is present in Huntington 240.

1. تعريف الجوهر والأقانيم

1 (|99v) قال: البيعة تعتقد أن البارئ[10] جوهر واحد موصوف بصفات ثلاث

2 وتعتقد فيه بأنه يوصف بثلاثة[11] أقانيم،

3 ويجب أن يفحص هذا الكلام ويسبر بالوجه الذي يعتقد من دلالة هذه الألفاظ ومن بعد نشرع في بيان ما نريد تبيينه

4 والجوهر يُشار به إلى ذات البارئ تعالى التي[12] قد بان أنها واحدة

5 والصفات (يشار بها) إلى معان موجودة لهذه الذات لا ذوات قائمة[13] بنفوسها هي أبوة وبنوة وانبعاث،

6 والأقنوم[14] يشار به إلى مجتمع الذات مع كل واحدة من الصفات. فإن الذات إذا أُخذت مع معنى الأبوة قيل في المجتمع (إنه)[15] أب وإذا أُخذت بعينها مع معنى البنوة قيل فيها أنها ابن وإذا أُخذت مع معنى الانبعاث قيل فيها أنها روح القدس.

7 فذات البارئ ينظر فيها ثلاثة أنظار من قبل ذاتها والبيان أدى إلى أنها واحدة ومن قبل صفاتها[16] سنبين أنها ثلاث لا زائدة ولا ناقصة ومن قبل مجتمع الأمرين جميعاً وهذا النظر يؤدي إلى أنّها ثلاثة أقانيم لأنَّ الأقنوم ليس هو أكثر من مجتمع الذات مع الصفة.

8 ولأن الصفات ثلاث فإذا أخذت الذات مع كل واحدة منهن كان ذلك أقنوماً فيكون البارئ تعالي واحداً وكثيراً، واحداً من قبل الذات كثيراً من قبل الأقانيم.

9 ومثل ذلك يوجد في الشاهد فإن زيداً وهو واحد بالعدد توجد له ثلاثة أحوال: بياض وكتابة وهندسة.

10 وذاتها واحدة وهي[17] الشخص القائل[18] لهذه الأحوال وصفاته الموجودة فيه ثلاث،

---

10. الباري
11. في بعض الأحيان "ثلثة"
12. الذي
13. القايمة
14. لقنوم
15. غير موجودة في المخطوطة الأصلية
16. ثلثة
17. فذاته واحد وهو
18. القايل

11. If his essence is taken with each of the attributes, the result of joining of the essence with each of the attributes is different from the result of joining the same essence with a different attribute. The meaning of white is different from the meaning of the geometrist, but he is still Zayd.

2. The Legal Demonstration That the Attributes Are Three

12. With that elucidation, we must proceed to demonstrate that the attributes are three, no more, no less, and thus the statement that the hypostases are three, no more, no less, is true.
13. This is demonstrated in two ways: legal and rational.
14. First, the legal demonstration is carried out thus: the divine attributes can be categorized.
15. There are attributes peculiar to him that are not communicable beyond his essence.
16. [And there are] attributes that are communicable beyond his essence to his creatures.
17. These include the attributes of power, wisdom and bounty [communicable] from an abundance of grace, unforced.
18. [As for] the essence of the Creator and those communicable attributes, human minds do not need revelation of this, since the earth and the way it is fashioned lead to the acknowledgment that it has a Creator with the attributes of bounty, power and wisdom as well as other communicable attributes.
19. As for the essential attributes that are particular [to the essence] and do not go beyond it, they are hidden to human minds and there is no means to arrive at or perceive them.
20. These three attributes are paternity, filiation and procession.
21. The exalted Lawgiver gives us knowledge of them and reveals them to us. So these revealed attributes are granted to humankind by the Giver of the Law in addition to what he revealed to them concerning their deeds, thus granting them the goal of knowledge and labor.
22. The reason for which he revealed these attributes to humanity with no further elucidation of their meanings is that every period of time takes its rank from Christ.

11 وإذا أخذت ذاته مع كل واحدة من الصفات (100r|99v) كانت الجملة المعتقدة من الذات والصفة غير الجملة المعتقدة من الذات بعينها والصفة الأخرى فليس معنى الأبيض هو معنى المهندس وهو زيد.

2. البيان الشرعي ان الأقانيم ثلاث

12 ومع الإيضاح عن ذلك يجب أن ينتقل إلى البيان على أن الصفات ثلاث لا زائدة[19] ولا ناقصة فبهذا يصح القول إن الأقانيم ثلاثة لا زائدة ولا ناقصة،

13 وهذا يبين ببيانين شرعي وعقلي.

14 أما الشرعي فيجري على هذه الصفة، لما كانت صفات البارئ تعالى تنقسم

15 فمنها صفات تخصه لا تتعداه

16 ومنها صفات تتعدى ذاته إلى مخلوقاته

17 كصفة قادر وحكيم وجواد لفيضه النعمة من غير إضطرار

18 فذات [البارئ] وصفاته التي تتعداه إلى مخلوقاته عقول البشر تستغني عن موقف يوقفها عليها. إذ كان العالم وصنعته يؤدي[20] إلى الاقرار بأن له صانعاً وأن له صفة الجود والقدرة والحكمة وغير هذه من الصفات التي تتعدى إلى المخلوقات.

19 فأما صفات الذات التي تخصها ولا تتعداها وهي خفية عن العقول البشرية ولا طريق إلى الوصول إليها والوقوف عليها،

20 وهي هذه الثلاث الصفات الأبوة والبنوة والانبعاث

21 فصاحب الشريعة تعالى ومنحنا علمها ووقفنا عليها توقيفاً فهذه الصفات هي صفات توقيف منحها صاحب الشريعة للبشر مضافاً مع ما نهج لهم من الطريق الإلهية في أفعالهم وأعطاهم غاية العلم وغاية العمل.

22 فأما العلة التي من أجلها وقفهم عليها توقيفاً من غير إيضاح عن معانيها، من قبل أن لكل وقت من الزمان رتبة من المسيح.

---

19. زايدة

20. تؤدّي

23. The Old Testament led human beings to confess the divine essence alone without the attributes particular to it.
24. The New Testament granted human beings knowledge of the attributes of essence so that human beings would arrive at knowledge of the most blessed of all beings in essence and attributes according to humanity's capacity.
25. Because our minds in the coming world will be purer and more enlightened, our reward will be the knowledge of the most noble beings.
26. So he refrained from elaborating on them in this world so that the truths of their mysteries might be revealed to us in the coming world.
27. And we are like people who advance by degrees, moving from state to state until attaining the perfect, virtuous state, with complete expression [of the attributes].
28. And the reason for their being three, no more, no less, will become [evident] in the world to come.
29. And some say that he only brought them with symbols and signs so that our minds would seek their meanings and thus gain enlightenment by seeking, knowledge and profound graces.
30. People do not apprehend them all at once, but gradually. Also, it was not within the capacity of human minds to know them for there was no means to ascend to them among the created beings.
31. So the Lawgiver perceived this and thus perceiving, he designed the pursuit of them [the essential attributes] for human minds and the knowledge of their truths as the end of their capacity.
32. This first legal demonstration containing the reason for the attributes numbering three, no more, no less, is exclusively revelation.
33. Because the Revealer establishes his truthfulness by the miraculous, belief in his revelation is thus established.

23 فالسنة العتيقة قادت الناس إلى الإقرار بالذات نفسها من دون صفاتها التي تخصها

24 والسنة الجديدة منحت الناس الصفات التي تخصها من ذات[21] ليكون الإنسان عالماً بأشرف الموجودات ذاتاً وصفةً[22] (100v|100r) بقدر الطاقة الإنسانية في هذا العالم،

25 ولأن عقولنا في العالم المزمع تكون أصفى وأنور وجزاءنا[23] وهو العلم بأشرف الموجودات.

26 فأترك الإفصاح عنها في هذا العالم لتنكشف لنا حقائق[24] أسرارها في الآتي

27 فنكون كالمتدرجين الذين نقلوا من حال إلى حال إلى أن بلغوا الحال الكاملة الفاضلة بالإفصاح عنها،

28 والعلة في كونها ثلاث لا زائدة[25] ولا ناقصة تكون في العالم الآتي.

29 وقوم قالوا إنما أتي بها إيماء[26] ورمزاً حتى تتطلب عقولنا معانيها فتستنير بالطلب والعلم والنعم الجسيمة[27]

30 لا يحل الناس بها دفعة (واحدة)[28] لكن يتدرجون، وأيضاً لأن هذه لم تكن في طاقة العقول البشرية علمها إذ كان لا طريق إلى التسلق إليها من الموجودات

31 فصاحب الشريعة أشعر بها فلما أشعر بها صاغ للعقول البشرية البحث عنها ومعرفة حقائقها[29] بمبلغ الطاقة.

32 وهذا البيان الأول الذي من قبل الشرع المتضمن للعلة في كون الصفات ثلاث لا زائدة ولا ناقصة وهي التوقيف حسب،

33 ولان الموقف يثبت صدقه بالمعجز فيكون[30] التصديق بتوقيفه بهذا الطريق.

---

21. ذاتها
22. صفات
23. جزانا
24. حقايق
25. زايده
26. أيما
27. الجسام
28. الكلمة «واحدة» غير موجودة بالمخطوطة الأصلية
29. حقايقها
30. فايكون

3. The Rational Demonstration That the Attributes Are Three

34. The second interpretation, to which we now proceed, requires the rational demonstration that the attributes of essence are three. This is proven in the following manner.

35. It is established that the essence of the exalted Creator exists and that it is one.

36. It is understood that this essence has the attribute of knowledge and rationality.

37. It is aberrant to be other than that so there remains in it the attribute of knowledge and rationality because it is impossible for the Creator of sciences and minds to be unknowing and irrational.

38. So if it has this attribute, then it has the power to know and its essence is one of its known objects.

39. The essence knows itself as it is known to itself.

40. Therefore we infer an essence capable of knowing, that has known itself, and has become known to itself.

41. These attributes cannot be extended to a four-way knowledge or reduced to a binary knowledge. So the attributes are three.

42. Furthermore, if each of these attributes is taken together with the essence, the ensemble is a hypostasis.

3.1 The Names of the Hypostases

43. The attribute of the ability to know, referred to as fatherhood, when taken with the essence, is described as an essence who is concerned to know, and is called Father.

44. The attribute of self-knowledge, referred to as filiation, if taken with the essence, yields the knowing one spoken of as the hypostasis of the Son.

45. The attribute of being known, taken with the essence, yields an ensemble spoken of as the Spirit.

46. These names are names of revelation, names of law.

3. البيان العقلي ان الصفات ثلاث

34 لان التأويل[31] الثاني يقتضي بيان كونها ثلاث بالطريقة العقلية فننتقل إليها، والبيان العقلي في كون الصفات ثلاثاً تجري على هذه الصفة.

35 قد ثبت أن ذات الباري تعالى موجودة وأنها واحدة ،

36 ومعلوم أن هذه الذات لا تخلو أن تكون بصفة العالمين العاقلين.

37 (اولاً وحويشت من القسم الثاني[32] فبقي لها صفة العاملين العاقلين)[33] لأنه محال أن يكون خالق العلوم والعقول غير عالم ولا عاقل،

38 وإذا كانت بهذه الصفة (101r|100v) فلها قوة ان تعلم وذاتها إحدى[34] المعلومات

39 وهي تعلم ذاتها فتكون ذاتها معلومة لها

40 فتتحصل[35] لنا ذات فيها قوة على أن تعلم وقد علمت ذاتها وصارت معلومة لذاتها.

41 وليس يمكن ان تتجاوز هذه الصفات إلى معنى الرباعية ولا تنحط إلى معنى الثنائية[36] فصفاتها إذن ثلاث.

42 وإذا أخذت كل واحدة من هذه الصفات مع الذات كان من الجملة أقنوم[37]،

3.1 أسماء الأقانيم

43 فصفة القوة على العلم وهي المدلول عليها بالأبوة إذا أخذت مع الذات قيل في الذات أنها ذات من شأنها أن تعلم وهذا يعبر عنه أنه أب.

44 وصفة علمها لذاتها وهي المدلول عليها بالبنوة إذا أخذت مع الذات تقوم وهي من الجملة معنى العالم وهو المدلول عليه بأقنوم[38] الإبن.

45 وصفة كونها معلومه إذا أخذت مع الذات تقوم من الجملة معنى (الجميع جملةً) وهي المعبر عنها بالروح.

46 فتكون هذه الأسماء[39] أسماء توقيف وأسماء شريعة

31. التأول
32. التاني
33. لا يوجد هذه الجزء في مخطوطة Vat Ar. 145.
34. احد
35. يتحصل
36. التنايية
37. قنومًا
38. بقنوم الأبن
39. «أسما» في الثلاث مرات

47. They were only used so that the attributes particular to the essence of the Creator, which the Lawgiver revealed, would not be otherwise in word and meaning.
48. Indeed, these names are fitting as the church believes that one of these hypostases – the Father – is cause and the other two – Son and Spirit – are two effects.
49. The expression "Father" indicates an essence that is cause. The Son and Spirit are two effects.
50. These names were used for this reason. Generally, expressions connote their meaning.
51. The Lawgiver expressed these attributes using these names via revelation. The names are given by revelation and do not normally carry these meanings in common parlance.
52. Furthermore, when we say the Creator has the ability to know, it must not be understood that he was in a [former] state and then became knowing. Rather, the ability to know was inherent in him eternally; he was both knowing and known.

4. Objection to the Attributes Being Three

53. Another objection arises in regard to his attributes. If the hypostasis is the ensemble of the essence with the attributes, and the attributes of the Creator are very many, how is it said that the hypostases are three, no more, no less?
54. Why are they not more, given that the attributes exceed three? The Creator is described by bounty, power, wisdom, eternality and other attributes.
55. So if we join power to the essence, we arrive at a hypostasis called "the Almighty." Also, if we join bounty to the essence, we arrive at a hypostasis called "the Bounteous."

47 وإنما إستعملت حتى لا يكون الذي أفاده صاحب الشريعة من صفات البارئ الخاصة بذاته غيّرها من جهة اللفظ والمعنى

48 لأن في هذه الألفاظ مناسبة فإن البيعة تعتقد في هذه الأقانيم الثلاثة أن الواحد منها وهو الأب علة والإثنين[40] معلولان،

49 ولفظة الأب تدل على ذات هي علّة والابن والروح معلولان

50 فلهذه الجهة استعملت هذه الأسماء[41]، وبالجملة الألفاظ مصطلح عليها بالدلالة،

51 وصاحب الشريعة عبّر عن هذه الصفات[42] بهذه الأسماء على جهة التوقيف وهي أسماء شريعة[43] لا أسماء جرت بها العادة في الشاهد.

52 ولا يفهم[44] بسبب أنا نقول أن في البارئ تعالى قوة على أن يعلم[45] أنه (ما)[46] كان على هذه الحال ثم علم، بل لم تزل[47] فيه قوة (أن يعلم)[48] وهو عالم بها ومعلوم.

4. إعتراض على كون الصفات ثلاث

53 ويطرأ (101v|101r) الشك (على) [49] صفته هذه الصفة، إذا كان الأقنوم هو مجتمع الذات مع الصفة وصفات البارئ كثيرة جداً فكيف يقال إن الأقانيم ثلاثة لا زائدة ولا ناقصة،

54 ولِمَ لا تكون أكثر لكون الصفات أكثر من ثلاث فإن البارئ تعالى يوصف بالجود والقدرة والحكمة والقدم وغير ذلك من الصفات.

55 فإن القدرة إذا أضفناها إلى الذات إجتمع من الجميع أقنوم القادر وكذلك الجود[50] إذا أصفناه إلى الذات صارمن الجميع أقنوم الجواد.

---

40. الاتنان
41. الاسماء
42. الثلاث
43. شرعية
44. نفهم
45. تعلم
46. لا توجد الكلمة "ما"
47. يزل
48. لا توجد العبارة "أن يعلم"
49. شك صفته
50. الجواد

4.1 Response to the Objection

56. The response is that the attributes of the exalted Creator are of two types: an attribute that extends beyond the essence to the creatures and is not restricted to the substance of the essence but entails another substance [the first type of attribute].

57. For instance, the attribute of power entails the substance of the object of power. The attribute of goodness entails the substance of the recipient of goodness and the attribute of eternality entails time.

58. The Church believes that the exalted Creator is three hypostases, one substance.

59. Attributes exceeding this number do not enter into belief because the Creator has revealed the attributes that the human mind is unable to discover or investigate.

60. These attributes [the second type of attribute] are particular to the essence. Since the attributes that are particular to the essence are three, accordingly, the hypostases are three, no more, no less.

5. Objection That the Attributes Require a Separate Essence

61. There is a further objection concerning the attributes. If the attributes of essence, in your view, are only three – which are paternity, filiation and procession – and whatever is in addition to these goes beyond the essence, such as power, bounty and wisdom, then power requires the presence of an object of power and wisdom requires a wise concept. In general, each attribute, apart from these three, requires the existence of another substance and everything except the substance of the Creator is contingent.

62. This is necessary as power is inherently caused and comes into existence after having had no previous existence.

63. The same is true of the attribute of goodness and that of eternality which involves time and time is caused.

64. The attribute of the Creator cannot be caused within him. Such would require an existent cause that had no previous existent cause. Plainly this is reprehensible.

4.1 الرد على الإعتراض

56 والجواب أن صفات البارئ[51] تعالى على ضربين، صفة تتعدى[52] الذات إلى المخلوقين ولا تقف عند جوهرالذات بل بجرّ معها جوهرًا آخر.

57 كصفة[53] قادر فإنها صفة لله تعالى تجر معها جوهر المقدور وكذلك صفة الجواد تجر معها جوهر[54] المجود و(صفة)[55] القدم تجر معها الزمان.

58 البيعة تعتقد أن البارئ تعالى ثلاثة أقانيم جوهر واحد

59 فما كثر من صفات الذات[56] لا يدخل في الإعتقاد لأن صاحب الشريعة إنما وقفنا على الصفات التي لا تفي العقول البشرية بالوقوف عليها ولا استقصائها[57]،

60 وهذه هي التي تخص الذات، وهذه بأنها ثلاث أعني الصفات التي تخص الذات وبحسبها تكون الأقانيم ثلاثة لا زائدة ولا ناقصة.

5. إعتراض أن الصفات تتطلب ذاتاً مستقلةً

61 وشك آخر (في)[58] صفته هذه الصفة، إذا كانت الصفات التي تخص الذات عندكم ثلاث وهي الأبوة والبنوة والانبعاث وما سواها يتعدى الذات كالقدرة والجود والحكمة فإن القدرة تقتضي وجود المقدور والحكمة وجود المبدأ، وبالجملة كل واحدة من الصفات سوى الثلاث تقتضي وجود جوهر آخر وجميع ما سوى[59] جوهر البارئ محدث.

62 فيجب لأن القدرة معلقة به أن تكون محدثة وكائنة[60] بعد أن لم تكن،

63 وكذلك صفة الجود وصفة القدم لأنها معلقة بالزمان والزمان محدث،

64 ومن المحال أن تكون صفات البارئ محدثة فيه لأن هذه (102r|101v) تقتضي محدثاً وموجوداً وإن كانت بعد ان لم تكن، وهذه كلها شناعات قبيحة.

51. والجواب الصفات للباري
52. «تتعدا» تكتب عادة في المخطوطة بالألف كلما ذكرت
53. لصفة قادر
54. تُذكر "صفة المجود" وليس "جوهر المجود"
55. لا توجد كلمة "صفة"
56. الصفات للذات
57. استقصا
58. كلمة "في" غير موجودة
59. سواه
60. وكاينه

5.1 Response to the Objection

65. The response is that all existent things and the meanings by which they are described are of two types.

66. Either as potential,[61] and it is the nature of action to proceed from it,

67. or as action. Potential is that from which action originates [described as] "potential" if the thing has refrained from action though it is in its nature to act and [described as] action if it is active, engaging in that trait (i.e. if it is engaging in that trait).

68. So the Creator is described by these attributes in eternity because they are potentialities innate to him and faculties whose nature it is to act.

69. What is done (by the faculties) is present to them in eternity [but] past in potentiality.

70. As for power, so long as it exists in potentiality, its object exists in potentiality.

71. If it acts, its object becomes actuality and, after creating the world, [the Creator] is described as wise and bounteous in actuality because the object exists in actuality, skilfully wrought.

72. Neither amendment nor censure is required because the exalted Creator brought forth what he brought forth and did what he did from beneficence.

73. So when he saw it would benefit the world and this benefit presented itself to his foreknowledge, he proceeded to bring it forth.

74. One might say, "Why did he not do it earlier?" [The response:] Because it was conditioned by beneficence.

75. So the attributes of the Creator, except his essential attributes which are paternity, filiation and procession, exist in him in potentiality.

76. By this I mean his existent faculties and entities.

---

61. I have translated Ibn al-Ṭayyib's use of "power" by "potentiality" based on the meaning derived from context. To summarize his view, all objects can be classified either as active or potentially active. The fact that action issues from power confirms the impression that Ibn al-Ṭayyib is referring to potentiality or potential action. This bears resemblance to early Islamic division of the attributes into attributes of essence and attributes of act (see Cumming, "Ṣifāt al-dhāt," 7–8).

5.1 الرد على الإعتراض

65 والجواب أن الأمور الموجودة لكل شيء والمعاني التي يوصف بها هي على ضربين،

66 أما بالقوة وهذه شأن الفعل أن يصدر عنها

67 او بالفعل والقوة وهي التي يصدر الفعل عنها بالقوة إذا كان الشيء ممسكاً عن الفعل وشأنه أن يفعل وبالفعل إذا كان فاعلاً بتلك الملكة.

68 فالبارئ تعالى يوصف بهذه الصفات في القدم على أنها قوى فيه وملكات شأنها أن تفعل،

69 وما تفعله[62] فهو موجود لها في القدم بالقوة

70 أيضاً فإن القدرة ما دامت بالقوة فمقدورها بالقوة

71 وإذا فعلت صار مقدورها بالفعل وبعد إيجاد العالم يوصف بأنه حكيم وجواد بالفعل لأن المقدور وجد بالفعل والمتقن أيضاً.

72 وليس يلزم في هذا عدل ولا لوم لأن البارئ تعالى أوجد ما اوجده وفعل ما فعله على جهة المصلحة.

73 فالوقت الذي رأى فيه مصلحة العالم وتقدمت في سابق علمه أوجده فيه،

74 ولقائل أن يقول فلِمَ لم يقدم على ذلك إذ كان مقروناً بشرط المصلحة.

75 فتكون صفات البارئ سوى صفاته التي تخصه التي هي الأبوة والبنوة والانبعاث موجودة له بالقوة

76 أعني ملكات ومعان موجودة له.

62. يفعله

77. If these are potential in eternity, then what is related to them is also potential in eternity.
78. Since power is in potentiality in eternity, the skillful outworking is also in potentiality in eternity.
79. Also, if wisdom is in potentiality in eternity, the skillful outworking is also in potentiality in eternity.
80. If these attributes [i.e. power, wisdom] are actualized, then the object of power, the thing skillfully made and the object of goodness came into being as well.

6. Objection That the Attributes of Essence Can Be Inferred

81. One may not say: "an awareness of the attribute of God's creation, wisdom and goodness, from the objects of his power leads us to the confession of the Creator and his attributes, and that one can therefore also infer the attributes of essence on the basis of that which exists.
82. As the Creator has skillfully brought forth creation, from the objects of his knowledge, one may infer that he is knowing."

6.1 Response to the Objection

83. Our response: Some of the attributes' effects are plain to the senses; the effects of others must be inferred by the mind.
84. Those that are plain to the senses include what he has empowered and created.
85. Through our senses we observe the excellence of the world's creation,[63] its governance and the effects of [his] power in it such that our senses lead our minds to declare these attributes in its creation.
86. As for the attribute "knower," we need the grace of assured revelation and what has this need may fall into error.

63. There is a possibility that Ibn al-Ṭayyib is here speaking not of the world (العالَم) but of the knowing One (العالِم), i.e. God. If so this sentence would take on a slightly different meaning as follows: "We witness through our senses the excellence of the knowing One's creation and his principles and the effects of power in him such that our senses bring our minds to declare these attributes in his creation."

77 وإذا كانت بالقوة (فيما لم يزل)[64] فما يتعلق بها أيضاً[65] يكون بالقوة (فيما لم يزل)[66]

78 فلأنّ[67] القدرة بالقوة فيما لم يزل يكون المقدور بالقوة فما يتعلق بها ايضًا يكون بالقوة فيما لم يزل،

79 وكذلك إذا كانت الحكمة فيما لم يزل بالقوة يكون المتقن بالقوة فيما لم يزل،

80 وإذا برزت أفعالها صار المقدور بالفعل والمتقن والمجود عليه.

6. إعتراض ان الصفات الذاتية يمكن للعقل ان يقف عليها

81 وليس لقائل أن يقول لإنّنا[68] كما توصلنا إلى الوقوف على صفة صنعة الله وحكمته وجوده من المقدورات والمتقنات بأن قادتنا الموجودات إلى الإقرار بالموجد (102v|102r) وصفاته، هكذا[69] أيضاً الصفات التي ذكرتم أنها صفات للذات وقد يمكن أن يتوصل إليها من الموجودات.

82 فإنه كما أن البارئ تعالى متقن الموجودات فمن معلوماته يتوصل إلى الوقوف عليه بأنه عالم.

6.1 الرد على الاعتراض

83 فنقول إن من الصفات ما تكون آثارها بينة للحس ومنها ما تحتاج آثارها إلى استنباط العقل.

84 فالبينة للحس كالمقدورات والموجودات.

85 فإنما نحن نشهد بحواسنا حسن صنعة العالم واحكامه وآثار القدرة فيه فتؤدينا حواسنا إلى أن تقر عقولنا بهذه الصفات في صناعته.

86 فأما صفة عالم فانا نحتاج[70] فضل التوقيف وما يحتاج إلى ذلك ربما يقع فيه الزلل. إلى[71] أن نتطلب آثارها بالعقل لنتوصل إليها.

64. العبارة غير موجودة بالمخطوطة الأصلية

65. ايضًا بها

66. العبارة غير موجودة بالمخطوطة الأصلية

67. فإنّ

68. لانا

69. هكذي

70. يضيف هنتينجتون 240 "ان تتطلب أثارها بالعقل لنتوصل إليها وما يتطلب بالعقل يحتاج إلى..."

71. الكلمة "إلى" غير موجودة

87. Thus we need a revealer for these attributes but not for the others.

88. Even though we concede that the creation leads us to [perceive] God as knower of the creation from the effects we find therein.

89. Because the way to ascertain it is from the effects in creation as it [God's being knower] does not extend beyond his essence.

90. What does not extend beyond his essence is concealed from human minds so necessity requires revelation for assured knowledge.

7. Two Opinions Concerning the Divine Attributes

91. People have two views regarding the attributes of the Creator.

92. Some say that the attributes are characteristics of the one to whom they are attributed, stated or unstated, and these characteristics are eternally his.[72]

93. Others hold that being consists of no more than the essence and that the attributes are only the sayings of those who describe him.

94. The essence cannot be described by characteristics in it which violate it.

95. They are a means by which inadequate minds arrive at that essence, speaking of it in customary, conventional and appropriate ways to describe it.

96. The second opinion is that of the philosophers while the first is that of the church.

97. The first opinion is correct and the second is incorrect.

98. Its incorrectness is seen in a question we may ask of the describer: Is what you mean by "good" the same as what you mean by "wise"?

99. It is impossible to answer this question in the affirmative as the two meanings are differentiated in the mind.

100. So if what is meant by the one attribute is not what is meant by the other, the difference must be attributed either to the essence described or to the speaker.

---

72. The root form of the word attribute (*ṣifa*) is *wasafa* وصف . The words translated as "describe" and "describer" are also derived from this word. Seeking to preserve this similarity renders the following awkward translation: "Some say that the attributes are meanings [*ma'ānī*] of him who is attributed whether an attributer has attributed them or not and these meanings are eternally his [*qadīma ma'hu*]."

87 فلهذا أحتجنا في هذه الصفات إلى موقف ولم نحتاج في تلك إلى موقف.

88 على أنا إن سلمنا أن الموجودات تؤد بنا إلى أن الله عالم بها من آثار نجدها فيها[73]

89 لأنّ الطريق إلى (أن) نقف عليه من آثار في الوجود إذ كان ذلك ما لا يتعدى ذاته.

90 وما لا يتعدى ذاته فهو خفي عن العقول البشرية والحواس فضرورة تدعو في الوقوف عليه إلى التوقيف.

7. رأيان فيما يخص الصفات الإلهية

91 وآراء الناس في صفات البارئ على ضربين.

92 منهم من قال إن الصفات هي معاني الموصوف سواء وصفه بها الواصف أو لم يصفه قديمة معه،

93 ومنهم من قال إن الموجود ليس فيه أكثر من الذات حسب والصفات أقاويل الواصفين.

94 لا توصف الذات بمعان موجودة فيها مخالفة[74] للذات

95 بل هو طريق تتوصل بها العقول الناقصة إلى تلك الذات فقالت بالمعهود المألوف واللائق[75] بأن توصف[76] بمثله.

96 والرأي الثاني رأي الفلاسفة والرأي الأول رأي البيعة،

97 والرأي[77] الأول يصح والرأي (102v|103r) الثاني يبطل.

98 أما بطلانه فمن قبل أنا نسأل[78] الواصف هل ما يفهمه[79] من صفة جواد هو ما يفهمه من صفة حكيم

99 ومن المحال أن يقول نعم لأن المعنيين مختلفان في العقل.

100 فإذا كان ما يفهم من هذه الصفة ليس هو ما يفهم من الصفة الأخرى فلا يخلو أن يكون هذا الإختلاف عائداً[80] إلى الذات الموصوفة أو إلى قول القائل.

73. هنتينجتون 240 يضيف "علمه بنفسه"
74. مخالصه. تعديل طرحه "تروبو" ويبدو لي مقبولًا.
75. اللايق
76. يوصف
77. واري
78. نسل
79. تفهمه - مرتان في ذات الجملة
80. عايدًا

101.If it is attributed to the speaker, it can only be attributed to the judgment of the speaker and there is no truth in it, for the truth of sayings is evidenced by their correspondence to existent beings.

102.In this view, there is no difference between what is described as a "wise one" and [what is described as] a "powerful one," because they refer to one power in which there is no differentiation.

103.But they do not say that the meaning of "wise one" is the same as the meaning of "powerful one"

104.so it is established that this difference is to be attributed to the essence.

105.However, it is impossible for it to be attributed to the essence itself as it has been established that it is one.

106.Therefore the difference is attributable to meanings existing in the essence, and inherent in it.

107.These are the attributes that Christians hold to be inherent in the essence of the Creator from his eternity past.

108.However, these attributes divide [into two groups]: those that concern the essence, and they are three, which we have learned by means of revelation and reason, and those that extend beyond the essence to attract another essence, and these latter attributes include all the exalted Creator's attributes except the aforementioned three.

8. Names of the Divine Attributes

109.Churchmen name the three qualities which are paternity, filiation and procession, "begetting, being begotten and emanating."

110.They make the attribute of the Father that he begot and that of the Son that he was begotten and the Spirit, that he emanated.

111.They also say that the Father is begetter unbegotten, and the Son is begotten not begetter, and the Spirit emanates.

112.All these names are from revelation and divine law and their meanings are not to be understood as they are in common parlance for any aspect or reason.

113.These refer to a singular essence that is the reason for all existence and all that has been formed.

101 فإن كان ذلك عائداً إلى قول القائل فيكون هذا الإختلاف إنما هو عائد إلى قول القائل ولا حقيقة له. لأن حقائق[81] الأقاويل تعلم من انطباقها على الموجودات.

102 ويكون بحسب هذا لا فرق بين الموصوف بأنه حكيم وبأنه قادر إذا كانا جميعاً يعودان إلى قوة واحدة لا خلاف فيها.

103 وليس يقولون إن معنى حكيم معنى قادر

104 فبقي أن يكون هذا الإختلاف عائداً إلى الذات

105 ومحال أن يكون عوده إلى نفس الذات لأنه ثبت أنها واحدة

106 فبقي أن يكون عوده إلى معان موجودة لها ومتعلقة بها،

107 وهذه هي الصفات التي[82] تعتقد النصارى بأنها موجودة مع ذات البارئ قديمة بقدمه،

108 سوى أن هذه الصفات تنقسم فمنها ما يخص الذات وهي ثلاث التي علمناها بطريق التوقيف والعقل، ومنها ما يتعدى ويجذب مع الذات ذاتاً [83] أخرى وهذه هي كل صفة يوصف بها البارئ تعالى سوى الثلاث المذكورة.[84]

8. أسماء الصفات الذاتية

109 والبيعوّن يسمون الخواص الثلاث التي هي الأبوة والبنوة والانبعاث ايلاداً وتولداً وانبعاثاً.

110 يجعلون صفة الأب أنه أولد والابن أنه ولد والروح أنه انبعث.

111 ويقولون إن الأب هو والد غير[85] مولود والابن مولود غير والد والروح منبعث،

112 وكل هذه الأسماء هي أسماء توقيف وشريعة وما يراد بمعانيها (ما) جرت (103r|103v) به العادة في الشاهد على وجه ولا سبب

113 والعود بها كلها إلى ذات واحدة بالعدد وهي سبب كل موجود وكل متكون.[86]

---

81. وقايلًا، وحقايق
82. وهذه التي
83. الكلمة غير موجودة في المخطوطة الأصلية
84. المذكورات
85. غيره
86. وتكون كل متكون

114. This essence has three attributes spoken of using these terms. Each of these attributes, if added to the essence, yields an ensemble which is the hypostasis and so on.

115. If we refer to the Father as "cause" and the Son and Spirit as "caused," we do not thereby mean "cause of existence" because the essence is one in number.

116. However, the Father, who is the essence itself with the potentiality of knowledge, is the cause of the Son and Spirit.

117. By this, I mean that the essence, in that it is knower and known, is the ground of its being, but not the cause of its existence.

118. If we compare the essence of the Creator with all beings other than itself, it is the cause of their existence, their being and their producing.[87]

119. For churchmen, there is no difference between calling the hypostasis of the Son "Son" and "Word."

120. Their saying the "Word of God" is a reference to the eternal hypostasis of the Son who is the essence of the Creator taken with the attribute of filiation.

121. We will explain why he was called "Word" at the beginning of the commentary on John's Gospel.

122. Our speaking of the Creator as "living" is a reference to his existence.

123. We do not say he is a body with a soul, with senses and moved by the will as is meant by [the term] "living" in common speech. He is far above that.

124. Some say that the meaning of "he is living" is the same as "he is knowing."

87. The word may also be *aḥdāthiha* meaning "their events."

114 لها صفات ثلاث يعبر عنها [88] بهذه العبارات، وإذا أضيف كل[89] واحدة[90] من هذه الصفات إلى الذات صار منها جملة وهي الأقنوم ونحوه.

115 ونحن[91] وإن قلنا في الأب أنه علة وفي الإبن والروح أنهما معلولان فلا يفهم منا أنا نريد علة وجود إذ كانت الذات واحدة بالعدد.

116 إلا ان الأب وهو الذات نفسها مع القوة على العلم وهو علة الابن والروح

117 أعني الذات نفسها في أن تكون عالمة ومعلومة فتكون ذاتاً واحدة علة لنفسها لا في الوجود .[92]

118 فأما اذا قسنا ذات البارئ إلى باقي الموجودات سواها فإنها تكون علة لوجودها وكونها واحداثها.

119 ولا فرق عند البيعيين من تسمية أقنوم الابن ابناً وكلمة

120 فقولهم كلمة الله اشارة إلى أقنوم الإبن [93] الأزلي وهو ذات البارئ إذا اخذت مع صفة البنوة.

121 وسنشرح لِمَ سمي كلمة في أول تفسير إنجيل يوحنا.

122 وقولنا في البارئ أنه حي اشارة إلى كونه موجوداً

123 وليس ذلك على المعنى الذي جرت بمثله العادة في الشاهد بأن يقال فيه انه[94] جسم ذو نفس حساس متحرك بارادة كما يقال في الحي في الشاهد. تعالى عن هذا.

124 وقوم قالوا معنى أنه حي معنى أنه عالم.

---

88. عنهن
89. غير موجودة بالمخطوطة الأصلية
90. واحد
91. ونحوه ونحن
92. الموجود
93. غير موجودة في المخطوطة الأصلية فتأتي في النص الأصلي "إشاره على قنوم الازلي"
94. بأنه

9. Objection That Attributes Lead to Compositeness

125. Someone might say that, if we join the meaning of an attribute to the essence of the Creator, the resulting entity is a composite.

126. Then, the essence of the knowing one would not be a simple essence but would resemble other composite beings. Perhaps it is also said that compositeness requires one who assembles.

127. The response is that compositeness is of two types: true and not true.

128. True compositeness is like that of natural bodies composed of the four elements.

129. The meaning of their compositeness is only the mixing of the four elements one with another.

130. Far be it from the Creator that his essence should have this attribute. This type [of compositeness] requires one who assembles.

131. Compositeness that is not true is called concurrent, such as the concurrence of the attribute with that to which it is attributed.

132. This does not require true composition of essence nor does it require an assembler because the essence and the attribute with it are from eternity past.

133. The church holds to the latter view, not the former.

10. Objection That the Attributes Are Accidents

134. One might object that if the essence of the Creator has attending attributes, then it has accidents and accidents are attributes of [created] beings.

135. The response: some of what is inherent in a thing is called accident and some is called property.

136. These are called "properties following the essence" and not "accidents."

9. إعتراض ان الصفات تؤدي إلى التركيب

125 ولقائل أن يقول أنا إذا قرنا إلى ذات البارئ معنى الصفات حصل لها معنى التركيب

126 ولا يكون في العالم ذات بسيطة وتشبه ايضًا ساير الموجودات المركبات وربما قيل إن التركيب يحتاج إلى مركب.

127 والجواب أن التركيب على ضربين حقيقي وغير حقيقي

128 فالحقيقي مثل تركيب هذه الأجسام الطبيعية المركبة من الأسطقسات الأربعة

129 فإنما معنى تركيبها هو اختلاط بعضها ببعض

130 وحوشي البارئ تعالى من أن تكون ذاته بهذه الصفة (104r|103v) وهذا القسم هو الذي يلزم أن يوجد له مركب،

131 وغير الحقيقي يسمى اجتماعياً مثل اجتماع الصفة مع الموصوف

132 وهذا لا يلزم أن تكون الذات مركبة تركيباً حقيقياً ولا ان يكون لها مركب لأن الذات والصفة قديمة معها،

133 والبيعة إنما تعتقد في الأقانيم المعنى الثاني لا الأول.

10. إعتراض ان الصفات هي أعراض

134 ولقائل ان يقول إن كانت لذات البارئ صفات موجودة لها فمعها أعراض والأعراض من صفات الكائنات.[95]

135 والجواب أن الموجود في الشيء منه ما يسمى عرضاً ومنه ما يسمى خاصة.

136 وهذه تسمى خواصًا تتبع الذات ولا تسمى أعراضاً.

95. الكاينات

Bibliography

Abd al-Jabbār. *Tathbīt dalā'il al-nubuwwa.* Dar al-Arabiya: Beirut, n.d.

Abīd, A. a.-L. *al-Bayān al-ṣarīḥ li-ḥawārīy al-Masīḥ*. Mansourieh, Lebanon: Dār kitābinā li-al-nashr, 2016.

Abramowski, L., and A. E. Goodman. *A Nestorian Collection of Christological Texts*, vol. 2. Cambridge: Cambridge University Press, 1972.

Abu-Nimer, M. S. M. *Interfaith Dialogue: A Guide for Muslims*. International Institute of Islamic Thought, 2007.

Accad, M. "The Gospels in the Muslim and Christian Exegetical Discourse from the Eighth to the Fourteenth Century." DPhil. diss, Oxford University, 2001.

———. "The Gospels in the Muslim Discourse of the Ninth to the Fourteenth Centuries: An Exegetical Inventorial Table; Part 1." *Islam and Christian–Muslim Relations* 14, no. 1 (2003): 67–91.

———. "The Ultimate Proof-Text: The Interpretation of John 20.17 in Muslim–Christian Dialogue (Second/Eighth–Eighth/Fourteenth Centuries)." In *Christians at the Heart of Islamic Rule*, vol. 1, edited by D. Thomas, 199–214. Leiden/Boston: Brill, 2003.

Afnan, S. M. *Avicenna: His Life and Works*. London: George Allen & Unwin, 1958.

al-Ash'ari. *Maqalat al-islamiyiin wa-ikhtilaf al-musallin*, vol. 1. Edited by H. Ritter. Leipzig: Brockhaus, 1930.

al-Basri, A. *Kitab al-burhan wa Kitab al-masa'il wa al-ajwiba.* Edited by M. al-Hayek. Beirut: Dar al-Mashriq, 1977.

al-Hāshimī, A. A., and A. a.-M. al-Kindī. "Ḥiwār dīnī bayn al-Amīr 'Abd Allāh al-Hāshimī wa-al-Amīr 'Abd al-Masīḥ al-Kindī fī 'ahad al-Khalīfa al-Ma'mūn (813–834)." Also found online: http://alkalema.net/kenedy.htm.

al-Khoury, B. *Ibn Rushd: Ibn 'Adi: al-Imaam wa al-Masiih.* Jounieh, Lebanon: The Pauline Library, 2004.

al-Niṣībīn, I. *al-Majlis al-thānī.* MS Paris Arabe 206, 14th century.

———. *Kitāb al-burhān al-ṣaḥīḥ*. MS Vatican Arabe 180, 13th century.

———. *Kitāb al-majālis*. Vat. Arabe 143 (1–149), 12th–13th century.

———. *Kitāb al-majālis*. Huntington 240. Bodleian Library, 1549.

———. *Kītāb daf' al-hamm.* Edited by Q. al-bāshā. Egypt: *maṭba' al-ma'ārif*, n. d.

———. "Risāla fī waḥdāniyyat al-Khāliq wa-tathlīth aqānīmihi." In *'Ashariyn maqalat diniyya*, edited by L. Cheikho. Beirut: Jesuit Publishers, 1920.

al-Niṣībīn, I., and A. al-Qasim. *Risāla ilā al-Wazīr al-Kāmil Abī al-Qāsim al-Ḥusayn ibn 'Ālī Ar. 318 [Sbath 1131]* (fols. 31a–71r). Hill Museum and Manuscript Library, 1924.

al-Niṣībīn, I., and D. Bertaina. *Establishing the Proof of Christian Monotheism from the Qur'an.* Unpublished article.

al-Ṭayyib, I. *al-Kalām fī al-ittiḥād*. Huntington 240 (104r–105r). Bodleian Library, 1549.

———. *al-Maqāla al-thālitha li-l-Shaykh Abū al-Faraj 'Abd Allāh bin al-Ṭayyib fī al-tathlīth wa-l-tawḥīd*. Huntington 240 (240). Bodleian Library, 1524.

———. *al-Maqāla al-thāniyya fī al-tathlīth li-Abū al-Faraj ʻAbd Allāh bin al-Ṭayyib*. Huntington 240 (95v–99v). Bodleian Library, 1549.

———. *Epistle on the Oneness of the Creator and Threeness of His Hypostases*. Huntington 240 (196r–199v). Bodleian Library, 1549.

———. *Ibn aṭ-Ṭayyib fiqh an-naṣrāniya*. Edited and translated by O. S. W. Hoenerbach, T Corpus Scriptorum Christianorum Orientalium collection, vol. 1–4. Louvain, Belgium: Imprimerie Orientaliste, 1956–1957.

———. *Tafsīr al-mashriqī*. Egypt: Principle of the Clerical School of the Coptic Orthodox Church, 1910.

al-Warrāq, and D. Thomas. *Anti-Christian Polemic in Early Islam: Abū ʻĪsá al-Warrāq's "Against the Trinity."* Cambridge: Cambridge University Press, 1992.

Allard, M. "Les Chrétiens à Baghdad." *Arabica* 9, no. 3 (1962): 375–388.

———. *Le problème des attributs divins dans la doctrine d'al-Aš'arī et de ses premiers grands disciples*. Beirut: Editions de l'Imprimerie Catholique, 1965.

Amedroz, H. F. *The Marwanid Dynasty at Mayyafariqin*. London: Royal Asiatic Society, 1903.

Andrews, J. *Identity Crisis: Religious Registration in the Middle East*. West Knapton, UK: Gilead Books, 2016.

Arnold, T. W. *The Caliphate*. Oxford: Clarendon Press, 1924.

Atiya, A. S. *A History of Eastern Christianity*. London: Methuen, 1968.

Baukham, R. "Only the Suffering God Can Help." *Themelios* 9, no. 3 (1984): 6–12.

Baum, W. *The Church of the East: A Concise History*. London: RoutledgeCurzon, 2003.

Baum, W., and D. Winkler. *The Church of the East: A Concise History*. Translated by M. G. Henry. London: RoutledgeCurzon, 2003.

Beaumont, M. "ʻAmmār al-Baṣrī." In *Christian–Muslim Relations: A Bibliographical History, vol. 1: 600–900*, edited by D. Thomas and B. Roggema, 604–610. Leiden/Boston: Brill, 2009.

———. "ʻAmmar al-Basri on the Incarnation." In *Christians at the Heart of Islamic Rule: Church Life and Scholarship in ʻAbbasid Iraq*, vol. 1, edited by D. Thomas, 55–62. Leiden/Boston: Brill, 2003.

———. *Christology in Dialogue with Muslims: A Critical Analysis of Christian Presentations of Christ for Muslims from the Ninth and Twentieth Centuries*. Bletchley: Paternoster, 2005.

———. "Muslim Readings of John's Gospel in the Abbasid Period." *Islam and Christian–Muslim Relations* 19, no. 2 (2008): 179–197.

Beeston, A. F. L. "An Important Christian Arabic Manuscript in Oxford." *Orientalia Christiana Periodica* 19 (1953): 197–205.

Bertaina, D. *Christian and Muslim Dialogues: The Religious Uses of a Literary Form in the Early Islamic Period*, vol. 29. Piscataway, NJ: Gorgias Press, 2011.

———. "Salvation and Monotheism in the Qur'an: Hermeneutics and Historiography in Elias of Nisibis' Kitab al-Majalis." Unpublished article, 2012.

Bertolacci, A. *The Reception of Aristotle's Metaphysics in Avicenna's Kitāb al-Ṣifa*. Leiden: Brill, 2006.

Bishoy, M. "The Councils of Ephesus and Chalcedon: The Christological Controversies of the Fourth and Fifth Centuries." In *Christianity: A History in the Middle East*, edited by H. Badr, 191–217. Beirut: Oikumene, 2005.

Bosworth, C. E. "al-Ṭabarī." In *The Encyclopaedia of Islam: New Edition*, vol. 10, edited by P. J. Bearman, T. Bianquis, C. E. Bosworth, E. van Donzel and W. P. Heinrichs, 11–18. Leiden: Brill, 2000.

Brock, S. "Christology of the Church of the East Studies." In *Syriac Christianity: History, Literature and Theology*, 125–152. Aldershot: Variorum, 1992.

———. "The 'Nestorian' Church: A Lamentable Misnomer." *Bulletin of the John Rylands University Library of Manchester* 78 (1996): 23–35.

———. "Two Millennia of Christianity in Iraq." *Islam and Christian–Muslim Relations* 21, no. 2 (2010): 175–184.

Budge, E., and B. Hebraeus. *The Chronography of Gregory Abul Faraj the Son of Aaron, the Hebrew Physician Commonly Known as Bar Hebraeus: Being the First Part of His Political History of the World*, vol. 1. Piscataway, NJ: Gorgias Press, 2003.

Cahen, C. "Buwayhids or Buyids." In *The Encyclopaedia of Islam*, vol. 1, edited by H. A. R. Gibb, J. H. Kramers, E. Levi-Provencal and J. Schacht, 1350–1357. Leiden: Brill, 1986.

Caspar, R., A. Charfi, M. De Epalza, A. T. Khoury, P. Khoury and S. K. Samir. "Bibliographie du dialogue islamo-chrétien." *Islamochristiana* 2 (1976): 187–249.

Caspar, R., A. Charfi and S. K. Samir. "Bibliographie du dialogue islamo-chrétien (XIe–XIIe siècles)." *Islamochristiana* 3 (1977): 256–284.

Charfi, A. "La fonction historique de la polémique islamochrétienne à l'époque abbasside." In *Christian Arabic Apologetics During the Abbasid Period (750–1258)*, edited by S. K. Samir and J. S. Nielsen, 44–56. Leiden/New York/Cologne: Brill, 1994.

Chediath, G. *The Christology of Mar Babai the Great*. Kottayam, India: Oriental Institute of Religious Studies, 1982.

Cheikho, L. "Majalis Iliyya mutran Nasibin." *Al-Mashriq* 20 (1922): 35–44 (First Session); 112–117 (Second Session); 117–122 (Third Session); 267–270 (Fourth Session); 270–272 (Fifth Session); 366–377 (Sixth Session); 425–434 (Seventh Session).

"A Common Word between Us and You." Amman, Jordan: The Royal Aal al-Bayt Institute for Islamic Thought, 2007.

Cumming, J. "The Meaning of the Expression 'Son of God.'" 2004. Joseph Cumming personal website, http://www.josephcumming.com/links/index.html.

———. "The Problem of Divine Unity and Human Pluralism." 2007. Joseph Cumming personal website, http://www.josephcumming.com/links/index.html.

———. "Ṣifāt al-dhāt in al-Ashʿarī's Doctrine of God and Possible Christian Parallels." In *Toward Respectful Understanding and Witness among Muslims*, edited by E. Reisacher, 111–145. Pasadena, CA: William Carey Library, 2012.

———. "What Do We Mean When We Say 'God Is Love'?" 2008. Joseph Cumming personal website, http://www.josephcumming.com/links/index.html.

"The Definition of Chalcedon." In *The Oxford Dictionary of the Christian Church*, edited by F. L. Cross and E. A. Livingstone. Oxford: Oxford University Press, 2005.

Delly, E. K. *La théologie d'Elie bar-Senaya*. Rome: Apud Pontificiam Universitatem Urbanianam de Propaganda Fide, 1957.

Dennett, D. C. *Conversion and the Poll Tax in Early Islam*. Cambridge: Harvard University Press, 1950.

Dick, I. "Deux écrits inédits de Théodore Abuqurra." *Le Muséon* 72 (1959): 53–67.

Diez, M. "The Profession of Monotheism by Elias of Nisibis: An Edition and Translation of the Fifth Session of the Kitāb al-majālis." *Islam and Christian–Muslim Relations* 28, no. 4 (2017): 493–514. doi: 10.1080/09596410.2017.1362801.

Ehrman, B. D. *The Apocryphal Gospels: Texts and Translations*. Oxford: Oxford University Press, 2011.

Fattal, A. *Le statut légal des non-musulmans en pays d'Islam*. Beirut: Imprimerie Catholique, 1958.

Faultless, J. "Ibn al-Ṭayyib." In *Christian–Muslim Relations: A Bibliographical History, vol. 1: 600–900*, edited by D. Thomas and B. Roggema, 667–697. Leiden/Boston: Brill, 2009.

———. "The Prologue to John in Ibn al-Tayyib's Commentary on the Gospels." PhD diss., University of Oxford, 2001.

———. "The Two Recensions of the Prologue to John in Ibn al-Tayyib's Commentary on the Gospels." In *Christians at the Heart of Islamic Rule: Church Life and Scholarship in 'Abbasid Iraq*, edited by D. R. Thomas, 177–198. Leiden/Boston: Brill, 2003.

Fyzee, A. A. A. *A Shi'ite Creed*, vol. 9. London: Humphrey Milford, 1942.

Gaudeul, J.-M. "The Correspondence between Leo and 'Umar: 'Umar's Letter Re-discovered?" *Islamochristiana* 10 (1984): 109–157.

Gimaret, D. *La doctrine d'al-Ash'ārī*. Paris: Editions du Cerf, 1990.

———. "Mu'tazila." In *The Encyclopaedia of Islam: New Edition*, vol. 7, edited by C. E. Bosworth, E. van Donzel, W. P. Heinrichs and C. Pellat, 783–793. Leiden: Brill, 1993.

———. "Ru'yat Allah." In *The Encyclopaedia of Islam: New Edition*, vol. 8, edited by C. E. Bosworth, E. van Donzel, W. P. Heinrichs and G. Lecomte, 649. Leiden: Brill, 1995.

———. "Sifa." In *The Encyclopaedia of Islam*, vol. 9, edited by C. E. Bosworth, E. van Donzel, W. P. Heinrichs and G. Lecomte, 551–552. Leiden: Brill, 1997.

———. "Tawḥīd." In *The Encyclopaedia of Islam*, vol. 10, edited by P. J. Bearman, T. Bianquis, C. E. Bosworth, E. van Donzel and W. P. Heinrichs, 389. Leiden: Brill, 2000.

Goddard, H. *A History of Christian–Muslim Relations*. Chicago: New Amsterdam Books, 2000.

Griffith, S. "ʿAmmar al Basri's *Kitab al-burhan*: Christian *Kalam* in the First Abbasid Century." *Le Muséon* 96 (1983): 145–181.

———. "Answers for the Shaykh: A 'Melkite' Arabic Text from Sinai and the Doctrines of the Trinity and the Incarnation in 'Arab Orthodox' Apolgetics." In *The Encounter of Eastern Christianity with Early Islam*, History of Christian–Muslim Relations 5, edited by E. Grypeou, M. Swanson and D. Thomas, 277–309. Leiden: Brill, 2006.

———. *The Church in the Shadow of the Mosque: Christians and Muslims in the World of Islam.* Princeton, NJ: Princeton University Press, 2008.

———. "The Concept of *al-Uqnūm* in ʿAmmār al-Baṣrī's Apology for the Doctrine of the Trinity." In *Actes du premier congrès international d'études arabes Chrétiennes*, edited by S. Khalil, 169–191. Rome: PISO, 1982.

———. "From Patriarch Timothy I to Hunayn ibn Ishaq: Philosophy and Christian Apology in Abbasid Times; Reason, Ethics and Public Policy." In *Christians and Muslims in Dialogue in the Islamic Orient of the Middle Ages*, edited by M. Tamcke, 75–98. Beirut: Ergon Verlag Wurzburg, 2007.

———. "The Monk in the Emir's Majlis: Reflections on a Popular Genre of Christian Literary Apologetics in Arabic in the Early Islamic Period." In *The Majlis: Interreligious Encounters in Medieval Islam*, Studies in Arabic Language and Literature 4, edited by H. Lazarus-Yafeh, 13–65. Wiesbaden: Harrassowitz Verlag, 1999.

———. "The Qur'an in Arab Christian Texts: The Development of an Apologetical Argument; Abu Qurrah in maglis of al-Ma'mun." *Parole de l'Orient* 24 (1999): 203–234.

———. *Theodore Abu Qurrah: The Intellectual Profile of an Arab Christian Writer of the First Abbasid Century.* Tel Aviv: Tel Aviv University, 1992.

———. "The View of Islam from the Monasteries of Palestine in the Early Abbasid Period: Theodore Abū Qurrah and the *Summa Theologiae Arabica*." *Islam and Christian–Muslim Relations* 7, no. 1 (1996): 9–28. doi: 10.1080/09596419608721064.

Grillmeier, A. S. J. *Christ in Christian Tradition: From the Apostolic Age to Chalcedon (451)*, vol. 1. Translated by J. Bowden. London: Mowbray's, 1975.

Grudem, W. *bi-Mātha yufakir al-Injīliyūn fī asāsāsiyāt al-īmān al-Masīḥī*, vol. 3. Cairo: Eagles Group, 2009.

Haddad, R. *La Trinité divine chez les théologiens arabes: 750–1050*. Paris: Beauchesne, 1985.

Haddad, W. *Christian–Muslim Encounters*. Gainesville, FL: University Press of Florida, 1995.

Hayek, M. "ʿAmmār al Baṣrī: La première somme de théologie chrétienne en langue arabe, ou deux apologies du christianisme." *Islamochristiana* 2 (1976): 69–133.

———. *Apologie et controverses*. Beirut: Dar al-Mashriq, 1977.

Hillenbrand, C. "Marwanids." In *The Encyclopaedia of Islam: New Edition*, vol. 6, edited by C. E. Bosworth, E. van Donzel and C. Pellat, 626–627. Leiden: Brill, 1991.

Hirvonen, H. *Christian–Muslim Dialogue: Perspectives of Four Lebanese Thinkers*. Leiden: Brill, 2013.

Husseini, S. L. *Early Christian–Muslim Debate on the Unity of God: Three Christian Scholars and Their Engagement with Islamic Thought (9th Century C.E.)*, vol. 21. Leiden: Brill, 2014.

Ibn Adī, Y. y. "Maqāla al-Shaykh Yaḥyā Ibn ʿAdī." In *maqālāt dīniyya qadīma li ba'ḍ mashāhīr al-kataba al-naṣāra*, edited by L. Cheikho, 70–74. Beirut: The Jesuit Fathers, 1920.

Ibn al-ʿAssāl, A.-M. t. *Majmūʿ usūl al-dīn wa-masmūʿ maḥṣūl al-yaqīn*, vol. 6a (bāb 1–18). Translated by A. Wadi. Cairo/Jerusalem: Franciscan Centre of Christian Oriental Studies, 1998.

———. *Majmūʿ usūl al-dīn wa-masmūʿ maḥṣūl al-yaqīn*, vol. 7a (bāb 20–70). Cairo/Jerusalem: Franciscan Publishers for Christian Oriental Studies, 1999.

Ibn Furak, A. B. M. *Mujarrad Maqālāt al-Shaykh Abī al-Ḥasan al-Ash'ārī*. Edited by D. Gimaret. Beirut: Dar al-Mashriq, 1987.

Jaṭlāwī, a.-H. *al-Ma'nā al-ṣaḥīḥ li-Injīl al-Masīḥ*. Mansourieh, Lebanon: Dār Kitābinā li-al-Nashr, 2017.

Jenkins, P. *The Lost History of Christianity: The Thousand-Year Golden Age of the Church in the Middle East, Africa, and Asia – And How It Died*. New York: HarperOne, 2009.

Keating, S. T. *Defending the "People of Truth" in the Early Islamic Period: The Christian Apologies of Abū Rā'iṭah*, History of Christian–Muslim Relations 4. Leiden/Boston: Brill, 2006.

Khalifeh, F. E. "The Maronites." In *Christianity: A History in the Middle East*, edited by H. Badr, 271–291. Beirut, Lebanon: Oikumene, 2005.

Khallikan, I. *Ibn Khallikan's Biographical Dictionary*, vol. 1. Edited by M. G. D. Slane. Paris: Oriental Translation Fund of Great Britain and Ireland, 1842.

Kraemer, J. *Humanism in the Renaissance of Islam*. Leiden: Brill, 1986.

Kuhn, M. "Early Islamic Perspectives of the Apostle Paul as a Narrative Framework for *Taḥrīf*." In *Arab Christians and the Qur'an from the Origins of Islam to the Medieval Period*, History of Christian–Muslim Relations 35, edited by M. Beaumont, 150–173. Leiden: Brill, 2018.

———. "Ibn al-Ṭayyib's Trinitarian Formulation in the Islamic Milieu." *Islam and Christian–Muslim Relations* 29, no. 2 (2018): 123–143.

———. "The Third Treatise of Shaykh Abū al-Faraj ʿAbd Allāh Ibn al-Ṭayyib on Unity and Trinity." *Islam and Christian–Muslim Relations* 29, no. 3 (2018): 269–287.

Küng, H. *Islam: Past, Present and Future*. Oxford: Oneworld, 2007.

Landron, B. "Apologétique, polémique et attitudes Nestoriennes vis-à-vis de l'Islam entre le 8ème et le debut du 14ème siècle." Doctorat d'Etat, Université de Paris IV, Paris, 1973.

———. *Chrétiens et musulmans en Irak : attitudes nestoriennes vis-à-vis de l'Islam*. Paris: Cariscript, 1994.

Lane, A. N. S. "Christology beyond Chalcedon." In *Christ the Lord*, edited by H. H. Rowdon, 282–298. Leicester: Inter-Varsity Press, 1982.

Lane, E. W., ed. *An Arabic-English Lexicon*. London: Williams & Norgate, 1863.

Lapidus, I. M. *A History of Islamic Societies*. Cambridge: Cambridge University Press, 2002.

Levy-Rubin, M. *Non-Muslims in the Early Islamic Empire: From Surrender to Coexistence*. New York: Cambridge University Press, 2011.

———. "The Pact of 'Umar." In *Christian–Muslim Relations: A Bibliographical History, vol. 1: 600–900*, edited by D. Thomas and B. Roggema, 360–364. Leiden/Boston: Brill, 2009.

Lewis, B. "Abbasids." In *The Encyclopaedia of Islam: New Edition*, vol. 1, edited by H. A. R. Gibb, J. H. Kramers, E. Levi-Provencal and J. Schacht, 15–23. Leiden: Brill, 1986.

———. *Islam and the West*. Oxford: Oxford University Press, 1993.

———. *What Went Wrong?* New York: Perennial-Harper Collins, 2002.

Liddell, H. G., and R. Scott. *A Greek–English Lexicon*. Edited by H. S. Jones. Oxford: Clarendon Press, 1966.

Maas, A. "Communicatio Idiomatum." 1908. New Advent. Retrieved 11 March 2015, http://www.newadvent.org/cathen/04169a.htm.

Massignon, L., and G. C. Anawati. "Ḥulūl." In *The Encyclopaedia of Islam: New Edition*, vol. 3, edited by B. Lewis, V. L. Menage, C. Pellat and J. Schacht, 570–571. Leiden: Brill, 1971.

Mikhail, W. "ʿAmmār al-Basrī's Kitāb al-burhān: A Topical and Theological Analysis of Arabic Christian Theology in the Ninth Century." PhD diss., University of Birmingham, 2013.

Mingana, A. "The Apology of Timothy the Patriarch before the Caliph Mahdl." Woodbrooke Studies 3. *Bulletin of the John Rylands Library* 12 (1928): 171–191.

———. *Commentary of Theodore of Mopsuestia on the Nicene Creed* 5. Cambridge: W. Heffer & Sons, 1932.

Moffett, S. H. *A History of Christianity in Asia*, vol. 1. New York: Orbis, 1998.

Moltmann, J. *The Trinity and the Kingdom*. Kindle ed. Minneapolis: Fortress, 1993.

Monferrer Sala, J. P. "Elias of Nisibis." In *Christian–Muslim Relations: A Bibliographical History, vol. 2: 900–1050*, edited by D. Thomas and A. Mallett, 727–741. Leiden/Boston: Brill, 2010.

Newman, N. A. "Al-Kindi's Apology." In *The Early Christian–Muslim Dialogue: A Collection of Documents from the First Three Islamic Centuries (632–900 AD)*, edited by N. A. Newman, 355–546. Hatfield, PA: Interdisciplinary Biblical Research Institute, 1993.

———. "The Dialogue of the Patriarch Timothy I with Caliph Mahdi." In *The Early Christian–Muslim Dialogue: A Collection of Documents from the First Three Islamic Centuries (632–900 AD)*, edited by N. A. Newman, 163–268. Hatfield, PA: Interdisciplinary Biblical Research Institute, 1993.

Norris, R. A. J. *The Christological Controversy*. Philadelphia: Fortress, 1980.

Parry, K. *The Blackwell Companion to Eastern Christianity*. Oxford: Blackwell, 2007.

Parry, K., D. J. Melling, D. Dimitri, S. Griffith and J. F. Healey, eds. *The Blackwell Dictionary of Eastern Christianity*. Oxford: Blackwell, 1999.

Pelikan, J. J. *The Spirit of Eastern Christendom (600–1700)*. Chicago: University of Chicago Press, 1974.

Perier, A. *Petits traités apologétiques de Yaḥyā Ben 'Adī: Texte Arabe*. Edited and translated by A. Perier. Paris: J. Gabalda; P. Geuthner, 1920.

Peters, F. E. *Aristotle and the Arabs: The Aristotelian Tradition in Islam*. London: New York University Press, 1968.

Platti, E. "Yaḥyā Ibn ʿAdī." In *Christian–Muslim Relations: A Bibliographical History, vol. 2: 900–1050*, edited by D. Thomas and A. Mallett, 390–438. Leiden/Boston: Brill, 2010.

———. "Yaḥyā b. 'Adī and His Refutation of al-Warrāq's Treatise on the Trinity in Relation to His Other Works." In *Christian Arabic Apologetics during the Abbasid Period (750–1258)*, edited by H. G. Kipenberg and E. T. Lawson, 172–191. Leiden: Brill, 1994.

———. *Yaḥyā Ibn 'Adī: Théologien chrétien et philosophe arabe*. Leuven: Orientaliste, 1983.

———. "Yahya Ibn 'Adi and the Theory of *Iktisab*." In *Christians at the Heart of Islamic Rule: Church Life and Scholarship in 'Abbasid Iraq*, vol. 1, edited by D. Thomas, 151–157. Leiden/Boston: Brill, 2003.

Putman, H. *L'église et l'islam sous Timothée I (780–823) : étude sur l'église nestorienne au temps des premiers 'Abbasides ; avec nouvelle édition et traduction du Dialogue entre Timothée et al-Mahdi*. Beirut: Dar el-Machreq éditeurs, 1975.

Renard, J. *Islamic Theological Themes*. Oakland, CA: University of California Press, 2014.

Reynolds, G. S. *A Muslim Theologian in the Sectarian Milieu: 'Abd al-Jabbar and the Critique of Christian Origins*, Islamic History and Civilization: Studies and Texts 56. Leiden: Brill, 2004.

Reynolds, G. S., and S. K. Samir, eds. *Abd al-Jabbar: Critique of Christian Origins; A Parallel English–Arabic Text*. Provo, UT: Brigham Young University Press, 2010.

Rissanen, S. *Theological Encounter of Oriental Christians with Islam during Early Abbasid Rule*. Abo: Abo Akademi University Press, 1993.

Robinson, B. W. "Miʿradj." In *The Encyclopaedia of Islam: New Edition*, edited by C. E. Bosworth, E. van Donzel, W. P. Heinrichs, and C. Pellat. Leiden: Brill, 1993.

Samir, K. "Maqāla fī al-tahlīth li-Abū l-Faraj ʿAbd Allāh ibn al-Ṭayyib al-mutawaffā Sanat 1043." *Bayn al-Nahrayn* 16 (1976): 347–382.

Samir, S. K. "ʿAbdallâh b. aṭ- Ṭa yyib, Abû l-Farağ'." *Islamochristiana* 2 (1976): 201–242.

———. "Le Daf' al-hamm d'Elie de Nisibe: Date et circonstances de sa rédaction." *Orientalia Lovaniensia Periodica* 18 (1987): 99–119.

———. "Deux cultures qui s'affrontent: Une controverse sur L'I'rab au XIe siècle entre Elie de Nisibe et le vizir Abu l-Qasim." *Mélanges de l'Université St. Joseph* 48–49 (1975–76): 619–640.

———. "Entretien d'Elie de Nisibe avec le vizir Ibn 'Ali al-Maghribi sur l'unité et la Trinité." *Islamochristiana* 5 (1979): 31–117.

———. *Foi et culture en Irak au XIe siècle: Elie de Nisibe et l'Islam*. Aldershot, UK/Bookfield, VT: Variorum, 1996.

———. *Maqāla fī al-tawḥīd li-l-Shaykh Yaḥyā Ibn 'Adī*. Junieh, Lebanon: Bulusia, 1980.

———. "La place d'Ibn at-Ṭayyib dans la pensée arabe." *Journal of Eastern Christian Studies* 58, no. 3–4 (2006): 177–193.

———. "Ṣafaḥāt min maqāla mafqūda li-Ibn al-Ṭayyib." *Bayn al-Nahrayn* 17–19 (1977): 247–262.

———. "Un traité nouveau d'Elie de Nisibe sur le sens des mots *Kiyan* et *Ilah*." *Parole de l'Orient* 14 (1987): 109–153.

———. "L'unicité absolue de Dieu: regards sur la pensée chrétienne arabe." In *Foi et culture en Irak au XIème siècle*. Aldershot, UK: Variorum, 1996.

Sbath, P. ed. "Entry 1130:1." In *Bibliothéque de Manuscripts Paul Sbath*, vol. 3, 10–19. Cairo: Bibliotheque de Manuscripts, 1934.

Shaḥāda, I. *al-Āb wa-al-Ibn wa-al-Rūḥ al-Qudus – Ilāh wāḥid amīn: ḍarūrat al-ta'adudiyya fī al-waḥdāniyyat al-ilāhiyya*. al-Mansourieh, Lebanon: Dār Manhāl al-Ḥayāt, 2009.

Simʿān, ʿA. *Allāh bayn al-falsafa wa-al-Masīḥiyya*. Stuttgart: Call of Hope, 2010.

———. *Allāh fī al-Masīḥiyya*. al-ʿubūr. Egypt: Kanīsat Qaṣr al-Dūbāra al-injīliyya, 2004.

Sirry, A. a.-M. "Early Muslim–Christian Dialogue: A Closer Look at Major Themes of the Theological Encounter. *Islam and Christian–Muslim Relations* 16, no. 4 (2005): 361–376.

Sourdel, D. "Al-Kadir bi'llah." In *The Encyclopaedia of Islam: New Edition*, vol. 4, edited by E. van Donzel, B. Lewis and C. Pellat, 378–379. Leiden: Brill, 1997.

Stott, J. *The Cross of Christ*. Leicester: Inter-Varsity Press, 1986.

Swanson, M. "Beyond Prooftexting: Approaches to the Qur'an in Some Early Arabic Christian Apologetics." *The Muslim World* 88, no. 3–4 (1998): 297–319.

———. "Folly to the *Hunafa'*: The Crucifixion in Early Christian–Muslim Controversy." In *The Encounter of Eastern Christianity with Early Islam*, History of Christian–Muslim Relations 5, edited by E. van Donzel, B. Lewis and C. Pellat, 237–256. Leiden: Brill, 2006.

———. "The Trinity in Christian-Muslim Conversation." *Dialog: A Journal of Theology* 44 (2005): 256–263.

"Theopaschites." In *The Oxford Dictionary of the Christian Church*, edited by F. L. Cross and E. A. Livingstone. Oxford: Oxford University Press, 2005.

Thomas, D. "ʿAbd al-Jabbār." In *Christian–Muslim Relations: A Bibliographical History, vol. 2: 900–1050*, edited by D. Thomas and A. Mallett, 594–610. Leiden/Boston: Brill, 2010.

———. "Abū ʿĪsā l-Warrāq." In *Christian–Muslim Relations: A Bibliographical History, vol. 1: 600–900*, edited by D. Thomas and B. Roggema, 695–701. Leiden/Boston: Brill, 2009.

———. "Al-Bāqillānī." In *Christian–Muslim Relations: A Bibliographical History, vol. 2: 900–1050*, edited by D. Thomas and A. Mallett, 446–450. Leiden/Boston: Brill, 2010.

———. "Ali Ibn Rabban al-Ṭabari: A Convert's Assessment of His Former Faith." In *Christians and Muslims in Dialogue in the Islamic Orient of the Middle Ages*, edited by M. Tamcke, 137–156. Beirut: Ergon Verlag Wurzburg, in Kommission, 2007.

———. "ʿAlī l-Ṭabarī." In *Christian–Muslim Relations: A Bibliographical History, vol. 1: 600–900*, edited by D. Thomas and B. Roggema, 669–674. Leiden/Boston: Brill, 2009.

———. *Christian Doctrines in Islamic Theology*. Leiden/Boston: Brill, 2008.

———. "Christian Theologians and New Questions." In *The Encounter of Eastern Christianity with Early Islam*, History of Christian–Muslim Relations 5, edited by E. Grypeou, M. Swanson and D. Thomas, 257–276. Leiden: Brill, 2006.

———. *Early Muslim Polemic against Christianity: Abū ʿĪsá al-Warrāq's "Against the Incarnation."* Edited and translated by D. Thomas. Cambridge: Cambridge University Press, 2002.

———. "Early Muslim Responses to Christianity." In *Christians at the Heart of Islamic Rule*, History of Christian–Muslim Relations 1, edited by E. van Donzel, B. Lewis, and C. Pellat, 231–254. Leiden/Boston: Brill, 2003.

———. "The Miracles of Jesus in Early Islamic Polemic." *Journal of Semitic Studies* 39 (1994): 221–243.

———. "Muslim Regard for Christians and Christianity, 900–1200." In *Christian–Muslim Relations: A Bibliographical History, vol. 2: 900–1050*, edited by D. Thomas and A. Mallett, 15–27. Leiden/Boston: Brill, 2010.

———. "The Past and the Future in Muslim–Christian Relations." *Islam and Christian–Muslim Relations* 18, no. 1 (2007): 33–42.

Thomas, D., and A. Mallett, eds. *Christian–Muslim Relations: A Bibliographical History, vol. 2: 900–1050*. Leiden/Boston: Brill, 2010.

Thomas, D., and B. Roggema, eds. *Christian–Muslim Relations: A Bibliographical History, vol. 1: 600–900*. Leiden/Boston: Brill, 2009.

Tritton, A. S. *The Caliphs and Their Non-Muslim Subjects*. London: Humphrey Milford/Oxford University Press, 1930.

Troupeau, G. "Le traité sur la Trinité et l'unité de 'Abd Allāh Ibn al-Tayyib." *Bulletin d'Etudes Orientales* 25 (1972): 105–123.

———. "Le traité sur l'union de 'Abd Allāḥ Ibn al-Ṭayyib." *Parole de l'Orient* 8 (1977–1978): 141–150.

———. "Le traité sur l'unité et la Trinité de 'Abd Allāh Ibn al-Ṭayyib." *Parole de l'Orient* 2 (1971): 71–89.

Tyan, E. "'isma." In *The Encyclopaedia of Islam: New Edition*, vol. 6, edited by E. van Donzel, B. Lewis and C. Pellat, 182–184. Leiden: Brill, 1997.

Volf, M. "A Common Word for a Common Future." In *A Common Word: Muslims and Christians on Loving God and Neighbor*, edited by M. Volf, G. bin Muhammad and M. Yarrington, 18–27. Grand Rapids: Eerdmans, 2010.

———. *Allah: A Christian Response*. New York: HarperOne, 2010.

Watt, M. *Islamic Creeds: A Selection.* Edinburgh: Edinburgh University Press, 1994.

———. *The Majesty That Was Islam: The Islamic World 661–1100*. New York: Praeger, 1974.

Weinandy, T. "Does God Suffer?" First Things (website of the Institute on Religion and Public Life). 2001. https://www.firstthings.com/article/2001/11/does-god-suffer.

Wensinck, A. J. *The Muslim Creed: Its Genesis and Historical Development*. Cambridge: Cambridge University Press, 1932.

Wigram, W. A. *History of the Assyrian Church: The Church of the Sassanid Persian Empire 100–640 AD*. London: SPCK, 1910.

Williams, R. "Archbishop's Address at al-Azhar al-Sharif, Cairo." 11 September 2004. http://rowanwilliams.archbishopofcanterbury.org/articles.php/1299/archbishops-address-at-al-azhar-al-sharif-cairo.

———. "Response by the Archbishop of Canterbury to *A Common Word between Us and You*," 123–172. Jordan: The Royal Aal al-Bayt Institute for Islamic Thought, 2009. http://www.acommonword.com/downloads/CW-Booklet-Final-v6_8-1-09.pdf.

Wilmshurst, D. *The Martyred Church: A History of the Church of the East.* London: East & West, 2011.

Winkler, R. *The First Thousand Years: A Global History of Christianity.* London: Yale University Press, 2012.

Yeor, B. *The Decline of Eastern Christianity under Islam: From Jihad to Dhimmitude, Seventh–Twentieth Century*. Madison, NJ: Fairleigh Dickinson University Press, 1996.

Index

Langham PARTNERSHIP

Langham Literature and its imprints are a ministry of Langham Partnership.

Langham Partnership is a global fellowship working in pursuit of the vision God entrusted to its founder John Stott –

> ***to facilitate the growth of the church in maturity and Christ-likeness through raising the standards of biblical preaching and teaching.***

Our vision is to see churches in the majority world equipped for mission and growing to maturity in Christ through the ministry of pastors and leaders who believe, teach and live by the Word of God.

Our mission is to strengthen the ministry of the Word of God through:

- nurturing national movements for biblical preaching
- fostering the creation and distribution of evangelical literature
- enhancing evangelical theological education

especially in countries where churches are under-resourced.

Our ministry

Langham Preaching partners with national leaders to nurture indigenous biblical preaching movements for pastors and lay preachers all around the world. With the support of a team of trainers from many countries, a multi-level programme of seminars provides practical training, and is followed by a programme for training local facilitators. Local preachers' groups and national and regional networks ensure continuity and ongoing development, seeking to build vigorous movements committed to Bible exposition.

Langham Literature provides majority world preachers, scholars and seminary libraries with evangelical books and electronic resources through publishing and distribution, grants and discounts. The programme also fosters the creation of indigenous evangelical books in many languages, through writer's grants, strengthening local evangelical publishing houses, and investment in major regional literature projects, such as one volume Bible commentaries like *The Africa Bible Commentary* and *The South Asia Bible Commentary*.

Langham Scholars provides financial support for evangelical doctoral students from the majority world so that, when they return home, they may train pastors and other Christian leaders with sound, biblical and theological teaching. This programme equips those who equip others. Langham Scholars also works in partnership with majority world seminaries in strengthening evangelical theological education. A growing number of Langham Scholars study in high quality doctoral programmes in the majority world itself. As well as teaching the next generation of pastors, graduated Langham Scholars exercise significant influence through their writing and leadership.

To learn more about Langham Partnership and the work we do visit **langham.org**

CPSIA information can be obtained
at www.ICGtesting.com
Printed in the USA
BVHW061438240619
551796BV00026B/2566/P

9 781783 685769